Texas Wildscapes
Gardening for Wildlife

by
Noreen Damude
Kelly Conrad Bender

With contributions from:
Diana Foss, Judit Gowen, John Herron,
Matt Wagner and Elena Cano Camarillo

Edited by:
Kelly Conrad Bender

Wildlife Diversity Program

TEXAS PARKS *and* WILDLIFE PRESS

Publisher
  Georg Zappler

Printing Coordination
  Mike Diver

Design
  Debra Morgan

Cover Illustration
  Rob Fleming

Other Illustrations
  Jeremy George Boehm

Cover Photograph
  © Lou Jost

Other Photographs
  Frank Aguilar, Reagan Bradshaw, Kelly Bryan, Neal Cook,
  Martin Fulfer, Ron George, Judit Gowen, John Herron,
  Chuck Kowaleski, Campbell Loughmiller, William McCarley,
  Glen Mills, Paul Montgomery, Richard Moree,
  National Wildflower Research Center, Earl Nottingham,
  Bill Reaves, Sid and Shirley Rucker, Rufus Stephens,
  Teaming With Wildlife, Texas Parks and Wildlife, Matt Wagner,
  Jim Whitcomb, Leroy Williamson, Jim Yantis

ISBN: 1-885696-30-2

Acknowledgments

This book was funded through the TPW Nongame and Endangered Species Fund. Special thanks are extended to Sally Wasowski (*Native Texas Plants, Landscaping Region by Region,* and *Native Texas Gardens*) and John Tveten (*The Birds of Texas, Wildflowers of Houston,* and *Butterflies of Houston*) for their review of and comments on the manuscript. Thanks also to Melanie Pavlas-Wynns and Mark Lockwood for their constructive comments.

Preface

The Texas Wildscapes Backyard Wildlife Habitat Program was developed by the Nongame and Urban Program (now the Wildlife Diversity Program) of Texas Parks and Wildlife in 1994. A major goal of the program is to create a greater amount of good wildlife habitat in urban and suburban areas by providing the public with the tools necessary to understand and appreciate the kinds of wildlife they can attract to their own backyards. Texas Wildscapes works by incorporating three key components necessary to support wildlife: food, water, and shelter. In addition, the program requires the use of at least 50% native Texas plants to provide good wildlife habitat in a landscape.

While your Wildscapes habitat might only support a few different species, whole neighborhoods full of Wildscape habitats will create a tapestry of habitat suitable to sustain wildlife. By creating and linking habitats to form a "patchwork quilt" of Wildscape habitats, a much larger area for wildlife can be provided.

When we watch nature programs on television, we may cheer as the nearly starving cheetah overtakes the gazelle, and watch with sad satisfaction as the cheetah then feeds the animal to her cubs. This, we reason, is nature. But nature does not cease when native animals enter our backyard sanctuaries. Caterpillars need to eat leaves in order to become butterflies, mammals need to raise their young, and hawks need to capture their bird and small mammal prey. All these animals are simply doing the things they need to do in order to survive and reproduce, just as we do. A caterpillar isn't "bad" because it eats the parsley plant, the snake isn't "bad" because it eats the eggs in a bird's nest, and humans aren't "bad" because we eat the eggs of a chicken and, to add insult to injury, the chicken too! When providing habitat for wildlife, we must keep an "ecosystem" frame of mind, realizing that animals simply do what they do, with neither valor nor malice, in order to survive and reproduce. When animals visit Wildscapes, whether for short periods to feed and bathe, or for longer periods to reside and nest, we can be assured that their habitat is complete.

Contents

Part One: Welcome to Wildscaping!

Chapter One: Creating a Wildscape 1
Why Wildscaping is Necessary 2
Benefits of Wildscaping 3
The Trouble with Lawns 4
Texas Wildscapes Backyard Habitat Certification Program 5
Related Texas Parks and Wildlife Programs 5

Chapter Two: The Ecological Regions of Texas 9
The Ten Ecoregions of Texas 12

Chapter Three: The Basics of Wildlife Habitat 23
Food 24
Cover 25
Water 26

Chapter Four: Designing Your Wildscape 33
Taking Inventory 34
Evaluating Current Use 34
Evaluating Future Needs 35
Designing for Function 36
Selecting Plants 37
Design Checklist 37
The Importance of Soil 37
Maintaining a Wildscape 39

Valuable Resources 47

Part Two: Gardening Tips for Texas Critters

Chapter Five: Birds 51
Creating a "Bird-friendly" Yard 52

Chapter Six: Common Texas Birds 59

Chapter Seven: Hummingbirds 69
Designing a Hummingbird Garden 70
Plants that Attract Hummingbirds 70
Hummingbird Feeders 72

Chapter Eight: Mammals, Reptiles & Amphibians 81
Mammals 82
Reptiles and Amphibians 84
Poisonous Texas Snakes 88
Amphibians 89

Chapter Nine: Insects & Spiders 91
Butterflies 93

Valuable Resources 101

Part Three: Garden Troubleshooting

Chapter Ten: Gate Crashers & Unwanted Guests 105

Chapter Eleven: Special Areas 115
Shady Areas 116
Wet Area Gardening 117
Dealing with Deer 118

Chapter Twelve: Watch Out for Exotics! 125
The Problem with Exotics 126
Common Exotic Plants to Avoid 126
Other Problem Plants 128

Part Four: Appendix

Bibliography 135

Glossary 139

Table A.1: Birds of Texas 148

Table A.2: Hummingbirds of Texas 186

Table A.3: Mammals of Texas 188

Table A.4: Amphibians and Reptiles of Texas 194

Table A.5: Native Plants of Texas 206

Part One: *Welcome to Wildscaping!*

Chapter One: *Creating a Wildscape*

© TPW, Judit Gowen

© TPW, Rufus Stephens

We often imagine wildlife as exotic creatures from faraway lands. After all, what could be more exciting than African lions, polar bears, and birds of paradise? Those of use who live in urban and suburban areas may even forget that our very own Texas has any wildlife at all. Where we now have tracts of single family dwellings, sprawling malls, and concrete parking lots, wildlife such as kit foxes, meadowlarks, whiptail lizards, and bobcats once roamed. Where we now have seas of St. Augustine, pansies, and begonias, there were once waves of Indiangrass, Gulf Coast muhly, purple asters, butterfly-weed, and winecups. Wildscapes is a program that can help us restore our private lands to these native plants and animals. By creating a Wildscape, we can produce a well-balanced habitat which invites native wildlife into our own backyards.

Why Wildscaping is Necessary

Texas is blessed with nearly 170 million acres of mostly rural countryside from the Chihuahuan Desert to pine forests. As a public land steward, Texas Parks and Wildlife has been engaged in habitat restoration on wildlife management areas, state parks, and state natural areas totaling over one million acres. The remaining land, over 97% of the total acreage, is managed by private land-owners. In order to sustain habitat for all species, both game and nongame, we must also address areas of land held by the private landowners. Private land stewardship insures the perpetuation of wildlife habitat through sustainable agricultural and wildlife management practices.

Changes in wildlife populations today are a reflection of progressive alteration and loss of habitat over time. As grasslands are converted to shrub lands and forests to pasture, wetlands are drained, and bottomland hardwoods are lost, dramatic changes in wildlife populations have also occurred. The physical structure of a habitat reflects the function of that habitat and the types of species that will find a home there. As a habitat changes, either due to natural factors such as flood or fire, or by the hand of man, so will the wildlife populations that depend on that habitat.

Ecologists today frequently use the term "habitat fragmentation." Habitat fragmentation occurs where discontinuous land use creates irregular patches of habitats across the landscape, breaking up large blocks of pristine habitat such as forests, grasslands and marshes. Today, habitat fragmentation is occurring rapidly in suburban fringe areas as development expands into former farm and ranch operations. Large land holdings are being increasingly subdivided. Roads, boundary fences, and utility easements are being constructed. If habitats become fragmented enough, the survival of many organisms will be threatened. Many exotic plants initially intended for backyard landscapes can also escape into the wild, with a devastating effect on both native plant and wildlife populations. Seemingly harmless exotic landscaping plants such as Chinese tallow have been known to completely replace native plant species, for instance; while introduced insects such as the red imported fire ant have altered entire ecosystems by preying on native insects, as well as the eggs and young of small reptiles, birds, and mammals.

Establishing Wildscapes creates habitat for wildlife. This spider on a Maximilian sunflower is part of a healthy ecosystem.

More than three quarters of the population of Texas is located in six cities: Austin, Dallas, El Paso, Fort Worth, Houston, and San Antonio. As these urban areas have grown, the land has changed from forests, prairies, and agricultural areas to suburban development. This transformation has resulted in extensive habitat fragmentation, creating land that is rendered nearly unusable to native wildlife because of the lack of connecting corridors. As Texas' human population continues to soar, more and more space is consumed to suit our needs. As a consequence, wildlife has been progressively squeezed out of the habitat they need to survive. Happily, private residences and other developed properties hold a great potential for restoring quality, quantity, and richness of the wildlife habitat that has been displaced. Wildscapes can provide the bridges, corridors, and buffers to link privately owned lands to natural areas, parks, and green belts. Wildscaping translates into a total increase in healthy wildlife habitat and natural beauty.

Urban development is one major cause of habitat loss.

Benefits of Wildscaping

There are educational, environmental, economic, and aesthetic benefits to creating backyard habitat to attract wildlife. To realize the educational benefits of Wildscapes, simply observe young children encountering nature in the backyard for the first time. A wildlife garden can become the setting for learning about the life histories of birds, small mammals, insects, plants, and other creatures. By observing first-hand migration, hibernation, reproduction, and predation, children will likely learn more about the workings of nature than they could glean from books. By discovering the intricate balances in the natural world, Texans of all ages become better able to make informed decisions concerning the future of our community and the world. We can better understand important local environmental issues and how they impact our lives.

By maintaining a healthy wildlife habitat, we create healthier living for people. Plants in richly vegetated open spaces in urban and suburban areas absorb carbon dioxide and give off oxygen, thus renewing our air supply. Plant foliage captures dust and other pollutants, thus purifying the air we breathe. Vegetated areas aid in erosion control and the conservation of soils. Plant roots hold soils in place while plant parts above ground impede water runoff. A diverse landscape containing many species of native plants not only supports an abundance of wildlife, it also is less prone to large-scale devastation from insect pests or diseases. Planting coniferous and deciduous trees, shrubs, and especially native grasses is an excellent erosion control measure, while also providing much needed cover and nesting sites for resident birds.

© Paul Montgomery

The economic benefits of creating a backyard habitat are also significant. Maintaining expansive manicured lawns, clipped hedges, and water-guzzling exotic plants can be many times more expensive than caring for native vegetation. Once established, native plant species require only minimal attention from the home gardener. This translates into a reduction of extensive soil amendments, less watering, and a reduced need for chemical pest control, chemical fertilizers, and pampering. Not only that, properly placed trees and shrubs can save home heating and cooling costs. Planted on the west or southwest side of a home, large deciduous shade trees will shelter the home from the onslaught of the hot summer sun. In the winter, the trees lose their leaves and allow the sun's rays to warm the house. Finally, planting or preserving vegetated slopes with cover for wildlife will also slow water and wind movement, decrease soil erosion, help replenish ground water reserves, reduce runoff, and decrease stream flow fluctuation. Conserving soils and safeguarding water quality improves overall ecosystem stability and saves money in the long run.

One has only to watch hummingbirds flying anxiously from flower to flower, chickadees and titmice snatching seeds from a feeder, or dazzling butterflies tilting lazily from blossom to blossom to understand that wildlife habitat is not only functional, but also aesthetically pleasing. People yearn to get back to nature. They have a compelling need for contact with the natural world. A Wildscape gives us a sense of place, keeps us in touch with the passing seasons, and affords an avenue of escape from the chaos of everyday life.

The Trouble with Lawns

To observe the wonders of wildlife, we need to entice their presence. Unfortunately, expansive, well-manicured yards with clipped turf and only tall trees do not support a great diversity of wildlife. Despite the allure of a rich carpet of plushness under your feet, the truth is that a neatly manicured lawn extending from property line to property line will be nearly as devoid of wildlife as a parking lot. Unfortunately, the only species which particularly benefit from oceans of closely cropped turf are those "weedy," undesirable species such as grackles, starlings, and house sparrows. The greater the habitat diversity your property provides, the more types of wildlife will choose to visit your yard. A primary method to increase habitat diversity is to replace expansive lawns with a selection of native wildflowers, shrubs, and trees in a well thought-out arrangement.

A multilayered landscape containing many species of native plants not only supports an abundance of wildlife, it also provides insurance against the depredation of insect pests. Landscapes that contain single species (monocultures) are impoverished systems and are highly vulnerable to diseases which can sweep in and wipe out everything.

Natural habitats can be outdoor learning labs for children of all ages.

Planting a variety of coniferous and deciduous trees, shrubs, and especially native grasses is an excellent way to diversify your habitat. It will also provide much needed cover and nesting sites to resident birds and other wildlife. Flowering plants in the legume family (those plants which produce a dry fruit, such as bean plants) provide nectar for bees and butterflies, while grasses offer larval food sources to several species of butterflies, particularly skippers. Both legumes and grasses also protect soils from erosion and excessive leaching.

Another good reason for growing less lawn is that fertilizers and lawn chemicals invariably make their way into ponds and streams. Excess fertilizers foul our waters by increasing nutrient levels and encouraging heavy algal blooms. Finally, watering lawns accounts for 40-60% of residential water consumption, making lawn maintenance not only a chore but also a drain on the pocketbook and the water supply.

Consider reducing the size of your lawn areas and replacing them with natural ground covers, native grasses, trees, shrubs, vines, and wildflowers. If you desire to have areas of turf grass, try grasses that are appropriate for your soil and climate. Buffalograss (*Buchloe dactyloides*), for example, is an excellent choice. It is native to many areas of Texas and is quite drought-tolerant. Mow any turf at a higher blade setting (no shorter than three inches) to reduce water use, and resist the urge to bag the clippings. Allow the clippings to remain in the turf to return nutrients to the soils. Less lawn means less water and chemical application, and less mowing. Who can argue with that?

For more information on caring for lawns, see *A Green Guide to Yard Care*, an informative brochure produced by the Texas Natural Resource Conservation Commission, and the "Don't Bag It" program sponsored by the Texas Agricultural Extension Service.

Male great-tailed grackles display to each other in one of their favorite habitats: a well manicured lawn.

Texas Wildscapes Backyard Habitat Certification Program

As you watch your Wildscape habitat develop, let the world (or at least your neighborhood) know about your efforts. Texas Parks and Wildlife is awarding official Texas Wildscape certifications to sites that fulfill the minimum requirements of providing food, water, and shelter to wildlife. Simply fill out the Texas Wildscapes Certification Application explaining how you provided habitat for wildlife and return it to Texas Parks and Wildlife. Once your application is approved, you will receive a personalized certificate and weather-resistant backyard sign that identifies your property as an officially certified Texas Wildscape. To obtain an official Texas Wildscapes Certification Application, send a check or money order for $5.00 to:

 Texas Wildscapes
 4200 Smith School Road
 Austin, Texas, 78744

For more information, call:
 Texas Wildscapes Coordinator
 Wildlife Diversity Program
 512-389-4974

Related Texas Parks and Wildlife Programs

Texas Parks and Wildlife has introduced several programs which benefit Texas wildlife, wildlife habitat, and you. The goal of these programs is to help Texans become more involved in Texas wildlife. Many of these programs go hand-in-hand with Wildscaping, and you may wish to integrate these programs into your Wildscaping project.

For general information on Texas wildlife or park information, call 800-792-1112. For more information about nongame wildlife in Texas, call the Wildlife Diversity Program at 512-389-4403. To receive a subscription to the Wildlife Diversity Program newsletter, *Eye on Nature*, contact the Wildlife Diversity Program at 512-389-4403.

Texas Wildacres

An extension of the Texas Wildscapes program, Wildacres is designed to help small landowners (10-200 acres) manage their land for the benefit of wildlife.

For more information, contact:
 Texas Wildacres Coordinator
 Wildlife Diversity Program
 512-389-4403
or:
 Texas Wildacres
 4200 Smith School Road
 Austin, Texas, 78744

Once you have created a Wildscape, consider certifying it with Texas Parks and Wildlife.

Texas Hummingbird Roundup Survey

Join over 3500 other Texans to help us determine more about the range, distribution, favored sites, and feeding habits of Texas hummingbirds. When you join the survey, you help us learn more about these fascinating creatures by recording events that take place at your hummingbird feeder, such as which species you see, what flowers they prefer, and when each species arrives and departs for the season. The survey packet contains a survey form, information about Texas hummingbirds, a packet of native seeds for your hummingbird garden, and a hummingbird distribution map.

You can read about the results in the annual newsletter, and you will receive a colorful Hummingbird Roundup decal. The Hummingbird Wheel is a full-color hummingbird identification device that includes illustrations of all 16 Texas hummers, identification characteristics, and fun hummingbird facts, and is also available through the Wildlife Diversity Program for $11.95.

For more information, contact:
> Texas Hummingbird Roundup Coordinator
> Wildlife Diversity Wildlife Program
> 512-389-4470
> **or:**
> Texas Hummingbird Roundup
> 4200 Smith School Road
> Austin, Texas, 78744

Texas Partners in Flight

Texas Partners in Flight (PIF) is a nonprofit partnership of state and federal government agencies, nongovernment organizations, industries, communities, landowners, and individuals, and operates solely from the volunteer efforts and contributions of its partners to insure healthy populations of Texas' magnificent bird resources.

For more information, contact:
> State Coordinator of Texas Partners in Flight
> 512-389-4970
> **or:**
> Partners in Flight
> 4200 Smith School Road
> Austin, Texas 78744

Growing Wild

Growing Wild, a butterfly gardening program, is presented by Texas Parks and Wildlife in conjunction with community volunteers. It is designed to offer a hands-on learning program to selected elementary schools. Third and fourth grade students learn about the relationships between plants and animals by growing plants from seed and planting a butterfly garden on their school campus.

For more information, contact:
> Austin:
> Wildlife Diversity Program
> 512-389-4403
> Dallas/Fort Worth:
> Urban Fish and Wildlife Office
> 972-293-3841
> Houston:
> Urban Fish and Wildlife Office
> 281-456-7029
> San Antonio:
> Urban Fish and Wildlife Office
> 210-348-6350

Project WILD/Aquatic WILD

Project WILD/Aquatic WILD is "Wildlife in Learning Design." The environmental and conservation education program for kindergarten through twelfth grade students emphasizes awareness, appreciation, and understanding of wildlife and natural resources.

For more information contact:
> Project WILD/ Aquatic WILD Office
> 512-389-4369 or 800-792-1112
> **or:**
> Project WILD/ Aquatic WILD
> Texas Parks and Wildlife
> 4200 Smith School Road
> Austin, Texas 78744

Biologist removing exotic water hyacinth from Sheldon Lake.

Private Lands Enhancement Program

The goal of the Private Lands Enhancement Program is to provide expertise to land managers in the preservation and development of wildlife habitat and the proper management of the wildlife populations which utilize that habitat. Along with superb technical guidance, the program also offers the recent publication "Wildlife Management Associations and Co-ops."

For more information, contact:

    Program Director of Private Lands Enhancement
    Texas Parks and Wildlife
    800-792-1112

or:

    Private Lands Enhancement
    4200 Smith School Road
    Austin, Texas, 78744

Lone Star Land Steward

Texas Parks and Wildlife sponsors the Lone Star Land Steward Award Program to recognize private landowners for excellence in habitat management and wildlife conservation on their lands. Ranchers, farmers, foresters, and other land managers and cooperatives may participate in this statewide awards program.

To receive a nomination form contact:

    Texas Parks and Wildlife
    Private Lands Enhancement Program
    4200 Smith School Road
    Austin, Texas, 78744

Chapter Two: *The Ecological Regions of Texas*

© Paul Montgomery

© Paul Montgomery

One of the goals of a Wildscape is to provide food and shelter for native wildlife with the use of native plants. As you plan your wildlife habitat, keep in mind that Texas is blessed with ten very different ecological regions (also known as ecoregions). An ecoregion is any geographical area which encompasses a distinct grouping of plant, animal, geological, and environmental features.

When comparing two very different ecoregions such as the Trans-Pecos region of West Texas to the East Texas Pineywoods, it is easy to see the vast differences in Texas' landscapes. The Trans-Pecos is generally characterized as an area of low rainfall, high elevation, and sparse vegetation, while the East Texas Pineywoods is characterized by high rainfall, low elevation, complex soils, and lush vegetation. The animal and plant life adapted to each of these regions are completely different from one another as well. Therefore, a person in the western portion of the state would not want to create a habitat based on the wildlife and plant species of East Texas, nor would a person in East Texas be able to successfully establish a Wildscape based on the vegetation of West Texas.

Because most of Texas' major cities are situated in areas where different soil and vegetational regions meet, it is sometimes not easy to know in which ecoregion you are located. Many metropolitan areas like San Antonio, Houston, Austin, and the Dallas-Fort Worth metroplex, for example, have two or three ecoregions. To know in which ecoregion you reside, first consult the Texas ecoregion map (Figure 2a), then simply step outside your front door and take a look around. Compare your area with the following regional descriptions. Check your soils first to determine if they contain clays, gumbos, or sands. (For more information on soils and soil types, see Chapter Four.) Remember that in suburban developments, builders have often scraped the topsoil away and replaced it with soil from other areas. To find out what kind of soil is naturally found in your area, examine soils in greenbelt areas, along railroad tracks, creeks, and other undeveloped areas. These locations can give you a pretty good indication of the natural soils and dominant native vegetation of your area. You may already have wonderful native species of trees, shrubs, and grasses growing on your property. These should be left in place. Your local native plant nurseryman and soil conservation agent can also provide useful information for your particular area.

Gulf Coast seaoats.

Limestone is a prominent feature of Edwards Plateau landscapes.

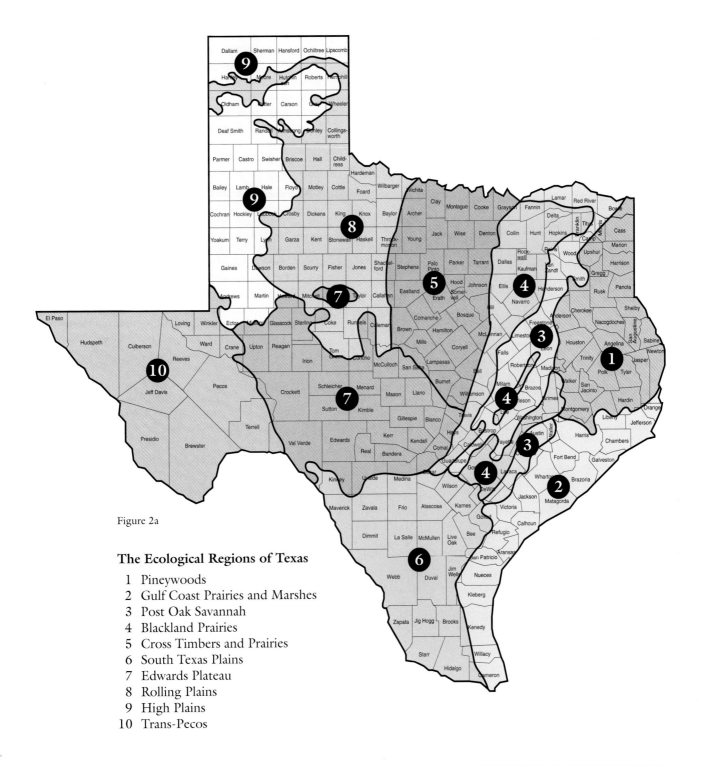

Figure 2a

The Ecological Regions of Texas

1 Pineywoods
2 Gulf Coast Prairies and Marshes
3 Post Oak Savannah
4 Blackland Prairies
5 Cross Timbers and Prairies
6 South Texas Plains
7 Edwards Plateau
8 Rolling Plains
9 High Plains
10 Trans-Pecos

The Ten Ecoregions of Texas
Region One – Pineywoods

Mostly deep, dark, and evergreen, the Pineywoods region of East Texas is an extension of the rich pine/hardwood forests of the southeastern United States. Gently rolling hills cloaked with pines and oaks and rich bottomlands with tall hardwoods characterize these forests, while intermittent pockets of evergreen shrub bogs, open seepage slopes, and cypress-tupelo swamps form a patchwork quilt throughout. Frequent long-term flooding plays an essential role in maintaining these bottomland hardwood communities. The region's plants are adapted to the characteristic ridge and swale formations in the bottomland caused by periodic and often severe flooding. Eliminating the flooding alters the plant and animal life that have formed a unique and diverse community in the area.

Flowering dogwood trees with their beautiful white bracts gleaming through the oak woodlands in the spring are scattered about the moist uplands. The region's thirty-five to sixty inches of rain each year support not only pines, including loblolly, shortleaf, and longleaf pines, but swamp and streamside stands of hardwoods including beech oaks, elm, and magnolia. In addition, the Pineywoods host a myriad of woodland specialties such as sphagnum mosses, ferns, pitcher plants, sundews, pipeworts, and orchids.

Elevations range from near sea level to almost 500 feet with an average annual temperature of 66° F. The growing season ranges from 250 days in the southern portion of the region to 230 days near the Red River in the north. Highly weathered soils are sandy or loamy and very deep. Most of the 15.8 million acres of the region is prime timber land, and conversion of these woodlands to plantations of loblolly or slash pine has permanently altered many of the natural forest communities.

East Texas boasts a rich diversity of wildlife. Fifteen species of Texas breeding birds nest predominantly in this ecoregion. Three of these species — the pine warbler, brown-headed nuthatch, and the endangered red-cockaded woodpecker — are confined almost exclusively, in Texas, to the Pineywoods forest for breeding. The Bachman's sparrow nests locally in Texas only in the longleaf pine uplands of this region, while wintering and nesting bald eagles set up roosts or nest sites in undisturbed woodlands near rivers and lakes. Other avian specialties of the Pineywoods include the wood thrush, hooded warbler, prothonotary warbler, and barred owl, the dark-eyed, noisy denizen of deep bottomland forests. Characteristic mammals of the region include the river otter, gray squirrel, flying squirrel, and possibly the Louisiana black bear. Although the Louisiana black bear is currently absent from the Pineywoods, suitable habitat still exists to support future populations of this East Texas specialty.

East Texas Pineywoods.

Region Two – Gulf Coastal Prairies and Marshes

The Gulf Coastal Prairies and Marshes follow the lip of the Texas coast and extend inland about sixty miles. This 9.5 million-acre swath of land traces a broad arc along the coast from the Sabine River to Baffin Bay. Elevations range from near sea level to almost 150 feet, and annual temperatures range from 70° F to 74° F. Soils of the marshy areas include acid sands, sandy loams, and clay. Soils of the Gulf prairies contain more clay than the marsh areas and are very rich in nutrients. The character of the coastline is shaped by the long and continuous confrontation with the sea, wind, and rain. Storms shape the shoreline as a sculptor works clay, creating shallow bays, estuaries, salt marshes, dunes, and tidal flats. Because of the proximity to the Gulf of Mexico, many plants are halophytic, or highly salt tolerant.

Much of the upland areas are dissected with numerous sluggish rivers, bayous, creeks, and sloughs. Between the rivers, little bluestem, Indiangrass, and various sedges dominate extensive open prairies. At one time, the coastal river bottoms of this area were clothed in woodlands of sugarberry, pecan, elm, and coastal live oak. Few such areas remain today, as most of these prairies are farmed or have been absorbed into urban areas. Much of the remaining native sod of the Coastal Prairies has been invaded by exotics such as Macartney rose and Chinese tallow or native woody species including mesquite, prickly-pear, acacias, and scrub oaks. Today cattle graze the Coastal Prairies, farmers use the rich soils to grow rice, corn, grain sorghum, and cotton, while the oil and petrochemical industries dominate the northeastern end of this region.

© Paul Montgomery

Gulf Prairies and Marshes.

The Coastal Bend begins at midcoast near Corpus Christi where the shoreline is edged by Mustang and Padre Islands, part of the longest chain of barrier islands in the world. Here, island dunes are dappled with seaoats, glasswort, beach evening-primrose, and railroad vine — hardy colonizers of the shifting beachhead sands. Sandy soils of the Coastal Bend also support distinctive chenier woodlands of scrub oaks, yaupon, red-bay, and wax-myrtle. Tallgrass and midgrass prairies, as well as Spartina grass marshes, make up a major portion of the coastal vegetation. Tallgrass prairies extending from the Great Plains to the Midwest are characterized by taller grasses, deeper soils, and more precipitation than short- or midgrass prairies further west.

Coastal areas are very rich in wildlife. Where treeless earth meets endless sky, coastal marshes harbor hundreds of thousands of wintering geese and ducks and provide critical landfall in the spring for neotropical migratory birds. The area is home to several important wildlife sanctuaries and refuges — notably those protecting the endangered Attwater's prairie-chicken and the whooping crane. In the fall, coastal dunes serve as sentry roosts for southward-bound migrating peregrine falcons, while at any season there are lone willets, mini-battalions of sanderlings, and congregations of gulls, terns, and black skimmers feeding or loafing near the surf.

Region Three – Post Oak Savannah

Lying immediately west of the East Texas Pineywoods, the Post Oak Savannah emerges almost imperceptibly, marked by subtle changes in soils and vegetation. Occupying approximately 8.5 million acres, the area's topography is gently rolling to hilly with elevations ranging from 300 to 800 feet, rainfall averages from 35 to 45 inches per year from west to east, with annual average temperatures ranging from 65° F to 70° F. Soils of the Post Oak Savannah are interesting and complex. They are usually acidic, with sands and sandy loams occurring on the uplands, clay to clay loams on the bottomlands, with a dense clay pan underlying all soil types. Because of this peculiarity, the Post Oak Savannah is sometimes referred to as the "Clay Pan Savannah." Clay pan soils are nearly impervious to water and underlie the surface layers of soil at depths of only a few feet. As a consequence, the moisture available for plant growth is limited, making the habitat surprisingly arid at times. One curious exception to the clay pan soils occurs in Bastrop County — home of the renowned Lost Pines. The Carrizo sands, a sandy inclusion of moist soils, harbor a unique community of loblolly pine, post oak, and blackjack oak and is also home to sphagnum bogs with ferns and carnivorous pitcher plants.

The Post Oak Savannah is punctuated by scattered oaks — mainly post oaks, of course — and blackjack oaks. Black hickory may also be locally abundant. Widespread trees of lesser importance include cedar elm, sugarberry, eastern red cedar, and common persimmon. Other important species of the region are Southern red oak, sassafras, flowering dogwood, yaupon, and winged elm. Some authorities believe that this region was once predominantly a tallgrass prairie, but that trees (mostly oaks) and brushy shrubs proliferated with the suppression of fires and the conversion of the land to farming and grazing. When fires were frequent, the land was not as it appears today. Historically, wide vistas of tallgrasses — little bluestem, Indiangrass, switchgrass — and a myriad of wildflowers, broken only by the occasional motte of venerable "giants," lent a parklike atmosphere to the landscape. Peat bogs, like the ones found in the Pineywoods, are also found here, mingled amongst stands of flowering dogwood, sassafras, bumelia, and yaupon.

Early European settlers were especially attracted to the Post Oak Savannah because it was clearly transitional between woodland and prairies. Today, the Post Oak Savannah is used largely for improved pasture, with vast acreages seeded to introduced grasses such as Bahia grass or Bermuda grass.

Mostly prairie animals with some woodland species abound in the Post Oak Savannah region. The distinctive sandy inclusion of the Lost Pines area also harbors one of the last refuges for the endangered Houston toad.

Post Oak Savannah.

Region Four – Blackland Prairies

Taking their name from the fertile, dark clay soil, the Blackland Prairies constitute a true prairie ecosystem and have some of the richest, naturally fertile soils in the world. Characterized by gently rolling to nearly level topography, the land is carved by rapid surface drainage. Pecan, cedar elm, various oaks, soapberry, honey locust, hackberry and Osage orange dot the landscape, with some mesquite invading from the south. A true tallgrass prairie, the dominant grass is little bluestem. Other important grasses include big bluestem, Indiangrass, eastern gammagrass, switchgrass and sideoats grama. While elevations from 300 to more than 800 feet match those of the Post Oak Savannah, the annual rainfall varies from thirty to forty inches west to east, and the average annual temperatures range from approximately 66° F to 70° F. Described as "black velvet" when freshly plowed and moistened from a good rain, true blackland soils are deep, dark, calcareous deposits renowned for their high productivity. Scientists believe the richness of the prairie soils is derived from the abundant invertebrate fauna and fungal flora found in the soils themselves. Like many of the prairie communities comprising the Great Plains of North America, the Blackland Prairies harbor few rare plants or animals. The Blackland Prairies are today almost entirely brought under the plow, with only 5,000 acres of the original 12 million remaining. For this reason, many authorities believe that the Blackland Prairies represent one of the rarest landscapes in Texas.

Blackland Prairies.

Cross Timbers and Prairies.

Region Five – Cross Timbers and Prairies

The Cross Timbers and Prairies region covers about 17 million acres of alternating bands of wooded habitat crossing throughout a mostly prairie region — thus the term Cross Timbers. Elevations range from about 600 to almost 1,700 feet while rainfall varies from about twenty-five inches in the west and thirty-five inches in the east. Average annual temperatures are about 67° F. The Cross Timbers share many of the same species with the Post Oak Savannah. Grassland species such as little bluestem, Indiangrass, and big bluestem are common to both, but there are a few notable differences in floral composition. Yaupon, sassafras, and dogwood which form dense understory thickets in the Post Oak Savannah are almost nonexistent in the Eastern Cross Timbers. Texas mulberry, American elm, and Osage orange become more common. In the understory are rusty blackhaw viburnum, American beautyberry, Arkansas yucca, and smooth sumac. In the Western Cross Timbers, which is drier still, live oak becomes more important, replacing the post oaks as you proceed westward. The decrease in moisture discourages trees from growing close together except along streams, resulting in more expansive pockets of prairies separating isolated stands of trees. Here flameleaf sumac, redbud, Mexican plum, rusty blackhaw viburnum, and eastern red cedar are more prevalent.

Fragrant sumac appears for the first time, a common shrub in the Western Cross Timbers, the Edwards Plateau, and further west. Wildlife consists of a mixture of eastern forest and prairie species.

Region Six – South Texas Plains

Bounded on the west by the Rio Grande and Mexico and on the north by the Balcones Escarpment, the South Texas Plains are vast, serene, and lightly populated. Elevations range from sea level to 1,000 feet and rainfall varies from 30 inches in the east to 16 inches in the west. Soils are varied and highly complex. Generally extremely basic to slightly acidic, they range from deep sands to tight clays and clay loams. With average annual temperatures around 73° F, the South Texas Plains boasts the longest growing season in Texas, lasting up to 365 days in some years at Brownsville. This warm region is, however, a land of recurrent droughts, a factor which distinctly marks the landscape. Nearly everything that grows here is drought-tolerant since rainfall is well below the amount needed for conventional forest trees. Sporadic rains, however, will trigger wildflowers to bloom unexpectedly at almost any time of year.

The Lower Rio Grande Valley is a highly distinctive subregion of the South Texas Plains. Usually defined as Cameron, Willacy, Hidalgo, and Starr counties, it contains the only subtropical area in Texas. Once supporting majestic groves of Sabal palms, Montezuma cypress, tall ebony-anaqua woodlands, and jungle-like expanses of Tamaulipan thorny shrubs, today much of it has been bulldozed, plowed, or paved. In fact, the once extensive groves of the native Sabal palm, which used to flourish here, are now reduced to only a few stands near Brownsville. Soils in this subtropical region range from sands to heavy clays. Clay soils and areas with extremely poor drainage dominate the resaca areas (old meandering paths of the Rio Grande).

Despite a history of land use which is the oldest in the state, the Rio Grande Plains harbor many rare species of plants and animals. It is here that a few wild tropical cats — ocelots and jaguarundis —

South Texas Plains.

The South Texas region owes its diversity to the convergence of the Chihuahuan desert to the west, the Tamaulipan thornscrub and subtropical woodlands along the Rio Grande to the south, and the coastal grasslands to the east. Essentially a gently rolling plain, the region is cut by arroyos and streams and is blanketed with low growing vegetation — mesquite, granjeno, huisache, catclaw, blackbrush, cenizo, and guayacan. Wherever conditions are suitable, there is a dense understory of smaller trees and shrubs such as coyotillo, paloverde, Mexican olive, and various species of cacti. The woody vegetation of the South Texas Plains is so distinctive that the area is also referred to as the "brush country."

still take refuge. Other special animals include ferruginous pygmy-owl, green jay, elf owl, Texas tortoise, indigo snake, and Mexican burrowing toad. There are also a surprising number of plants that occur here and nowhere else, especially among the cactus family, like Albert's black lace cactus, star cactus, and Runyon's cory cactus.

Region Seven – Edwards Plateau

Semi-arid, rocky, and beautifully rugged, the Edwards Plateau comprises nearly 24 million acres of land dominated by ashe juniper, various oaks, and occasionally, honey mesquite. Much of the region overlays a foundation of honey-combed Cretaceous limestone — and an immense underground reservoir called the Edwards Aquifer which spills out into many crystal clear springs. Caliche slopes, limestone escarpments, and thin clay soils are riddled with fossil remains of microscopic marine creatures, bearing testimony to the once massive sea that covered most of the state.

Topography is generally rough with elevations ranging from slightly less than 1,000 feet to over 3,000 feet and annual rainfall varies from a meager fifteen inches in the west to more than thirty-three inches in the east. Droughts can be prolonged, frequent, and often unpredictable. Sporadic flash floods can be devastating to those unaccustomed to their fury. Average temperatures range from 64° F to 67° F, and soils range from neutral to slightly acidic sands and sandy loams in the Llano Uplift, to thin, rocky, highly calcareous clays and clay loams over the rest of the Plateau.

It is a region of great floral diversity, with 100 of the 400 Texas endemic plants occurring only here, including Texas snowbells, bracted twist-flower, Texabama croton, Texas wildrice, and rock quillwort. Tucked away in protected valleys are relict populations of Texas madrone, Texas smoke tree, witch hazel, and big-tooth maple — trees normally found far to the northeast in Arkansas, to the west in the Trans-Pecos mountains, or to the south in the mountains of Mexico. The moist river corridors of the Colorado, Guadalupe, Blanco, and Nueces are lined with majestic bald cypress, pecan, hackberry, and sycamores. And perhaps nowhere else are the spring wildflowers so spectacular as in this region, with undulating tapestries of bluebonnets, Indian paintbrush, gaillardia, and golden-wave dazzling even the most jaded eye come April.

The region also hosts a number of terrestrial vertebrates. Here the white-tailed deer is king. Other common denizens of the Hill Country include armadillo, black-tailed jackrabbit, opossum, and Texas earless lizard. The purity and constant temperature of the waters provide ideal habitat for specialized spring dwellers such as the Clear Creek gambusia, the San Marcos gambusia, the fountain darter, and the San Marcos salamander. The unique Guadalupe bass and the Cagle's map turtle make their homes within the clear waters of the larger rivers. Thousands of caves of all sizes harbor cave shrimp and blind salamanders, which live only within the confines of these underground systems. Rare invertebrates like blind spiders, pseudoscorpions, mold beetles, and harvestmen are also found in caves, as well as Mexican free-tailed bats, which establish summer nursery colonies within several larger caves throughout the region. The Edwards Plateau also provides a meeting ground for birds typical of both eastern and western regions. The green kingfisher, cave swallow, black-capped vireo, and golden-cheeked warbler nest more commonly here than in any other region in the state.

© Paul Montgomery

Edwards Plateau.

Rolling Plains.

© Paul Montgomery

Region Eight – Rolling Plains

Marking the southern end of the Great Plains of the central United States, the red Rolling Plains represents the "last gasp" of a great continental prairie ecosystem. As its name suggests, topography of the Rolling Plains is gently rolling to moderately rough, with elevations ranging from 800 to 3,000 feet. Rainfall averages between thirty inches in the east to twenty-two inches in the west, the annual temperatures range from 60° F to 64° F. Most of the soils are neutral to slightly basic. The land is a varied and beautiful assortment of reds, from burnt sienna to the palest of pinks. East of the Cap Rock, on heavier clay soils, the native prairies of the Rolling Plains once consisted of midgrass and tallgrass communities nurtured by the intense summer rains and hot summer days. Pristine pockets of prairie are a rarity today, however. Much of what was once a sweeping expanse of sideoats grama, little bluestem, and blue grama has been tilled for grain fields or cotton. In many areas, overgrazing has allowed honey mesquite and shinnery oak to spread into the prairies, along with snakeweed and prickly-pear. Trees occurring along waterways and canyons of the Caprock include plains cottonwood, Mohr oak, netleaf hackberry, one-seed juniper, and Rocky Mountain juniper.

The gently rolling hills and broad flats of the Rolling Plains are the birthplace of many great Texas rivers, including the Canadian, the Colorado, the Concho, and the Red River, which originate in the brakes of the Cap Rock Escarpment and in the western reaches of the region. These rivers and their tributaries harbor their own unique inhabitants such as the Concho water snake and Brazos water snake which live only in a few restricted areas of the Colorado and Brazos river systems, respectively. Sand bars in the upper reaches of these rivers provide nesting habitat for the uncommon interior least tern and the snowy plover. Juniper woodlands, on the steep breaks of the canyons, are home to the Palo Duro mouse, a close relative of the pinyon mouse of the Rocky Mountains. Burrowing at the base of mesquite trees as they forage by night for seeds and greens, the Texas kangaroo rat is restricted to certain clay-loam soils of the Rolling Plains. This unique desert-adapted rodent still has scientists guessing as to its origins.

Region Nine – High Plains

Described as a sea of waving grasslands, the High Plains extends from the Panhandle south to the Pecos River. This 20 million-acre region fills most of the "handle" portion of the state and consists of a relatively high and level plateau of sandy to heavy dark, calcareous clay soils lying over an impervious layer of caliche. Soils consist mainly of outwash sediments from the Rocky Mountains. Elevations range from 3,000 to 4,700 feet, with an average annual temperature of approximately 59° F. Winters here are the coldest in Texas. Rainfall averages from twenty-one inches on the eastern edge of the region to as low as twelve inches on the southwestern edge, and sun and wind rob the soil of what little moisture it receives.

Today an arid, treeless plain, much of the High Plains is irrigated from the vast Ogallala aquifer, the chief source of fresh water in the region. Classified as mixed-prairie and short-grass prairie, the vegetation varies as a function of location. Hardlands, mixed lands, sandy lands, draws, or caliche lakes give rise to distinct differences in plant communities. Though characteristically free from trees or brush, honey mesquite and yucca have invaded some areas, while sandsage and shinnery oak have spread through the sandylands. Playa lakes play an essential role in this region, as they are among the prime waterfowl wintering grounds for the North American Central Flyway. The region's other name, Llano Estacado or "Staked Plains" is thought to derive from the first European settlers to traverse the High Plains who drove stakes into the ground to help guide them across the flat, featureless plain. These early pioneers found a vast carpet of short grasses, home to enormous herds of buffalo and pronghorn antelope. This was also home to the Comanches, who were known as the "Lords of the South Plains."

While the plow and barbed wire fence have forever changed the original character of the High Plains, unique areas still remain, including scattered sand dunes cloaked with Havard shin-oak, sandsage, and little bluestem. Tallgrass meadows still wave in the breezes along the Canadian River and its tributaries, nourished by underground water flowing through the sands. While few rivers actually cross the High Plains, the thin ribbons of meager water along the Canadian and Red Rivers once sustained luxuriant growths of tall willows and cottonwoods. Now two Old-World exotic plants, Russian olive and tamarisk, have supplanted the native trees that line the banks, providing alternate homes for versatile phoebes and kingbirds. Grasses still provide cover and nesting habitat for myriads of other birds, and belts of trees planted back in the 1930s provide shelter to an amazing diversity of wildlife. Whereas gray wolves, grizzly bears and elk no longer occur on the High Plains, mountain lions, the adaptable coyote, red-tailed hawk, and the diminutive swift fox now sit at the top of the food chain. And while the once vast populations of prairie dogs have dwindled, flocks of wintering waterfowl still frequent the ephemeral playa lakes, as do sandhill cranes and shorebirds which forage along the playa margins. Scattered bunches of lesser prairie-chickens still boom on the prairies, though their numbers are greatly reduced, while migrating flocks of lark buntings and horned larks still ply the skies over restless grassland seas.

High Plains meets the Rolling Plains.

Region Ten – Trans-Pecos

The Trans-Pecos is perhaps the most remarkable ecoregion of Texas, offering at once breathtakingly spectacular vistas and incredible biological diversity. Located west of the Pecos River are 19 million acres featuring an impressive array of habitats from desert grasslands, desert scrub, salt basins, sand hills, and rugged plateaus to wooded mountain slopes with summits that support mixed hardwood and coniferous forests. The Trans-Pecos as a whole represents the largest United States portion of true Chihuahuan Desert. This combination of Chihuahuan desert flats with more humid mountain ranges of diverse geological origin creates a living museum of biological wonders. More rare and endemic species are found among its desert valleys, grassy plateaus, wooded mountains, and protected canyons than in any other part of Texas. Indeed, one out of five Texas endemic plants occurs here and nowhere else.

Parts of this region are the hottest and driest in Texas with the western-most reaches receiving a scant eight inches of annual rainfall, sometimes even less. The average annual temperature of 64° F over the entire area does not reflect temperature extremes, heat being an important feature of the area. With elevations ranging from 2,500 feet to slightly over 8,500 feet, precipitation levels increase with increasing elevation giving rise to more moisture-loving communities in the mountainous areas. Soils are exceedingly complex, ranging from very alkaline limestone-derived soils to highly acidic volcanically derived soils.

The Trans-Pecos cannot really be considered a single unit at all. For what occurs on the summit of the south rim of the Chisos Mountains — alligator juniper, Texas madrone, ponderosa pine, for example — bears no resemblance to the vegetation of the surrounding desert which includes creosote, tarbush, ocotillo, and lechuguilla. Generally, the land is dominated by creosote-tarbush desert-scrub grasslands with scattered inclusions of montane ponderosa pine, pinyon pine, and oak forests along with yucca and juniper savannahs, grama grasslands, and saltbush and alkali sacaton-dominated salt basins. Much of the landscape is dominated by desert grassland, but many of the desirable grasses have been replaced by lower quality plants due to continuous overgrazing. Stream courses, or riparian areas, are the oases of the desert, yet few remain relatively undisturbed. These areas support stands of willows, cottonwoods, sycamores, ash, and little walnuts. In these spring canyons, plants that cannot tolerate the rigors of dry desert conditions find refuge in the cool, moist surroundings.

A total of fifty-four species of birds are primarily confined to this region, among them the crissal thrasher, the black-tailed gnatcatcher, Gambel's quail, and Lucy's warbler. In fact, the Chisos Mountains is the only place in Texas where one can reliably find the Lucifer hummingbird, Mexican jay, Hutton's vireo, and painted redstart. Reptiles abound, notably the eastern collared lizard, southwestern blackneck garter snake, and the Trans-Pecos rat snake. Mammals are equally diverse with Mexican long-tongued bat, spotted bat, Texas antelope squirrel, kit fox, and bighorn sheep occurring mainly in this region. Black bears and mountain lions still inhabit the region, although the native populations of wapiti and grizzly bear are long gone. Finally, unique species of desert-adapted and relict pupfish, mosquito fish, and shiners make their homes in the few remaining undisturbed desert watercourses and cienegas.

Trans-Pecos.

© Paul Montgomery

Primary source: Texas Diversity: From the Pineywoods to the Trans-Pecos. In *The Nature Conservancy News:* 32 (5) by S. Winkler.

Chapter Three: *The Basics of Wildlife Habitat*

© Teaming With Wildlife

© TPW

Step outside your back door and take a good look around. Chances are you will see a tree or two, a fence on your boundary line, maybe some clipped hedges, a few shrubs, and most probably a well-kept lawn over the vast majority of your backyard. Maybe there is a bird feeder hanging off a nearby tree limb. Overall, it is quite an attractive scene. However, your pretty backyard could be much more. It could be a haven for birds and other kinds of wildlife. Establishing a small wildlife sanctuary in your backyard will reward you by attracting a variety of animals for you to enjoy viewing. Many of these animals will visit, and some may actually stay to nest and rear their young in your backyard. The secret to attracting wildlife consists of supplying them with three basic requirements for survival: **food, cover,** and **water**.

Food

Naturally occurring vegetation or native species of plants can provide food to wildlife species in your area. A variety of trees, shrubs, grasses, and flowers are good food sources, providing acorns, nuts, berries, buds, fruit, nectar, and seeds that can be used by a variety of wildlife. For a year-round supply of food, choose different plantings that produce food throughout each of the four seasons.

Deciduous plantings generally bear the most fruit, nuts, and seeds for wildlife. In addition, they offer shady, leafy nest sites. However, they shed their sheltering leaves in autumn. Evergreens, which bear leaves throughout the year, offer a good source of berries and seed-filled cones. They also offer year-round shelter, protection, and some breeding sites.

When vegetation cannot supply enough food for wildlife, you can supplement with feeders. There are three main types of feeders: hanging feeders, ground feeders, and suet feeders. Regardless of what type of feeder you choose, regular maintenance and cleaning is important to keep the feeder disease-free and to keep the seeds, nectar, or suet from spoiling. Usually, no more than a two-day supply of food should be placed in the feeders at a time.

Hanging Feeders

Hanging feeders are exactly that: feeders that hang from a tree limb or other overhead support. Fill them with either sugar water for nectarivores such as hummingbirds, orioles, and some bats, or seeds for seed-eating birds and mammals such as chickadees, titmice, and squirrels. When providing a seed feeder for birds, it may be best to use sunflower seeds only. Sunflower seeds are the number one choice of most seed-eating birds, especially the easy to shell and high calorie black-oil sunflower seeds. If a feeder is filled with mixed seeds, wildlife will often toss aside unwanted seeds to get to their favorites. This practice can get expensive and create a mess under the feeder. Squirrels love sunflower seeds also, so you may have to protect your hanging feeder with a baffle — a dome-shaped cover placed above the feeder. This deters squirrels from jumping onto your feeder to eat the seeds and destroying your feeder. Place nectar feeders out for hummingbirds especially during the migration times of March through May, and August though early October.

During these times you will be almost guaranteed to see a few of these flying jewels. To minimize fighting between the belligerent birds, space the feeders widely around your yard.

By choosing your birdseed carefully, you can attract a wide variety of birds, such as these gregarious American goldfinches.

Ground Feeders

Ground feeders vary from an elevated feeding tray placed on the ground and filled with seeds to simply tossing seeds directly on the ground. When used along with hanging feeders, a ground feeder will often distract squirrels from the other feeders. Cracked corn provides an inexpensive source of starch for large ground-feeding birds and squirrels. You can also supply the feeder with mixed seeds such as millet and peanut kernels, which will keep squirrels and most ground-feeding birds busy and happy.

Suet Feeders

A suet feeder dispenses suet (hard beef fat from the kidneys and loins) which is a good high energy food source during winter months. Many birds enjoy a suet feeder, and you will attract a variety of them to your feeder, especially woodpeckers such as the downy, ladder-backed, red-bellied, golden-fronted woodpeckers, and yellow-bellied sapsuckers. To make this type of feeder, simply place hard fat in an old onion bag and hang it outside on a tree limb. Give birds a special treat by adding a variety of favorite seeds and raisins to the melted suet. For a decorative suet feeder, dip pine cones in the warm, melted fat mixture and allow it to cool and set. Vegetable shortening can also be used in place of beef fat. Suet feeders are ideal during cold weather, but suet becomes rancid very quickly during warm weather. In Texas, suet feeders should be watched closely for spoilage.

Cover

Wild animals are always on the alert for danger. Providing cover in your Wildscape will create wildlife refuges and safe havens for visitors. Understandably, wildlife that find shelter in your backyard habitat will feel safer and be more likely to eat, drink, and nest in your backyard habitat. By providing shelter, you can be assured that wildlife will find the one component that will most allow them to survive in your habitat: protection for themselves and their offspring from the weather and predators.

Shrubs

You can provide a variety of structures and objects that are readily used by wildlife. A few well-placed brushy shrubs are the perfect hiding place for frightened animals such as birds, squirrels, or rabbits.

The dense growth will not only keep these small animals out of sight of predators, but it also provides protection from adverse weather conditions. Shrubs are also useful to birds such as cardinals, mockingbirds, and thrashers, since these birds use the thickly growing branches as nesting habitat. Planting thick evergreen shrubs, such as juniper and yaupon holly, will give wildlife shelter even in the winter, when other vegetation has shed its leaves. While shrubs provide a safer retreat from predators, they can also serve as a hiding place for predators, as well. For this reason, shrubs should not be placed too close to areas where animals may be otherwise occupied, such as at bird baths, feeders, ponds, and nest boxes.

You can replace valuable shelter by constructing a brush pile, like this one, in locations such as along the edges of fields, forests, and wetlands.

Brush Piles

Another way to provide shelter for wildlife is to construct a brush pile by piling together loose brush, sticks, and small trees (such as old Christmas trees). Brush piles serve as a haven for small animals such as lizards, rabbits, woodrats, and even birds. The piles should be dense enough to protect wildlife from predators, cold wind, and rain, but loose enough to allow free passage into and out of the shelter. Some good locations for brush piles include forest edges and forest openings, field corners and edges, margins between streams and wetlands, near land that is being cleared, near forests that are being thinned, and along pond edges where the pile can be partially submerged. It is important to note that while brush piles are extremely valuable to wildlife, they may also attract household pests. For this reason, brush piles should not be located too close to your home.

Snags

Standing dead trees, called snags, provide for a great variety of wildlife. Woodpeckers excavate nesting cavities in soft, dead wood, and after the woodpeckers vacate their nests, other birds and mammals will enlarge the holes and nest there as well. Chickadees, nuthatches, titmice, bluebirds, some owls, wrens, tree swallows, raccoons, flying squirrels, and even some bats will nest or roost in these excavations. A few bats and the brown creeper, a tiny forest bird, will even roost under the loose bark of snags during the winter.

Originally, large hollow snags were the preferred nesting site of chimney swifts. Since much of this habitat has been cleared, they have adapted and moved to masonry chimneys which offer the same type of structure and are far more abundant than the hollow snags. Wide scale capping of residential chimneys on newer houses is reducing what was once a commonly available nest site.

Standing dead trees (snags) and fallen logs, like this one, are extremely valuable structures for wildlife.

Snags are also very attractive homes for insects, fungi, and microorganisms that help decompose the wood of the tree. Many of these species are eagerly hunted by various birds, reptiles, and mammals. Snags, therefore, not only provide roosting and nesting opportunities, but also provide a well-stocked "restaurant" for wildlife.

Nest Boxes

If there are no snags available on your property, you may want to construct a nest box to house one of the approximately fifty species of North American birds that are known to utilize bird houses for nesting. Most cavity-nesting birds are insectivorous and thus play an important part in the control of insect pests. Many small mammals also use nest boxes. To provide a nest box for the birds and mammals in your area, you must first decide which species you want to attract. Nest box and entrance hole dimensions for cavity

nesting birds vary depending on the size of the bird. If you decide to purchase a manufactured box, remember that commercial boxes are often designed to attract buyers more than birds. Each species has preferred nesting requirements, and the closer you match these preferences, the more likely it is that your nesting structures will attract the tenants you desire. (See Chapter Five for detailed information on nest boxes.)

Loose Stones and Fallen Logs

While many animals are attracted to conspicuous nest boxes, other types of wildlife prefer a more quiet, secretive place to nest, den, or hibernate. Many amphibians, such as frogs and toads, like the cool, moist areas under loose stones and fallen logs. You can provide loose stone simply by leaving such rock features as stepping stones, garden borders, and rock walls uncemented. The rocks will also be used by lizards, butterflies, and perhaps even a turtle or two for coveted basking spots. Fallen logs are especially useful to salamanders and frogs. They can be placed attractively in a number of locations in your garden, and look particularly nice with a few native ferns and perhaps even some volunteer bracket fungi growing on the dark bark.

Irregular Corners and Small Crevices

One final way of creating shelter for wildlife is by locating and preserving choice irregular corners and small crevices around the outside of your home. Some good examples include the loose bark on snags and logs, the space between rocks in a rock wall or garden border, and in the leaf litter. All sorts of wildlife are attracted to these areas, including beneficial insects, earthworms (a gardener's delight), butterflies, turtles, frogs, toads, salamanders, lizards, and small mammals including our enormously beneficial insect-eating bats.

Water

The final critical habitat component to include in a Wildscape is a dependable source of clean water. Many urban and suburbanites forget what a limiting factor water can be in an area that is far from lakes and streams. Because all animals need a source of water, waterscaping your yard will attract wildlife of all varieties, not just those species that come to feed at your feeders or nest in your nest boxes. Nothing attracts wildlife more effectively on a hot summer day than a supply of cool, fresh

Songbirds, such as this hermit thrush, need a source of fresh, dependable water.

water. Vireos, warblers, mockingbirds, cardinals, hummingbirds, bluebirds, orioles, grosbeaks, sparrows, doves, bobwhite, and buntings will flock to your yard. You may also see many varieties of turtles, tadpoles, dragonflies, squirrels, and beetles using your oasis. If you go a step further and add the sound of moving water by installing a mister, dripper, artificial stream or waterfall, you can almost guarantee that you will attract all sorts of wildlife. The sound of trickling or moving water is an irresistible lure to them. Any extra water feature you add to your basic bird bath or pond will attract a bounty of wildlife.

Designing a Backyard Pond

A backyard pond does not need to be an elaborate construction. It can be as small as a 1' x 2' depression or as large as an Olympic-sized swimming pool. Before you begin building the pond, though, consider the pond's placement, depth, and the surrounding habitat.

Placement: Locate your pond in an area that receives a good amount of sunlight and is not under a tree or bird feeder. The leaves and seed hulls from trees and feeders will fall into the water and decay, and the decaying material will use up much of the oxygen that is dissolved in the water. When a pond is depleted of oxygen, it becomes stagnant and supports very little aquatic life. Also, make sure the pond is not located in a very low part of the yard where pesticides, fertilizers, and other pollutants will drain into it and collect.

Depth: The depth of the pond is critical. If you want birds to be able to use your pond, leave a sloping area into the pond that has rough or rocky

sides and bottom and is no more that 2" to 3" deep. This will allow the birds to enter the water, without slipping, to bathe and drink. This is also helpful to small mammals such as squirrels and chipmunks. Provide a nice slope along an edge of the pond for turtles to enter the water and rest on the bank and for the tadpoles and polliwogs to exit their watery habitat. If you wish to include aquatic vegetation (good for a hiding place as well as for frog and toad eggs), be sure to include an area that is 15" to 24" deep.

Surrounding habitat: Plants, particularly flowering ones, in and around your pond will attract more wildlife than a pond with bare edges. However, predators can also lurk in the vegetation surrounding the pond, so include a sunny, grassy bank nearby which small wildlife, such as birds and small mammals, will use. Just outside of pouncing distance but just inside of flitting distance, place a shrub or small tree where birds and other wildlife can hide in case of danger, or simply to dry their feathers or fur. Aesthetically, it is also nice to curve your pond around a corner and camouflage it with native vegetation such as native ornamental grasses or flowering annuals.

Building a rubber-lined pond involves installing a coping shelf and padding the bottom with sand and other materials.

Building a Backyard Pond

Once you have planned the placement, depth, and surrounding habitat of your pond, you are ready to begin building it. Use the following list of steps as guidelines.

one
Use a garden hose or other flexible material to define the outline of your pond, experimenting with a variety of shapes. If you are using a prefabricated liner, use the hose to outline the contours of the liner on the ground.

two

Start digging around the edges of the pond outline. The edge should support a coping shelf, ledge, or lip of the pond. A coping edge made with cement will keep the shelf permanent, and should be dug about 10" or so deep. Later, heavy rocks can be added on top of the shelf to provide a natural look and help keep the shelf from falling or sagging.

three

Once the depth and width of the coping shelf is completed, place 1" x 4" stakes around the perimeter and attach "bender board," masonite, or other flexible material to create a wall (Figure 3a). This will remind you of a sidewalk being installed.

four

Dig several holes 4" deep around the perimeter of the shelf, close to the center of the distance between the board wall and the earth wall. These can be dug with a post hole digger or a spade shovel.

five

Sink rebar vertically into the holes. Place more sections of rebar around the shelf, tying each horizontal piece to the vertical rebar posts. Horizontal rebar should be a few inches from the ground.

six

Add a bit of sand to the bottom before pouring the cement. Sand helps to absorb moisture in the cement and assists with uniform drying of the cement.

seven

Pour the cement into the ditch to form the coping shelf. Level the top of the cement with a flat shovel or straight two-by-four.

eight

Let the cement dry for a day, then remove the board wall and stakes and dig out the center of the pond.

nine

Contour the bottom of the pond to produce specific topographic features (Figure 3b). Create a variety of depths for use by different plant and animal life. By sloping the bottom up, you allow gasses that build up under the pond to release without floating (and adding stress to) your liner.

Figure 3a

Figure 3b

Clemente Guzman III

ten

Add a layer of sand to the bottom of the dug-out pond (Figure 3c). This helps cushion the bottom of the pond and prevents sharp objects from penetrating the liner. If you have soil that does not drain, or doesn't drain well, you may consider an earth-bottomed pond.

eleven

Prepare your liner. You will want a very thick plastic, such as 45 mil EPDM rubber, which is available at many home repair, garden, and pond specialty shops. Stretch the liner out and repeatedly rinse the side that will face the water. Allow it to dry in the sun for a few hours. Be aware that grass will readily bake under the hot rubber, so if you have any unwanted grass or weeds, this is a good way to get rid of them.

When providing a water element, be sure to create shallow areas for smaller wildlife, such as butterflies, turtles, and songbirds.

© TPW, Judit Gowen

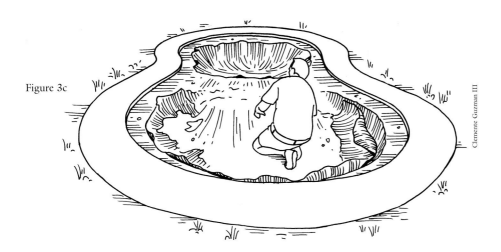

Figure 3c

Clemente Guzman III

twelve

To figure out how much liner you will need, measure the widest and longest part of the pond. Use the following equations:

$$\begin{array}{r} \text{(pond depth x 2)} \\ + \text{ (widest part of the pond)} \\ \underline{+ \text{ (24 inches ``fudge factor'')}} \\ = \textbf{Width} \end{array}$$

$$\begin{array}{r} \text{(pond depth x 2)} \\ + \text{ (longest part of pond)} \\ \underline{+ \text{ (24 inches ``fudge factor'')}} \\ = \textbf{Length} \end{array}$$

thirteen

Depending on how large your pond is, there are different ways to place your liner into the pond. If you are creating a large pond, simply roll the liner up, carry it to the pond, and unroll it in the pond. Try to conform to the corners and bends of the pond. Use heavy rocks to keep the liner in place as you work. If you have a smaller pond, simply stretch the liner over the top of the pond and hold it in place, suspended over the pond, with rocks. Slowly add water into the center of the liner, which will be pulled down into the pond with the weight of the water. By putting in the liner this way, the liner will automatically curve and pleat to fit the contours of the pond.

fourteen

Fill the pond to the top with water and let it sit for twenty-four hours. This will help you determine if there are any leaks in the liner.

fifteen

Now place the coping material into position. The most often used and most natural-looking coping material is native stone, but be sure that the stone is hard and will not break down in a few years. Place one layer of rocks down first, and puzzle-piece them together. Strive for a good, firm fit so that sun will not break down the liner material. Stack more rocks on top to create the look or height you desire (Figure 3d). The rocks should be firmly in place so that the children, who are certain to make a playground out of your Wildscape, will not fall off of an unstable rock.

sixteen

If you would like to add a waterfall or some other moving water element, place a water hose at various sites on the rocks to see where a waterfall would create the most appealing sound to invite wildlife to your newly created pond.

Once your pond is finished, add rocks, sand, and flowering plants to complete the scene.

seventeen

Add selected habitat elements to your pond, such as surrounding vegetation (see Chapter Eleven for suggestions for water plants), water lilies, bog plants, and native aquatic plants (Figure 3e). Add Gambusia or goldfish to help with mosquito control; however, fish will eat frog and toad eggs, as well, so if you are trying to create a frog pond, wait to add fish until the frog population is firmly established.

Figure 3d

Figure 3e

© William McCarley

Installing a Preformed Pond

When installing a preformed pond, follow the basic plan already outlined, but leave a ledge of about 1" depth to accommodate the lip of the pond form. After digging the pond, place a layer of sand on the bottom of the hole. Use this layer to help level the lowered pond form. Fill the spaces between the pond form and the sides of the soil with earth and/or sand. Let the pond settle for one week before adding other elements such as vegetation or animal life.

eighteen

Trim the liner around the edge of the pond back, or leave it as it is and place small pebbles, rocks, or sand on it to create a little beach (Figure 3f). The beach will be used by many animals as a basking area. Birds may even use it as a dust-bathing area. If you slope the beach down into the water, birds will use it for bathing, butterflies will use the margin for "puddling," and turtles will be able to enter and exit the pond with ease.

Figure 3f

Clemente Guzman III

Chapter Four: *Designing Your Wildscape*

© Chuck Kowaleski

© TPW, Judit Gowen

Successful Wildscaping involves more than just throwing out a bunch of native plants in your garden. You will need to plan ahead, not only considering the needs of the wildlife you wish to attract, but also the needs of your family. Think of your Wildscape project as a journey. You wouldn't start on a long car trip before checking a map and familiarizing yourself with your route, so take the time to plan for your Wildscape journey as well. It isn't a difficult trip, but it will require a little forethought.

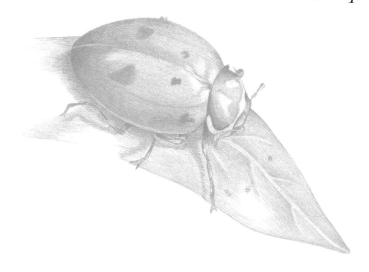

A plan will help you assess your needs and desires and prevent costly mistakes such as installing a pond where you someday want to build a deck. The plan will also help you design a functional habitat to meet the needs of the wildlife you want to attract. Finally, a well-designed plan creates a harmonious, unified garden rather than a piece-meal project. By planning ahead, you can establish your priorities and consider physical and financial limitations.

Design and plan your Wildscape now, and then you can complete the project in stages over several months or years. If your preferences change over time, you can always update and alter your plan to meet your changing needs.

A "before" photograph of an un-Wildscaped yard. There's no habitat for colorful songbirds here!

Taking Inventory

To begin your Wildscape plan, take inventory of your yard to determine existing structures, plantings, and environmental conditions. Use the following steps to gather information about your existing yard and sketch the information you gather to form a scaled map (see Figures 4a- 4f at the end of this chapter).

one
Determine property dimensions and decide on a scale for your map. Example: $^1/_2$ in. = 1 ft. Include an arrow pointing north on your map.

two
Show the location of physical features of your property, including the house, garage, storage shed, other buildings, driveway, sidewalks, and other hard surfaces on the map to scale. Note locations of doors and windows (Figure 4a).

three
Determine possible hazards to gardening, such as utility lines, and mark locations on the map (Figure 4b).

four
Add existing vegetation, flower beds, and lawn areas to your landscape plan. Measure trees and large shrubs from the middle of the trunk out to the tip of a branch to estimate tree spread and mark these on your map. Note any plants that affect energy conservation and comfort in your home such as shade trees and windbreaks.

five
Mark down environmental conditions. Show soil conditions and areas that are sunny, shady, wet, dry, windy, or sloped.

six
Identify special wildlife features such as feeding areas, tree cavities, thick cover, or water sources.

seven
Show neighboring property features that have an effect on your yard, such as roads, fences, noisy pets, or overhanging trees.

eight
Make several copies of your scaled inventory map to use throughout the planning stages.

Evaluating Current Use

Once you have completed your property inventory, you can evaluate what you have to work with and how these features are currently being used. You need to consider current usage by both your family and wildlife in the area. Using one copy of your inventory map, sketch in circular areas to represent family, service, and wildlife use to construct a "current use" map.

Family Needs

Consider how you and your family currently use your yard to determine your family needs. What activities do you and your family enjoy that involve your yard? Do you entertain friends on the patio? Do your children like to play in the yard?

Service Areas

Service areas include the storage shed, garbage can storage, fire-wood stack, air conditioning units, garden shed, and vegetable garden. Do these areas need to be shaded, open, accessible? Would you prefer that they be hidden? How close do they need to be to the primary residence?

Wildlife Considerations

Since the primary object of Wildscapes is to attract native wildlife to your yard, think about the wildlife already utilizing your property. How does wildlife use your yard now? Where does wildlife congregate in your yard? What types of wildlife visit? View your yard from an animal's perspective. What does your yard provide now in terms of food, water, cover, and travel corridors?

Evaluating Future Needs

After finishing the property inventory and current use assessment, you can begin to decide future uses for your property. This is an opportunity to create the yard you have always wanted — on paper at least. Using another copy of your inventory map and referring to your current use map, plan your "future use" map by sketching in tentative ideas and notes (Figure 4c). Include locations of your water sources, brush or rock piles, bird feeders, or other wildlife features you plan to add (Figure 4d). While you brainstorm, consider the following future use of public, private, service areas.

Many birds, such as this Eastern screech owl, require a cavity in which to nest.

Public Areas

Public areas are visible to the public and may be accessed by people other than your family. What are your future plans for public areas around your yard? Does your front yard need a more manicured look to conform to neighborhood standards? Can it have islands of color for hummingbirds and butterflies? Do you need additional trees or shrubs?

Private Areas

Private areas are designated spaces for family use, such as the patio, deck, or backyard. Where do you need privacy screens? What are the desirable views from your windows? Do you need more shade over the back patio? Would you like to reduce yard maintenance and mowing by decreasing the amount of lawn? Do you need designated children's play areas?

Service Areas

Will your service areas alter with changes in the yard? Do you need more room or can you scale down the space designated to these areas? Plan adequate access to these areas and consider ways to screen them from direct view.

Designing for Function

Before selecting plants for your Wildscape, think of the "big picture." Plants are more than pretty, they are also functional, providing shelter, nesting areas, and source of food (nectar, fruit, nuts, and berries). Consider your future plants' functions and how and where they can best be utilized in your yard.

one

Starting at one corner of your "future use" map, sketch in beds and rough shapes to represent general types of plants you want (to scale) considering how they will function to attract wildlife (Figure 4e).

two

As you work, refer to your "current use" map. Think about your needs such as privacy hedging, shade, flowing trees, or understory shrubs and include them on the map.

three

Sketch in locations of your water sources, brush or rock piles, bird feeders, or other wildlife features you plan to add.

Design Tips

one

Curves replicate nature better than straight lines. Curved lines fool your eyes to make spaces seem larger or more distant.

two

Disguise boundaries. A small space looks more confined when its edges are obvious. Use vines or shrubs to soften the straight lines of a fence, or use open fencing materials, such as chain link, split rail, or lattice.

three

Colors affect your perception of space. Cool colors (blue, green, violet) retreat visually to give the impression of greater space. Warm colors (yellow, red, orange) seem to surge forward, making the space look small. If you plant warm and cool colors together, use four times more cool color to balance the warm.

four

Growers define "full sun" as six hours or more of direct sunlight daily, including four hours of hot afternoon sun. "Full shade" is defined as four hours or less of direct sunlight per day. "Partial sun" and "partial shade" fall somewhere in between. (For information on predominately shady yards, see Chapter Eleven.)

five

Remember to design your yard vertically with layers of vegetation, including trees, shrubs, and groundcovers. Place shorter plants in the foreground with taller plants in the background.

six

If you are lacking shade in some areas, consider planting a few fast growing, short-lived trees mixed together with slow growing, longer-lived trees.

Selecting Plants

Choosing plants for your Wildscape is not as difficult as it may seem, but does take some thought. Having already chosen the general types of plants for your plan, you are ready to select specific plants to accomplish your objectives.

one

Concentrate on plants native to Texas that provide food and shelter for wildlife. Remember that not every plant native to Texas is adapted to your area. Refer to the range map (Figure 2a, page 11) and Chapter Two to determine the ecological region in which you are located and the plants and growing conditions that are typical for your area.

two

Study your Wildscape plan to establish your planting needs. Begin thinking about specific plants that serve each function. See the native plants table in the appendix for suggested plants suitable for your region.

three

Refer to your inventory map to check existing light, water, and soil conditions. Make sure to choose plants that are appropriate for those areas.

four

Consider each plant's mature height and width, hardiness, color, and blooming and fruiting period during plant selection. Remember to create layers of vegetation.

five

Note interesting features about each plant. Be aware of potential problems associated with each plant, such as sap or pollen that might cause allergies, leaves or berries that might be poisonous to children or pets, maintenance problems such as messy fruit or invasive roots, or aggressive plants that may grow out of control.

six

Once you have identified specific plant species for each area, use another copy of your base map to write in the actual plants that will accomplish the functions you determined (Figure 4f).

Design Checklist

Before beginning actual work on your Wildscape make sure your design plan includes:
- Native plants
- Water source (shallow areas, reliable)
- Plant diversity
- Winter shelter
- Layers of vegetation
- Snags or nest boxes
- Year-round food sources
- Optimal viewing spots for your family

Planning and planting a Wildscape is a wonderful activity in which to include children.

The Importance of Soil

Soils are the foundation of life. They serve as an anchor for plant roots and are the storehouse for the nutrients, organic matter, air, and water needed for plant growth. Good soils will grow healthy and vigorous plants, which will, in turn, produce an abundance of food and cover for a wide array of wildlife. Knowing what type of soil you have and how to condition it can help you plan and plant a successful Wildscape.

Texas is blessed with a wonderful variety of soils. They are different in mineral composition, particle size, organic matter, pH, and even color. But all good, healthy soils are a dynamic mixture and balance of air, water, minerals, organic matter, and living organisms. The destruction of this balance through the relatively recent agricultural practices of applying harsh synthetic fertilizers and chemicals and removal of dead organic matter has reduced our living soils to dry, sterile dirt.

Before you prepare your soil for your Wildscape plants, you may wish to determine its chemical characteristics by having it tested. The tester should be a company which will give you detailed information about your soil's chemical composition as well as organic fertilizer recommendations. Local nurseries or Agricultural Extension offices may be able to furnish this service.

Another company which can provide this service is:

Texas Plant and Soil Labs
Route 7, Box 213 Y
Edinburg, Texas 78539

Preparing your Soil

To begin replenishing the health and vigor of your soils, concentrate on two main components of the soil: air and humus. Air is extremely important for soil health, for without it, humus formation cannot occur. To increase the air in your soil, turn the soil mechanically with a hand cultivator for ornamental beds, use a mechanical aerator for lawns, or rip or chisel plow larger acreage. Encourage or introduce earthworms to your gardens, as they will provide both the necessary components of air and humus. Humus is the dead, decaying organic matter in the soil which acts as a water reservoir and a slow-release plant food. The best source of humus for lawn and garden is compost. Apply four to six inches of compost over new gardens and watch your soil and plants come alive. By correcting your soil's aeration and humus content, the other elements of healthy soil (microorganisms and chemical nutrients) will naturally be improved.

Determining your Soil Type

The soils of Texas are often described in a variety of terms, which can sometimes be confusing. The most common soil types of Texas include:

Sand: Sandy soil is soil that readily accepts water and that readily releases water. Plant roots grow easily through sandy soil, and can find oxygen pockets even when the soil is wet. The pH of most sandy soil is neutral or acidic, and therefore acid-loving plants such as flowering dogwood and pine will thrive in it. In areas of low rainfall such as South and West Texas, though, sandy soil will be slightly alkaline.

Loam: Loam is a mixture of sand and clay soils, which also contains a hefty amount of organic matter. This combination is the ideal soil which will grow just about anything. Loam is generally neutral or slightly acidic.

Clay: Clay soils are dense, heavy soils. You may also have heard this soil referred to as "gumbo," especially in the Houston area. This is the thick, gummy stuff that will suck your boots off when its wet and be rock hard when it is dry. Most prairie plants do very well in clay soil. Do not try to keep your clay soil consistently wet, as it will literally suffocate sand and loam loving plants. Wet areas that receive more than forty-five inches of rainfall annually will have slightly acid clay soils. With less rainfall, the soil will be slightly alkaline.

An excellent source of information and recommendations on organic gardening and soil health is *The Dirt Doctor's Guide to Organic Gardening* by J. Howard Garrett.

By installing a Wildscape, you automatically reduce the amount of time, money, and chemicals necessary to maintain the health and beauty of your garden.

Maintaining a Wildscape

Maintenance of your newly planted Wildscape is vital for success. Through regular maintenance, you will become familiar with the vital ecosystem developing in your yard. The good news is that by using native plants you have already reduced the long-term maintenance required, but your new plants will need your assistance most during the first year or two.

Water

Plants must have water. Your Wildscape will need regular watering for the first one to three years until the plants become established. For clay-based soils, frequent but brief waterings are necessary. You may need to water more often during the hot summer months. Remember to water below the flowers of nectar-producing plants so you don't wash away the nectar. Ponds and bird baths will lose water through evaporation and may need periodic refilling.

Mulching

Mulching conserves water, adds humus and nutrients to the soil, discourages weeds, and gives your beds a nice, finished appearance. Flower beds and trees should have a 3" blanket of roughly-shredded wood or other organic material. Continue to add a layer of aged mulch to your Wildscape beds and around bases of trees each year. Avoid placing freshly shredded material around your plants. This fresh mulch may be too acidic and can actually burn your plants. Allow the mulch to compost in a pile for a few months before adding it to your Wildscape. A layer of pine needles can be applied around acid-loving plants each fall.

Fertilizers

A good application of mulch should take care of the nutrients your plants require and therefore reduce the need for fertilizers. In fact, many native plants dislike chemical fertilizers and grow better without fertilizers of any kind. If you decide your plants need fertilizing, one application of an organic fertilizer to the soil before the growing season begins should be sufficient.

Mowing

Wildflower patches look beautiful while blooming, but may look "weedy" when the flowers have gone to seed. Mow the wildflower patch with the mower blade four to six inches above the ground after the spring bloomers have dropped their seeds. This allows the summer and fall bloomers to continue growing while trimming the spent stalks. In some areas, you may want to allow the spent flower heads to remain since birds enjoy the seeds over the winter.

Pruning

Native plants may need occasional trimming to remove damaged branches or maintain proper shape. Prune only those branches which are rubbing other branches and causing injury, broken and damaged limbs, diseased limbs, limbs with mistletoe, dangerous limbs, and suckers. Avoid pruning trees during the first year in order to allow them time to become established. In February, trim off the stalks of perennials which die down to the ground each winter and wait for the plant to resprout from the roots in the spring. Or, by leaving the stalk in place over the winter, you allow the seeds to scatter and supply birds with a winter food source. Other perennials die back to the ground and overwinter (survive the winter) as a small rosette of green leaves. Try not to disturb these green clumps through the winter. You will be rewarded with colorful blooms in the spring.

Many people buy beneficial insects, such as these ladybugs, to help control pests in their garden.

Pest Management

Controlling pests in your Wildscape involves different strategies to maintain the health of your backyard ecosystem. Integrated pest management combines the use of natural predators, proper plant selection, and other biological and chemical methods to discourage pests. Wildscaping encourages respect for all aspects of nature. The presence of insects in your Wildscape shows that you have been successful in attracting a key component of

A Wildscape is a beautiful and beneficial addition to any area, no matter how large or small.

the food web. Birds, such as the mockingbird, purple martin, and woodpecker, feed on these insects. Other creatures, including ladybugs, frogs, lizards, spiders, and bats also eat insects. By leaving the insects in your Wildscape, you are maintaining a reliable food source for those insectivorous wildlife species.

The most important step in pest management is to maintain healthy soil. Good, healthy soil produces healthy plants which are better able to withstand plant diseases and insect damage. The second step is plant selection, with emphasis on hardy plants. Native plant species are generally less susceptible to native insect damage and disease. The third step is diligence and active warfare. By frequently observing your plants, you can conquer insect problems in the early states. Nontoxic methods of insect control include manually removing the pests, spraying them with strong jets of water, and maintaining or releasing native beneficial predatory insect populations. Use soapy water, insecticide soap, diatomaceous earth, pyrethrum, and BT bacteria as alternatives to more conventional insecticides, but do so judiciously. By avoiding the use of insecticides, you are also protecting the butterflies and caterpillars residing in your Wildscape. Learn to recognize the caterpillars, ladybugs, and other desirable invertebrates visiting your Wildscape.

Composting

Compost is an integral part of your Wildscape. Compost improves soil structure, texture, and aeration and increases the soil's water holding capacity. Compost loosens clay soils and helps sandy soils retain water. Adding compost promotes soil fertility and stimulates healthy root development in plants.

To create compost, you will need equal amounts of "browns" and "greens." Browns are dry materials, such as dried leaves, wood chips, and small twigs. Greens are fresh, moist materials, such as grass clippings, weeds, and food scraps. Avoid using woody stalks, large branches, pet excrement, fats, and meats. These items will take much longer to decompose and may attract nuisance animals. Make sure to keep your compost moist. A good rule of thumb is to keep the material as moist as a wrung out sponge. Composting may take a month to a year, depending on the amount of aeration, moisture, and composting materials you use. Turning compost is necessary to ensure proper aeration, which promotes aerobic decomposition. Turn the compost once a week or whenever you add new material. To contain the compost material, construct your own container by surrounding it with chicken wire or other open mesh fencing, enclosing three sides with hay bales or wooden pallets, or simply heaping the material in a pile. You can also purchase one of several styles of composting bins on the market. For additional composting information, contact the Texas Natural Resources Conservation Commission, the Agricultural Extension Service in your county, Native Plant Society, or the Texas Committee on Natural Resources (Dallas). Your city or town may also have composting programs which will provide you with information.

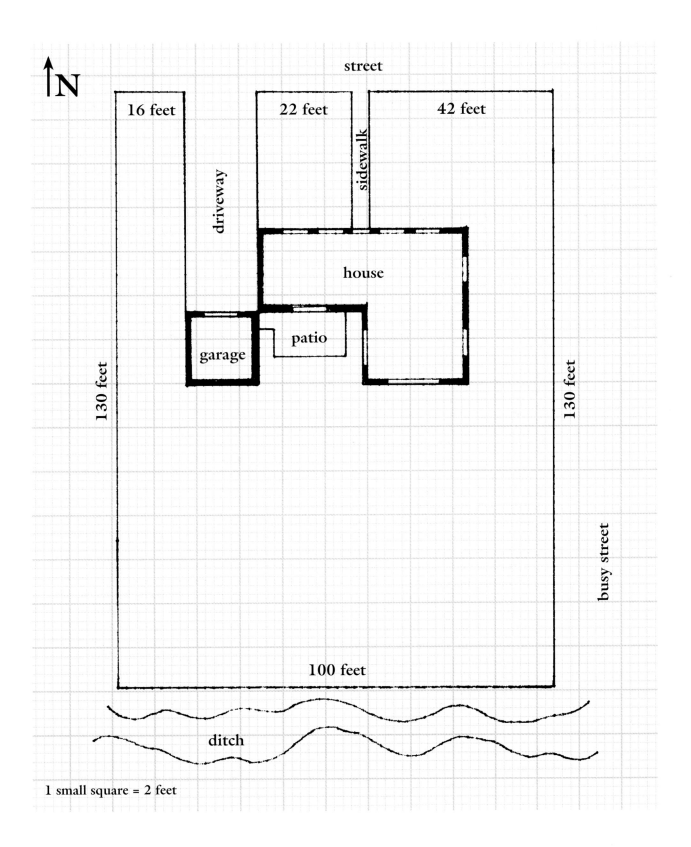

street

N

16 feet   22 feet   42 feet

driveway   sidewalk

house

130 feet   130 feet

garage   patio

busy street

100 feet

ditch

1 small square = 2 feet

Figure 4a. Base map of your property, showing dimensions and buildings to scale.

Source: *Designing a Wildscape,* Diana Foss, Texas Parks and Wildlife, 1997.

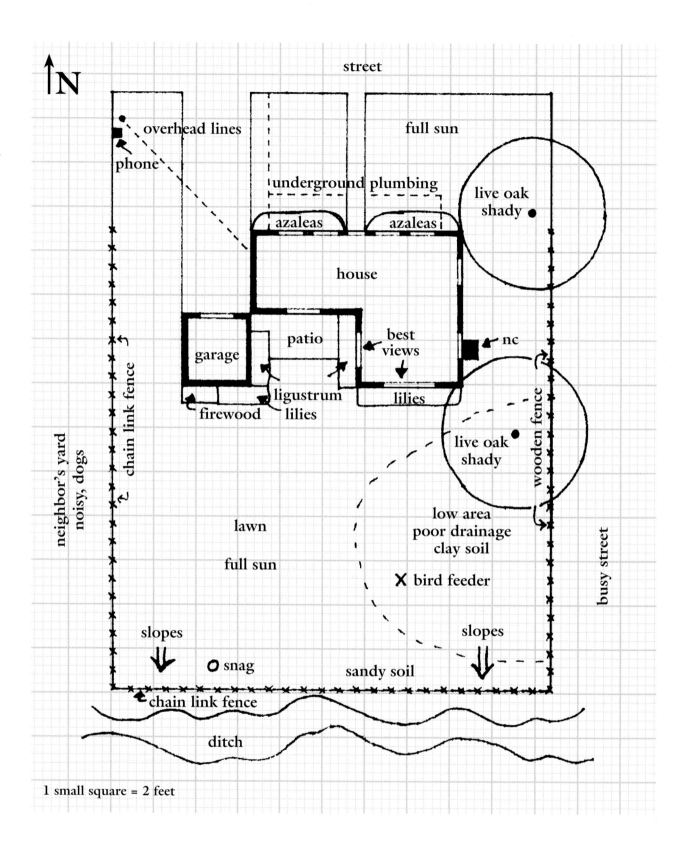

Figure 4b. Inventory map of your property, including existing vegetation, environmental conditions, potential gardening hazards, and other special features.

Source: *Designing a Wildscape,* Diana Foss, Texas Parks and Wildlife, 1997.

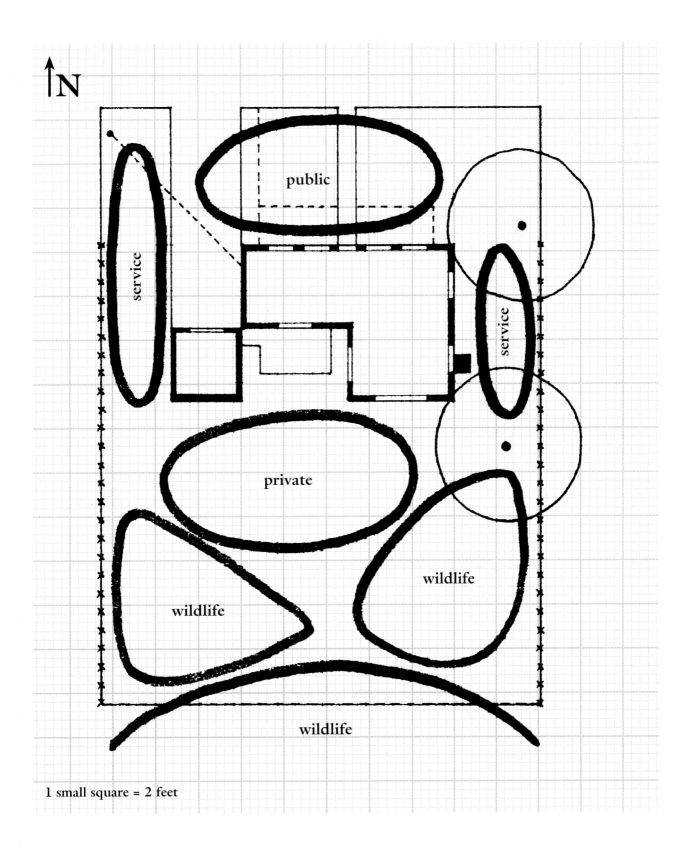

N

public

service

service

private

wildlife

wildlife

wildlife

1 small square = 2 feet

Figure 4c. Future uses sketched on a copy of the base map. Try various layouts on paper (see Figure 4d).

Source: *Designing a Wildscape,* Diana Foss, Texas Parks and Wildlife, 1997.

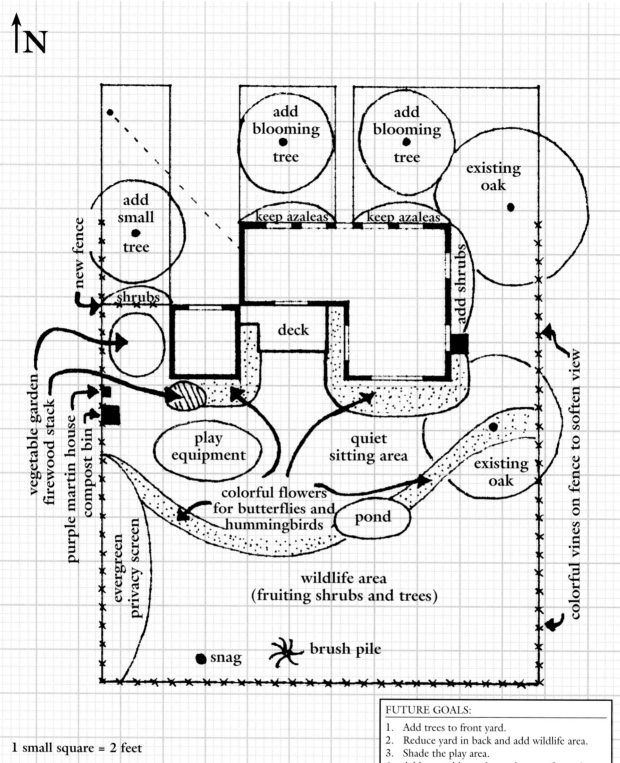

N

add blooming tree

add blooming tree

existing oak

add small tree

new fence

keep azaleas   keep azaleas

add shrubs

shrubs

deck

vegetable garden

firewood stack

purple martin house

compost bin

play equipment

quiet sitting area

existing oak

colorful vines on fence to soften view

evergreen privacy screen

colorful flowers for butterflies and hummingbirds

pond

wildlife area
(fruiting shrubs and trees)

snag   brush pile

1 small square = 2 feet

FUTURE GOALS:
1. Add trees to front yard.
2. Reduce yard in back and add wildlife area.
3. Shade the play area.
4. Add vegetable garden and screen from view.
5. Screen fences with vines and shrubs.
6. Leave dying tree as snag.
7. Add other wildlife features, such as brush pile, purple martin house, and rock wall.
8. Add pond near seating area.
9. Replace lilies and ligustrum with colorful nectar plants.

Figure 4d. Future uses sketched on a copy of the base map. Try various layouts on paper (see Figure 4c).

Source: *Designing a Wildscape,* Diana Foss, Texas Parks and Wildlife, 1997.

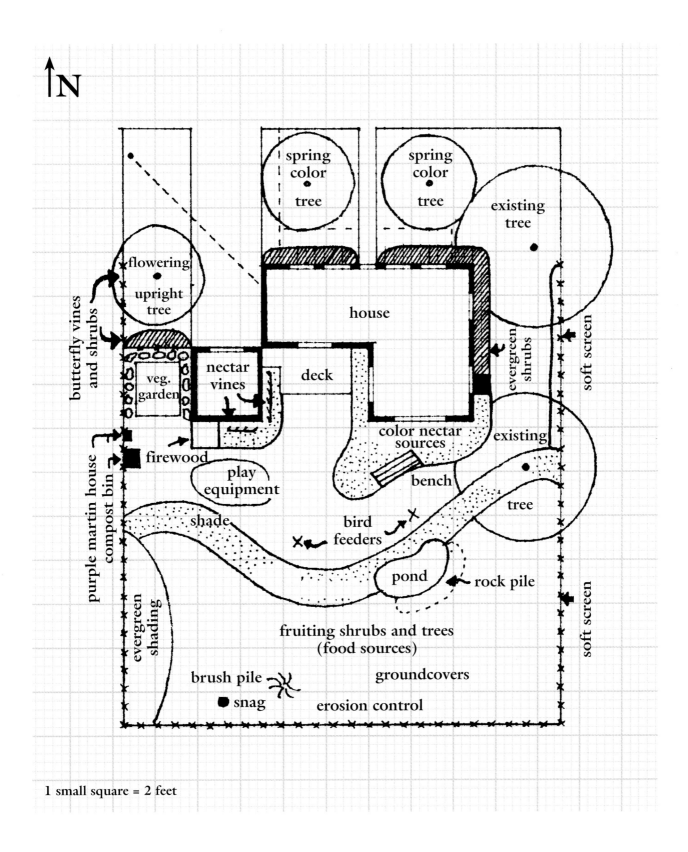

N

spring color tree

spring color tree

existing tree

flowering upright tree

butterfly vines and shrubs

house

evergreen shrubs

soft screen

nectar vines

deck

veg. garden

color nectar sources

existing

purple martin house compost bin

firewood

play equipment

bench

tree

shade

bird feeders

pond

rock pile

evergreen shading

fruiting shrubs and trees (food sources)

groundcovers

brush pile

snag

erosion control

soft screen

1 small square = 2 feet

Figure 4e. Wildscape plan focusing on the function of each plant, rather than individual species.

Source: *Designing a Wildscape*, Diana Foss, Texas Parks and Wildlife, 1997.

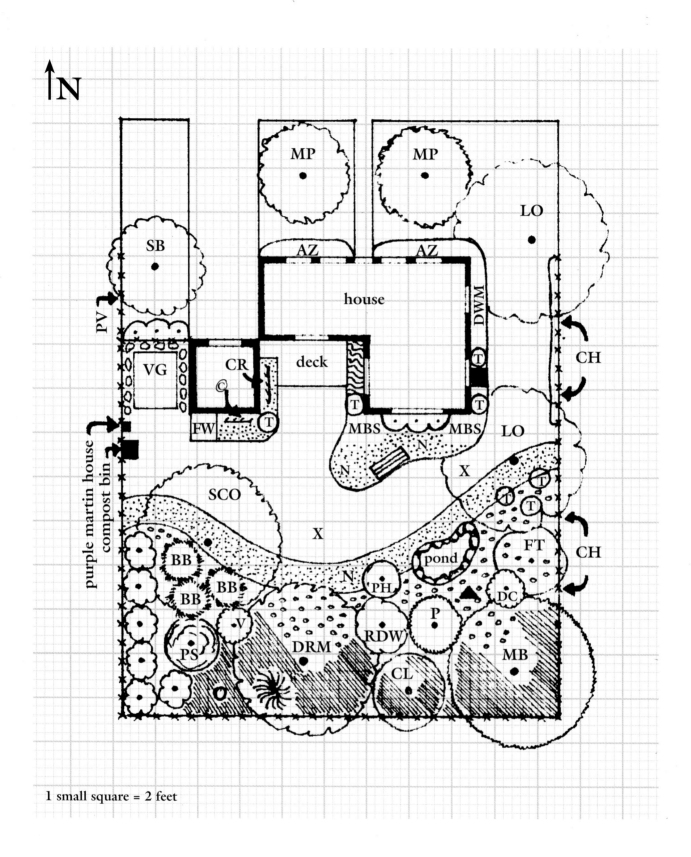

Figure 4f. Wildscape plan for a Houston home, featuring specific plants that perform the functions specified in Figure 4e. See legend at right.

Source: *Designing a Wildscape,* Diana Foss, Texas Parks and Wildlife, 1997.

Ajilvsgi, G. 1984. *Wildflowers of Texas*. Bryan, Texas: Shearer Publishing Company.

Ajilvsgi, G. 1991. *Butterfly Gardening for the South*. Dallas, Texas: Taylor Publishing Company.

Cox, P. and P. Leslie. 1988. *Texas Trees, a Friendly Guide*. San Antonio, Texas: Corona Press.

Ellis, B. 1997. *Attracting Birds and Butterflies: How to Plan and Plant a Backyard Habitat*. Boston, Massachusetts, and New York, New York: Houghton Mifflin Company.

Garrett, J. H. 1995. *The Dirt Doctor's Guide to Organic Gardening*. Austin, Texas: University of Texas Press.

Henderson, C. L.1992. *Woodworking for Wildlife*. St. Paul, Minnesota: Minnesota's Bookstore. (A product of Minnesota Department of Natural Resources. Call Minnesota's Bookstore at 800-657-3757)

Knopf, J., S. Wasowski, J.K. Boring, G. Keator, J. Scott, and E. Glasener. 1995. *Natural Gardening: A Nature Company Guide*. Berkeley, California: The Nature Company.

Loughmiller, C. and L. Loughmiller. 1988. *Texas Wildflowers*. Austin, Texas: University of Texas Press.

Simpson, B.J. 1989. *A Field Guide to Texas Trees*. Austin, Texas: Texas Monthly Press.

Tufts, C. and P. Loewer. 1995. *Gardening for Wildlife: How to Create a Beautiful Backyard Habitat for Birds, Butterflies, and Other Wildlife*. Emmaus, Pennsylvania: Rodale Press.

Wasowski, S. and A. Wasowski. 1989. *Native Texas Plants: Landscaping Region by Region*. Austin, Texas: Texas Monthly Press.

Wasowski, S. and A. Wasowski. 1997. *Native Texas Gardens*. Austin, Texas: Texas Monthly Press.

Green Builder Program, Austin, Texas. www.greenbuilder.com

Texas Department of Agriculture and Texas Agricultural Extension offices in your area. Consult the blue government pages in your local telephone book for the office in your area.

Figure 4f Legend

NECTAR SOURCES

N	Black-eyed Susan	MBS	Mealy Blue Sage
C	Clematis Vine	N	Mexican Hat
CR	Cross-vine	N	Mexican Milkweed
N	Indian Blanket	N	Mistflower
N	Katie's Ruellia	N	Scarlet Sage
	Lantana, New Gold	T	Turk's Cap
	Lantana, Texas	N	Verbena

WILDLIFE AREA

groundcovers		**trees**	
	Partridgeberry	CL	Cherry Laurel
	Wood Violets	FT	Fringe Tree
		MP	Mexican Plum
shrubs		PH	Parsley Hawthorn
BB	American Beautyberry	PS	Persimmon
	Coralberry	P	Possumhaw
DC	Dwarf Cherry Laurel	MB	Red Mulberry
V	Rusty Blackhaw	RDW	Rough-leaf Dogwood
	Viburnum	SCO	Swamp Chestnut Oak
		SB	Sweet Bay Magnolia

SCREENING

CH	Coral Honeysuckle	PV	Passionflower Vine
DWM	Dwarf Wax Myrtle		Southern Wax Myrtle

POND AREA

Buttonbush	Lizard's-tail
Cardinal Flower	Louisiana Iris
False Indigo	Obedient Plant
Gulf Coast Penstemon	Swamp Lily
Halberd-leaf Hibiscus	Swamp Sunflower
Horsetail	Water-lily

MISCELLANEOUS

AZ	Existing Azalea Bushes	FW	Firewood
▲	Bat House	■	Purple Martin House
	Bench		Vine Trellis
X	Bird Feeder	o	Snag
	Brush Pile		

Part Two: *Gardening Tips for Texas Critters*

© TPW

© Teaming With Wildlife

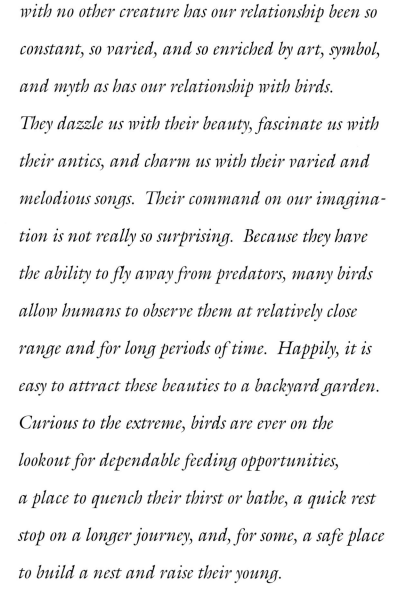

Since the dawn of human existence, birds have evoked wonder and a sense of mystery. Perhaps with no other creature has our relationship been so constant, so varied, and so enriched by art, symbol, and myth as has our relationship with birds.

They dazzle us with their beauty, fascinate us with their antics, and charm us with their varied and melodious songs. Their command on our imagination is not really so surprising. Because they have the ability to fly away from predators, many birds allow humans to observe them at relatively close range and for long periods of time. Happily, it is easy to attract these beauties to a backyard garden. Curious to the extreme, birds are ever on the lookout for dependable feeding opportunities, a place to quench their thirst or bathe, a quick rest stop on a longer journey, and, for some, a safe place to build a nest and raise their young.

Providing for the birds is easy, and you can make your garden more attractive to them in a variety of ways. The key to success is to offer the proper combination of the avian amenities of food, water, and shelter. With planning, it may require only a few additions or changes to transform your yard into an oasis for the birds.

A thick, lush understory has attracted this American robin.

Creating proper habitat for birds will encourage them to stay for more than just dinner!

Creating a "Bird-friendly" Yard

one

Make a literal "bird's-eye view" inventory of your yard; you may already have a number of native trees, shrubs, and flowers attractive to various species of birds. Oaks, cedars, sycamores, elms, and hackberries provide the architecture of a fine habitat. They also furnish food, cover, and nesting sites.

two

Supplement with a wide selection of native fruiting trees, shrubs, and vines. Plants that bear fruit and berries are particularly alluring to bluebirds, cardinals, and mockingbirds in the summer, not to mention cedar waxwings and robins in the winter. Favorites include ashe juniper, yaupon, deciduous holly, viburnum, elderberry, lance-leaf and evergreen sumacs, Mexican plum, Virginia creeper, rough-leaf dogwood, and red mulberry.

three

Create a layered and multi-tiered effect, increase edge, and provide a rich understory. This will increase bird species diversity. Ground-nesters and birds that nest in low, thick shrubs may consider your garden as a potential site to raise their young.

four

Make sure to provide ample clean water. A formal bird bath or even an overturned garbage can top will do. A dripping system that makes a gurgling sound is highly attractive to passing birds. We all know that water is essential for life, but it also provides an area for bathing, which is important to feather maintenance. Elevating the bird bath helps protect birds from cats and other predators. Provide cover and perch sites nearby for quick getaways and places to hide from predators, such as cats and hawks.

Berries like these from a deciduous yaupon (Ilex decidua) *will feed birds during the lean winter times.*

five

Reduce the area occupied by the lawn. Wide expanses of turf grass are sterile habitats attracting less desirable "generalist" species, such as feral pigeons, starlings, cowbirds, and grackles.

six

Provide splashes of color in different areas of the garden. Birds, like butterflies, are highly visual creatures and are attracted by brightly colored wildflowers and fruit. Those glitzy hummingbirds are especially fond of red and orange tubular flowers. Red salvias, penstemons, standing cypress, trumpet creeper, and flame anisacanth will draw a bevy of birds, especially during migration.

seven

Use native grasses as accent plants and in wildlife meadow patches. House finches, painted buntings, goldfinches, native sparrows, and doves readily eat seeds of native grasses and composites, such as sunflowers. Also, consider letting your garden flowers go to seed. Doing so provides a wealth of nutritious food for many species of seed-eating birds.

Birds are attuned to the sound of water. By providing fresh, clean, and dependable water, you can attract a variety of bird life.

eight

Reduce or avoid the use of pesticides in your yard. Many insecticides remove all insects, including beneficial insects as well as pests, that serve as the prey base for insectivorous birds. Using plants native to your region reduces the need for pesticide use since the native plants are resistant to local pests and diseases. Besides, let your birds do the pest control. Mockingbirds, warblers, vireos, and wrens relish insect pests and gobble them up with fervor.

nine

Supplement with feeders. There are several styles of feeders on the market that cater to the tastes of different species of birds: nectar feeders for hummingbirds, tubular feeders for chickadees and titmice, platforms feeders for cardinals, house finches, and white-crowned sparrows, suet feeders for woodpeckers and other winter insectivores, and impaled oranges and other fruit for orioles, mockingbirds, and other fruit mongers. Keep your feeders clean and dry. Seed feeders that get wet often harbor mold and bacteria which can be harmful or fatal to birds, and feeders that are not cleaned regularly will spread avian diseases.

A variety of birds can be attracted to seed feeders. This American goldfinch is enjoying black oil sunflower seed from a hanging feeder. They also love thistle seeds.

ten

Protect your birds from feral and domestic cats. Your beloved cat, no matter how well fed, plays havoc with newly-fledged birds — and their parents, too. It is unfair to attract birds to your yard if you have cats on the prowl.

eleven

Resist removing large old trees with cavities. These standing dead trees, or snags, are used by woodpeckers who make their nests in the soft wood. Many other species of birds, including chickadees, titmice, some flycatchers, and bluebirds, depend on deserted woodpecker holes to raise their young. If there are very few snags in your area, consider putting up a few nest boxes.

A proper backyard bird habitat will have a dependable source of water, multi-layered vegetation, and a variety of food sources including flowering and fruiting trees, shrubs, and forbs, and even supplemental feeders.

Nest Box Guidelines

one

Build the house for a specific species (Figure 5a) with the proper entrance size, cavity depth, and height (see Table 5.1 at the end of this chapter).

two

Use $^3/_4"$ durable woods like cypress, cedar, redwood or exterior-grade plywood as building materials. Avoid pressure-treated lumber or wood with a green-tinted preservative, since the preservative releases toxic vapors.

three

Avoid using plastic or metal boxes, which become lethally hot in Texas summers.

four

When building nest boxes, attach the boards using wood screws, or concrete-coated or ring-shank nails. Galvanized nails tend to loosen as wood expands and contracts.

Figure 5a

Eastern bluebird returning to the nestbox to feed hungry nestlings. Nestboxes can be a valuable commodity to cavity nesting species.

five

Build a wooden roof extending over all sections of the house for maximum protection.

six

To help birds climb out of the box, provide cleats or roughen the surface beneath the entrance hole with a wood chisel.

seven

To provide ventilation, leave gaps between the roof and sides of the box, or drill a few $1/4"$ holes in the sides just below the roof. To ensure proper drainage, cut the corners off the floor or drill $1/4"$ holes in the box floor.

eight

Provide an easy way to clean out the box.

It is essential to provide an easy method to clean out and monitor nestboxes. You will need to clean out nest parasites, old nesting material, and invasive exotic species such as house sparrows or European starlings.

nine

Except for purple martin houses, most nest boxes do not need to be painted. Paint purple martin houses white (on the outside only) to increase chances of house occupation. If you do paint other boxes, choose muted colors that blend in with the natural environment, and don't stain houses with materials like creosote or lead-based paint. If you need to apply a water-proofing agent, apply only on the outside

ten

Don't provide perches, since starlings and house sparrows often take over houses with this accessory. (For more methods of deterring pests and predators, see Chapter Ten.)

eleven

Monitor nest boxes for signs of house sparrow or European starling occupation, and promptly evict these invasive, exotic species. To deter wasps from building in the box, coat the ceiling of the box with bar soap. If you notice blowfly larvae infesting the nest, gently lift up the nest and tap out the insects, brushing the pests out of the box before lowering the nest. To deter ants, coat a section of the post or pole with axle grease. Be sure to wrap the section of post with tape before applying grease if you do not want it to soak into the wood.

twelve

Houses mounted on metal poles are less vulnerable to predators than houses nailed to wood posts or trees. Clear tall vegetation from the base, and wrap sheet metal around wooden poles to deter predators from climbing into boxes.

thirteen

Use no more than four small nest boxes for any one species or one large box per acre. Separate bluebird houses by 100 yards, and do not put any houses near bird feeders. In areas with hot summers, face the entrance holes of your boxes north or east to avoid overheating the box.

Table 5.1
Nest Box Requirements
(Measurements in inches except where indicated)

Species	Floor	Depth	Entrance height above floor	Entrance diameter	Height above ground (feet)	Habitat
Eastern Bluebird	5x5	8	6	$1\,^1/_2$	5	Short grassy areas, with scattered trees for perches.
Carolina Chickadee	4x4	8-10	6-8	$1\,^1/_8$	4-15	Yards, etc., with mature hardwood trees, 40%-60% sunlight.
Carolina Wren	4x4	6-8	1-6	$1\,^1/_2$	6-10	Open deciduous woodland, especially with good cover, and farmland and suburbs.
House Wren	4x4	8-10	1-6	$1\,^1/_4$	6-10	Wooded, shrubby habitats. Place box under eaves or in a tree.
Bewick's Wren	4x4	8-10	6-8	$1 - 1\,^1/_4$	6-15	Open woodland, shrubland, farms, and suburbs.
Tufted Titmouse	4x4	8-10	6-8	$1\,^1/_4$	6-15	Woodlands and forests including parks.
Red-headed Woodpecker	6x6	12	10	2	10-20	Open woods, farmlands, bottomlands, parks, and backyards. Place wood chips in box.
Golden-fronted Woodpecker	6x6	12-15	9-12	2	12-20	Dry woodlands, pecan groves, mesquite brushlands, towns and parks.
Ladder-backed Woodpecker	6x6	12-15	9-12	$1\,^1/_2$	12-20	Dry country including brushlands, mesquite, and cactus, often associated with towns and rural areas. Place wood chips in box.
Downy Woodpecker	4x4	9-12	6-8	$1\,^1/_4$	6-20	Will nest in deciduous and mixed conifer woodlands, riparian woodlands, orchards, and parks. Place wood chips in box.
Northern Flicker	7x7	16-18	14-16	$2\,^1/_2$	6-20	Open woodlands and suburban areas.
Barn Owl	10x18	15-18	4	6	12-18	Mixed agricultural land: meadows, haylands and pastures

Species	Floor	Depth	Entrance height above floor	Entrance diameter	Height above ground (feet)	Habitat
Eastern Screech Owl	8x8	12-15	9-12	3	10-30	Variety: woodlots, forests, swamps, orchards, parks, suburban gardens, especially edges. Use 2-3" wood chips in box.
Wood Duck	10x18	10-24	12-16	4(w)x3(h)	10-20	Bottomland woodlands and wetlands. Place 4" cedar shavings in box.
Black-bellied Whistling Duck	10x18	10-24	12-16	4	10-20	Trees near woodland streams, ponds, and marshes of South Texas.
American Robin	6x8	8	nesting shelf	nesting shelf	6-15	Nests under eaves or soffits of buildings, or on top of light fixtures. Also in trees and shrubs.
Barn Swallow	6x6	6	nesting shelf	nesting shelf	8-12	Farmsteads, on rafters, under eaves, or on top of light fixtures
Purple Martin	6x6	6	1	2 1/2	15-20	Form colonies. Place boxes in open area, at least 30' away from trees, and preferably near open water.
Eastern Phoebe	6x6	6	nesting shelf	nesting shelf	8-12	Build mud-pellet nests in a variety of human-built structures, especially beneath bridges, in culverts, wells, and under eaves and soffets.
Great-crested Flycatcher	6x6	8-10	6-8	1 9/16	8-20	Hardwood forests, orchards, and parks. Prefer pines, mixed conifers, or hardwood stands. Sometimes uses nest boxes.
Ash-throated Flycatcher	6x6	8-10	6-8	1 1/2	8-20	Variety: deserts, chaparral, and woodlands.
Prothonotary Warbler	6x6	6	4	1 1/2	3-5 above surface of water	Bottomland hardwood forests. Nests in flooded backwater habitats, in snags above water, or facing water.

Chapter Six: *Common Texas Birds*

Over 600 species of birds have been recorded in Texas. The diversity of Texas' habitats, as well as its vast size, account for this phenomenon. The following are a few of the more common and best-loved species of the state that may visit your Wildscape.

Northern Mockingbird
Mimus polyglottos

Texas' state bird, the mockingbird, is a talented mimic.

A feisty defender of home territory, this vociferous mimic will often nest in shrubs and trees near your home. Sometimes known to sing by the light of the full moon, or even bright streetlights, the Texas state bird is a great lover of fruit and will defend a berry-laden shrub from all who would dare to trespass. The northern mockingbird is perhaps best known for its singing abilities. Not only can it perform thirty-nine species' songs and fifty call notes, but it can also mimic sounds such as a barking dog, squeaky hinges, notes from a piano, and even a cackling hen. The mockingbird performs so expertly that even an electronic analysis cannot tell the difference between the mockingbird and the original source of the sound. The medium-sized songbird is dull gray above with paler underparts, and is easily identified by the flash of white produced in flight by its wings and outer tail feathers.

Though territorial all year, mockingbirds are especially aggressive during the nesting season, which falls between March and August. If they feel threatened, they may attack starlings, grackles, and even cats. Nests are a bulky cup constructed of dry leaves, stems, cotton, paper, grass, and other handy materials. Females incubate the three to six blue or green eggs, which are spotted with brown. Incubation lasts from eleven to fourteen days, and the young leave the nest after they are ten to twelve days old.

The northern mockingbird is widely distributed and has extended its range much farther north in recent years. They range throughout North America from southern Canada south to Mexico, and have even been introduced and established in Hawaii. Mockingbirds live in Texas all year round and they frequent lawns and gardens in urban and rural environments, edges of open woods, farmland, streamside thickets, and brushy deserts.

Scissor-tailed Flycatcher
Tyrannus forficatus

The beautiful and acrobatic scissor-tailed flycatcher is one of Texans' favorite birds.

Despite being the state bird of Oklahoma, the scissor-tailed flycatcher probably ranks number one as Texans' favorite bird. Its great beauty and aerial maneuvers make it a marvel to behold. On their summer breeding grounds they are birds of open country, where scattered shrubs and trees serve as convenient lookout perches. Males will valiantly defend their territory from crows, caracaras, ravens, hawks, and other birds much larger than themselves. Often seen perched on telephone wires, they seem oblivious to passing traffic.

Males and females are generally similar in appearance, females being slightly smaller with shorter tails. Upper parts are pearly gray while underparts are whitish with salmon pink sides. The male performs one of the most spectacular courtship displays imaginable as he wheels and dives in an elaborate sky ballet to attract the female's attention. For all the intensity of the courtship display, these birds make little fuss about their nest. Females lay five creamy eggs in bulky nests which are placed about fifteen feet high in isolated trees. Scissor-tailed flycatchers winter from Mexico south to Panama. During the fall migration, motorists may count hundreds perched on telephone wires.

Chuck-will's-widow
Caprimulgus carolinensis

The long, mournful song of the Chuck-will's-widow has lulled countless rural Texans to sleep.

Our largest nightjar (a family of long-winged, nocturnal birds), this southern cousin of the whip-poor-will used to be fairly common through most of the eastern two-thirds of Texas. Mottled buff-brown overall with a long tail and rounded wings, its intricate plumage serves as a perfect camouflage. The male differs from the female in having white on the end of the outer tail feathers and a poorly-defined white band across the lower throat. The Chuck-will's-widow is active mainly after dark. Named for its call, this persistent singer seems to clearly pronounce its name: *Chuck, Will's wid-ow*. While hunting, it is also known to utter an eerie growl or croak.

Most feeding is done on the wing, close to the ground, with silent flight. Preferred food consists of beetles and moths that the bird scoops out of the air as it flies the night skies with its mouth wide open. A very effective feeding mechanism, its 2-inch-wide gape is lined with a fringe of stiff bristles that act as a funnel. It will also occasionally take small birds during migration, including hummingbirds, swallows, and warblers. By day, it spends most of its time crouching on or near a fallen log, on a horizontal limb, or on the leaf litter blanketing the forest floor. The female builds no nest but lays two eggs directly on the ground in the leaf litter. She lures predators away from the eggs by feigning injury. If the eggs are disturbed, the female will pick each one up in her mouth and transfer it to a safer location — an unusual behavior in birds. This chunky nightjar winters from Cuba, the Bahamas, and Guatemala south to northern Columbia. Sadly, this nighttime songster, which is heard more often than seen, is being heard less and less. Ground nesting birds are very vulnerable to the increased numbers of predators, especially house cats, found in fragmented woodland habitats. Outright loss of habitat has also taken its toll.

One of Texas' most popular and beautiful birds, the scissor-tailed flycatcher is the state bird of Oklahoma.

Blue Jay
Cyanocitta cristata

© TPW, Kelly Bryan

The beauty of the blue jay is often overlooked. Commonly found in eastern Texas gardens, the jay is a noisy and boisterous inhabitant.

Sometimes a mischievous rascal, this robin-sized blue and white bird with the jaunty crest is a frequent inhabitant of suburban gardens. In wilder places, they still dwell in woodlands along streams and groves of trees on prairies. In Texas, blue jays occur mainly in the eastern half of the state. Exuberant and raucous, the blue jay is mostly a vegetarian, feeding on acorns, nuts, seeds, and fruit. Some of these nuts are not eaten immediately but "cached" in the ground for use later. Blue jays will also glean a variety of insects, some spiders, and other small invertebrates from tree limbs and branches. Not particularly shy, this wily bird will often lord over the other birds at the feeder, supplanting smaller foragers when the opportunity arises. They are also known to periodically help themselves to the contents of any unguarded nests they happen to encounter.

Except during the breeding season, jays tend to troop noisily through parks and woodlands in loose bands. Oddly, you will often see jays "mobbing" large predatory birds such as crows, hawks, and owls. A frenzied flock of jays will surround the beleaguered raptor and harass it unmercifully until it finally leaves. Another favorite pastime is basking in the sun. On cool winter days, you might spot one in a sunny patch of lawn, breast facing the sun, raising its wings to expose its belly feathers to the warming rays. Or it will lie breast down on the ground with its wings spread to warm its back and rump. Blue jays are equally enthusiastic bathers and give themselves with abandon to their daily ablutions in the bird bath or shallow pool. Lucky observers might even catch one excitedly rubbing ants over its feathers, a ritual of feather maintenance and surface bug-removal operation practiced by several songbirds.

Blue jays, while not highly gifted musicians, have a number of distinctive calls — a loud, harsh *jay* call uttered in three's, a distinctive rusty-gate note, and a curious gurgle yodel. They are also skilled mimics and reproduce a version of the red-shouldered hawk call that is almost impossible to distinguish from the real thing. In the spring, the female constructs a round bulky cup-nest made of twigs and bark strips five to twenty feet up in a tree. Nests are often garnished with plastic strips and string to lend an air of distinction. Males help with both nest construction and material supply. The female then lays four to five greenish buff eggs. Both male and female care for the young which fledge in seventeen to twenty days. While perhaps not a model of "perfect" behavior, blue jays will afford the observer hours of enjoyment as they congregate enthusiastically at your feeder.

Carolina Chickadee
Poecile carolinensis,
formerly *Parus carolinensis*

© TPW, Leroy Williamson

The delightful Carolina chickadee can be found throughout the eastern half of Texas.

Black-capped, black-bibbed, and decidedly cute, this agile gleaner of insects and snatcher of seeds is a delight to behold. Speaking its name to announce its presence, this mite of a bird is the southern look-alike of the black-capped chickadee. Carolina chickadees are fairly common through most of the eastern half of Texas south to the Nueces River. A frequent visitor to backyards, chickadees are mainly denizens of woodlands, edges of clearings, and brushy streamsides. They are especially attracted to tube-shaped feeders tailored to their small size which discourage larger, more aggressive seed-eating birds.

In the fall and winter, chickadees will band together with other small woodland birds such as the tufted titmouse, ruby-crowned kinglet, brown creeper, and downy woodpecker. These small mixed flocks comb the countryside in search of food, finding protection and better foraging opportunities by joining forces. Favorite food items include insects and their larvae and eggs, along with seeds and berries. There is perhaps nothing more mesmerizing than to watch a small group of chickadees flitting from branch to branch, working rapidly in a variety of positions, deftly nabbing morsels from the outer branch tips. You will rarely ever see a chickadee feed on the ground, but they will bathe periodically in your birdbath.

Male chickadees begin singing their four-note nuptial song, *fee-bee, fee-bay,* as early as late January and early February. Chickadees prefer to nest in deserted woodpecker holes or other tree cavities found in your yard or nearby woodland. They will also utilize nest boxes with appropriately-sized entrances. Females lay from five to eight white eggs lightly marked with reddish brown. Males and females take turns feeding the young, which leave the nest in thirteen to seventeen days. This small, plump, short-billed bird, at once tame and acrobatic, will provide you with loads of viewing pleasure as it makes quick trips to the feeder and back to its favorite perch in the nearby tree.

Tufted Titmouse
Baeolophus bicolor, formerly *Parus bicolor*

© Sid and Shirley Rucker

The distinctive "peter! peter! peter!" call of the tufted titmouse can be heard in woodlands and suburban areas through most of Texas. This little mite sports the black crest typical of tufted titmouse found in the western part of its range.

With a perky black crest and jaunty air, this small member of the tit family is all business and efficiency at the tube feeder. A quick learner and a problem solver, the smart little titmouse will be the first to learn how to negotiate a new feeder or find a way to retrieve a hard-to-reach morsel. Texas hosts two versions of the tufted titmouse, the gray crested form of the east and black crested form of the west. Tufted titmice are common to fairly common throughout most of the state. Bold and lively, the birds frequent oak groves and other woodland habitats. They can also be found along forest and prairie edges, in streamside thickets, and sparsely wooded pastures. They are common denizens of backyards in towns and cities as long as large trees and thick shrubbery are present.

Like the chickadees, titmice are important members of the wintering foraging flocks that roam the woodlands in search of food. The tufted titmouse has a bounding, quick, and slightly irregular flight as it pops from tree to tree, landing with a slight flourish of the tail. Unlike the Carolina chickadee, tufted titmice periodically descend to the ground to hunt for insects, their larvae, and eggs. They have a special yen for caterpillars and wasps, but will also snap up seeds, nuts, wild fruits, and berries when available.

Highly inquisitive and definitely not shy, they respond positively to whistles and *pishing* noises and will come immediately to investigate the situation. Their most common vocalization is the *peter, peter, peter* song. They also belt out a cardinal-like series of three to five notes all on the same pitch. Titmice have various scold notes, some of them sounding very chickadee-like, and they can produce all sorts of chortling sounds. During the nesting season these usually gregarious birds become aggressively territorial as they defend their nest site against potential intruders. As is the case for all cavity nesters, suitable snags are in high demand and very short supply. Like the Carolina chickadee, titmice will accept artificial nest boxes as long as the entrance is the proper size. An interesting facet of their nest construction behavior, titmice line the inside of the nest hole with all kinds of fur and animal hair and can sometimes be seen pulling the fur from live animals standing or sleeping nearby. Titmice maintain long-term pair bonds. Females lay from five to seven creamy white eggs which hatch in approximately fourteen days. Both males and females tend the nestlings, which fledge after fifteen to eighteen days. Interestingly, young of a previous brood will occasionally help at the nest.

Carolina Wren
Thyrothorus ludovicianus

The Carolina wren is a versatile little bird which will nest in almost any available space, including this abandoned barn swallow nest.

Dressed in rich rufous with a golden ochre breast, the Carolina wren sings gloriously for its supper: an enticing array of insects, with caterpillars a special treat. Having a fondness for hanging baskets of flowers, these close-sitting wrens will flush abruptly, often startling home gardeners who are merely watering their plants. For such a tiny bird, the Carolina wren belts out a resounding and insistent song: a clear *teakettle, teakettle, teakettle* or *cheery, cheery, cheery*. Its varied repertoire of scolds and calls keeps homeowners aware of nesting progress.

Northern Cardinal
Cardinalis cardinalis

One of the brightest sights in winter is the crimson northern cardinal, seen here in its preferred brushy habitat.

With a cone-shaped reddish bill and conspicuous crest, the redbird and his tawny consort are favorites of the backyard garden. With a distinctive black patch at the base of its bill, the cardinal is the only all red-bodied bird in the United States that sports a crest. In Texas, cardinals occur throughout much of the state, though less regularly in the Trans-Pecos and western Panhandle. Highly adaptable to habitats altered by man, cardinals have continued to increase their range, especially northward. The proliferation of bird feeders may be partly responsible for this spread, as cardinals have an inordinate fondness for black oil sunflower seeds. In the more humid areas of Texas, cardinals frequent woodlands or open habitats with scattered trees, bushes, and an abundance of tall weeds. In the more arid regions to the west, cardinals tend to show up around vegetated stream-bottoms and residential areas landscaped with shade trees, shrubs, and water features. Preferring to forage on the ground, cardinals dine on a large variety of wildflowers and grass seeds. They will also eat wild fruits and berries, supplementing their diet with insects, snails, slugs, and mollusks, when available.

Strangely enough, both male and female cardinals will do heated battle with car mirrors and reflective windows, defending territory against the pale reflections of themselves. Both males and females sing, though the male's nuptial song is more insistent and elaborate. Loud, clear, rich, and mellifluous, the song is a sustained series of variable, distinctively phrased whistles. The call note is a sharp and emphatic chip which is easy to recognize once you have heard it. Come nesting time you will notice the male providing tasty courtship feedings to his wing-fluttering mate. While the pair bond is maintained throughout the year, he becomes much more attentive and solicitous at this time. Indeed, until she lays her eggs, he hardly lets her out of his sight. Nests are placed from five to ten feet off the ground, usually in a well-hidden spot toward the center of a thick shrub. Once the female has laid the three to four eggs in the scantily-lined cup-shaped nest, the male will bring her tidbits of food as she incubates. He also performs a good many of the nest chores such as feeding the young and removing fecal sacs. Young fledge about twelve days after hatching. At this time the male will take over the feeding of the youngsters while the female starts a new brood.

House Finch
Carpodacus mexicanus

Also known as the "Hollywood finch," the colorful and gregarious house finch is one of the earliest nesters of the season.

Otherwise known as the Hollywood finch, this gregarious cherry-colored finch with a brown cap and streaky belly sings a melodious song. Expanding its range to urban areas, it gives the ubiquitous house sparrow a good run for its money. House finches favor weed seeds but also flock to feeders where they plop themselves down to gorge on sunflower seeds, to the utter frustration of the titmice and chickadees who wait impatiently for the seed gluttons to leave.

Cedar Waxwing
Bombycilla cedrorum

A dapper gentleman, the cedar waxwing is so named for its fondness of cedar and juniper berries, and for the drop of what looks like red sealing wax on its wings.

Always impeccably groomed, this sleek and elegant bird is an abundant wintertime visitor. The cedar waxwing's silky brown-buff plumage is set off smartly by a black mask, perky dark brown crest, short, yellow-tipped tail, and yellowish underparts. Waxwings get their curious name from the red waxlike spot found on the secondary wing feathers of most birds.

Cedar waxwings tend to be rather gypsylike in their occurrence. Arriving in mid-October or November, they can stay as late as May. They are irregularly abundant to fairly common throughout most of the state. Flying in tight formations, these highly gregarious birds often alight en masse in a fruiting tree. Watch for the "pass the berry" game, in which one bird passes an uneaten fruit to the next bird down the line to the end of the limb, the final bird gobbling it up with delight. Preferred habitats include dense to open woodlands, valleys, swamps, and tree-cloaked hills. They readily frequent cultivated areas bordering fields and private residences, especially those with ornamental fruiting trees. In the western regions, they gravitate toward the brushy and tree-lined stream bottoms. A major fruit lover, waxwings gorge on ripe cedar and juniper berries, hackberries, and pyracantha berries. A large flock can strip a tree of nearly all its fruit in a matter of minutes. When winters are marked by great fluctuations in temperature from long-term hard freezes to abrupt thaws and warm spells, wild fruits and berries will often become fermented. Large flocks of waxwings feasting on the tainted fruit can become hopelessly drunk. Birds then fall to the ground or wheel deliriously about crashing into cars, windows, or the paws of an onlooking cat. Cedar waxwings don't have elaborate songs. They emit high-pitched lisping calls, *see, see, see, see, see,* which do not carry over a long distance. Cedar waxwings are one of the major delights of the winter landscape, and along with American robins, brighten up those somber winter days.

Red-bellied Woodpecker
Melanerpes carolinus

In the wild, red-bellied woodpeckers eat ants, beetles, berries, acorns, and corn. In backyards, the bird will partake of seeds, bread, fruit, suet, and even the sugar water set out for hummingbirds and orioles.

Also known as the "zebra" woodpecker, this noisy bird is the only bar-backed woodpecker with an entirely red crown. Favorite haunts in Texas include groves of deciduous trees, open stands of mixed coniferous forest, and stream and edge habitats in the eastern half of the state. Many Texans mistakenly call this bird with the red cap the red-headed woodpecker, and this is understandable because the so-called red-belly is really a very pale coral, rarely visible in the field. The red-bellied woodpecker, also known as the "Chad" or "Chack" for one of his calls, is often heard before it is seen. A noisy bird, it also utters a soft, *churr* several times in succession.

Not a gregarious species, red-bellies are usually seen singly or in pairs. In settled areas, this woodpecker will often frequent backyards and orchards. It is one of the few members of the family that consumes more vegetable matter than insects. Berries, acorns, and corn are favorite food items. They also take ants and beetles and sometimes store them in cracks and tree crevices for a later day. Many suburban red-bellies are attracted to backyard feeders, partaking of seeds, bread, fruit, suet, and even sugar water set out for hummingbirds. A fairly common nester in large back yards or nearby woodlands with suitable snags, both male and female excavate the nest cavity. Birds will also use an artificial nest box, lining it with small bits of wood chips or sawdust. The female lays four to five elliptical white eggs that are sometimes glossy and sometimes matte finished. The male incubates the brood at night, with the female taking over for the day shift. Young fledge from twenty-four to twenty-seven days after hatching and will remain around the nest tree or nest box for the time it takes to learn how to forage for themselves.

Downy Woodpecker
Picoides pubescens

The pint-sized downy woodpecker can often be seen feeding in mixed flocks with chickadees, titmice, and nuthatches.

Industrious and diligent, this smallest of our woodpeckers ranks as one of Texas' favorites. His cheerful *peek* call and his long, rattling, descending "whinny" resound from tree trunk and backyard suet feeders alike. This tame little bird hitches up a tree trunk headfirst by a series of hops and jumps, poking under a flake of bark here, looking into a crevice there, tapping attentively all the while in search of hidden insects. If you walk toward him as he pecks away at the trunk, he will merely circle coyly to the other side, then peer around to see if the coast is clear. He drills the trunk with his short awl of a bill and can often be seen dangling from twigs relieving the outer branches of any hapless insect or grub.

The downy ranges across North America, avoiding only the arid regions of the Desert Southwest. A year-round resident of eastern and northern Texas, he is one of the few of our woodpeckers whose range does not also extend into Mexico. Look for the downy feeding in mixed foraging flocks in open woodlots and parks in the company of chickadees, titmice, and nuthatches. Interestingly, downies go through a brief amorous stage in the fall. Heated rivalries, brief bouts of drumming and dancing soon give way, however, to renewed peaceful coexistence with the onset of cold weather. Birds excavate a new nest every year and often choose cottonwoods or other species found near water.

The downy lines the nest cavities with wood chips and dust and often camouflages it with surrounding moss, fungus, and lichens. The female lays four to five white eggs and both male and female incubate. After the eggs hatch the male is thought to do most of the brooding of the young. Young fledge approximately twenty-one days after hatching. Fledglings remain dependent upon their parents for their food and for learning how to forage until about three to four weeks after fledging.

Chapter Seven: *Hummingbirds*

© TPW, Earl Nottingham

© Sid and Shirley Rucker

Feisty hummingbirds zipping about from flower to flower like so many glittering dive-bombers are a delight to watch, and you can easily attract them to almost any backyard. Their shining, jewel-like colors and fascinating behavior make hummingbirds among the most welcome visitors to the wildflower garden. Curious to the extreme and ever on the lookout for new sources of food, hummers will boldly explore your garden for suitable nectar sources.

In the wild, hummingbirds frequent meadows, lowland forest edges, and woodland openings. The key to creating an attractive habitat for these small creatures is to provide them with conditions that most closely approach those found in the wild. Floral variety, rich nectar sources, overlapping bloom times, running water, and adequate cover are prime ingredients.

Hummingbirds utilize two major sources of food: flower nectar and the tiny insects and spiders that are attracted to it. The sweet sap which exudes from holes that sapsuckers have made in trees is another food source. Hummers will also frequent special feeders, well placed for easy viewing, which contain sugar water of the proper concentration. While hummingbirds obtain most of their water from flower nectar, it is good to provide an additional source of running water for them to bathe in and drink. Even though hummers can use beads of water on a leaf or even the spray from a garden sprinkler, putting up a bird bath with a small mister, dripper, or waterfall is perhaps the most effective method of providing water for hummingbirds. Make sure the bird bath has areas of very shallow water so the birds are able to stand in the water if they choose to do so. Place a few flat rocks in the water to create various depths. Watching hummers absorbed in their daily bathing routine can be lots of fun for the whole family.

Hummingbirds mainly feed on flower nectar and the tiny insects and spiders that are attracted to it.

Designing a Hummingbird Garden

Gardens designed to attract hummingbirds are easy to create. They can be as simple as a flower box of hummingbird plants arranged on a balcony or patio, or as elaborate and expansive as a formal parterre garden. Include native trees, shrubs, and vines along with native wildflowers. (See Table 7.1 at the end of this chapter for a list of plants that hummingbirds favor.) Flowering shrubs are very effective hummingbird lures, as are trellises and fences covered with flowering vines. Rather than scattering flowers about, plant them in clusters. Incorporate areas of shade, partial sun, and full sun. Include tall trees, short, thick shrubbery, and low grassy areas to create a multi-tiered effect. The multilayered arrangement not only affords a wide choice of suitable foraging, perching, and resting areas, it also provides easy access to all the flowers. Hummers will make use of this extra space around the blooms to hover and forage comfortably.

Coral honeysuckle is an ideal hummingbird plant, having orange-red tubular flowers that angle down, very tiny petals, very little scent, and copious nectar.

Plants that Attract Hummingbirds

One of the most important steps in creating a hummingbird garden is selecting and planting appropriate flowers. While hummingbirds will visit nectar-bearing flowers of all colors, they are particularly drawn to bright red and orange tubular flowers. A garden rich in scarlet penstemon, red sages, and bright orange trumpet vine will catch the eye of any hummingbird passing nearby. However, you do not need to plant an all red flower garden to attract them. Once the birds discover suitably shaped flowers with abundant nectar, they will return to them. And, while hummingbirds are attracted to a variety of plants, native wildflowers and flowering shrubs are recommended.

Before selecting particular native plants, it is good to review some of the structural characteristics of the classic hummingbird flower. Many "hummingbird flowers" hang down in pendant fashion or are held horizontally in widely spaced clusters of flowers. This configuration gives the bird plenty of room to feed easily and lessens the possibility of entanglement. Most hummingbird flowers have tubular or trumpet-shaped blossoms with thick petal walls and flexible stalks. Thick petal walls protect the delicate ovary at the base of the floral tube from the hummingbird's sharp bill, and also discourage cheaters, like carpenter bees, from nipping the base and stealing the nectar without pollinating the flower. Other blossoms have grooves which guide the cylindrical hummingbird bill to the nectar and away from fragile flower parts. Because hummingbirds have a very poor sense of smell, many hummingbird flowers save energy by not producing a fragrance.

Hummingbirds require a great deal of energy to maintain body temperature and sustain flight. For this reason, hummingbird flowers produce large amounts of nectar at frequent intervals. Unlike insects, hummingbirds do not require special floral platforms on which to land while feeding since the birds hover in the air in front of the flowers to drink the nectar.

This ruby-throated hummingbird hovers while sipping nectar from dangling bright red salvia.

The individual plants you select for the hummingbird garden will depend on which area in Texas you reside. Hummingbirds feed from a variety of different native plants. Ruby-throated hummingbirds, whose range extends throughout the eastern half of the United States, are especially attracted to red columbine, scarlet sage, coral honeysuckle, phlox, trumpet creeper, cross-vine, standing cypress, and various species of red, pink, and magenta penstemon. The black-chinned hummingbird, which summers throughout most of the western United States from central Texas to British Columbia, is attracted to ocotillo, tree tobacco, chuparosa, lantana, palo verde, butterfly bush, scarlet delphinium, paintbrushes, red columbine, agaves, scarlet gilia, various penstemons, and red yucca, to name a few. Many species of the hummingbirds that occur in the southwestern portion of the state include the blue-throated, broad-tailed, magnificent, lucifer, rufous, and the occasional Anna's hummingbirds. The broadbilled, calliope, green violet-ear, violet-crowned, and white-eared hummingbirds also show up sporadically in our state. Native wildflowers and shrubs of the southwest such as paintbrush, penstemons, columbines, sky-rocket, agaves, lupines, red salvias, ocotillo, lobelia, and monkey-flowers are highly attractive to these species.

It's easy to make the sugar-water nectar hummingbirds eagerly lap up: Just combine four parts water with one part granulated white sugar, boil, cool, and fill the feeder.

Hummingbird Feeders

It is easy to create a "fast food" hummingbird cafeteria by hanging one to several hummingbird feeders at various points around the outside of the house and in the yard. Position them for easy viewing from living room, bedroom, or kitchen windows so you can enjoy the show. If you are really enterprising, rig up a fluorescent spotlight to bring out the full iridescence of each species' body feathers as it comes to sip the nectar. It is important to purchase or construct the nectar-containing feeder in order to discourage ants and bees who will also be attracted to the sugary solution. You might also try to block pesky ants and bees from the feeder by applying Vaseline to the pole or the wire holding the feeder. Some feeders have specially designed bee guards that fit over the feeder holes making it difficult for bees to reach the fluid. Other feeders have even been designed with an "ant moat," a tiny bowl of water fitted around the feeder hanging wire that prevents the ants or other crawling insects from traveling down the wire to the feeding ports of the feeder.

Bottles or feeders hung among the blossoms of flowering shrubs are speedily discovered by hummingbirds. Hummingbirds are sometimes so bold that you may be able to attract one by simply holding a bright red flower in your hand while standing a short distance from a flowering shrub. Sitting quietly in a lawn chair wearing a red T-shirt or bright red cap may also arouse the curiosity of one of these feisty creatures.

After you purchase or construct your hummingbird feeder, you need to fill it with hummingbird food. There are commercial solutions available on the market which you can purchase, but it is just as simple to make your own at home. A good recipe for a homemade mixture is one part sugar to four parts water, which closely approximates the ratio of sugar to water in the nectar of many hummingbird flowers. White granulated sugar is best to use. Boil the mixture for one to two minutes and then let it cool. This process will help to delay fermentation. **Do not use honey** since it harbors a fungus that could be a health threat to the birds.

Fill the feeder and store the remaining liquid in the refrigerator. It is not necessary to add red food dye to the solution. Many feeders on the market are made of red plastic or have red somewhere on the plastic covering. This will be more than enough color to attract the birds. Make sure that you clean the hummingbird feeder every few days, as hummingbird liquid is highly susceptible to mold and bacteria, which may present a health hazard to the birds, especially in hot weather. Cleanse feeder bottles and nectar ports with soap and water, or a combination of baking soda and vinegar (watch out: this combination fizzes). Rinse feeders thoroughly to remove all residue. You will find that some designs of hummingbird feeders are easier to clean than others.

It is almost impossible to differentiate between the species of some female hummingbirds. This little female is either a ruby-throated or black-chinned hummingbird.

Since most species of hummingbirds are migratory, feeders should be set in place to coincide with the birds' arrival in the spring. The arrival date, of course, will depend on which part of Texas you live in and on the migratory patterns of the birds. Your local Audubon Society will have inexpensive bird check lists available for your region which will indicate average spring arrival and fall departure times of hummingbirds for your part of the state. To find your local Audubon Society chapter, call the National Audubon Society office in Texas at 512-306-8751. In addition, refer to any of several field guides to the North American birds. These sources will inform you about when you can expect to see hummingbirds and which species of hummingbirds to look for in your area.

It is a misconception that it is harmful to leave a feeder up too late in the fall. Doing this will not prevent a hummingbird from migrating. Feeders that are left up longer than usual may actually help late migrating hummers, since they will provide the birds with the critical extra energy they need to complete the journey in an environment that may be devoid of flowering nectar plants. If you choose to leave your feeders up only during migration periods, though, a good rule of thumb is to wait until one week after you see the last hummingbird before you remove your feeders.

Black-chinned hummingbirds are found throughout the western half of Texas.

Placement of feeders is very important. If possible, try to hang feeders in the shade and out of the wind. It is a good idea initially to place feeders near native wildflowers that are naturally attractive to hummingbirds. This may speed up the discovery process. It is better to have already created a habitat garden where hummingbirds are likely to visit before hanging up the feeders. The addition of feeders to the garden will simply increase the traffic by offering more foraging opportunities to more individuals.

Don't be disturbed to find out that hummers can be very aggressive and sometimes outright belligerent with one another when it comes to sharing a feeder. Chases abound and they may expend a good deal of energy in establishing a dominant position around well-placed feeders. It is always interesting to observe the hummers as they jostle for position in the pecking order. You will soon get to recognize which bird is the alpha individual, so to speak. To minimize spats, place feeders far apart in locations out of view from one another.

While most feeders are quickly attended by a host of hungry hummers, there are a few reasons a feeder may seem to go unused.

When Hummers Won't Come to a Feeder

Often people put up hummingbird feeders and are disappointed when birds don't appear. The reasons hummingbirds may not discover the feeders are numerous and complex. A few possible reasons for an absence of hummers are:

- Lack of patience. It may take a few weeks for hummingbirds to find feeders. Once discovered, however, they will return year after year. Be sure to keep the solution fresh and clean, even if you don't think the birds are around.

- The feeding solution level may be too low or may be fermented. This is often the case in a climate like Texas where the heat of only two or three afternoons can ferment the solution. If you have left your feeder empty for too long a period, hummers will go find food elsewhere.

- Sometimes it only appears that hummers are not using the feeder. Much of their time is spent perching and preening inconspicuously in a nearby tree. Hummers may then zip to the feeder when you are not looking.

- Hummingbirds will often use the feeders heavily during migration periods, but when it comes time for the females to build their nest, they will become much more secretive and inconspicuous. Again, be patient. Come the end of August, little migrants will be back looking for food to fuel their upcoming voyage to the tropics.

- There may be so much food in the wild that hummers do not need to supplement their diet. If given a choice, hummers prefer flowering plants and shrubs. When bloom periods are over, however, they will return faithfully to the well-supplied feeders.

- If your neighborhood does not have an abundance of wildflowers, hummingbirds may just not be attracted to that area. Neighborhoods with lots of nectar-rich flowers are a mecca for hummers.

Some species of sphinx moths, also called "hummingbird moths," mimic hummingbirds. Their wings hum like the hummingbird's, the proboscis (part of an insects mouthparts) extends out to resemble the hummingbird's beak, and they hover just like hummingbirds. Sphinx moths are also important pollinators.

- There may be too many aggressive bees and ants around your feeder which make foraging difficult and dangerous for the hummers. Try installing bee guards and ant moats (available at almost any shop that carries birdfeeders), or greasing the post or hanging wire. For the hummingbirds' protection, be sure to keep insecticides and other foreign substances away from the feeder ports.

Hosting hummers in your backyard will require work and planning, but once your hummer habitat is established and the birds have discovered it, they will repay you with hours of enjoyment. Their beauty more than makes up for the labor involved.

Ruby-throated Hummingbird
Archilocus colubris

The only hummingbird found in the eastern part of Texas and the United States is the colorful ruby-throated hummingbird.

The darting flight and insistent squeaks and chitters of a hummingbird are sure signs that spring has arrived. The male ruby-throated hummingbird is a tiny bird, sporting a bright red throat patch, or gorget, and a beautiful bronze-green back. Females are a little less fancy, with a white-gray throat and underparts, white spots on the outside tips of the tail, and the same beautiful bronze-green back. Neither male nor female weighs much more than a penny, and they are both lively additions to any rural, suburban, or urban garden.

The little ruby-throat migrates from Central America to the eastern half of the United States as well as southern Canada in the spring to breed. Many of the hummingbirds will migrate directly over the Gulf of Mexico, making a 650-mile nonstop flight on the energy of just a few grams of fat. Females construct their tiny nests primarily out of plant bud scales held together with spider silk, lined with plant down, and decorated with bits of lichen. Her two eggs resemble navy beans in size, shape, and color. In the fall and after the nesting period, the ruby-throat migrates again south to the wintering grounds of Central America. Since ruby-throated hummingbirds are very curious, providing feeders and flowers, especially red or orange flowers, in your garden is almost always rewarded with a visit from the little birds.

Black-chinned Hummingbird
Archilochus alexandri

The beautiful male black-chinned hummingbird sports a black chin and a blue-purple "collar."

Breeding from Texas, where it is the most common hummingbird, all the way up into British Columbia, the black-chinned hummingbird has the most extensive breeding range of any western hummingbird. As its name suggests, the black-chin is the only North American hummingbird to feature a black throat patch edged by a glittering band of amethyst-purple iridescence. Metallic green above with dull green sides and flanks and whitish underparts, black-chins closely resemble their eastern counterpart, the ruby-throated hummingbird — especially in poor light. When the telltale gorget is not visible, male black-chins can sometimes be distinguished by their slightly darker underparts and narrow white collar. Females of the two species, however, are almost impossible to distinguish in the field.

Over much of the west, this hummer is widespread in a variety of semi-arid habitats at lower elevations. It often frequents suburban gardens and will sometimes nest in backyards within its range. In addition to well-flowered residential areas, preferred habitats include semi-dry brush country, chaparral, and river groves. In Texas, black-chins are known to nest across the central and western counties, as far east as San Antonio, Austin, and Dallas.

The black-chin's feeding habits are similar to those of the ruby-throat, perhaps with a greater tendency to watch for small flying insects from a conspicuous perch, sallying out after them in the manner of a flycatcher. One of the more vocal hummingbirds, black-chins utter a cascade of high-pitched squeals and twittering notes. Some writers have compared its high-pitched song to a person whistling through his or her teeth. Call notes consist of a soft *tchew*, but when squabbling with others at a well-defended feeder, chip notes are spewed out in rapid-fire succession.

Males attract females by performing elaborate aerial courtship displays consisting of a series of deep looping dives and elaborate figure eights. After mating, the female assumes all nesting duties while the male seeks to impress other potential mates. Females build a tiny, walnut-sized nest of plant down and spider webs much like that of the ruby-throat except that they do not use lichens so extensively for adornment. The female alone incubates the two pea-sized white eggs until they hatch about sixteen days later. She feeds the tiny, helpless chicks a rich diet of nectar, insects, and spiders which she administers by regurgitation, inserting her bill deep into their throats. Chicks accept the food in the manner of a mini sword swallower, a disconcerting sight for almost anyone who first witnesses the process. Within two weeks, the chicks begin exercising their wings and are soon to fledge — two more incredible feathered flying machines set out into the world.

Table 7.1
Plants Favored by Hummingbirds

* Not native to Texas, but not invasive. ** Considered naturalized.
Note: Plants are listed alphabetically by family. Numbered regions correspond to the Texas Ecoregion map on page 11.

Common Name	Scientific Name	1	2	3	4	5	6	7	8	9	10
Acanthus Family	**Acanthaceae**										
Flame Acanthus	*Anisacanthus wrightii*							x			
Hummingbird Plant	*Anisacanthus insignis*										x
Shrimp Plant	*Beloperone guttata* *						x				
Agave Family	**Agavaceae**										
Century Plant	*Agave americana*		x				x			x	
Century Plant	*Agave neomexicana*										x
Red-flowered Yucca	*Hesperaloe parviflora*			x	x	x		x			
Catalpa Family	**Bignoniaceae**										
Cross-vine	*Bignonia capreolata*	x	x	x	x						
Trumpet-creeper	*Campsis radicans*	x	x	x	x	x	x	x			
Desert Willow	*Chilopsis linearis*						x	x			x
Yellow Trumpets	*Tecoma stans*							x			x
Borage Family	**Boraginaceae**										
Geiger Tree	*Cordia sebestana* *						x				
Pineapple Family	**Bromeliaceae**										
Air Pine	*Tillandsia bailleyi*						x				
Cactus Family	**Cactaceae**										
Hedgehog Cactus	*Echinocereus triglochidiatus*						x		x	x	x
Bluebell Family	**Campanulaceae**										
Cardinal Flower	*Lobelia cardinalis*	x	x	x	x	x	x	x	x	x	x
Honeysuckle Family	**Caprifoliaceae**										
Coral Honeysuckle	*Lonicera sempervirens*	x	x	x	x	x					
Pink Family	**Caryophyllaceae**										
Western Catchfly	*Silene laciniata*										x
Catchfly	*Silene subciliata*	x	x	x							

Common Name	Scientific Name	1	2	3	4	5	6	7	8	9	10
Morning Glory Family	Convolvulaceae										
Red Morning Glory	Ipomoea coccinea*	X	X								
Scarlet Morning Glory	Ipomoea cristulata										X
Cypress Vine	Ipomoea quamoclit*	X	X								
Heath Family	Ericaceae										
Hoary Azalea	Rhododendron canescens	X									
Texas White Azalea	Rhododendron oblongifolium	X									
Ocotillo Family	Fouquieriaceae										
Ocotillo	Fouquieria splendens										X
Horsechestnut Family	Hippocastanaceae										
White Buckeye	Aesculus glabra v. arguta	X		X	X	X		X			
Red Buckeye	Aesculus pavia	X	X	X	X			X	X		
Mint Family	Lamiaceae										
Prairie Brazoria	Brazoria scutellarioides			X	X	X		X			
Purple Horsemint	Monarda citriodora	X	X	X	X	X	X	X	X	X	X
Wild Bergamot	Monarda fistulosa	X	X	X							
Spotted Beebalm	Monarda punctata	X	X	X	X	X		X	X		
Tropical Sage	Salvia coccinia	X	X	X	X	X	X	X			
Autumn Sage	Salvia greggii					X		X	X		X
Crimson Sage	Salvia henryi										X
Big Red Sage	Salvia penstemonoides			X	X	X		X			
Cedar Sage	Salvia roemeriana							X			X
Mountain Sage	Salvia regla										X
Red Hedge-nettle	Stachys coccinia	X	X								
Legume Family	Leguminosae										
Lead-plant Amorpha	Amorpha canescens	X	X	X	X	X		X	X		
False Indigo	Amorpha fruticosa	X	X	X	X	X	X	X			
Smooth Amorpha	Amorpha laevigata	X	X								
Panicled Amorpha	Amorpha paniculata	X									

Table 7.1
Plants Favored by Hummingbirds

* Not native to Texas, but not invasive. ** Considered naturalized.

Note: Plants are listed alphabetically by family. Numbered regions correspond to the Texas Ecoregion map on page 11.

Common Name	Scientific Name	1	2	3	4	5	6	7	8	9	10
Legume Family continued											
Anacacho Orchid-tree	*Bauhinia congesta*			x	x	x		x			
Bird of Paradise	*Caesalpinia gilliesii**							x			x
False Mesquite	*Calliandra conferta*						x	x			x
Fairy Duster	*Calliandra eriophylla**						x	x			x
Eastern Coral Bean	*Erythrina herbacea*		x	x	x	x					
Scarlet Runner Bean	*Phaseolus coccineus**	x	x	x	x	x	x	x			
Bristly Locust	*Robinia hispida*	x									
New Mexico Locust	*Robinia neomexicana*										x
Rattlebush	*Sesbania drummondii*		x	x	x	x	x	x			
Showy Sesbania	*Sesbania punicea**	x									
Logania Family	**Loganaceae**										
Carolina Jessamine	*Gelsemium sempervirens*	x	x	x							
Pink-root	*Spigelia marilandica*	x		x							
Magnolia Family	**Magnoliaceae**										
Tulip Tree	*Liriodendron tulipifera**	x									
Mallow Family	**Malvaceae**										
Heart-leaf Hibiscus	*Hibiscus cardiophyllus*		x				x	x			
Scarlet Hibiscus	*Hibiscus coccineus**	x									
Turk's Cap	*Malvaviscus arboreus*	x	x	x	x	x	x	x			
Globe-mallow	*Sphaeralcea angustifolia*						x		x	x	x
Four-o'clock Family	**Nyctaginaceae**										
Hierba de la Hormiga	*Allionia incarnata*									x	x
Colorado Four-o'-clock	*Mirabilis multiflora*										x
Scarlet Four-o'-clock	*Mirabilis coccinea*										x
Scarlet Muskflower	*Nyctaginia capitata*		x	x	x	x		x	x	x	x
Phlox Family	**Polemoniaceae**										
Scarlet Standing Cypress	*Ipomopsis aggregata*										x
Standing Cypress	*Ipomopsis rubra*	x		x	x	x	x	x			

Common Name	Scientific Name	1	2	3	4	5	6	7	8	9	10
Phlox Family	**Polemoniaceae**										
Drummond's Phlox	*Phlox drummondii*	x	x	x	x	x	x	x			
Polemonium	*Polemonium pauciflorum*										x
Buttercup Family	**Ranunculaceae**										
Texas Clematis	*Clematis texensis*			x	x	x		x			
Wild Columbine	*Aquilegia canadensis*	x		x	x	x		x			
Buckthorn Family	**Rhamnaceae**										
Mexican Buckeye	*Ungnadia speciosa*	x	x	x	x	x		x			x
Rose Family	**Rosaceae**										
Prairie Rose	*Rosa setigera*	x		x	x	x					
Madder Family	**Rubiaceae**										
Trompetilla	*Bouvardia ternifolia*										x
Orange Hamelia	*Hamelia patens**						x				
Figwort Family	**Scrophulariaceae**										
Indian Paintbrush	*Castilleja indivisa*	x	x	x	x	x	x				
Grassland Paintbrush	*Castilleja integra*										x
Woolly Paintbrush	*Castilleja lanata*										x
Cenizo	*Leucophyllum frutescens*						x	x			x
Snapdragon Vine	*Maurandya antirrhiniflora*	x	x	x	x	x	x	x			x
Havards' Penstemon	*Penstemon havardii*										x
Cup-leaf Penstemon	*Penstemon murrayanus*	x	x	x							
Three-flower Penstemon	*Penstemon triflorus*							x			
Wright's Penstemon	*Penstemon wrightii*										x
Nightshade Family	**Solanaceae**										
Shrubby Tobacco	*Nicotiana glauca***			x	x	x	x	x			x
Verbena Family	**Verbenaceae**										
Lantana	*Lantana horrida*	x	x	x	x	x	x	x	x		x

Chapter Eight: *Mammals, Reptiles & Amphibians*

© TPW

© TPW, Jim Whitcomb

A surprising number of Texas mammals will show up in backyard settings given the appropriate conditions. Deer, jackrabbits, cottontail rabbits, shrews, fox and gray squirrels, armadillos, foxes, raccoons, opossums, moles, and bats are some of the mammals you may observe in a well-rounded backyard habitat. Cute and furry, backyard mammals are generally more shy and skittish than their avian neighbors. Often, evidence of their dens and food caches (collections) can be found in sheltered areas under decks, piled debris, dog houses, in large clumps of grass and fallen logs, or in burrows dug beneath the ground, under large tree roots, and excavated high up in trees.

Texas also hosts an exceedingly rich array of native herptiles or "herps," for short. Indeed, the Lone Star state boasts approximately 70 species of amphibians and 165 species of reptiles. Most of them are small, secretive, and need a little bit of "wildness" in which to hide and find food. If you are lucky enough to live near a stream or pond close to woods, you could observe various salamanders, frogs, turtles, lizards, and snakes in your backyard or wildflower garden.

While it is more difficult to observe mammals because of their secretive and often nocturnal habits, with a little extra effort and by knowing where and when to look, you can often catch glimpses of their activities.

Mammals

If you live in an urban area, you shouldn't expect to attract larger mammals such as mountain lions or bobcats. However, if you happen to live within their range in isolated wilderness areas, or have extensive stands of suitable habitat adjoining your neighborhood, these animals may pass within viewing range. While it is more difficult to observe mammals because of their secretive and often nocturnal habits, with a little extra effort and by knowing where and when to look, you can often catch glimpses of their activities.

To attract small mammals to your yard, provide special areas of cover to protect them from predators. Brush piles are especially good means of providing a habitat structure for cottontail rabbits and squirrels, especially if vegetative cover is scarce. It is also important to give special protection to cavity trees on your land. Nest boxes can substitute for natural cavities if your property is snag-poor. Protect nearby streams, marshes, and swamps from water pollution and degradation. Create extensive edge areas with maximum habitat diversity. Plant native trees, shrubs, and vines with edible fruits and nuts, such as oaks, pines, junipers, wild cherries, mulberries, and wax myrtles. Provide sufficient areas of low cover to serve as protective shelter from dogs and cats, as well as from adverse weather. Erect special bat houses to attract Mexican free-tailed bats.

Eastern Fox Squirrel
Sciurus niger

Fox squirrels prefer to nest in hollow trees, but will also inhabit large, leafy, and globe-shaped nests high up in trees.

Either you love the fox squirrel or you hate him. This little fellow is undeniably cute, but tends not to endear himself to those who love to feed wild birds. As any bird watcher can tell you, the fox squirrel is almost impossible to deter from bird feeders. Inquisitive and intelligent, the fox squirrel is adept at learning how to manipulate devices such as bird feeders in order to obtain food.

The fox squirrel is a large tree squirrel with rusty or reddish underparts and brownish or grayish upperparts. The tail is fluffy, less than half of its body length, and is colored with a mix of cinnamon, black, and cream. Fox squirrels dwell in most of the eastern two-thirds of Texas, and are very commonly seen in open woodlands as well as suburban areas. Folks often spot the large, leafy, globe-shaped nests the squirrels build high up in trees; however, they prefer hollow trees as nesting and denning sites. Acorns constitute the majority of their diet, but the squirrels also eat a variety of nuts, insects, green shoots, fruits, seeds, and buds. Females give birth to an average of four naked, blind, and helpless young per year. The young develop slowly, beginning to venture out of the nest at about seven to eight weeks. At ten to eleven months, the young are fully mature. Their frenzied chasing and boisterous barking are often the first happy signs to us that the young have left the nest and have ventured out on their own.

Ringtail Cat
Bassariscus astutus

While it looks like a cross between a raccoon and a domestic cat, the ringtail cat is a species in its own right. It occurs throughout Texas and is cousin to the raccoon.

Some people falsely profess that the ringtail cat is a cross between a domestic cat and a raccoon. While closely related to the raccoon, the ringtail is its own species and is an exceptionally attractive cat-sized carnivore easily identified by its long, bushy, black and white ringed tail and slim body. Although the ringtail is rarely seen, it can be found throughout Texas, preferring rocky areas such as rock piles, stone fences, and canyon walls. Ringtails will also occupy hollow trees and logs, and are exceptional climbers. The ringtail is primarily active at night, and will spend most of the day in its den. Like its wily cousin, the raccoon, the ringtail will eat a variety of foods, including small birds, mammals, "herps" such as snakes, lizards, toads and frogs, crickets and grasshoppers, spiders, scorpions, and centipedes, and fruits of native plants, such as persimmon, hackberry, and mistletoe. California gold miners of the late 1940s thought the ringtail was an admirable substitute for their mousing domestic cats back home and would often encourage them to take up residence near their homes to make nightly "mouse hunts."

Bats

Texas records the largest number of bat species in the nation: thirty-two out of a possible forty-one species. While most bats live in caves, tree foliage, and bark, some species will take up residence in mines, tunnels, bridges, old buildings, and bat houses. Most bats in the United States weigh less than one ounce, but they may appear larger due to the size of their wings.

In Texas, most species of bats are very beneficial, feeding on a variety of insects and arachnids including moths, beetles, mosquitoes, crickets and scorpions.

In the United States, all but three species of bats primarily feed on a variety of insects and arthropods, including moths, crickets, mosquitoes, and scorpions. These prey items are hunted both in the air and on the ground. Bats are particularly important in the United States for their contribution in the control of night-flying insects. According to Bat Conservation International, many bats consume 2,000 or more insects in just one night, and some can gobble up 600 mosquitoes in just one hour. Many of the insects that bats devour are considered agricultural pests such as the corn borer and cutworm moths. For this reason, large colonies of bats are extremely important for insect control. A flourishing bat population is a good alternative to chemical insect control, which is a threat to both personal and environmental health.

People have been putting up bat houses for over sixty years. Providing artificial roosts for the winged mammal is becoming increasingly important to their survival as their traditional roosts in old trees and buildings are becoming more and more scarce. Bat houses are commercially available in nature stores, or you can find plans to build one in woodworking books.

Mexican Free-tailed Bat
Tadarida brasiliensis

Mexican free-tailed bats are extremely beneficial mammals: each bat consumes up to 2000 insects each night!

Squeaking and swooping in the evening, Mexican free-tailed bats are the most common of our bats in Texas. The three-ounce free-tailed bat is medium-sized with dark brown or dark gray fur. It is also a member of a family of bats known as Molossidae, or free-tailed bats, which are so named because their tails extend beyond the uropatagium, the thin membrane that spans the two hind legs like the webbing between the toes of ducks.

Mexican free-tailed bats typically inhabit caves or unoccupied parts of buildings, crevices in large rocks, or nooks in structures such as buildings, bridges, and signs. These bats are also migratory and during migration, may stop over to roost in old cliff swallow nests. Bat excrement, known as "guano," has been harvested since the nineteenth century for use as fertilizer and fuel. The Mexican free-tail represents a very real threat to insects: they feast nightly on the swarms of the pesky critters. They have been found to prey on moths, flying ants, June beetles and leaf beetles, leafhoppers, and other bugs, and are estimated to consume from 6,000 to 18,000 metric tons of insects annually in Texas.

One key to providing habitat for many reptiles and amphibians is to provide easily accessible water and moist soil areas.

Reptiles and Amphibians

While many people think of reptiles and amphibians as slimy, slithery, creepy, or scary critters, they are really fascinating animals in their own right. Moreover, they perform an important ecological service for us by preying on noxious insects and rodents. If the idea of attracting these wonderful creatures appeals to you, there are a few things you can do to make your yard attractive to them.

Texas is home to a variety of lizards such as geckos, skinks, iguanids, glass and alligator lizards, as well as whiptail lizards. This little prairie lizard is found in a variety of habitats of central and western Texas.

Luring Reptiles and Amphibians to your Yard

- Leave stones, stumps, and rotting logs in place. They can be creatively and attractively incorporated into almost any garden and provide valuable shelter and food resources for a variety of herps.

- Create brush piles and wood piles at the edge of your yard to provide valuable shelters and basking sites for these cold-blooded creatures.

- For borders around flower beds and ponds, consider constructing a wall of loose stones instead of using mortar. The crevices, nooks, and crannies will be home and hideout to a variety of amphibians and lizards.

- Reduce lawn area. Reptiles and amphibians prefer native ground covers, grasses, and wildflowers to a finely manicured carpet of St. Augustine grass.

- Keep your cat indoors. Cats, both domestic and feral, are serious predators of amphibians and reptiles. Poikilotherms (cold-blooded animals) are often sluggish, especially on cooler days, and are no match for the speed and stealth of these efficient hunters.

- When possible, avoid the use of pesticides and lawn chemicals. Amphibians and their prey are especially sensitive to these chemicals.

- Allow leaf litter, which is coveted habitat for many herps, to accumulate in flower beds or odd corners of a yard.

- Provide easily accessible water and moist soil areas.

- Well-aerated, friable soils (ones that crumble easily) are best for burrowing herptiles.

Reptiles

Texas hosts 165 species of reptiles, including 1 crocodilian, 35 turtles, 61 lizards, and 68 snakes. Turtles are highly distinctive with their peculiar bony shells and skeletons, scaly skin, toothless heads, and wide variety of pattern and color. All turtles have shells. The upper shell (carapace) and a lower shell (plastron) are connected at the sides by bony bridges. All turtles lay eggs which are deposited in a shallow nest which the female has constructed out of damp soil.

Sixty-one lizards call Texas home, among them are the geckos, skinks, iguanids, glass and alligator lizards, and whiptail lizards. Lizards are highly variable in color, pattern and size. They all have scaly skin, most have external ear openings (except for the earless lizards) and claws on their toes (except for the glass lizard, which has no legs). Lizards can be found in a variety of habitats, and while the majority lay eggs, some bear live young. Most lizards are diurnal, remaining active throughout the day.

The sixty-eight species of Texas snakes include blind snakes, colubrid snakes (the large majority of Texas snakes), elapid snakes (coral snakes), and vipers (rattlesnakes, copperheads, and cottonmouths). Snakes are thought by some herpetologists to be the most successful of all living reptiles, ranging farther north and to higher altitudes and adapting to a wider range of habitats than crocodiles, turtles, or lizards. Snakes are specialized for capturing particular kinds of prey such as earthworms, snails, slugs, amphibians, and small reptiles. Of the 113 species and subspecies of snakes, less than 15% are venomous. Indeed, the majority are totally harmless. Snakes fill very special roles in our ecosystem by controlling rodent and other pest species populations.

Red-eared Slider
Trachemys scripta elegans

The red-eared slider is almost exclusively aquatic, but is often seen basking on logs, exposed rocks, or vegetation.

The red-eared slider is perhaps the best known and most recognizable of turtles. The top of the shell is smooth and gently curved and is olive to black with yellow stripes and bars. It is a medium-sized turtle, best identified by the red or sometimes yellow patch found just behind its eye.

It is at home in quiet, freshwater systems that have muddy bottoms and abundant aquatic vegetation. They range from Indiana to New Mexico down through Texas to the Gulf of Mexico. They are widely distributed throughout Texas except the far western region.

The red-eared slider is almost exclusively aquatic, and only rarely ventures out of water to lay its eggs or to migrate to a new body of water. Young turtles generally eat insect larvae and small fish, but as they age, their favorite food gradually switches to vegetation. The slider is commonly seen basking in the sun on logs, exposed rocks, or atop masses of vegetation. When basking sites are in short supply, they may even pile on top of each other up to three turtles deep.

Red-eared sliders may produce up to three clutches of four to twenty-three eggs in a single year. The female constructs each nest on the shore by digging a shallow depression, three to ten inches wide. She deposits her eggs in these excavations and subsequently covers them up. Although the young turtles may spend the winter in the nest, they generally hatch sixty to seventy-five days after being laid.

Ornate Box Turtle
Terrapene ornata ornata

The ornate box turtle is an extravagantly marked reptile found throughout most of Texas. It dines on insects, berries, and carrion.

This beautifully marked diurnal turtle spends most of its time on the land. With a dome-shaped, elegantly-patterned carapace, squared off snout, hooked beak, and front legs sporting large orange spots, the ornate box turtle is certainly an attractive reptile. When alarmed, it closes its shell

tightly at both ends in defense. It prefers sandy soils in semi-arid regions on grasslands, plains, and in tame pastures throughout most of Texas, except for the extreme western portion of the Trans-Pecos. Males are distinguished from females by eye color; males have red eyes while the eyes of females are yellow. This interesting turtle dines on a variety of insects, with a special taste for dung-beetles, as well as berries and carrion. Females lay two to eight eggs in a shallow, flask-shaped nest she digs in sandy soils any time from May to July.

Green Anole
Anolis carolinensis

Commonly incorrectly called a chameleon, the green anole will change its color in response to a variety of situations, including light quality, temperature, and emotion.

Another common inhabitant of backyard gardens is the elegant green anole, sometimes incorrectly called the chameleon for its ability to change color from green to brown. Color change can be triggered by a number of factors including light quality, temperature, and emotion. Often seen during breeding season rhythmically extending its flashy rose to orange dewlap (fold of skin under its neck), combative males both attract mates and establish territories which they defend vigorously against all rivals. This arboreal lizard is common throughout the eastern half of Texas with a separate population occurring in extreme South Texas along the Rio Grande. It is active during the day, climbing high into trees, shrubs, and vines and also on fences and walls in the garden. Very sensitive to low moisture levels, this attractive lizard requires shade, shelter, and a moist environment to survive the long hot Texas summers.

Texas Rat Snake
Elaphe obsoleta lindheimeri

The nonvenomous Texas rat snake is the serpent most often found up in the rafters of barns, lofts, and attics in rural and suburban areas.

A powerful constrictor, the Texas rat snake is a feisty, long, bluish black and olive brown blotched serpent ranging from forty-two to seventy-two inches long. Its background color is gray or yellowish and the head is usually black. Sometimes there may be a hint of red on the skin between the scales. The underside of the tail tip is commonly solid gray. This species exhibits considerable individual variation in pattern and coloration within its range in Texas. Adults are fairly unmistakable, but juveniles may resemble other rat snakes like the Great Plains rat snake and Baird's rat snake. It is also similar to the prairie kingsnake and the bullsnake.

In Texas, this snake is commonly found in rural and suburban areas from the central through the eastern half of Texas in a wide variety of habitats including pine forests, deciduous woodlands, pasturelands, stream valleys, and rocky canyons. In suburban areas, they tend to hide out in barn rafters, lofts, attics, or abandoned machinery and automobiles. The Texas rat snake prefers to prey on birds, their nestlings and eggs, as well as rodents, other small mammals, and lizards. The Texas rat snake is a highly agile climber, making its way up and down trunks of large trees with relative ease, thanks to high-traction belly scales. It is also an accomplished swimmer and is often found patrolling river banks from the water.

The Texas rat snake is not venomous; however, it does tend to have an aggressive temperament. When threatened, it will rear its head, hiss, simulate a rattle by vibrating its tail in dry grass, and sometimes strike at the offender. The bite rarely succeeds in inflicting serious injury since the pressure of its jaws is insufficient to cause major damage.

Hawks are one of the main predators of the Texas rat snake, though it is also preyed upon by various mammals and other snakes. Hawks can easily locate the rat snake since it is often the subject of noisy mobbing activity by small birds when the snake is in the process of raiding a bird's nest.

Checkered Garter Snake
Thamnophis marcianus marcianus

The elegant checkered garter snake is found through north, central, and the southern coastal plains of Texas.

The checkered garter snake is a brown, olive, or tan snake with a bold checkered pattern of large, squarish black spots over its body that diminishes toward the tail. Uppermost spots impinge upon the creamy yellow central back stripe, and side stripes are also light in color. The best field mark is a pale yellowish crescent moon shape just behind a large black spot on the side of the neck. The belly is yellow with no pattern. Most grow about two feet long and look very similar to the Western plains garter snake, superficially like the Texas and blackneck garter snakes, and somewhat like the ribbon snakes.

The checkered garter snake occurs throughout the western two-thirds of the state and is also commonly found in much of the southern part of the state. This species is seen most often during late spring and early summer in Texas. They can be found in grassy upland areas near water in north and central Texas but are more common in thorn scrub and brushy habitats on the lower coastal plain. This species seldom appears to stray far from permanent water.

This moderately slender terrestrial snake preys on earthworms, toads, frogs, fishes, and sometimes small rodents. Most commonly seen on warm, humid nights, they tend to forage at dawn and dusk in the fall and spring, but are predominantly nocturnal during the hot summer months. Warm evening showers apparently encourage food-seeking activities. This species will often take refuge in burrows or rock crevices, as well as under logs, rocks, and piles of debris.

The checkered garter snake is not venomous, but may nip if handled in a rough manner. When picked up, they will release a foul-smelling splash of feces from their vent and anal glands. Coyotes, skunks, armadillos, snake-eating snakes, and raptors commonly prey on this snake.

Poisonous Texas Snakes

While the majority of snakes found in Texas are harmless, all should be treated with respect. It is important to distinguish between harmless snakes and venomous ones. The following snakes should be observed from a distance.

Texas Coral Snake
Micrurus fulvis tenere

"Black on yellow, kill a fellow" is an easy rhyme to remember the unique color pattern on the venomous coral snake.

The coral snake sports the familiar black, yellow, and red pattern that strikes fear into anyone's heart. While the pattern is mimicked by the harmless milk snakes, the coral snake's black on yellow band pattern is distinctive. Only about

50% of bites the coral snake inflicts actually contain venom, but all bites that break the skin should be considered venomous and treated immediately by a qualified physician.

Western Cottonmouth
Agkistrodon piscivorus leucostoma

The venomous western cottonmouth can be found both in the water or on land.

Like rattlesnakes and copperheads, the Western cottonmouth has a triangular head, vertical pupils (like cat eyes), and a pit or depression on each side of the head. The cottonmouth is often associated with water, but can be found on dry land as well. A heavy-bodied snake, it can be identified in the water by its habit of lazily swimming in the water with its head slightly raised. In contrast, other (nonvenomous) snakes are quick and agile in the water. When threatened on land, the snake will often adopt an open-jawed threat posture. With the mouth open, you can easily see the distinctive creamy-white mouth that gives the cottonmouth its name. Another name for this species is water moccasin.

Western Diamondback Rattlesnake and other Rattlesnakes
Crotalus spp.

The wide, triangular head, vertical pupils, and pits (depressions on the head that look like a second, lower set of nostrils) of this western diamondback rattlesnake indicate that this snake is a venomous pit viper.

In addition to having a triangular head, vertical pupil, and pits, rattlesnakes also possess a rattle at the end of their tails. Rattlesnakes are often considered temperamental, and great care should be taken to avoid them.

The Copperheads
Agkistrodon spp.

Copperheads also have a triangular head, vertical pupils, and pits, but are distinctively colored and have light eyes.

Copperheads have the triangular head, vertical pupils, and pits of the other vipers, but are also colored with the distinctive brownish bands on a khaki background. Copperheads also have light eyes, which make the dark, vertical pupils easy to observe, even at a comfortable distance.

Amphibians

The chirping chorus of spring peepers or the booming throng of bullfrogs is a familiar sound from our childhood, recalling memories of spring campouts and sultry summer evenings. Amphibian species include toads, treefrogs, true frogs, spadefoot toads, burrowing toads, and salamanders. Frogs and toads are some of the easiest animals to attract to watery habitats since they need water for at least one part of their life cycle. Since frogs and salamanders breathe through their skin as well as with their lungs, provide these garden-friendly visitors with a fresh, clean source of water.

Amphibians like this spotted salamander are very beneficial to the garden, feeding on a variety of insects and spiders.

In addition, providing sturdy aquatic vegetation will give the frogs, toads, and salamanders a place to lay their eggs, and for the hatched young to grow to adulthood.

Gulf Coast Toad
Bufo valliceps valliceps

The Gulf Coast toad is found throughout east, central, and south Texas.

Marked by a broad dark stripe down each side and bordered above by a light stripe, this medium-sized flatish toad is found in most of East Texas and throughout Central and South Texas. Preferring a variety of moist habitats including backyard gardens, man-made ditches, dump sites, and storm drains, it is most active at twilight, but can often be observed under street lights at night feasting on the insects attracted to the light. Breeding takes place from March to September.

Cope's Gray Treefrog and Green Treefrog
Hyla chrysoscelis, Hyla cinerea

The call of the delightful little green tree frog can be heard throughout east Texas on warm nights just before dark.

These two species are almost identical in physical appearance, range, habitat, and behavior patterns, and can be differentiated only by close analysis of calls. These angular-looking treefrogs range in color from bright greenish yellow during the breeding season to dark gray when inactive or during cold weather. A showy white or pale yellow stripe runs along the side from the jaw to the groin, though sometimes this field mark is absent. Many have small golden flecks on their backs and their slim body is small and flat with prominent eyes and flashy white lips. They are found mainly in the eastern third of the state and prefer habitats with water, sandy banks, and dense vegetation. They call just before dark as they congregate in large choruses near the water. Preferring a variety of insects for food, they are frequently drawn toward lighted windows where insects are apt to be present.

Southern Spadefoot
Scaphiopus multiplicatus

Spadefoot toads are so named for the short, hard spade located on the rear heel which is used for digging.

Spadefoot toads take their name from the small, wedge-shaped "spade" found on their back legs which is used for digging. Found throughout West Texas and north through the Panhandle region, the southern spadefoot is a gray or brown (sometimes deep green or black) toad with a short body, short snout, and large eyes. The generally smooth skin is speckled with "warts" which are tipped with orange or yellow, and their underparts are white. This toad is nocturnal and is found in sandy, gravelly soils. It digs into the soil using its spades to push the soil up as it rocks from side to side and backs down into its hole. The southern spadefoot is adapted to a variety of conditions and lives on shortgrass prairies, floodplains, alkali flats, and areas with open vegetation.

Texas tortoise.

Chapter Nine: *Insects & Spiders*

© William McCarley

© TPW, Leroy Williamson

Often referred to as "creepy-crawlies," most insects and spiders are actually very beneficial to back-yard habitats. Flying insects, such as honeybees and butterflies, drink the nectar from flowers as they pollinate. Wasps are often responsible for ridding the garden of a great deal of other pesky bugs such as ants, flies, spiders, and caterpillars. Beetles will often hunt for caterpillars, slugs, snails, and ants. Spiders prey on a variety of insects, using the familiar flying insect web trap of most spiders, or even actively hunting them down as the wolf spider does.

Green Lacewing
Family: Chrysopidae

The larval form of the green lacewing feeds on all sorts of aphids, mealybugs, scale, and other small insects.

The green lacewing adult is the "Tinker Bell" of the garden, with a clear green body and transparent wings laced with delicate green. While the adults, which grow to $^3/_4$ inch in length, are certainly the beauties, it is their less-than-pretty young that provide the most benefit to our gardens. The $^1/_2$-inch long, alligator-like larval forms of the lacewing delight in devouring all sorts of aphids, mealybugs, scale, and other small insects.

Antlions
Family: Myrmeleontidae

The antlion larva waits in merciless ambush, but the adult form resembles a weak-flying damselfly.

All insects are interesting both in form and in behavior, but the antlion is a summer insect that can really pique your curiosity. The antlion most people recognize is not the adult, which resembles a weak-flying damselfly, but actually the larval form. The larvae spend their time at the bottom of a small, inverted cone-shaped pit built in fine-grained sand. You can often find the pits clustered together in sheltered areas near houses, rock ledges, and bridges. The pit is the "bug trap" that gives this diminutive insect its name. The edges of the pit are smooth, and ants, caterpillars, or other small crawling insects that venture too close to the pit fall in and have a great difficulty escaping. When the prey reaches the bottom of the pit, the antlion larva, which is buried just slightly under the surface, grasps it with its pinchers and injects it with a paralyzing venom, then sucks out the prey's juices. You can observe this action by using a piece of grass, pine needle, or other object to simulate a bug falling into the pit. You will observe the larva tossing dirt on top of the "capture," thus bringing it closer to the bottom. Once down at the bottom of the pit, the larva might even attempt to grasp the makeshift "prey."

The small inverted cones formed in fine-grained sand are often the only evidence of antlion larvae.

Black-and-yellow Argiope or Garden Spider
Family Araneidae, subfamily Argiopinae

This striking garden spider, the black-and-yellow Argiope, is a beautiful and beneficial addition to any Wildscape.

This large, colorful, and extremely visible creature is one of the more familiar spiders found in the garden. Known generically as the "garden spider," it is actually one of many brightly colored spiders that primarily inhabit grassy or weedy areas. The striped spiders construct large, vertical, orb-shaped webs which have a characteristic zigzag pattern running down the center. Called a "stabilimentum," this structure was once thought to provide stability to such a large web. Scientists now speculate that the structure is an adaptive device which makes the web more visible to larger animals, such as birds, which might otherwise move through the web and destroy it. The Argiopes are especially beneficial creatures, and should be treasured in any Wildscape.

Butterflies

The image of butterfly wings flitting gingerly from flower to flower like so many bits of confetti bobbing in the sun can bring a smile to any gardener's face. Butterflies add an ethereal beauty to flower gardens and meadows and are second in importance only to bees as plant pollinators. Together with the moths, butterflies make up the second largest order of insects, the Lepidoptera (from the Greek combining forms "Lepido," meaning scale, and "ptera," meaning wing). More than 17,500 species of butterflies have been identified worldwide. While the greatest numbers are found in the tropical regions of the globe, approximately 700 species of butterflies occur in North America. Each region of the United States has

The early-blooming Mexican plum tree (Prunus mexicana) *is a favorite with butterflies, such as this painted lady.*

its characteristic butterfly fauna, and the butterflies of a particular region often are specifically adapted to the native plants of that region. Local field guides and butterfly lists are increasingly available to those wishing to know which species of butterflies are common to an area and which native plant species they use as nectar sources and larval host plants. (See Table 9.1 at the end of this chapter for a list of adult and larval butterfly food sources in Texas.)

Butterflies and native plant species depend on one another and help each other survive. While butterflies pollinate the flowers, the plants provide butterflies with food, housing, and sometimes chemical protection. The butterflies lay their eggs on appropriate host plants whose leaves provide ample food for the larvae. Nectar plants provide fuel for adults in their quest to find a mate and reproduce.

Planting local native plant species in a rich, well-planned butterfly garden will provide essential corridors between remaining patches of habitat and help repair the patchwork of healthy ecosystems that still exists. Every square meter devoted to a butterfly garden will also provide habitat for many other species of beneficial insects. Besides the conservation benefit, there is the added delight of watching butterflies flutter about the garden from the first warm days of spring to the last warm days of fall. As Robert Pyle, noted butterfly conservationist, expressed it, "The beauty of a swallowtail-studded patch of phlox confers a deep sense of pleasure that flowers alone are unable to match."

Some plants, such as this butterfly milkweed (Asclepias tuberosa), *can serve as both larval host plants and adult nectar sources.*

Designing a Butterfly Garden

Building a butterfly garden sanctuary around your home is not difficult. Whether you have a large house with extensive gardens and fields or a small garden apartment with a modest plot of yard space, anyone can attract and play host to butterflies. Much will depend on how enthusiastic you are and how strongly you can keep your need for neatness and order under control. Remember, though, that the design possibilities are limitless and need not conform to any particular model. You are completely free to create your own special vision, so experiment and have fun.

Many different types of flowers can provide nectar to butterflies. This Queen butterfly is feeding from a buttonbush (Cephalanthus occidentalis).

It is important to make the most of your natural setting. Butterflies like edges, for instance, so planting low flowers at the edge of a lawn, and high flowers at the edges of trees or along a fence is a way to enhance edge habitat. Locate a major part of the garden in a sunny, protected area. Butterflies are ectothermic (cold-blooded) and need sun to warm their body temperature. Place flat stones for butterflies to bask upon at various sunny locations in the garden. During cool mornings or cold spells, butterflies will perch on these stones or on bare soil to sun themselves. This behavior is necessary to raise their body temperature enough to allow them to fly. A few species of butterflies, such as the wood nymph and satyrs, prefer shady conditions, and if your yard has a wooded area, you might consider laying out special potions to attract these species. Geyata Ajilvsgi, in her publication *Butterfly Gardening for the South*, has a number of effective and apparently irresistible recipes.

Butterflies avoid high winds and appreciate windbreaks. If there are any natural structures to block the wind, leave them standing as butterflies will often congregate there on blustery days to get out of the wind. You may want to add tall plants to buffer the wind if your garden area does not possess natural barriers.

You can provide butterflies with shelter by planting densely growing shrubbery, windbreaks, and by leaving snags and other cozy nooks in your Wildscape.

Native wildflowers serve as butterfly lures. Growing native species not only restores habitat, but also provides special nectar and larval food sources for the butterflies. When selecting wildflowers, it is always best to select those native to your region, though a few non-natives that do not become pesky weeds such as West Indian bloodroot (Ascelpias curassavica) and common butterfly-bush (Buddleia spp.), or marigolds, do a magnificent job at attracting butterflies.

Most butterflies wander from place to place, stopping off temporarily at your garden to partake of food, water, and shelter on their way to somewhere else. When food sources disappear, butterflies go elsewhere. A combination of wildflowers and grasses that bloom from early spring through early fall will keep butterflies well fed throughout the seasons. Gardeners from the southeast and southwest Texas regions can enjoy amazingly extended flowering seasons with many attendant butterfly species, both residents and migrants.

In designing the layout of your garden, try to use large splashes of color. Butterflies are first attracted to flowers by their color, and a large mass of blooms is easier for them to spot. According to some experts, their favorite color is purple, followed by blue, yellow, white, pink, and orange.

Members of the composite family of flowers, such as asters, coreopsis, boneset, goldenrods, and sunflowers are excellent nectar sources. How you group your colors, however, depends on your own preferences.

If you love butterflies, you will have to learn to love and provide for their larvae, too. Adult butterflies will definitely hang around if you feed and house their caterpillars. Admittedly, caterpillars look rather like worms — a life form not held in high regard by many people. It is important, however, to provide a good quantity of larval host plants for them, as larval food plants lure females into the garden to lay their eggs. Don't get overly attached to the larval host plants though, or you will be upset when you watch the hungry caterpillars eat them to shreds. That's how caterpillars grow. They will repay the plants indirectly by performing pollination duties at the next stage. It all evens out in the long run.

It is important to provide food for both larval (caterpillar) and adult butterflies in a Wildscape. Both the wooly bear caterpillar and the adult sulfur butterfly enjoy this salvia.

It is important to leave old trees as well as some younger trees, as butterflies like to perch on them and their larvae may use them for food. For instance, the beautiful swallowtail caterpillar prefers munching on the leaves of wild cherry. Mourning cloak caterpillars feed on elms and willows as well as hackberries. Spicebush caterpillars prefer, in addition to spicebush, red bay and sweet bay trees. Small trees, such as hawthorns, buckeyes, and sumacs offer nectar sources and shelter, as well. Try to leave thick brush under some of the trees, for this is where butterflies can find shelter and warmth on colder days or when it rains. These are also the areas where many species of caterpillars go to pupate.

A permanent wet patch or seep with various species of sedges and moisture-loving wildflowers will attract a multitude of butterflies. Provide damp areas or shallow puddles. If at all possible, install a seep irrigation system instead of sprinklers since sprinklers wash the nectar out of the flowers. A damp patch of sand, baited with a touch of manure or fermented fruit, will attract butterflies in a "puddle assemblage." Soil enriched by ashes from fires are especially attractive to them. Large congregations of "puddlers," mostly males who derive important elements from this foul feast, will descend to partake of the goodies. They will be less wary of observers here, and so it makes a good spot to take photos.

People who want to go all out might well choose to offer butterfly "delicacies" — which are anything but delicate. Beautiful butterflies do not always behave the way we might expect. Shunning our most prized roses, many prefer to feed on rotten fruit, carrion, mud puddles, oozing sap, human sweat, and even animal scat (fecal matter). Of course, this step is not for everyone, but if you choose to take it, you can attract species you might not otherwise see such as the dazzling red-spotted purple, hackberry, and goatweed butterflies. In fact, many attractive members of the Nymphalidae (brush-footed butterfly family) are attracted to these noisome buffets.

It is imperative that you not use insecticides anywhere near your butterfly garden, the larval food plants, or the adult nectar sources. These chemicals will kill butterflies in both the adult and larval stages. Treat any pest problem you have manually. If you have fire ants, try to use a juvenile growth hormone such as Logic, nontoxic insecticides like diatomaceous earth, or boiling water. Integrated pest management (see Chapter Four) is the best technique in any situation.

Remember, butterfly gardens develop gradually. They are not made overnight or even in one year. Each year you can increase the number of nectar plant selections and lengthen the blooming period to span the seasons. Planning, patience, and persistence are the keys to success. The more home gardeners add to the interactive communities of butterflies and native plants, the more stable and colorful the habitat will become.

Spicebush Swallowtail
Papilio troilus

This beautiful, slow fluttering butterfly is a member of the Papilionidae family of butterflies. It is a black butterfly that measures about four inches from the tip of one wing to the other, and sports an iridescent patch of blue green on the hindwing. Pale yellow or green spots line the lower edges of the wings, and there is a small, spoon-shaped projection on the bottom edge of the hindwing. The range of the spicebush includes central and eastern Texas, and it prefers second-growth woods, deciduous woodlands, edges, wooded swamps, and pine barrens as habitat. You will often see the adult lazily fluttering about from April through October in search of its favorite nectar plants, including lantana, asters, cardinal flower, crownbeard, and salvias. The spicebush caterpillar prefers the vegetation of the spicebush, redbay, and sweetbay.

American Snout
Libytheana carinenta

The unusual-looking American snout butterfly is a common inhabitant of Texas.

This little two-inch butterfly is easily recognizable by its "snout," which actually is its enlarged and beaklike labial palps (mouth parts). It flutters about at an incredible rate of speed, flashing a splash of orange on its upper wings. The underside of the wing, which you will see when the butterfly alights on a flower, is a mottled or solid gray. A typical behavior for the snout is to perch, head down, on a twig or small branch where it will mimic a dead leaf.

Look for the first brood of snouts flying in mid-May through June, and a second round of snouts in early August. The adults overwinter in South Texas and Florida, and the species sometimes will engage in spectacular migrations. The preferred larval food sources include desert hackberry and sugarberry species. The adult butterflies prefer dogwood, dogbane, and goldenrod for nectar.

Monarch
Danaus plexippus

With its large, easily identifiable wing patterns and spectacular migrations, the monarch butterfly is one of the most easily recognized butterflies in the United States.

The monarch butterfly is perhaps the most commonly recognized butterfly in North America. Ranging in size from $3^{1}/_{2}$ to $4^{1}/_{2}$ inches, the monarch's wings are a beautiful bright orange with black veins and a black border with two rows of white dots. The monarch is found throughout Texas and undergoes dramatic migrations. Millions of adult butterflies spend their winter in colonies in central Mexico. The larval monarch butterflies are dependent on milkweed plant species for food, and the adults store a poison from the milkweed which, in turn, makes them extremely unpalatable to birds. The adult butter-

flies feed on a variety of flowers, including lantana, boneset, frostweed, sunflowers, and groundsel. The habitat of the Monarch includes open, weedy areas, roadsides, pastures, marshes, and other similar areas.

The monarch butterfly caterpillar is an unpalatable creature even to the hungriest birds.

With its thread of "gold," even the monarch chrysalis is beautiful.

Table 9.1
Common Texas Butterfly Species and Nectar Plant Sources
* Not native to Texas, but not invasive.

Species	Larval Food Plants	Adult Food Plants (Nectar Sources)
Black Swallowtail	Prairie parsley, Dutchman's breeches, bishop's weed, dill*, parsley*, fennel*, carrot*	Fruit tree blossoms, lantana, boneset, asters, thistles, milkweeds, clover
Bordered Patch	Sunflower, crownbeard, ragweeds, straggler daisy, cockleburs	Sunflowers, crownbeard, ragweeds, straggler daisy, cockleburs, composites
Buckeye	Purple gerardia, paintbrush, frog-fruit, ruellia, snapdragon, plantain, toadflax	Purple gerardia, paintbrush, frog-fruit, ruellia, lantana, composites
Cloudless Giant Sulphur	Senna species, partridge pea, cassia	Lantana, hibiscus, turk's cap, cardinal flower tropical sage, goldenrod
Common Checkered Skipper	Globe mallow, common mallow, sida, hollyhocks, hibiscus	Milkweeds, dandelions, asters, frog-fruit, and fleabane
Dogface	Leadplant, clover species, alfalfa, prairie clover	Verbena, golden-wave, bur-clover, salvias
Falcate Orange-tip	Rockcress, peppergrass, rocket mustard	Violet species, chickweed, and Prunus species
Giant Swallowtail	Lime prickly-ash, hop-tree, cultivated citrus, trifoliate orange, Hercules'-club	Lantana, butterfly-bush, milkweeds, honeysuckles. Also partakes of fruit juices and manure.
Great Southern White	Peppergrass, members of the mustard family, shepherd's purse	Eclectic tastes
Great Purple Hairstreak	Mostly mistletoe, eastern cottonwood, mesquite, sycamore	Roosevelt weed, creek plum, Mexican plum, goldenrods, ragweeds
Gulf Fritillary	Passion-flower species, passion-vine	Butterfly bush, lantana, boneset, golden-eye, asters
Goatweed Butterfly	Silver croton, one-seed croton, woolly croton	Likes tree sap, juices of fruits, moisture from decaying wood
Hackberry Butterfly	Hackberry species	Prefers carrion, dung, tree sap, rotting fruit, and mud
Janais Patch	Flame acanthus	Flame acanthus, bee-brush, annual sunflower
Julia	Passion-flower, passion vine	Lantana species
Large Wood Nymph	Wild petunia, waterwillow and various grasses	Boneset, milkweeds, thistles, golden-eye, clematis, button-bush
Long-tailed Skipper	Legumes and mustards	Legumes and mustards
Monarch	Milkweed species, milkweed vine	Lantana, boneset, frostweed, sunflowers, groundsels, Roosevelt weed, goldeneye
Mourning Cloak	Black willow, eastern cottonwood, hackberries	Milkweeds and goldenrods

Species	Larval Food Plants	Adult Food Plants (Nectar Sources)
Painted Lady	Thistles, milfoil, globemallow, and mugwort	Thistles, milfoil, mugwort, gayfeathers, asters
Palamedes Swallowtail	Red bay, sweet bay, and sassafras	Thistles, phlox, verbenas, azaleas*, pickerel-weed, yellow iris, purple loosestrife
Pipevine Swallowtail	Dutchman's pipe	Lantana, phlox, frostweed, cardinal flower, thistles, butterfly bush, sand-verbena, and frost-weed
Queen	Milkweed species	Milkweed species, frog fruit, blue mistflower, boneset
Question Mark	Nettles, hackberries, cedar elm	Likes mud, tree sap, carrion, also asters and milkweeds
Red Admiral	Nettles, false nettle, pellitory	Milkweeds, asters, dogbanes, bonesets, tree sap, ripe fruit, animal dung
Red-spotted Purple	Black cherry, eastern cottonwood, basswood, ironwood, hop-hornbeam	Eclectic tastes, likes carrion, dung, floral nectar, rotten fruit, tree sap, insect honeydew
Snout Butterfly	Hackberry species	Dogwood, dogbane species, goldenrods
Spicebush Swallowtail	Spicebush, red bay, sweet bay, sassafras, and tulip tree	Lantana, asters, cardinal flower, phlox, verbenas, crownbeard, salvias, bee balm, and bergamot
Texas Crescentspot	Flame acanthus, orega de raton, dicliptera, ruellia	Kidneywood, boneset, golden-eye, Indian blanket
Tiger Swallowtail	Green ash, Mexican plum, blackcherry, eastern cottonwood, camphor-tree	Butterfly weed, butterfly bush, abelia*, azaleas*, salvias, milkweeds
Variegated Fritillary	Stiff-stem flax, violets, pansies, purselane, and passion flowers	Flax species
Zebra Longwing	Passion-flowers, passion flower vines	Mistflower, lantana, bonesets, golden-eye, varied tastes
Zebra Swallowtail	Common pawpaw, dwarf pawpaw, big flowered pawpaw	Pawpaw, turk's cap

© TPW, Leroy Williamson

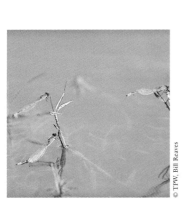

© TPW, Bill Reaves

The following books and field guides will help you become more familiar with the wildlife in your area.

Garrett, J.M. and D.G. Barker. 1987. *Texas Monthly Field Guide Series: A Field Guide to Reptiles and Amphibians of Texas.* Houston, Texas: Gulf Publishing Company.

Davis, W.B. and D.J. Schmidly. 1994. *The Mammals of Texas.* Austin, Texas: Texas Parks and Wildlife Press.

Milne, L. and M. Milne. 1980. *The Audubon Society Field Guide to North American Insects and Spiders.* New York: Alfred A. Knopf

National Geographic Society. 1987. *Field Guide to the Birds of North America.* Washington, D.C.: National Geographic Society.

Opler, P.A. 1994. *Peterson First Guides: Butterflies and Moths.* Boston, Massachusetts, and New York, New York: Houghton Mifflin Company.

Opler, P.A. 1992. *Peterson Field Guide Series: A Field Guide to Eastern Butterflies.* Boston, Massachusetts and New York, New York: Houghton Mifflin Company.

Schmidly, D.J. 1991. *The Bats of Texas.* College Station, Texas: Texas A&M University Press.

Tennant, A. 1985. *Texas Monthly Field Guide Series: A Field Guide to Texas Snakes.* Houston, Texas: Gulf Publishing Company.

Tveten, J.L. 1993. *The Birds of Texas.* Fredericksburg, Texas: Shearer Publishing.

Tveten, J. and G. Tveten. 1996. *Butterflies of Houston.* Austin: University of Texas Press.

Wright, A.B. 1993. *Peterson First Guides: Caterpillars.* Boston, Massachusetts and New York, New York: Houghton Mifflin Company.

Part Three: *Garden Troubleshooting*

Chapter Ten: *Gate Crashers & Unwanted Guests*

© Chuck Kowaleski

© TPW, Bill Reaves

While the benefits of establishing a backyard habitat to attract wildlife are substantial, there are a few drawbacks. As our towns grow and suburbs expand, there will be inevitable conflicts between the needs of people and the needs of animals. And, while wildlife is a source of enjoyment for most urban residents, some wildlife species can be a source of frustration, annoyance, and even fear for people.

The sight of white-tailed deer browsing nonchalantly on your prized flowering shrubs or cottontails munching in your garden is unsettling to say the least. Beavers clogging up streams or drainage ways, raccoons invading your attic to raise their families, opossums camping out in your garbage can, armadillos rooting for insects, and snakes under the house are outright nuisances. These types of problems may arise whether you landscape for wildlife or not, but a well-designed Wildscape can help you attract desirable species and deter nuisance behavior of others.

Of course, no plan can eliminate all problems. Tolerance for small levels of inconvenience and frustration may be the price we need to pay for the benefits we receive in bringing wildlife into our lives. Fortunately, the Texas Department of Agriculture has an effective program called Texas Wildlife Services with a staff of biologists trained in methods to control or deter nuisance animals. Wildlife Services staff can also offer technical assistance in trapping unwanted wildlife. Your local office can be located by calling the state office in San Antonio at 210-472-5451.

Raccoons

The comical raccoon is an increasingly common wild animal in urban and suburban areas.

The wily raccoon, at once an endearing charmer and mischievous masked bandito, can be a delightful source of entertainment, but also an extreme annoyance. The autumn begins with a restless search for a winter den, and in the summer the female seeks out a safe haven to rear her young. If your house or apartment is not well sealed or if

your garbage cans are not battened down well, you can count on faithful families of raccoons sharing your living space. These masked critters are driven by an insatiable curiosity and a voracious appetite to rummage through your garbage or your pet's outside food bowl for leftovers. They will pick through the booty, examining the best pieces with their forepaws, then wash them in the dog's water bowl before eating.

The nightly raids can be entertaining to watch when it takes place on your porch, but their persistent thumping and scratching about in your attic or kitchen is disturbing. If you want to deter raccoons, equip your garbage cans with screen door spring guards, don't leave cat or dog food and water outside at night, and make sure your home is securely sealed. A convenient pet entrance for your dog or cat is like an open invitation to these clever explorers who will quickly gain access to and rummage through your cabinets. Control methods include trapping and repellents, but prevention is more than half the cure. Screen attic and foundation access points to prevent them from getting in or under the house. Feed your pets during the day and remove leftovers before nightfall. Take bird feeders down and empty water bowls at night.

Armadillos

The prehistoric-looking armadillo digs in the soil looking for grubs, tubers, and roots.

These armored creatures are really quite interesting — until you wake up one morning and see the damage they've done to your gardens and yard. From the armadillo's point of view, rooting around looking for succulent roots, bulbs, and tasty insects is the normal thing to do. But what a mess it leaves! Some homeowners tolerate the digging, while others resent the intrusion. About the size of an opossum, armadillos normally produce one litter a year. They are active primarily from twilight through early morning hours in the summer and during the day only during the winter. Their favorite diet consists of larval beetles, termites, ants, and other invertebrates. They may also eat fruit and vegetable matter. Because of their diet they are actually beneficial animals, but unfortunately lawns, gardens, and flower beds are often their preferred hunting grounds.

When armadillo damage is significant, control methods can be effectively applied. Live trapping and exclusion are the best strategies. Since armadillos normally dig burrows in areas that have cover, removing brush, rock piles, and tall grass will discourage them from becoming established. However, by destroying these areas, you will be removing good cover and nesting areas for other desirable species. Live trapping is an effective way to capture armadillos but is often used only as a last resort. Animals should be moved to areas at least two miles away. This technique should be avoided when they are raising young.

Beavers

Because beavers are actually rodents, they must continually gnaw to wear down their front teeth.

The beaver is the largest rodent in North America and an industrious dam builder, admirable for his work ethic and engineering skills. Beavers commonly reside in lakes, rivers, streams, and other aquatic environments that contain an adequate flow of water for damming. Beavers must continually gnaw trees to keep their front teeth from growing into their skulls.

Beaver can cause property damage by gnawing on and killing ornamental trees.

The major concern of homeowners and farmers is that as the land behind a beaver dam is flooded, shorelines can also be damaged. The animals also build caches (hiding places for food piles) with the branches of deciduous trees and will sometimes injure or kill ornamental or fruit trees. On many streams and ponds, you can encourage beavers to go elsewhere by removing food trees and dam construction material from the water's edge. Try excluding beavers from a plot of land by erecting a metal fence around property and by fencing of culverts, drain pipes, or other structures. Shield ornamental trees by wrapping each one in wire mesh, hardware cloth, or tree wrap. You can also mix a recipe of one tablespoon of hot pepper sauce in a gallon of water and spray it on tree trunks to reduce gnawing damage to the trees. When beavers are active during warm months, you need to reapply the compound periodically. If trapping is used, special traps must be used due to the beaver's size, strength, and sharp incisors. Traps are expensive and take skill to set properly, and it is often it is hard to catch all members of the family.

Nutria

The nutria is an introduced species originally from South America.

Introduced from South America as "aquatic weed cutters," nutria are large, semiaquatic rodents that resemble beavers and muskrats. Almost exclusively vegetarian, they consume about three pounds of food a day. Nutria damage occurs when they eat desirable vegetation and girdle ornamental trees. They can also dig their burrows into pond dams, levees, or watershed structures which may weaken the structures and cause them to collapse. Habitat manipulation and good farming practices such as aquatic weed control and proper drainage maintenance are good strategies for discouraging nutria from getting established in the first place. Nutria are classified as furbearers in Texas, but it is legal to trap them if they are causing damage. There are several trap styles available. Snares are sometimes used when other trapping methods are not feasible.

Opossums

The Virginia opossum is North America's only marsupial.

Our only marsupial, opossums are especially appealing when they are young. While they sport a mouth full of teeth, they are really shy and inoffensive animals. However, they can be a nuisance when they raid the garbage. Opossums are omnivores and will consume a wide range of animal and plant foods. They will also scavenge any carrion and garbage available. Opossums are furbearers and are classified as a game species in some states, but not in Texas. While they sometimes cause damage similar to skunks and raccoons, overall the level of damage they cause is slight, and they are beneficial as scavengers. The best control measure for opossums is exclusion. Many of the same methods used for raccoons will work for opossums: secure trash containers with tight-fitting lids and pick up leftover pet food at night if you feed your pets outside.

Rabbits

The Eastern cottontail finds a home in brushy hedgerows, woody edges with dense cover, and urban and suburban areas with shrubs, gardens, and lush lawns.

There is no doubt about it, bunnies are cute, but they can also be quite destructive in the backyard vegetable garden. Eastern cottontails and their relatives are generally found in brushy hedgerows and wood edges with dense cover. They also do well in urban areas and suburbs with shrubs, gardens, and lawns. Renown for their reproductive capabilities, rabbits feed on leafy plants during the growing season and the buds and bark of woody plants during the winter. Sometimes in the spring they do damage to vegetable and flower gardens. A well-constructed fence around your garden is the most effective permanent protection against rabbit damage. It need only be two feet high and made of one-inch poultry wire stretched from post to post. The lower edges should be staked securely to the ground or slightly buried. Protect small garden plots and individual plants by applying chemical repellents that rabbits find distasteful, or consider modifying the habitat. Rabbits avoid areas with little cover because of the danger from predators. Live trapping of rabbits and relocating them is a temporary solution, since replacements will soon arrive. Locate trapped rabbits to suitable locations immediately to avoid self-inflicted injuries.

Bats

The Mexican free-tailed bats, which are common in central Texas, can consume 2,000 insects per bat per night.

There are thirty-two species of bats recorded in Texas, each with distinctive physical characteristics and lifestyle. Those few species that roost in or on buildings, whether in colonies or singly, are the only bats people are likely to encounter. These species are attracted to suburban and urban areas where there are substantial populations of flying insects. Most bats feed on insects which they catch in flight. Bats are particularly important in the control of night-flying insects. A single bat can consume 2,000 or more insects in one night. Large colonies of bats are thus extremely important for insect control. Like any mammal, bats are

susceptible to rabies. However, less than one-half of one percent of bats in North America ever contract the disease.

If you have bats in your attic, the only permanent way to remove them is by excluding their entrances after they have vacated the premises. Chemicals should never be used. They are expensive, temporary, and cause worse problems by exposing the neighborhood to sick and dying bats. Any removal of bats should be done by the methods described in Merlin Tuttle's book, *America's Neighborhood Bats*. These techniques are very effective and inexpensive. For more information about bats, call Bat Conservation International at 512-327-9721.

Starlings and Grackles

Grackles thrive in the vast expanses of lawn in suburban and urban areas.

Often forming huge roosts in urban areas, starlings and grackles flock together during the fall, winter, and early spring. While individual birds normally do not pose much of a problem, they can be a real nuisance when they flock together and roost in trees near homes and public facilities. While grackles can consume or destroy some farm crops, the smaller European starlings are far more aggressive. They were introduced into New York from Europe in the late 1800s. This was an unfortunate idea and a harmful introduction, as this opportunistic bird has out-competed many of our native species such as woodpeckers and bluebirds for nesting spots. They can also cause damage to orchards and gardens. There are several methods available for discouraging roosting birds. Thinning roost vegetation and decreasing lawn area, thereby making it less attractive to the birds, often produces longer lasting results than scare tactics. For additional information and technical assistance with the control of roosting birds, contact your local Texas Wildlife Services specialist.

Snakes

Snakes are an important component of ecological systems.

Texas has many different kinds of snakes — only the Western cottonmouth, the Texas coral snake, copperheads, and rattlesnakes are poisonous to humans. Of those snakes that share human habitats, most are harmless. Snakes perform many valuable ecological services and are often maligned due to fear and misinformation. Many harmless snakes are killed for no better reason than it seems the thing to do.

Like other reptiles, snakes are ectothermic (cold-blooded). They cannot tolerate extremely cold temperatures, and they will normally hibernate during the winter months. Since most are active at night and during early morning and late evening hours, they usually escape notice. If you absolutely cannot tolerate the presence of snakes, there are various control methods available. One of the most effective methods is to remove their shelter. Eliminating rock piles, brush piles and tall grass will cause them to seek a more suitable habitat elsewhere. Store wood piles and lumber at least eighteen inches off the ground. You can eliminate their food supply by controlling insect and rodent populations around the house. Exclusion is another important strategy in deterring snakes. Keep snakes out of houses and other buildings by sealing all points of entry. Trapping is also an effective method of catching snakes which have taken up residence inside the house. Captured snakes can then be released elsewhere.

Deer

An overpopulation of white-tailed deer can devastate suburban gardens.

The sight of a white-tailed deer feeding in the front yard is a delight to many. However, in some suburban areas of Texas where human habitation has benefited deer, the population of these animals has gotten out of control. Many times, deer will exceed the carrying capacity, or the maximum population numbers that a given area can support. When this happens, they are forced into yards and gardens to get the food they need to survive. Well-tended, well-watered gardens are a delicious bonanza for these animals, especially during the drought periods of summer when the browse (thin branches) in the wild has been seriously diminished. Exclusion by deer-proof fencing is probably the best method of keeping hungry deer from eating your plants and trees. If you feed deer, it only makes the situation worse by producing more deer than the habitat can support since food is immediately translated into new fawns which creates even larger deer populations. Without natural population controls, such as mountain lions, wolves, and screw-worm disease, the land can soon be overrun with a glut of deer. (See the list of "deer-resistant" native plants in Chapter Eleven.)

Cats

Domestic cats are efficient hunters of native wildlife. Keeping a cat indoors will help prevent excessive predation.

Cats today rank as American's favorite pet, and there are over three million domestic cats in Texas. Many of these cats are free-ranging pet cats, stray cats, and feral cats (domestic cats living in the wild). As beautiful and playful as they might be, domestic cats are efficient predators of birds, small mammals, reptiles, and amphibians when left to their own devices. While loss of habitat and pollution of the air and water are cited as major causes of declines of bird species, domestic and feral cats are also a factor, especially in urban and suburban areas. No matter how well a cat is fed, it will still kill birds. That is the nature of cats. Indeed, after sleeping, hunting is the favorite pastime of cats. However, cats are not "natural" predators since they occur in higher numbers than would be possible for a wild predator. Many cats are fed by humans, and so are not totally dependent on prey numbers to support their growing population.

Cats first accompanied the British colonists as early as 1614 when they arrived on American shores and were imported again in the 1800s to assist in rodent control. The introduction of foreign species into a new territory frequently has negative effects on native species' populations. Domestic cats are no exception. Feral cats have caused their share of damage, especially on small islands where they have brought about the extinction of native birds. Ground-nesting birds like the wood thrush and chuck-will's-widow are especially vulnerable, and young fledglings are literally "sitting ducks" to a cat. Feral, stray, and free-ranging pet cats roaming Texas is a very real problem. Unwanted kittens cast off into the woods must fend for themselves and live off the land. Their expanding population puts tremendous pressure on native wildlife. Cat prey items include rodents, birds, rabbits, reptiles and amphibians, and insects. In fact, a rural cat will kill an average of eighty-three animals per year, and an urban cat will kill an average of twenty-six animals a year. This is tremendous predation, especially considering that cats outnumber all other mammalian predators combined. It is unfair to attract birds to your backyard if cats are allowed to stalk them at will.

Curbing the Cat Problem

If you have a cat, there are several things you can do to help save birds and other wildlife while also watching out for the best interest of your cat.

- Make your kitty an indoor cat. Remember, bells are ineffective wildlife warning devices, and by keeping your cat inside, you are protecting him from disease, parasites, fleas, ticks, and serious injury. Cats gradually introduced back into home-life will not only be much healthier than their outdoor compatriots, but will also be quite happy and content.

- Only about 20% of America's cats have been spayed or neutered, yet cats are prolific breeders. Have your cat neutered or spayed in a timely manner.

- Support programs to remove cats that are living off the land in parks and refuges.

- Never dump unwanted kittens into the nearby woods. Take them to the humane society or have a kitty sale. Dumping kittens into the wild is cruel both to the kittens and to the birds, reptiles, and small mammals that will serve as their food.

- Don't abandon a pet cat when moving to new premises. Take the time to find it a new home.

Discouraging Nest Box Predators

Nest boxes and feeders undeniably offer much-needed feeding and nesting resources in our backyards, but by providing these predictable, easily recognized structures for animals to feed at and nest in, we also provide easily patrolled hunting areas for predators such as snakes, raccoons, opossums, and house cats. Moreover, these coveted areas are often scouted out by aggressive species such as house sparrows, European starlings, and grackles, who then oust desirable species from the nesting cavities or chase them from their feeding areas.

Prevent snakes, raccoons, and other predators from accessing nest boxes by installing a baffle around the nest box pole (Figure 10a). Construct the baffle out of 26-gauge sheet metal in either a cone or cylinder shape. Place the baffle on the nest box pole, as high off the ground or water surface as possible and about six to twelve inches below the nest box for a cylinder-type baffle, and at least three feet from the ground or water surface for a cone-type baffle. To prevent predation by snakes and mammals, place a 6" length of appropriate diameter PVC pipe into the entrance hole of the nest box (Figure 10b).

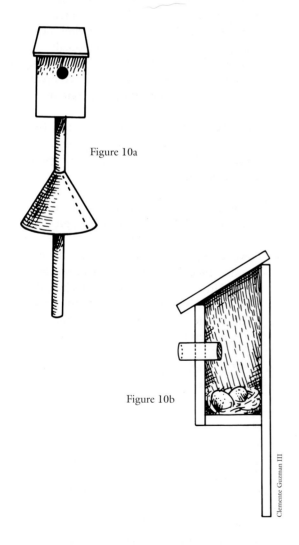

Figure 10a

Figure 10b

Clemente Guzman III

House Sparrows and European Starlings

© TPW, Frank Aguilar

The house sparrow is a cheerful exotic bird that has adapted well to urban life. Unfortunately, it is also very aggressive, and takes over the nesting sites of many native birds.

House sparrows and European starlings are both aggressive and exotic (not native to Texas or the United States) species that aggressively run off other native species from both natural and artificially provided nesting areas. These avian tyrants sometimes even kill the native species to retain the coveted nesting spot. Neither the house sparrow nor the European starling is protected in the United States, and should be evicted from nest boxes. Often, you will have to remove the same pair several times before they get the message and leave your area for good.

© TPW, Bill Reeves

The European starling is an introduced bird which competes directly with native birds for suitable nest sites.

Entrances to nest boxes are accessible to house sparrows if they are at least $1 \frac{3}{8}$" in diameter, and to European starlings if they are at least $1 \frac{1}{2}$" in diameter, so be sure to construct nest box entrances at the smallest size possible. Also, do not provide perches for bird nest boxes, since the sparrows and starlings seem to prefer houses with this feature.

Wasp Nests

Prevent wasps from attaching their nest to the roof of nest boxes by rubbing layers of liquid soap or rubbing a bar of soap on the inside ceiling.

If wasps or other insects invade the nest box before it can be occupied by birds, try to remove the nest manually (armed with a can of insecticide for self-protection), or spray the box with pyrethrin which is not toxic to birds, and plug the hole for twenty-four hours. To prevent wasps from attaching a nest to the roof of the nest box, apply a layer of liquid soap to the surface.

Fire Ants

The red imported fire ant is not only a bother at picnics, it is also deadly to many species of native wildlife.

The red imported fire ant *(Solenopsis invicta)* is an introduced species which is extremely detrimental to many species of native wildlife, including nesting birds. You can protect your nesting birds from fire ants in three ways. One effective method is to "grease" the support pole with a mixture of five pounds chassis grease and one quart of turpentine (mixed well). If the support pole is wooden, apply a layer of duct tape first to prevent the wood from absorbing the mixture. Be sure to check the application periodically to ensure that it is still tacky and effective. Another way to prevent ants from crawling up to the nest box is to apply a layer of DE (Diatomaceous Earth), which is a nontoxic product that kills many different insects by cutting the insects' waxy exoskeleton and absorbing the insects' body liquid. DE kills a wide variety of insects, including beneficial insects, so its use should be restricted to areas of infestation or where potential infestation would cause great harm (such as around a nest box). The third method of fire ant control is to use Logic insect growth regulator. Since Logic is specific to ants, it does not harm "nontarget" organisms. Logic can be used either as a single mound treatment or as a broadcast application, and is typically targeted at the red imported fire ant and big-headed ant *(Pheidole megacephaia)* colonies.

Chapter Eleven: *Special Areas*

© Chuck Kowaleski

© TPW, Glenn Mills

In Texas, there is no such thing as a "typical yard." Our landscapes have shaded areas, soggy spots, and sections that are overrun with hungry deer. What do you do with these problem areas when planting a Wildscape? Turn your trouble spots into assets by accentuating them, flaunting them, and making them the highlight of your garden!

Those shaded areas, when properly planned, can be transformed into the jewels of your yard. Turn that dappled shade garden into a hideaway that replicates a deep forest draped in bracken fern *(Pteridium aquilinum)*, carpeted with delicate partridgeberry *(Mitchella repens)*, and punctuated with vibrant widow's tears *(Commenlina* sp.*)* Turn soggy areas into shallow bogs or wetlands just big enough to entice butterflies to "puddle" or gather by the moist edges. Your wetland might also attract a few wading birds anxious to gobble up the invertebrates, such as dragonfly larvae, in the mud. For that matter, why try to do battle with the deer? By planting vegetation that deer avoid, you will enjoy a hardy, beautiful, and mostly "unmunched" garden.

Shady Areas

This lovely shrubby boneset will thrive in areas with dappled shade.

Selecting plant species for shaded areas can present a real challenge for home gardeners. You may have a few areas that are so shady that even the most shade-tolerant species won't thrive. While some Texas natives do well under a variety of lighting conditions, the majority of plants have distinct lighting preferences.

Full Sun: Full sun means that the plants grow best when exposed to direct sunlight all day long. Many native Texas wildflowers prefer full sun, yet some of these sun lovers can tolerate shade for a couple of hours (but no more than that).

Partial Shade: Plants in this category prefer the morning sun, which is less intense, from four to six hours per day.

Dappled Shade: Dappled shade occurs when sunlight is filtered through the leaves of trees and is patchy most of the time. Many shade-loving plants thrive and bloom in a half-day or more of dappled shade.

The American beautyberry is a wonderful understory plant. In the spring the loosely-shaped shrub produces delicate pink flowers. In the fall, the flowers yield vibrant purple berries.

Shade: Shade-loving species can tolerate as little as two hours of direct sun or four hours of dappled sunshine per day. Many of these species also require additional moisture if placed in sunnier spots. Various native forbs (nonwoody, nongrassy plants, such as wildflowers), grasses, vines, and shrubs will thrive in shady or semishady situations.

Selecting Shade Tolerant Plants

Before purchasing and planting new vegetation, analyze how much shade your yard gets in various locations during different seasons, then learn which plants will grow and thrive under these conditions (see Table 11.1 at the end of this chapter).

Wet Area Gardening

It is obvious that Texas is blessed with scenic vistas, rolling prairies, and towering forests. However, the quantity and variety of aquatic habitats found within Texas' borders are also impressive. Swiftly moving streams, quiet bogs, and gently flowing rivers are only part of the rich diversity of Texas' aquatic habitats. Recreate natural aquatic habitat in your yard by turning soggy areas and water sources into wetlands and oases. Select native Texas plants, and make your yard abuzz with wildlife activity.

Aquatic Plants

Lady fern
Athyrium filix-femina var. *asplenioides*

Buttonbush
Cephalanthus occidentalis

Crinum lily
Crinum americanum

Titi
Cyrilla racemiflora

White-topped sedge
Dichromena colorata

Horsetail
Equisetum hyemale

Swamp sunflower
Helianthus angustifolius

Waterleaf
Hydrolea ovata

Chain fern
Lorinseria areolata

© TPW, John Herron

Ponds edged and filled with plants will provide habitat for a variety of birds, amphibians, dragonflies, and more!

Yellow lotus
Nelumbo lutea

White water-lily
Nymphaea odorata

Floating-heart
Nymphoides aquatica

Sensitive fern
Onoclea sensibilis

Cinnamon fern
Osmunda cinnamomea

Royal fern
Osmunda regalis var. *spectabilis*

Tuckahoe
Peltandra virginica

Pickerel-weed
Pontederia cordata

Arrowhead
Saggittaria lancifolia

Lizard's-tail
Saururus cernuus

Powdery thalia
Thalia dealbata

Meadow-rue
Thalictrum sp.

Narrowleaf cattail
Typha angustifolia

Floating bladderwort
Utricularia radiata

Virginia chain fern
Woodwardia virginica

Dealing with Deer

The white-tailed deer *(Odocoileus virginianus)* is by far the most abundant large native herbivore in Central Texas. In fact, deer are more numerous today than they were when North America was first settled by Europeans. Several factors have contributed to the burgeoning deer population in our region, including the eradication of screw-worm disease, the reduction of natural predators such as wolves and mountain lions, and the widespread practice by well-meaning homeowners of setting out supplemental food for them.

As creatures of the forest edge, deer are highly adaptable to the environmental changes wrought by man. White tails prefer a diverse habitat with a mixture of forage and cover. If there is an adequate supply of natural browse (tender shoots, twigs, and leaves) in the deer's usual feeding ground, they will likely not touch a homeowner's ornamental or vegetable garden. If, on the other hand, the natural food supply is low due to extended drought or other adverse environmental conditions, deer will boldly invade our well-tended domestic gardens.

© TPW, Glen Mills

The white-tailed deer has adapted very well to the environmental changes brought on by humans.

Highly Palatable Plants

Deer, like most animals, are selective in their foraging, avoiding some species while seeking out others with relish. They eat a wide variety of vegetation and change their diet according to what is available. A hungry deer will avoid a particular plant depending primarily on the availability of other food; but you can better your odds of growing a green Wildscape by eliminating those plants that deer find absolutely irresistible.

Palatable Plants to Avoid

Roses
Pansies
Pyracantha spp.
Spirea spp.
Hibiscus
Petunias
Euonymous
Photinia spp.
Geraniums

Selecting Deer-resistant Plants

Only a few plants are so toxic or distasteful that deer will avoid them altogether. Others are avoided only at certain stages of growth, with palatability varying with the plant's age or with the seasons. Under stress, however, few plants are totally resistant to the white-tailed deer. And where deer pressure is very high, even unpalatable plants will be devoured. Selecting wildflowers in an effort to "deer-proof" your planting may improve their survival, but nothing will guarantee their safety after a hard winter or spring in an area of intense population pressure (see Table 11.2 at the end of this chapter).

Mexican hat.

Table 11.1
Plants that Accept Variable Degrees of Shade

Common name	Scientific name	Shade	Dappled	Partial	Full sun
Flowers					
Wild Red Columbine	*Aquilegia canadensis*	x	x	x	
Annual Aster	*Aster subulatus*				x
Texas Aster	*Aster texanus*		x	x	x
Winecup	*Callirhoe involucrata*			x	x
Straggler Daisy	*Calyptocarpus vialis*	x	x	x	x
Wild Hyacinth	*Camassia scilloides*		x	x	
Day-flower	*Commelina erecta*		x	x	
False Day-flower	*Commelinantia anomala*		x	x	
Rainlilies	*Cooperia* spp.	x	x	x	
Spectacle-pod	*Dithyrea wislizenii*		x	x	
Wild Buckwheat	*Eriogonum multiflorum*		x	x	
Blue Mistflower	*Eupatorium coelestinum*		x	x	
White Avens	*Geum canadense*	x	x	x	
Standing Cypress	*Ipomopsis rubra*		x	x	x
Copper Lily	*Habranthus texanus*		x	x	
Cardinal Flower	*Lobelia cardinalis*		x	x	
Coral Honeysuckle	*Lonicera sempervirens*			x	
Partridgeberry	*Mitchella repens*	x	x	x	
Baby Blue-eyes	*Nemophila phacelioides*		x	x	
Yellow Passionflower	*Passiflora lutea*		x	x	
Rose Pavonia	*Pavonia lasiopetala*			x	x
Gulf Coast Foxglove	*Penstemon tenuis*		x	x	x
Blue Curls	*Phacelia congesta*		x	x	x
Drummond's Phlox	*Phlox drummondii*		x	x	x
Fragrant Phlox	*Phlox pilosa*		x	x	
Texas Frog-fruit	*Phyla nodiflora*		x	x	x
Obedient Plant	*Physostegia angustifolia*		x	x	
White Milkwort	*Polygala alba*		x	x	x
Pidgeonberry	*Rivina humilis*	x	x	x	
Common Ruellia, Wild Petunia	*Ruellia nudiflora*		x	x	
Meadow-pink	*Sabatia campestris*		x	x	x
Scarlet Sage	*Salvia coccinea*		x	x	x
Autumn Sage	*Salvia greggii*			x	
Lyreleaf Sage	*Salvia lyrata*		x	x	
Golden Groundsel	*Senecio obovatus*	x	x	x	
Blue-eyed Grass	*Sisyrinchium* spp.		x	x	
American Germander	*Teucrium canadense*	x	x	x	
Spiderworts	*Tradescantia* spp.	x	x	x	
Western Ironweed	*Vernonia baldwinii*		x	x	x
Hairy Zexmania	*Wedelia hispida*		x	x	x

Common name	Scientific name	Shade	Dappled	Partial	Full sun
Grasses and grasslike plants					
Cedar-sedge	*Carex planostachys*	X	X		
Inland Seaoats	*Chasmanthium latifolia*	X	X	X	
Canada Wildrye	*Elymus canadensis*		X	X	
Vines					
Crossvine	*Bignonia capreolata*	X	X	X	X
Trumpet-vine	*Campsis radicans*			X	X
Scarlet Clematis	*Clematis texensis*	X	X	X	
Snapdragon Vine	*Maurandya antirrhiniflora*		X	X	
Virginia Creeper	*Parthenocissus quiquefolia*	X	X	X	
Shrubs					
American Beautyberry	*Callicarpa americana*	X	X	X	
Chili Pequín	*Capsicum annuum*	X	X	X	
New Jersey Tea	*Ceanothus americanus*		X	X	
Deciduous Holly	*Ilex decidua*		X	X	
Yaupon	*Ilex vomitoria*		X	X	X
Wax-myrtle	*Myrica cerifera*	X	X	X	
Texas Mock Orange	*Philadelphus texensis*		X	X	X
Fragrant Sumac	*Rhus aromatica*		X	X	X
Pidgeonberry	*Rivina humilis*		X	X	
Eve's Necklace	*Sophora affinis*		X	X	X
Carolina Cherry Laurel	*Prunus caroliniana*		X	X	
Texas Mountain Laurel	*Sophora secundiflora*	X	X	X	
Mexican Buckeye	*Ungnadia speciosa*		X	X	X
Texas Persimmon	*Diospyros texana*	X	X	X	X
Rusty Blackshaw Viburnum	*Viburnum rufidulum*			X	X
Woods Rose	*Rosa woodsii*		X	X	X
Coralberry	*Symphoricarpos orbiculatus*		X	X	
Virginia Sweetspire	*Itea virginica*	X	X	X	
Ferns					
Maidenhair Fern	*Adiantum capillus-veneris*	X	X	X	
Ebony Spleenwort	*Asplenium resiliens*	X	X	X	
Alabama Lipfern	*Cheilanthes alabamensis*	X	X	X	
Powder Cloakfern	*Notholaena dealbata*	X	X	X	
Southern Shield Fern	*Thelypteris ovata* var. *lindheimeri*	X	X	X	

Table 11.2
Deer-Resistant Plants

Common name	Scientific name	Highly resistant to deer	Deer avoid most of the time	Unpalatable
Annual Sunflower	*Helianthus annuus*			x
Ashe Juniper	*Juniperus ashei*		x	
Bald Cypress	*Taxodium distichum*			x
Beargrass	*Nolina* spp.			x
Black-eyed Susan	*Rudbeckia hirta*			x
Blackfoot Daisy	*Melampodium leucanthum*			x
Cardinal Flower	*Lobelia cardinalis*			x
Cenizo	*Leucophyllum frutescens*			x
Cherry Laurel	*Prunus caroliniana*		x	
Clematis	*Clematis* spp.			x
Columbine	*Aquilegia* spp.			x
Cow-itch Vine	*Cissus incisa*			x
Cross-vine	*Bignonia capreolata*			x
Damianita	*Chrysactinia mexicana*	x		
Deciduous Holly	*Ilex decidua*			x
Drummond's Skullcap	*Scutellaria drummondii*			x
Ferns	Almost all except *Pellaea* spp.		x	
Flame-leaf Sumac	*Rhus lanceolata*			x
Fleabane	*Erigeron* spp.			x
Four O'clocks	*Mirabilis* spp.			x
Gayfeather	*Liatris* spp.		x	
Germanders	*Teucrium* spp.			x
Indian Blanket	*Gaillardia pulchella*		x	
Kidneywood	*Eysenhardtia texana*			x
Lantana	*Lantana horrida*		x	
Larkspur	*Delphinium carolinianum*			x
Lemon Mint	*Monarda citriodora*		x	
Maidenhair Fern	*Adiantum capillus-verneris*		x	
Maximilian Sunflower	*Helianthus maximiliani*			x
Mealy Sage	*Salvia farinacea*		x	
Mexican Hat	*Ratibida columnifera*		x	
Milkweeds	*Asclepias* spp.	x		
Mountain Pink	*Centaurium beyrichii*			x
Penstemons	*Penstemon* spp.			x
Pink Evening Primrose	*Oenothera speciosa*		x	
Pink Wood Sorrel	*Oxalis drummondii*		x	
Prickly Pear Cactus	*Opuntia lindheimeri*			x
Purple Coneflower	*Echinacea purpurea*			x
Queen's Delight	*Stillingia texana*		x	

Common name	Scientific name	Highly resistant to deer	Deer avoid most of the time	Unpalatable
Plateau Liveoak	*Quercus fusiformis*		X	
Red Yucca	*Hesperaloe parviflora*		X	
Eastern Redbud	*Cercis canadensis*			X
Rockcress	*Arabis petiolaris*			X
Shrubby Skullcap	*Scutellaria wrightii*			X
Nightshades	*Solanum* spp.		X	
Shrubby Boneset	*Eupatorium havanense*		X	
Slender Greenthread	*Thelesperma filifolium*			X
Snow-on-the-Mountain	*Euphorbia marginata*		X	
Snow-on-the-Prairie	*Euphorbia bicolor*		X	
Texas Mountain-laurel	*Sophora secundiflora*		X	
Texas Persimmon	*Diospyros texana*			X
Texas Sage	*Salvia texana*			X
Verbenas	*Verbena* spp.			X
Yaupon	*Ilex vomitoria*		X	
Yucca	*Yucca rupicola*		X	
Yellow Wood Sorrel	*Oxalis dillenii*		X	
Zexmenia	*Wedelia hispida*			X

Chapter Twelve: *Watch Out for Exotics!*

© Paul Montgomery

© Paul Montgomery

Exotics are foreign plants or animals imported and introduced into a new environment. Most gardens in Texas host a number of exotic species of plants. Many have been brought into the United States because of their unusual flowers or fruit, special fragrance, extravagant color, or bizarre appearance. Some may even be horticultural favorites from long ago such as azaleas, roses, and peonies.

The Problem with Exotics

Exotics will sometimes surprise you. While many of them require pesticides, extra water, or cold protection to survive the seasons, some exotics find their new home a dream come true. While not all introductions become invasive, the few that do can become serious problems. Every so often a plant whose origins are continents away will spread unchecked in their new environment, and become "naturalized" in the wild. Slowly and surely, these aliens often out-compete our natives and change the face of the landscape.

Reasons for such unbridled success are manyfold. The most important is the lack of natural controls — no pathogens, no herbivores, or no natural enemies to keep the newcomers down. Because they are foreigners, they have left their native predators and parasites behind and now have little to keep them in check in their new home. Invasive aliens become particularly obnoxious weeds, moving boldly into new habitats and reproducing rapidly.

While a well-planned wildlife garden can have carefully selected exotic plants to serve as accents and supplemental wildlife food sources, using native plants is preferable. The less labor devoted to making ornamental plants survive, the more time to observe the birds and butterflies that frequent your garden. Besides, native plants form the food base for local wildlife species. Their presence in your garden will attract a diversity of animals that do not ordinarily come into residential areas. Gardeners interested in providing habitat for native wildlife should avoid planting exotic plants, and should consider eradicating the ones that have made their way into the landscape.

Common Exotic Plants to Avoid

Chinese Tallow
Sepium sebiferum

Its attractive fall foliage and quick growth habit make the exotic Chinese tallow a very popular landscape tree.

The Chinese tallow, an attractive member of the Spurge family, has become the scourge of the Gulf Coast. Spread by birds, this aggressive plant has dramatically altered the landscape of the Upper Texas Coast, out-competing native vegetation at every turn. Like many members of its family, it has milky sap which is poisonous. Originally cultivated in China for the wax from the seed covering which was used for soap, it has now become popular for landscaping because of its fall color and pretty white berries.

Chinese Privit
Ligustrum sinensis

Birds relish the berries of the Chinese privit, another aggressive shrub which is an oriental upstart member of the Olive family. It supplants yaupon and other valuable natives as an understory plant in the wild. Common on the Upper Gulf Coast, this native of southeast Asia is a popular landscape plant grown for its ornamental value.

Chinaberry Tree
Melia azedarach

The ubiquitous Chinaberry tree produces pale, fragrant lavender flowers, but is a real pest to native trees.

A native of Asia, the chinaberry is an introduced ornamental that has escaped cultivation and is growing wild over wide areas of Texas east to Florida. It especially thrives in waste places and along rivers, squeezing out native trees as it spreads. A member of the Mahogany family, its yellow fruit is attractive to birds which disperse the seeds far and wide.

The Chinaberry tree can also be recognized by its distinctive bright yellow fall foliage.

Water-Hyacinth
Eichhornia crassipes

The beautiful blooms of the water-hyacinth belie the danger it poses to rivers, lakes, and streams.

There is no denying that a carpet of water-hyacinth spread across sluggish streams or lakes is a beautiful sight to behold. It also is a mess to remove, making passage impossible and completely changing the aquatic environment it has overrun.

Japanese Ligustrum
Ligustrum lucidum

With thick leathery leaves and attractive arrangements of blue berries, the Japanese ligustrum is an ornamental shrub whose spread is aided and abetted by the birds. A member of the Olive family, it has become an all too common invader of Central Texas landscapes, replacing beautiful natives in its wake. Native to China, Korea, and Japan, this aggressive ornamental is commonly planted in the warmer regions of Texas.

Purple Loosestrife
Lythrum salicaria

Purple loosestrife was introduced into North America from Europe at the beginning of the 19th century, and it has progressively spread westward. It aggressively invades wetlands where it displaces native vegetation. While attractive, it takes over moist environments and does not let go. This plant is more of a problem in the northern states, but gardeners should still avoid planting it in Texas.

Yellow Star-Thistle
Centaurea melitensis

Yellow star-thistle is a thorny, noxious weed. This knee-high composite can take over pastures, replacing native forbs and grasses in its path. This aggressive alien is as hard to get rid of as it is unattractive. Many other exotic members of the thistle group, such as nodding thistle and small-flowered thistle, have also become noxious weeds in Texas.

Japanese Honeysuckle
Lonicera japonica

© Paul Montgomery

The Japanese honeysuckle vine is a fragrant summer bloomer, but will take over an area if you let it.

A clambering, smothering vine, the fragrant exotic honeysuckle can overrun an area once it gets started. Filling the air with a sweet perfume that reminds us of summer and warm weather, it lulls us into thinking that nothing has gone awry. But just try to find another species of plant under a stand of honeysuckle!

Other Problem Plants

Troublesome and aggressive plant species are frequently cultivated in central Texas and often escape into the wild where they replace and out-compete native species. The following species should be avoided as landscape plants and should not be introduced into any Texas habitat, natural or man-made. The notation "(non-native)" indicates a variety or species which is not native to Texas. There are other varieties or specific species of these groups of plants that are native to the state, which you may include in a Wildscape without harm.

Trees and Shrubs

Tree-of-heaven
  Ailanthus altissima

Mimosa tree
  Albizzia julibrissin

Paper mulberry
  Broussonetia papyrifera

Chinese loquat
  Eriobotrya japonica

Common fig
  Ficus carica

Chinese parasol-tree
  Firmiana simplex

Golden rain-tree
Koelreuteria paniculata

Lantana (non-native)
Lantana spp. (non-native varieties)

Wax-leaf ligustrum
Ligustrum quihoui

White mulberry
Morus alba

Heavenly bamboo
Nandina domestica

Oleander
Nerium oleander

Red-tip photinia
Photinia serrulata

White poplar
Populus alba

Kudzu
Pueraria lobata

Firethorn
Pyracantha spp.

Salt cedar
Tamarix spp.

Siberian elm
Ulmus pumila

Periwinkle
Vinca major

Lilac chaste-tree
Vitex agnus-castus

Herbaceous Plants

Many-flowered thistle
Carduus tenuiflorus

Nodding thistle
Carduus nutans

Distaff thistle
Carthamus lanatus

Malta star-thistle
Centaurea melitensis

Chickory
Cichorium intybus

Tickseed, tick-clover
Desmodium spp.

Pink
Dianthus spp.

Bush-clover
Lespediza spp. (non-native varieties)

The bright red berries of a nandina provide much needed color in winter, but the plant can be rather aggressive when it escapes cultivation.

Birdsfoot trefoil
Lotus corniculatus

Common horehound
Marrubium vulgare

Sweet clover
Melilotus albus

Sour clover
Melilotus indicus

Yellow sweet clover
Melilotus offinalis

Childing pink
Petrorhagia prolifer

Wild mustard
Rapistrum rugosum

Castor-bean
Ricinus communis

Tumbleweed
Salsola kali

Milk thistle
Silybum marianum

Sow thistle
Sonchus asper

Beggar's ticks
Torilis arvensis

Goats's beard
Tragopogon dubius

Low hop-clover
Trifolium campestre

White clover
Trifolium repens

Pink clover
Trifolium pratense

Brazilian vervain
Verbena brasiliensis

Persian speedwell
Veronica persica

Grasses

Giant reed
Arundo donax

KR Bluestem
Bothriochloa ischaemum

Rip-gut brome
Bromus diandrus

Rescuegrass
Bromus unioloides

Bufflegrass
Cenchrus ciliaris

Bermudagrass
Cynodon dactylon

Kleberg bluestem
Dichanthium annulatum

Angleton bluestem
Dichanthium aristatum

Silky bluestem
Dichanthium sericeum

Southern crabgrass
Digitaria ciliaris

Goosegrass
Eleusine indica

Mediterranean lovegrass
Eragrostis barrelieri

Tall fescue
Festuca arundinacea

Meadow fescue
Festuca elatior

Kleingrass
Panicum coloratum

Bahiagrass
Paspalum notatum

Johnsongrass
Sorghum halepense

Guineagrass
Panicum maximum

© Paul Montgomery

Johnsongrass is used extensively in agriculture, but will also invade native prairies, meadows, and even urban landscapes.

Aquatic Plants

Elephant ears
  Colocasia spp.

Water hyacinth
  Eichhornia crassipes

Hydrilla
  Hydrilla verticillata

Yellow flag
  Iris pseudacorus

Purple loosestrife
  Lythrum salicaria

Milfoil
  Myriophyllum spp. (non-native)

Japanese honeysuckle (Lonicera japonica).

Part Four: *Appendix*

Bibliography

Ajilvsgi, G. 1991. *Butterfly Gardening for the South*. Dallas, Texas: Taylor Publishing Company.

Ajilvsgi, G. 1979. *Wildflowers of the Big Thicket, East Texas, and Western Louisiana*. College Station, Texas: Texas A&M Press.

Ajilvsgi, G. 1984. *Wildflowers of Texas*. Bryan, Texas: Shearer Publishing Inc.

Amos, C. and F. Gehlbach, eds. 1988. *Edwards Plateau Vegetation: Plant Ecological studies in Central Texas*. Waco, Texas: Baylor University Press.

Brown, C.A. 1972. *Wildflowers of Louisiana and Adjoining States*. Baton Rouge, Louisiana: Louisiana State University Press.

Cannatella, M. 1985. *Plants of the Texas Shore: A Beachcombers Guide*. College Station, Texas: Texas A&M University Press.

Correll, D. and M. Johnston. 1979. *Manual of the Vascular Plants of Texas*. Richardson, Texas: University of Texas.

Cox, P. and P. Leslie. 1988. *Texas Trees; A Friendly Guide*. San Antonio, Texas: Corona Press.

Davis, W.B. and D.J. Schmidly. 1994. *The Mammals of Texas*. Austin, Texas: University of Texas Press.

Duncan, W.H. and M.B. Duncan. 1987. *The Smithsonian Guide to Seaside Plants of the Gulf and Atlantic Coasts*. Washington, D.C.: Smithsonian Institution Press.

Ellis, B. 1997. *Attracting Birds and Butterflies: How to Plan and Plant a Backyard Habitat*. Boston, Massachusetts: Houghton Mifflin Company.

Enquist, M. 1987. *Wildflowers of the Texas Hill Country*. Austin, Texas: Lone Star Botanical.

Everitt, J.H. and D.L. Drawe. 1993. *Trees, Shrubs, and Cacti of South Texas*. Lubbock, Texas: Texas Tech University Press.

Fisher, C.D. 1984. Texas birds: diversity and preservation. In: *Protection of Texas Natural Diversity: An Introduction for Natural Resource Planners and Managers.* (eds.) E.G. Carls and J. Neal. College Station, Texas: Texas A&M University Press.

Flores, D.L. 1990. *Caprock Canyonlands: Journeys into the Heart of the Southern Plains.* Austin, Texas: University of Texas Press.

Garrett, J.H. 1995. *The Dirt Doctor's Guide to Organic Gardening.* Austin, Texas: University of Texas Press.

Garrett, J.H. 1996. *Plants for Texas.* Austin, Texas: University of Texas Press.

Garrett, J.M. and D.G. Barker. 1987. *A Field Guide to Reptiles and Amphibians of Texas.* Houston, Texas: Gulf Publishing Company.

Gould, F. 1975. *The Grasses of Texas.* College Station, Texas: Texas A&M University Press.

Gould, F., G.O. Hoffman, and C.A. Rechenthin. 1960. *Vegetational Areas of Texas.* College Station, Texas: Texas Agricultural Experiment Station L-492.

Great Plains Flora Association. 1977. *Atlas of the Flora of the Great Plains.* Ames, Iowa: Iowa State University Press.

Ham, H. 1984. *South Texas Wildflowers.* Kingsville, Texas: The Conner Museum, Texas A&I University.

Hatch, S.L. and J. Pluhar. 1995. *Texas Range Plants.* College Station, Texas: Texas A&M University Press.

Jones, F. 1975. *Flora of the Texas Coastal Bend.* Corpus Christi, Texas: Mission Press.

Kirkpatrick, Z.M. 1992. *Wildflowers of the Western Plains.* Austin, Texas: University of Texas Press.

Lonard, R.I., J.H. Everitt, and F.W. Judd. 1991. *Woody Plants of the Lower Rio Grande Valley Texas.* Misc. Paper #7. Austin, Texas: Texas Memorial Museum, University of Texas at Austin.

Lonard, R.I., and F.W. Judd. 1981. *The Terrestrial Flora of South Padre Island, Texas.* Misc. Paper #6. Austin, Texas: Texas Memorial Museum, University of Texas at Austin.

Loughmiller, C. and L. Loughmiller. 1984. *Texas Wildflowers: A Field Guide.* Austin, Texas. University of Texas Press.

Lynch, Brother D. 1981. *Native and Naturalized Woody Plants of Austin and The Hill Country.* Austin, Texas: Saint Edward's University.

Mahler, W.F. 1988. *Shinner's Manual of the North Central Texas Flora.* Fort Worth, Texas: Botanical Research Institute of Texas.

Martin, A.C., H.S. Zim, and A.L. Nelson. 1951. *American Wildlife and Plants - A Guide to Wildlife Food Habits.* New York: Dover Publications.

National Geographic Society. 1987. *Field Guide to the Birds of North America, Second Edition.* Washington, D.C.: National Geographic Society.

Nixon, E. 1985. *Trees, Shrubs, and Woody Vines of East Texas.* Nacogdoches, Texas: Bruce Lyndon Cunningham Productions.

Peterson, R.T. et al. 1974. *Gardening with Wildlife.* Washington, D.C.: National Wildlife Federation.

Pope, T., N. Oldenwald, and C. Fryling. 1993. *Attracting Birds to Southern Gardens.* Dallas: Taylor Publishing Company.

Powell, M.A. 1988. *Trees and Shrubs of Trans-Pecos Texas Including Big Bend and Guadalupe Mountains National Park.* Big Bend National Park, Texas: Big Bend Natural History Association, Incorporated.

Rappole, J.H. and G.W. Blacklock. 1985. *Birds of the Coastal Bend: Abundance and Distribution.* College Station: Texas A&M University Press.

Richardson, A. 1990. *Plants of Southernmost Texas.* Brownsville, Texas: University of Texas at Brownsville.

Rose, F. and R. Strandtmann. 1986. *Wildflowers of the Llano Estacado.* Dallas, Texas: Taylor Publishing Company.

Simpson, B.J. 1989. *A Field Guide to Texas Trees.* Austin, Texas: Texas Monthly Press.

Stokes, D. and L. Stokes. 1989. *The Hummingbird Book.* Boston, Massachusetts: Little, Brown, and Company.

Tennant, A. 1985. *A Field Guide to Texas Snakes.* Houston, Texas: Gulf Publishing Company.

Texas General Land Office. 1980. "The Natural Heritage of Texas." Austin, Texas: Nature Conservancy.

Toops, C. 1992. *Hummingbirds: Jewels in Flight.* Stillwater, Minnesota: Voyageur Press, Incorporated.

Tufts, C. 1988. *The Backyard Naturalist.* Washington, D.C.: National Wildlife Federation.

Tveten, J and G. Tveten. 1993. *Wildflowers of Houston.* Houston, Texas: Rice University Press.

Tveten, J.L. 1993. *The Birds of Texas.* Fredericksburg, Texas: Shearer Publishing.

Vines, R.A. 1982. *Trees of North Texas.* Austin, Texas: University of Texas Press.

Vines, R.A. 1960. *Trees, Shrubs, and Woody Vines of the Southwest.* Austin, Texas: University of Texas Press.

Warnock, B.H. 1970. *Wildflowers of the Big Bend Country, Texas.* Alpine, Texas: Sul Ross University Press.

Warnock, B.H. 1977. *Wildflowers of the Davis Mountains and the Marathon Basin, Texas.* Alpine, Texas: Sul Ross University Press.

Warnock, B.H. 1974. *Wildflowers of the Guadalupe Mountains and the Sand Dune Country, Texas.* Alpine, Texas: Sul Ross University Press.

Wasowski, S. and A. Wasowski. 1997. *Native Texas Gardens.* Austin, Texas: Texas Monthly Press.

Wasowski, S. and A. Wasowski. 1989. *Native Texas Plants: Landscaping Region by Region.* Austin, Texas: Texas Monthly Press.

Wauer, R.H. 1980. *Naturalist's Big Bend.* College Station, Texas: Texas A&M Press.

Weaver, J.E. 1954. *North American Prairie.* Lincoln, Nebraska: Johnsen Publishing Company.

Wilson, J. 1991. *Landscaping with Wildflowers.* Boston: Houghton Mifflin Company.

Winckler, S. 1982. Texas Diversity: From the Piney Woods to the Trans-Pecos. In: *The Nature Conservancy News.* 32(5).

achene: A small, dry, one-seeded fruit with no seams, as in a sunflower.

acid soil: Soils which have a low pH; deficient in lime.

alkaline soil: Soils rich lime; having a high pH.

alternate: Any leaf arrangement along the stem that is not opposite or whorled. Only one leaf arising from the node.

angiosperm: Plants that produce seeds enclosed in a fleshy, papery, or woody fruit; a flowering plant.

annual: A plant that germinates from seed, flowers, sets seed, and dies in the same year.

antenna (plural antennae): Paired structures on the head of the butterfly, probably used for smelling, touching, and orientation. In butterflies the antennae are clubbed or barely thickened. In skippers they are hooked at the end like a shepherd's crook. Moths can have plumed antennae.

anther: The pollen-bearing part of the stamen.

Apodiformes: The avian order that includes swifts and humming-birds. The name refers to the characteristic of both swifts and hummingbirds as having extremely weak legs and feet suitable for perching or clinging, but not for walking.

aposematism: Vivid coloration or striking pattern, often in reds, yellows, oranges, and black, that identifies an animal as having distasteful or unpleasant properties. Warning coloration.

aquatic: Primarily inhabiting water.

arid: Areas where annual precipitation is less than the potential evaporation and transpiration. An area which typically has very little soil moisture.

aromatic: Fragrant, spicy or pungent in smell. Usually refers to a scent given off when you crush the leaves.

arroyo: A gully generally found along valley floors in an arid or semi-arid region. The gully has steep walls cut into fine-grained sediments. The floor is flat and is generally sandy. In the United States, arroyos are typically found in the Southwest.

ascending: Rising or curving obliquely in an upward direction.

axil: The angle formed between the leaf and the stem to which it is attached.

barbs: The individual subunits of a feather, which extend diagonally outward in pairs from the central shaft. Barbs contain the pigments which are responsible for the feather's color.

Batesian mimicry: Resemblance of a palatable species to one that is unpalatable or has effective defenses. This may trick a predator into passing up an otherwise tasty prey item.

beneficial insects: Insects that feed on other insects that are destructive to plants.

biennial: A plant that completes its life cycle in two years.

bog: A plant community in acidic, wet areas. Decomposition rates are very slow, which favors the development of peat.

bract: A reduced or modified leaf found just underneath the flower cluster. Looks like a petal but is not.

bulb: Underground storage organ filled with resources formed during the previous growing season to nurture the next season's blooms.

bulb scales: The fleshy, overlapping segments on the bulbs of lilies.

calcareous: Consisting of a large portion of calcium carbonate. Used when referring to soils.

caliche: A white to cream-colored carbonate soil made from decomposed limestone.

calyx: Refers collectively to the outer whorl of flower parts, usually green. The sum of the sepals.

campanulate: Shaped like a bell. Refers to flower shape.

canebrake: A thicket of cane.

capsule: A dry fruit that consists of two or more parts that split open.

carpel: Also called pistil, the female part of the flower which bears the ovules.

catkin: A scaly spike of reduced flowers.

chaparral: An area of vegetation characterized by plants having leaves which are evergreen, hard, thick, leathery, and usually small.

chenier: A beach or sandy ridge that is built on a marsh area. Formed by the working of waves on river sediment in the Gulf Coast of Texas.

chitin: The tough material that makes up a major part of an insect's inner cuticle or procuticle. The procuticle is part of the insect's outer skeleton (exoskeleton).

cienega: A spring-fed wetland. In Texas, used for such areas in the Southwest portions of the state.

clutch: In egg-laying animals, a complete set of eggs laid and incubated at one time.

complete metamorphosis: Striking changes between larva and adult, with an intervening pupal stage, as in insects.

compost: The rotting down of organic material for use as humus.

compound leaf: A leaf composed of smaller, distinct, bladelike parts called leaflets.

coniferous: Applies to trees or shrubs that are mostly evergreen and generally bear seeds in cones.

connate: United at the base. Usually refers to the joining of the bottom part of blades of opposite leaves. Fusion of like parts.

contour feathers: The body feathers in general, not including the more specialized types of feathers such as down.

cordate: Heart-shaped, especially when referring to a leaf.

corolla: The inner, colored whorl of flower parts. Refers to all the petals collectively.

crepuscular: Active during the twilight hours of dawn and dusk.

cultivars: Plant varieties found only under cultivation.

deciduous: Applies to trees that shed their leaves seasonally.

deltoid: Triangular in shape, especially when referring to a leaf.

desert: An area in which the amount of precipitation is exceeded by the amount of evaporation for most of the time. Plants and animals that occupy deserts have adapted to long periods of drought or lack of free water.

diapause: A state of arrested growth, development, and behavior that occurs at a particular stage in an insect's life cycle.

disk flower: A small tubular flower that is found on the central disk of a flower in the Sunflower family (Compositae).

display: Behavior patterns that have evolved to provide a means for one organism to communicate with another. Displays are often stereotypic and exaggerated. Territoriality or mate suitability are often the message.

diurnal: Active during the daylight hours, as opposed to nocturnal.

drupe: A fleshy fruit with one stonelike seed in the center, as in a plum or a peach.

ecosystems: An interdependent community of organisms and the environment in which they live.

edge: The transitional zone where two habitats meet.

elliptic: Narrowly oval in shape, most often twice as long as wide, when talking about leaf shape.

endemic: Referring to a species of animal or plant which is native to and restricted to a particular region.

entire: When speaking about the margin of a leaf, completely smooth and unbroken; no teeth.

estuary: A coastal area in which salt water from the sea and fresh water from inland rivers mix. Estuaries are often subject to tidal action, and the ebb and flood currents avoid one another, forming separate channels.

exoskeleton: A skeleton external to the remainder of the body, with the muscles attaching to its inner surface, as in an insect.

exotic: A plant that has been introduced into an area; a non-native.

fascicle: A compact cluster or bundle, as of pine needles.

filament: In flowers, the stalklike structure that bears the anther in a stamen.

filiform: Shaped like thin threads.

fledgling period: The period between the first flight and gaining independence.

follicle: In plants, a type of fruit that is dry, opens automatically and along one line.

forest: A vegetated area in which the tree crowns touch, and so form a continuous canopy.

generalist: A species with broad foraging or habitat requirements. Such an animal would not be dependent on a single environmental resource, such as only one or two plant species. Most hummingbirds are generalists.

germination: The beginning of growth of a seed, usually after a period of dormancy.

glabrous: Smooth and lacking hairs.

gland: A structure on or beneath a surface which secretes a substance.

globose: Round or spherical in shape.

gorget: The brightly colored, iridescent throat patch of a hummingbird which shines brightly when the light hits it at the proper angle.

gymnosperm: Plants that produce seeds held in woody or fleshy cones.

habitat: The physical characteristics of a specific environment.

halophytic: A plant that is adapted to salty environments.

hawking: The act of capturing insects while in flight.

head: In plants, a dense flower cluster that rises from a common point on a stem.

herbaceous: Herblike. Leafy and green, definitely nonwoody.

holometabolous: Having complete metamorphosis. Passing through egg, larval, pupal, and adult stages. Butterflies are holometabolous.

humus: Partially decomposed organic matter.

imago: The terminal instar, or the adult stage, of an insect.

incised: Deeply cut.

incubation period: In birds, the period between the laying of eggs and hatching, when one or both parents actively sit on the nest to warm the eggs.

inflorescence: The flower cluster or flower head of a plant consisting of many smaller florets.

infructescence: The inflorescence in its fruiting stage.

innate: Inherited, such as instinctive patterns of behavior.

instar: The stage of an insect's development between molts, the first being between hatching and the first larval molt.

invasive plants: Plants that spread aggressively into areas where other plants are growing.

iridescence: A spectral color formed by selective interference and reflection of specific wavelengths of light, as in hummingbird feathers.

laciniate: Cut into slender lobes or segments.

lateral: On the side of something.

leaching: The process of removing material from a substrate with percolating liquid (liquid passing through a porous substance).

leaf litter: A layer of fallen and decaying leaves.

legume: A plant in the pea family that produces a dry pod opening along two lines.

Lepidoptera: The order to which butterflies and moths belong. Second in size only to Coleoptera, to which the beetles belong.

lepidopterist: A person who studies butterflies and moths.

linear: Narrow and long.

loam: A soil composed of a balanced mixture of silt, sand, and clay.

lyrate: Having or suggesting the shape of a lyre.

mangrove forest: A forest located in a swamp of saline or brackish (mixture of both fresh and saline) water. Typically, the forest has a tangle of roots which project above the surface of the water. Mangrove forests can reach over ninety feet tall, but in Texas they are short and not common.

margin: The outer edge of a leaf.

marine: Having to do with the sea.

marsh: An ecosystem of more or less continuously waterlogged soil dominated by emersed herbaceous plants, but without a surface accumulation of peat.

mesa: A flat-topped hill that is similar in form to but smaller than a plateau. Both are smaller than a butte, which is a flat-topped hill where the diameter of the caprock is less than the height of the land from above the surrounding country.

mimicry: The resemblance of one organism to another or to an object in its surroundings for concealment and protection against predators.

mobbing: An aggressive behavior of small birds often associated with the presence of a predator. Birds will fly at, peck, and harass the predator until it leaves the area.

montane forest: A forested area at high elevations as on a mountain. It is comprised of vegetation that is different from vegetation at the same latitude but lower altitude. Trees are smaller and species diversity is generally reduced.

morphology: The form and structure of any object, especially organisms, without the consideration of function.

mucronate: A leaf having a small, short projection at the tip.

mudflat: An area along the coast where fine-grained silt or sediment and clay accumulates. It is an early state in the development of a salt-marsh or mangrove forest.

Muellerian mimicry: The similarity in appearance of one species to another, where both are unpalatable.

mulch: A protective layer of organic material placed around the plant to retain soil moisture and restrict weed growth. Leaves, straw, or peat help prevent evaporation and freezing of the roots.

native plants: Plants that grow naturally in an area without human influence or interference.

naturalized plants: Non-native or introduced plants adapted sufficiently enough to an area to be able to reproduce in the wild.

nectar guide: A streak on a flower that guides the pollinating agent such as a bee, moth, butterfly, or hummingbird to the nectar source. It may also work to guide the sharp bill of the hummingbird away from the delicate ovary of the flowering plant. Some nectar guides are invisible to humans, but are plainly evident to insects sensitive to ultraviolet light.

nectarivorous: Organisms adapted for foraging on nectar.

nematodes: Minute, unsegmented soil-inhabiting worms of the phylum Nematoda.

nerve: In a leaf blade, the vein, groove, or rib on the upper or lower surface.

nesting period: The period between hatching and initial flight in birds.

niche: The role that a species occupies in nature; that is, its precise habitat plus its behavior in that habitat. (Its profession, as opposed to its address.)

nocturnal: Active primarily at night. Compare to diurnal and crepuscular.

node: The point on a stem from which the leaves arise. Looks like a swollen bump along the stem.

nuptial plumage: Plumage associated with the breeding season. Also called alternate plumage.

oblong: Much longer than broad in shape, usually with parallel sides.

old growth: A mature ecosystem characterized by the presence of old woody plants and the wildlife and smaller plants associated with them.

ommatidium (plural ommatidia): A functional unit of the compound eye, expressed externally as a facet.

opposite leaves: Paired leaf arrangement, with one leaf on either side of the stem at the node.

orbicular: More or less round in shape, as in a leaf.

ornithophilous: Refers to a special class of bird-pollinated plants with special floral adaptations such as distinctive coloration, high nectar production, thick-skinned tubular blossoms and general lack of fragrance, which are attractive to birds. In the Western Hemisphere, humming-birds are the principal beneficiaries of these special adaptations.

outcrop: That part of a geologic formation, like a limestone ledge, that projects out from the surrounding soil.

ovary: The ovule-bearing lower part of a pistil that ripens into fruit.

ovule: In flowers, the minute structure that, after fertilization, becomes the seed.

palpus (plural palpi): In insects, a paired, segmented appendage arising on the maxilla or labium (mouth area) and serving sensory functions associated with taking in food.

panicle: A branched cluster of flowers in which the branches are racemes.

parasite: A plant or animal that derives its nour-ishment from another living plant or animal (host) and that completes its development on or in another host. The parasite does not normally kill its host.

parasitoid: An insect that lives its immature stages in or on another insect, which it kills after completing its own feeding.

peat: An accumulation of unconsolidated partially decomposed plant material in a more or less waterlogged area. See marsh.

pedicel: The supporting stalk of a single flower in a flower cluster.

peduncle: A general term for the stem of a single flower or a group of flowers.

peltate: A leaf having its stem attached to the center of the lower surface of the blade as in Pennywort.

pendulous: Hanging or drooping.

perennial: A plant of indefinite life span, flowering and setting seed each year.

perfect: In plants, flowers that have both male and female sex organs present and functioning.

petiole: The stalk of a leaf.

pH: A measure of the acidity or alkalinity of a medium. High pH is basic or alkaline, low pH is acidic.

pheromone: An external chemical messenger that passes between individuals of the same species and controls intraspecific interactions, i.e. attracting mates, recognizing mate, responding to mating signals, etc.

pinnate: A compound leaf with the leaflets symmetrically arranged on both sides of a common stem.

pistil: Includes the stigma, style and ovary of the flower. It bears the ovules, like carpel.

playa: A nearly level area at the bottom of an undrained basin that frequently floods, afford-ing excellent habitat for breeding ducks and shore birds.

plumose: Featherlike in appearance.

pod: A dry fruit that opens along seams like a legume.

pollen: Collectively, the mass of microspores or pollen grains produced by the male parts (anthers) of flowering plants or male cones of gymnosperms (like pine trees).

pollination: The transfer of pollen from the anther to the stigma of the same flower or of another flower, by wind, insects, or hummingbirds.

prairie: An area of vegetation in North America dominated by drought-resistant grasses. Prairies are characterized by the height of their domi-nant grasses, i.e. shortgrass, midgrass, and tallgrass.

prickle: A sharp outgrowth of the bark or epidermis of a plant. Compare to spine and thorn.

proboscis: A slender, strawlike tube, used by the butterfly to drink nectar and other fluids. When not feeding, it is kept tightly coiled underneath the insect's head. The length varies from species to species.

procumbent: In plants, trailing on the ground but not rooting.

prostrate: Lying flat on the ground. Often used when referring to the habits or character of plants.

pubescent: Covered with hairs.

raceme: A spikelike floral arrangement consisting of a central axis stem bearing a number of flowers on pedicels of equal length. The basal flower opens slightly earlier than its neighbors. Two good examples of racemous flowers are the blue larkspur (*Delphinium carolinianum*) and pale lobelia (*Lobelia appendiculata*).

ray flower: In the composite flower of the Sunflower family, the outer, nonfertile straplike flowers surrounding the fertile disk flowers.

reniform: Shaped like a kidney, especially when referring to a leaf, as in Texas redbud.

reticulate: Having a netlike pattern, as on the undersurface of a leaf.

rhizome: A horizontal underground stem that develops roots and sends up leaves and flowering stems.

riparian: Pertaining to a riverbank.

roost: A place to rest or sleep, especially in birds.

samara: A winged fruit, as in a maple tree or an ash.

savannah: An extensive area dominated by grasses and accompanied by tall bushes or trees. Characterized as "open," a grassland with a scattering of tress and shrubs.

scape: A flower stalk rising up from the ground and bearing one or more flowers, but no leaves, as in a rainlily.

secondary succession: The type of vegetation that appears after an environmental disturbance, such as burning.

sepal: A green, leaflike segment of the calyx.

serrate: A toothed margin of a leaf with the teeth pointing forward.

sessile: A condition where the leaf blade attaches directly to the stem without a petiole or stalk.

sexual dimorphism: Refers to species in which the two sexes differ markedly as adults, either in size, color, or behavior.

silique: The fruit of many members of the Mustard family. A capsule which peels away from a central dividing membrane.

simple: An undivided, nonbranched leaf which is not compound.

sinuate: Deeply or strongly wavy along the leaf margin.

slough: An inlet from a river, backwater, creek in a marsh, or tidal flat.

snag: Standing dead tree.

specialist: A species with narrow foraging or habitat adaptations. A specialist, unlike a generalist, will exploit a single resource.

spine: A sharp-pointed, rigid structure which is really a highly modified leaf. Compare to prickle and thorn.

spiracle: An external opening of the tracheal system that takes in air. Insects, such as butterflies, breathe through these tiny holes which are located in a row along each side of the thorax and abdomen.

stamen: The part of the flower that produces pollen, including the anthers and filaments. The male component of the flower.

stellate: Having radiating arms or shaped like a star.

stigma: The surface of the female flower part or pistil that receives the pollen.

stipules: Pairs of very reduced leaflike appendages that are found at the base of the petiole of a leaf.

striate: Having very fine grooves, ridges or lines along the axis.

succession: The process of change by which a stable, natural plant community is reached, progressing from initial disturbance to climax.

succulent: Very fleshy, juicy, and soft, as in a cactus pad.

swale: A low-lying, wet stretch of land.

swamp: A wet area that is more or less permanently covered in water, not drying out in the summer. A seasonally flooded bottomland with more woody plants than a marsh.

taproot: A large, central root.

taxonomy: The practice of classifying organisms and arranging them in an ordered system that reflects natural relationships.

tendril: A coiling or twining organ by which the plant climbs, seen often in vines.

tepals: Collectively, the petals and the sepals, especially when they cannot be differentiated.

terrestrial: Primarily inhabiting land. Compare with aquatic.

territoriality: The advertisement and aggressive behavior associated with establishing and defending a territory, especially during the breeding season.

territory: An area having resources that are controlled or defended by an animal against others of its species. For example, hummingbird territories usually contain important food sources which are vigorously defended by the territory holder.

thermoregulation: Temperature regulation. Many insects and reptiles are cold-blooded, or ectothermic, organisms. On cool days, these animals can absorb heat from the sun several ways, including basking or shivering. On warmer or hot days, warm-blooded, or endothermic organisms avoid or release heat by hiding in shade, panting, and sweating.

thorax: The central segment of an insect's body, bearing the legs and wings.

thorn: A modified branch that is sharp-pointed. Compare to spine and prickle.

thorn forest, thorn scrub, thorn woodland: An area of vegetation that is dominated by thorny shrubs and bushy trees, perhaps with a few taller trees. Ground plants generally do not include grasses, which reflects the more arid nature of thorn scrub habitat. Common in south Texas.

throat: In a flower, the central opening of the flower in a corolla composed of fused petals.

tidal flat: In coastal areas, a sand flat, mud flat, or marsh developed in tidal areas, estuaries, or protected bays of some lagoons.

torpor: A sleeplike state of reduced body temperature and metabolism, often entered into during the night or during cold periods of the year. An excellent energy conserving strategy. Used by poorwills and hummingbirds, for example.

trachea: A delicate system of air tubes. Insects, such as butterflies, do not have lungs as we do, so the tracheal system supplies oxygen to every cell.

Trochilidae: The family of birds to which hummingbirds belong.

tuber: A short, thickened underground stem which bears many buds.

umbel: A flat-topped or convex flower cluster in which the pedicels arise from a common point, as in many flowers of the parsley family.

undulate: Wavy, often used when speaking about a leaf margin.

unifoliolate: Having only one leaf or leaflet.

vein (of a wing): In insects, a hardened rod supporting the wing membrane (collectively called venation).

vesicle: A cavity or bladder.

wetlands: Collectively, an area that is covered in water permanently or seasonally. A general term that includes swamps, bogs, fens, marshes, lakes, ponds, rivers, and estuarine habitats.

whorl: A circular arrangement of three or more petals or leaves at one node (joint).

wing: In plants, a ribbonlike membrane bordering a stem or around seeds.

woodland: An area in which the widely spaced, mature tree crowns do not necessarily touch, giving a more or less open appearance. Under the trees, grasses, heath, and scrub communities often develop, giving the area a parklike appearance.

xeric: Referring to arid or desert conditions. Not needing much water for survival. Compare to mesic and hydric.

xeriscape: To landscape with plants that require little or no supplemental water.

Table A.1
Birds of Texas

More Americans feed their backyard birds annually than watch the Superbowl! The easiest way to identify the birds in your area is to learn which birds are most common. Use this list in conjunction with the descriptions in a field guide to help you identify the birds most often found in your area.

x - regular occurrence, abundant to uncommon   o - more difficult to find, scarce to rare   x/o - can be common in parts of the region, but rare in others

Species	Ecological Region 1 2 3 4 5 6 7 8 9 10										Notes	Habitat
	1	2	3	4	5	6	7	8	9	10		
Cormorant Family												
Double-crested Cormorant	x	x	x	x	x	x	x	x	x	x	Locally abundant inland, abundant winter resident on coast.	Lakes, ponds, coastal waters.
Anhinga Family												
Anhinga	x	x	x	x		o					Uncommon summer resident along coastal plain, east & central Texas.	Lakes, ponds, rivers, sloughs.
Heron Family												
American Bittern	x	x	x	x	x	x	o	o	o	o	Rare summer to fairly common winter resident; rare to common migrant throughout.	Freshwater & brackish marshes.
Great Blue Heron	x	x	x	x	x	x	x	x	x	x	Common permanent resident.	Rivers, lakes, marshes, bays.
Great Egret	x	x	x	x	x	x	x	x	x	x	Very common resident along coast, locally common summer resident in eastern 1/2 of state.	Estuaries, bays, marshes, lakes.
Snowy Egret	x	x	x	x	x	x	x	x	o	o	Common permanent resident along coast, uncommon summer resident in eastern 1/2 of state.	Ponds, marshes, bays, estuaries.
Little Blue Heron	x	x	x	x	x	o					Common summer resident east 1/3 of Texas, uncommon winter resident on coast.	Inland marshes, ponds, & lakes.
Cattle Egret	x	x	x	x	x	x	x	x	x	o	Abundant summer resident in eastern 1/3 of state.	Savannahs & grasslands, often in presence of cattle.

Species	Ecological Region 1	2	3	4	5	6	7	8	9	10	Notes	Habitat
Green Heron	x	x	x	x	x	x	x	x	x	x	Summers throughout Texas, most common in the eastern 2/3. Solitary.	Wooded areas around quiet ponds, dense swamps, & marshes.
Black-crowned Night-Heron	x	x	x	x	x	x	x	x	x	x	Common resident along coast, locally common inland.	Marshes, lakes, & bays.
Yellow-crowned Night-Heron	x	x	x	x	x	x	x	o	o	o	Locally common summer resident in eastern 1/2 of state, winter resident along coast.	Wetlands, fields near ponds.
Duck Family - Goose Subfamily												
Greater White-fronted Goose	x	x	x	x	x	x	x	x	o	o	Common migrant statewide, locally abundant winter resident.	Croplands, grasslands, marshes, lakes.
Snow Goose	x	x	x	x	x	x	x	x	x	x	Common migrant statewide, abundant winter resident along coast.	Lakes, marshes, grasslands, & croplands.
Canada Goose	x	x	x	x	x	x	x	x	x	x	Locally abundant to common migrant & winter resident throughout the state east of the Trans-Pecos, especially along coast & in Panhandle.	Lakes, ponds, bays, marshes, fields.
Duck Family - Duck Subfamily												
Wood Duck	x	x	x	x	x	x	x	x	x	o	Uncommon to common summer resident, uncommon to common winter resident in eastern 1/2 of state.	Mostly wooded rivers and swamps, & ponds.
Green-winged Teal	x	x	x	x	x	x	x	x	x	x	Common to abundant migrant, common winter resident, abundant on upper coast.	Lakes, ponds, marshes, estuaries.
Mottled Duck	o	x	o	o							Locally common resident at coast, rarer inland.	Lakes, ponds, bays, & marshes.

Table A.1
Birds of Texas

x - regular occurrence, abundant to uncommon   o - more difficult to find, scarce to rare   x/o - can be common in parts of the region, but rare in others

Species	Ecological Region										Notes	Habitat
	1	2	3	4	5	6	7	8	9	10		
Duck Family - Duck Subfamily												
Mallard	x	x	x	x	x	x	x	x	x	x	Fairly common migrant & winter resident statewide.	Lakes, ponds, marshes, bays, estuaries.
Northern Pintail	x	x	x	x	x	x	x	x	x	x	Locally uncommon to abundant winter resident throughout.	Shallow ponds, flooded fields, & swales.
Blue-winged Teal	x	x	x	x	x	x	x	x	x	x	Common migrant throughout, common winter resident in southern 1/3 of state.	Ponds, marshes, lakes, & estuaries.
Cinnamon Teal	o	x	o	o	o	x	x	x	x	x	Locally common migrant & winter resident in western Texas, uncommon winter resident along coast.	Lakes, marshes, ponds, & estuaries.
Northern Shoveler	x	x	x	x	x	x	x	x	x	x	Abundant migrant & winter resident throughout.	Lakes, bays, ponds, & estuaries.
Gadwall	x	x	x	x	x	x	x	x	x	x	Common migrant & winter resident throughout.	Lakes, ponds, bays, & estuaries.
American Wigeon	x	x	x	x	x	x	x	x	x	x	Common to abundant migrant & winter resident throughout.	Ponds, bays, lakes, estuaries, & fields.
Canvasback	x	x	x	x	x	x	x	x	x	x	Uncommon/locally common migrant & winter resident throughout.	Lakes & bays.

Species	Ecological Region 1	2	3	4	5	6	7	8	9	10	Notes	Habitat
Redhead	x	x	x	x	x	x	x	x	x	x	Uncommon to common migrant throughout, winter resident along central & lower coast.	Ponds, lakes, & saltwater bays.
Ring-necked Duck	x	x	x	x	x	x	x	x	x	x	Uncommon to locally common migrant & winter resident throughout. Most numerous in northern $1/2$ of state during spring & fall.	Lakes & ponds.
Lesser Scaup	x	x	x	x	x	x	x	x	x	x	Abundant migrant & winter resident throughout the state.	Lakes & bays.
Common Goldeneye	o	x	o	o	o	o	o	x	x	o	Uncommon to common winter resident in most of Texas, especially on coast.	Lakes, bays, reservoirs, coastal waters.
Bufflehead	x	x	x	x	x	x	x	x	x	x	Locally common winter resident throughout the state. Locally common to scarce in western $1/2$, uncommon to rare in eastern $1/2$.	Lakes, bays, & estuaries.
Hooded Merganser	x	x	x	x	x	x	x	x	x	o	Irregularly, uncommon to common migrant & winter resident in eastern $2/3$ of state including Panhandle, rare in Trans-Pecos.	Bays, estuaries, wooded lakes, ponds, & rivers.
Common Merganser	o	o	o	o	o	o	o	x	x	x	Irregularly, common winter resident in the Panhandle & Trans-Pecos, scarce to rare throughout the rest of the state.	Woodlands, rivers, & lakes, sometimes brackish water.
Red-breasted Merganser	x	x	x	o	o	o	o	o	o	o	Rare to uncommon winter resident inland, common on coast.	Marine, bays, lakes.
Ruddy Duck	x	x	x	x	x	x	x	x	x	x	Common migrant & winter resident throughout the state, rare summer resident.	Lakes, ponds, & bays.

x - regular occurance, abundant to uncommon   o - more difficult to find, scarce to rare   x/o - can be common in parts of the region, but rare in others

Species	Ecological Region 1	2	3	4	5	6	7	8	9	10	Notes	Habitat
Vulture Family												
Black Vulture	x	x	x	x	x	x	x			o	Common resident in eastern 1/2 of state, rare in Panhandle & Trans-Pecos away from the Rio Grande.	Savannahs, thornscrub, second growth.
Turkey Vulture	x	x	x	x	x	x	x	x		x	Common summer resident throughout, rare to locally common winter resident in southeastern 1/4 of state.	Ubiquitous except in agricultural areas.
Hawk Family - Osprey Subfamily												
Osprey	x	x	x	x	x	x	x	o	o	o	Rare to uncommon migrant throughout, rarer in west. Rare summer visitor & locally common to scarce winter visitor.	Rivers, lakes, & coasts.
Hawk Family - Hawk Subfamily												
Mississippi Kite	x	x	x	x	x	x	x	x		o	Common summer resident in Panhandle, common to uncommon migrant.	Riparian & oak woodlands, savannahs.
Bald Eagle	x	x	x	x	x	x	x	o	o	o	Rare to uncommon migrant & winter resident throughout. Rare summer resident.	Lakes, rivers, estuaries.
Northern Harrier	x	x	x	x	x	x	x	x	x	x	Common migrant throughout, locally common winter resident.	Marshes, prairies, savannahs, & fields.
Sharp-shinned Hawk	x	x	x	x	x	x	x	x	x	o	Uncommon to fairly common migrant & winter resident throughout, rare summer resident.	Forests, woodlands, & thickets.
Cooper's Hawk	x	x	x	x	x	x	x	x	x	x	Uncommon to rare summer resident throughout, fairly common to uncommon winter resident, & migrant.	Forests, broken woodlands, & river groves.

Species	Ecological Region 1 2 3 4 5 6 7 8 9 10	Notes	Habitat
Harris' Hawk	x . . . . x o . . x	Locally common resident in South Texas, West Texas & to a lesser extent the southern Edwards Plateau, vagrant on coast.	Arid scrub & thorn forest.
Red-shouldered Hawk	x x x x x x x o o o	Common permanent resident in east & central Texas, rare to uncommon further north & west.	Riparian forest, woodlands, & swamps.
Broad-winged Hawk	x x x x x x x o o .	Common migrant in east $\frac{1}{2}$ of Texas, uncommon summer resident in east $\frac{1}{3}$.	Forests & woodlands, during "kettles" (large flock of swirling birds) in migration.
Swainson's Hawk	o o o o x x x x x x	Common summer resident/migrant in West Texas & Panhandle to north South Texas, rare in eastern $\frac{1}{3}$ of state.	Prairies, savannahs, desert scrub.
Red-tailed Hawk	x x x x x x x x x x	Common resident throughout, common migrant & winter resident throughout.	Woods with nearby open country, plains.
Ferruginous Hawk	o o o o x o o x x x	Rare summer resident in west Panhandle, locally common winter resident in Panhandle & Trans-Pecos; locally uncommon on coast.	Shortgrass prairies, savannah, plains, & desert.
Falcon Family			
Crested Caracara	x x x x x o x . . x	Locally common to rare resident in South Texas, southern Edwards Plateau, & Trans-Pecos.	Thornscrub, prairies, rangeland, & savannahs.
American Kestrel	x x x x x x x x x x	Common migrant & winter resident throughout, rare summer resident in northern part of state.	Open grasslands, roadsides, suburbs, farmland.
Guan Family			
Plain Chachalaca	. . . . . x	Uncommon to locally common resident in Lower Rio Grande Valley.	Riparian forest, thickets, second growth.

Table A.1
Birds of Texas

x - regular occurance, abundant to uncommon   o - more difficult to find, scarce to rare   x/o - can be common in parts of the region, but rare in others

Species	Ecological Region 1	2	3	4	5	6	7	8	9	10	Notes	Habitat
Pheasant Family - Pheasant Subfamily												
Ring-necked Pheasant	o								x	x	Common resident in north & west Panhandle, rare eastward. Introduced species.	Agricultural fields & pastures.
Pheasant Family - Turkey Subfamily												
Wild Turkey	x	x	x	x	x	x	x	x		x	Formerly common resident in east 2/3 of state, common in South Texas, Central Texas.	Oak woodlands, deciduous forest, thornscrub.
Pheasant Family - Quail Subfamily												
Northern Bobwhite	x	x	x	x	x	x	x	x	x	o	Uncommon to common throughout except Trans-Pecos.	Savannah, brushy fields, prairie, pastures.
Scaled Quail					x	o	x	x			Uncommon to locally common in Trans-Pecos, Panhandle, South Texas, western Edwards Plateau.	Arid scrub, desert, thornscrub.
Rail Family - Rail Subfamily												
Virginia Rail	x	x	x	x	x	x	x	x	x	x	Common but secretive migrant, & uncommon winter resident along Gulf Coast.	Freshwater & brackish marshes & wetlands, & coastal salt marshes.
Sora	x	x	x	x	x	x	x	x	x	x	Locally common migrant throughout, winter resident on coast. Summer records rare.	Brackish & fresh water marshes, wet meadows.
Common Moorhen	x	x	x	x	x	x	x	x	x		Uncommon permanent resident from central Texas to South Texas coast, rare in west.	Fresh water marshes.
American Coot	x	x	x	x	x	x	x	x	x	x	Uncommon to common summer resident throughout, abundant winter resident throughout.	Marshes, bays, ponds, & lakes.

Species	Ecological Region 1	2	3	4	5	6	7	8	9	10	Notes	Habitat
Crane Family - Crane Subfamily												
Sandhill Crane	x	x	x	x	x	x	x	x	x	x	Common migrant in western ½ of state, uncommon in east. Common winter resident on coast.	Grasslands, prairies, savannahs, pastures.
Plover Family - Plover Subfamily												
Semipalmated Plover	x	x	x	x	x	x	x	x	x	x	Common winter resident on coast, rare in north, common migrant throughout.	Estuaries, mudflats, beaches.
Killdeer	x	x	x	x	x	x	x	x	x	x	Common permanent resident throughout, higher numbers in winter in central & south Texas.	Open areas, golf courses, shortgrass areas.
Mountain Plover	x					o	x		x	x	Rare summer resident in higher elevation grasslands of Trans-Pecos & Panhandle, winter resident on coastal plains.	Shortgrass prairies, plowed fields, pastures.
Stilt Family												
Black-necked Stilt	x	x	x	x	x	x	x	x	x	x	Common winter resident, uncommon summer resident along coast. Uncommon inland.	Marshes, estuaries, ponds, & mudflats.
American Avocet	x	x	x	x	x	x	x	x	x	x	Common winter resident, rare summer resident along coast. Uncommon summer resident in west.	Flooded pastures, mudflats, estuaries, prairie ponds.
Sandpiper Family - Sandpiper Subfamily												
Greater Yellowlegs	x	x	x	x	x	x	x	x	x	x	Common migrant throughout, common winter resident on coast, rare summer resident in southern ⅔ of state.	Mudflats, marshes, prairies, estuaries.
Lesser Yellowlegs	x	x	x	x	x	x	x	x	x	x	Common migrant throughout, common winter resident on coast, rare summer visitor along coast.	Pond borders, mudflats, swales, estuaries.
Solitary Sandpiper	x	x	x	x	x	x	x	x	x	x	Rare to common migrant throughout, rare winter resident along coast, South Texas to Central Texas.	Ponds, rivers, lakes, & streamsides.

Table A.1
Birds of Texas

x - regular occurance, abundant to uncommon   o - more difficult to find, scarce to rare   x/o - can be common in parts of the region, but rare in others

Sandpiper Family - Sandpiper Subfamily

Species	Ecological Region										Notes	Habitat
	1	2	3	4	5	6	7	8	9	10		
Willet	o	x	o	o	o	o	o	o	o	o	Common permanent resident on coast, uncommon migrant throughout.	Coastal ponds, beaches, marshes, mudflats.
Spotted Sandpiper	x	x	x	x	x	x	x	x	x	x	Common to uncommon migrant & winter resident throughout, rare in west.	Streams, rivers, ponds, beaches.
Upland Sandpiper	x	x	x	x	x	x	x	x	x	o	Common spring migrant, rare fall migrant, rare summer resident in Panhandle.	Prairie, pastures, plowed fields, open meadows.
Long-billed Curlew	x	x	x	x	x	x	x	x	x	x	Fairly common, winters in central, South, & coastal areas of Texas. Some breed in the northwestern Panhandle.	Wet & dry uplands, coastal & lake beaches, salt marshes, & grainfields.
Whimbrel	o	x					o	o	o	o	Rare to uncommon migrant throughout eastern ½ of state, more common on coast.	Salt marshes, estuaries & tallgrass prairies.
Semipalmated Sandpiper	x	x	x	x	x	o	o	o	o	o	Rare to locally common migrant & summer visitor on coast, rare inland.	Ponds, lakes, mudflats, & beaches.
Western Sandpiper	x	x	x	x	x	x	x	x	x	x	Common migrant & winter resident on coast, uncommon inland, rare in northwest.	Beaches, mudflats, ponds, lakes, & swales.
Least Sandpiper	x	x	x	x	x	x	x	x	x	x	Common migrant throughout, uncommon winter resident on coast, Trans-Pecos, north-central Texas.	Mudflats, ponds, lakes, & swales.

Ecological Region

Species	1	2	3	4	5	6	7	8	9	10	Notes	Habitat
Baird's Sandpiper	x	x	x	x	x	x	x	x	x	x	Uncommon to common migrant in all parts of state.	Ponds, lakes, & swales.
Pectoral Sandpiper	x	x	x	x	x	x	x	x	x	x	Locally common migrant in all parts of state, summer straggler.	Wet prairies, ponds, lakes, & swales.
Dunlin	x	x	x	x	x	x	x	x	x		Rare to local migrant throughout, mostly on coast, winter resident on coast.	Lakes, ponds, beaches, mudflats, & muddy pools.
Stilt Sandpiper	x	x	x	x	x	x	x	x	x	x	Locally common migrant in eastern 1/2 of state, including the Panhandle, rare in west.	Flooded pastures, lakes, ponds, marshes, & shallow pools.
Short-billed Dowitcher	x	x	x	x	x	x	x	o	o	o	Common migrant & locally common winter resident along coast, uncommon inland.	Mudflats, flooded pastures, ponds, lakes, & tidal marshes.
Common Snipe	x	x	x	x	x	x	x	x	x	x	Common migrant throughout. Common winter resident in eastern 2/3 of state, uncommon in west.	Marshes, flooded pastures, wet ditches, & wet meadows.
Gull Family - Gull Subfamily												
Laughing Gull	o	x			o					o	Abundant permanent resident along coast, rare visitor throughout, especially in eastern 1/2 of state.	Bays, lakes, agricultural fields, & beaches.
Franklin's Gull	x	x	x	x	x	x	x	x	x	o	Uncommon migrant throughout, rare winter visitor on coast & inland.	Tallgrass prairie, pastures, flooded fields.
Ring-billed Gull	x	x	x	x	x	x	x	x	x	x	Common migrant nearly throughout. Common winter resident on coast & inland.	Lakes, bays, estuaries, beaches.

Table A.1
Birds of Texas

x - regular occurrence, abundant to uncommon   o - more difficult to find, scarce to rare   x/o - can be common in parts of the region, but rare in others

Species	Ecological Region 1	2	3	4	5	6	7	8	9	10	Notes	Habitat
Gull Family - Gull Subfamily												
Herring Gull	x	x	x	x	x	x	x	x	x	x	Common migrant & winter resident along coast, locally uncommon inland.	Beaches, bays, lakes, rivers, marine environments.
Gull Family - Tern Subfamily												
Gull-billed Tern	x								x		Common resident on coast, fewer in winter, rare visitor inland.	Wet fields, marshes, & prairies.
Forster's Tern	x	x	x	x	x	x	x	x	x	x	Common resident along coast, uncommon migrant & locally common winter resident.	Marine, beaches, bays, marshes, lakes.
Least Tern	x					x				o	Common summer resident on coast, uncommon migrant in eastern $^2/_3$, rare in winter.	Beaches, bays, rivers, ponds, & lakes.
Black Tern	x	x	x	x	x	x	x	x	x	x	Common migrant throughout, very rare visitor along coast.	Ponds, marshes, bays, estuaries, lakes.
Pigeon Family												
Rock Dove	x	x	x	x	x	x	x	x	x	x	Feral species from Europe occurs in most areas of Texas.	Cities, towns, suburbs, agricultural areas.
White-winged Dove	o	o	x	o	x	o	x	o	o	x	Common summer resident north to Waco, east to coast, & the South Texas & Trans-Pecos regions along the Rio Grande.	Residential & agricultural areas, mesquite thornscrub.
Mourning Dove	x	x	x	x	x	x	x	x	x	x	Common permanent resident throughout the state, many winter here.	Prairie, thorn forest, woodlands.

Species	Ecological Region 1	2	3	4	5	6	7	8	9	10	Notes	Habitat
Inca Dove	x	x	x	x	x	x	x	x		x	Common resident in South Texas, Central Texas to lower Rolling Plains & Panhandle, range is expanding.	Residential areas, thornscrub, savannah.
Common Ground-Dove	x	x				x	x			x	Uncommon to locally common permanent resident from South Texas, Gulf Coast, Central Texas, lower Rolling Plains.	Thornforest, thornscrub, savannah.
Parrot Family - Amazon Subfamily												
Monk Parakeet		x			x		x				Introduced. Locally common in a number of metropolitan areas.	Open woodlands, savannahs, residential areas.
Cuckoo Family - New World Cuckoo Subfamily												
Yellow-billed Cuckoo	x	x	x	x	x	x	x	x	x	x	Common migrant & summer resident throughout the state.	Deciduous forest & thornscrub, savannah.
Cuckoo Family - Roadrunner Subfamily												
Greater Roadrunner	x	x	x	x	x	x	x	x	x	x	Uncommon to common permanent resident throughout, rare in northeastern part.	Thorn forest, desert, savannah.
Cuckoo Family - Ani Subfamily												
Groove-billed Ani		x					x				Common summer resident in Lower Rio Grande Valley, uncommon fall & winter visitor on coast.	Farmlands grasslands with woody component.
Barn Owl Family												
Barn Owl	x	x	x	x	x	x	x	x	x	x	Rare to locally common permanent resident throughout, except in Trans-Pecos mountains.	Woodlands, groves, farms, barns, towns, & cliffs.
Owl Family												
Eastern Screech-Owl	x	x	x	x	x	x	x	x	x	o	Common resident throughout, less so in western 1/3 of state.	Woodlands, thorn forest, residential areas.
Western Screech-Owl								x		x	Uncommon & local resident in Trans-Pecos & western Edwards Plateau.	Oak woodland & riparian forest.

Table A.1
Birds of Texas

x - regular occurrence, abundant to uncommon   o - more difficult to find, scarce to rare   x/o - can be common in parts of the region, but rare in others

Species	Ecological Region 1 2 3 4 5 6 7 8 9 10										Notes	Habitat
Owl Family												
Great Horned Owl	x	x	x	x	x	x	x	x	x	x	Common resident throughout state, uncommon in East Texas woodlands.	Woodlands, suburbs, streamsides, & woodlots.
Elf Owl						x	x			x	Uncommon to locally common summer resident in Lower Rio Grande Valley, Trans-Pecos, west Edwards Plateau.	Desert scrub, thorn forest, pinyon-juniper.
Burrowing Owl	o	o	o	o	o	o	x	x	x		Uncommon/common permanent resident on open western prairies, rare migrant/vagrant eastward.	Prairies, pastures, agricultural areas, open grasslands.
Barred Owl	x	x	x	x	x	x	x		x		Uncommon to common permanent resident from east Panhandle to East Texas & Gulf Coast.	Deciduous & mixed forest, wooded streams.
Long-eared Owl	o	o	o	x	o	o	o	x	x		Rare to locally uncommon migrant & winter resident in most areas, except east.	Coniferous & mixed woodland.
Short-eared Owl	x	x	x	x	x	x	x	x	x	x	Rare to locally uncommon migrant & winter resident throughout, rare in far west.	Prairies, marshes, estuaries, savannahs.
Nightjar Family - Nighthawk Subfamily												
Lesser Nighthawk	x				x	o				x	Common migrant & summer resident in Trans-Pecos east to Edwards Plateau & south to Gulf Coast & South Texas.	Desert scrub & thorn forest.
Common Nighthawk	x	x	x	x	x	x	x	x	x	x	Uncommon to common migrant throughout state, summer resident in all but far East Texas forests.	Grasslands, savannah, thorn forest, open areas.

Species	1	2	3	4	5	6	7	8	9	10	Notes	Habitat
	Ecological Region											
Pauraque		x				x					Common permanent resident in South Texas to lower coast.	Arid scrub & thorn forest.
Common Poorwill		o			x	x	x	x	x	x	Common summer resident from Trans-Pecos to Edwards Plateau, High Plains, Rolling Plains, South Texas.	Dry thorn forest, dry hills, & open brush.
Chuck-will's-widow	x	x	x	x	x	x	x	o			Common migrant & summer resident in east & central Texas to South Texas.	Deciduous & mixed hardwood forest.
Whip-poor-will	x	x	x	x	o	o	o			x	Common migrant in east $^{1}/_{3}$ of state & locally common summer resident in Trans-Pecos mountains.	Woodlands.
Swift Family - Chimney Swift Subfamily												
Chimney Swift	x	x	x	x	x	x	x	x	x	o	Common migrant & summer resident throughout most of state except Lower Rio Grande Valley & Trans-Pecos areas.	Most habitat types with suitable nesting areas.
Swift Family - Swift Subfamily												
White-throated Swift										x	Common summer resident & locally common winter resident from Trans-Pecos to Palo Duro Canyon in Rolling Plains.	Montane regions.
Kingfisher Family - New World Kingfisher Subfamily												
Belted Kingfisher	x	x	x	x	x	x	x	x	x	x	Uncommon to locally common permanent resident throughout state.	Rivers, lakes, ponds, bays.
Green Kingfisher						x	x				Uncommon resident of the lower Rio Grande, & also of the Edwards Plateau.	Banks of freshwater streams & resacas.
Woodpecker Family - Woodpecker Subfamily												
Red-headed Woodpecker	x	x	x	x	x			o	o		Uncommon permanent resident in Panhandle & East Texas to Calhoun County, irregular in winter along lower coast.	Deciduous forest, oak woodlands, savannah.

Note: Hummingbird species listed in Table A.2, page 186.

Table A.1
Birds of Texas

x - regular occurrence, abundant to uncommon   o - more difficult to find, scarce to rare   x/o - can be common in parts of the region, but rare in others

Woodpecker Family - Woodpecker Subfamily

Species	Ecological Region 1	2	3	4	5	6	7	8	9	10	Notes	Habitat
Golden-fronted Woodpecker	x/o				x	x	x	x	x	x	Common resident from South Texas to Edwards Plateau to southern Panhandle, Gulf Coast & far eastern Trans-Pecos.	Mesquite thorn forest, riparian woodlands.
Red-bellied Woodpecker	x	x	x	x	x		x	x			Common resident in eastern 1/2 of state.	Mixed woodlands & riparian forests.
Yellow-bellied Sapsucker	x	x	x	x	x	x	x	x	x	x	Uncommon to locally common migrant & winter resident throughout, rare in western Trans-Pecos.	Riparian forest, woodlands, savannahs, scrub habitat.
Ladder-backed Woodpecker	x				x	x	x	x	x	x	Rare to common permanent resident throughout western 2/3 of state.	Thorn forest, riparian forest, oak woods.
Downy Woodpecker	x	x	x		x	x	x	o	o		Common permanent resident eastern 1/2 of state to Edwards Plateau, rare migrant & winter visitor in west.	Forests, woodlands, second growth, park lands.
Hairy Woodpecker	x	x				x				x	Uncommon permanent resident in eastern 1/3 of state, also in Trans-Pecos mountains & Rolling Plains.	Forested areas, woodlands, river groves.
Northern Flicker	x	x	x	x	x	x	x	x	x	x	Rare to locally common permanent resident of Panhandle, Trans-Pecos, northeast East Texas, winter resident elsewhere.	Open forests & woodlands, groves, semi-open country.
Pileated Woodpecker	x	x	x	x	x						Rare to common permanent resident in forests of East & Central Texas.	Forested regions.

Tyrant Flycatcher Family

Species	Ecological Region 1	2	3	4	5	6	7	8	9	10	Notes	Habitat
Olive-sided Flycatcher	x	x	x	x	x	x	x	x	x	x	Rare to common migrant throughout, uncommon summer resident in Trans-Pecos.	Coniferous forest, thorn forest, riparian woods.
Eastern Wood-Pewee	x	x	x	x	x	x	x				Common summer resident in eastern Texas, west through north-central Texas, Edwards Plateau, Panhandle.	Woodlands, groves.
Yellow-bellied Flycatcher	x	x	x								Uncommon to common migrant in eastern $1/2$ of state.	Riparian forest, thorn forest.
Acadian Flycatcher	x	x	x			x					Common migrant & summer resident in eastern $1/3$ of state west to Real County.	Swamp forest, oak woodland, riparian woods.
Alder Flycatcher	x	x	x			x					Uncommon migrant in eastern $1/2$ of state, also Lower Rio Grande Valley.	Brushy swamps & swales; wetter areas.
Willow Flycatcher	x	x	x	x	x	x	x	x	x	x	Formerly bred in Trans-Pecos, rare/uncommon migrant in all parts of state.	Bushes, willows, thickets, brushy fields; drier areas.
Least Flycatcher	x	x	x	x	x	x	x	x	x	x	Common migrant in all parts of state except far west, more in eastern $1/2$.	Open woodlands, thorn forest.
Hammond's Flycatcher									o	x	Migrant through the Trans-Pecos.	Nests in coniferous forests.
Eastern Phoebe	x	x	x	x	x	x				o	Uncommon to common summer resident in northern $2/3$ of state, common migrant & winter resident.	Riparian forests, thorn forests, near nest sites.

Table A.1
Birds of Texas

x - regular occurrence, abundant to uncommon   o - more difficult to find, scarce to rare   x/o - can be common in parts of the region, but rare in others

Tyrant Flycatcher Family

Species	*Ecological Region* 1	2	3	4	5	6	7	8	9	10	Notes	Habitat
Say's Phoebe						x	x	x	x	x	Rare to common resident of High Plains, Rolling Plains, Trans-Pecos, South Texas, Edwards Plateau, very rare in east.	Desert scrub & dry thorn forest.
Vermilion Flycatcher		x				x	x				Summer resident from Trans-Pecos, Edwards Plateau, south to central coast, Lower Rio Grande Valley.	Mesquite thorn forest, dry thorn scrub near water.
Ash-throated Flycatcher		x				x	x	x	x	x	Uncommon to common summer resident in western ½ of state, rare migrant on coast.	Dry thorn forest, mesquite thornscrub, savannah.
Great Crested Flycatcher	x	x	x	x	x						Uncommon/common summer resident & migrant in eastern ½ of state, rare migrant in west.	Mesquite thorn forest, broadleaf forest.
Great Kiskadee		x				x	o				Locally common in Lower Rio Grande Valley to Aransas & Val Verde counties.	Mesquite thorn forest, riparian forest, near water.
Couch's Kingbird		o				x					Common summer resident in Lower Rio Grande Valley, rare in Trans-Pecos, Edwards Plateau & along coast.	Tropical thorn forest.
Western Kingbird	o	x	o	o	x	x	x	x	x	x	Common summer resident in all parts of state east to Harris, Hunt & Lamar counties.	Grasslands & savannah, avoids forested areas.
Eastern Kingbird	x	x	x	x	x	x	x		o		Rare to common summer resident in eastern ½ of state west to Edwards Plateau & Panhandle.	Wood margins, open farmland & savannahs.

Species	Ecological Region 1 2 3 4 5 6 7 8 9 10										Notes	Habitat
Scissor-tailed Flycatcher	x	x	x	x	x	x	x	x	x	o	Common summer resident except in Trans-Pecos where uncommon. Rare in winter.	Agricultural lands with scattered trees, prairies.
Lark Family												
Horned Lark	x	o	o	x	x	x	x	x	x	x	Rare/common permanent resident in High Plains & Gulf Coast. Migrant/winter resident throughout, rare in east.	Shortgrass prairie, sand flats, roadsides, plowed fields.
Swallow Family - Swallow Subfamily												
Purple Martin	x	x	x	x	x	x	x	x	x		Common summer resident in most of state, local in High Plains & Rolling Plains, rare in Trans-Pecos.	Farms, towns, open or semi-open country, often near water.
Tree Swallow	x	x	x	x	x	x	x	x	x	x	Common migrant throughout state, breeds in Delta, Mason, & Wood counties.	Open areas during migration, lakes, marshes, ponds.
Northern Rough-winged Swallow	x	x	x	x	x	x	x	x	x	x	Rare to locally common summer resident/migrant throughout, absent from Rolling Plains in summer.	Ponds, rivers, lakes, streams & open areas.
Bank Swallow	x	x	x	x	x	x	x	x	x	x	Migrates throughout, locally common summer resident along the Rio Grande.	Ponds, rivers, lakes, mostly open areas in migration.
Cliff Swallow	x	x	x	x	x	x	x	x	x	o	Rare/locally common summer resident throughout, common migrant throughout.	Open areas with bridges, culverts near water.
Cave Swallow	o	o	o	o	x	x				x	Locally common summer resident in Edwards Plateau, Lower Rio Grande Valley west to Trans-Pecos.	Open areas, near water, nests in culverts & caves.
Barn Swallow	x	x	x	x	x	x	x	x	x	x	Rare to common summer resident throughout. Common/abundant migrant throughout.	Prairies, savannah, open areas near water & buildings.

Table A.1
Birds of Texas

x - regular occurrence, abundant to uncommon   o - more difficult to find, scarce to rare   x/o - can be common in parts of the region, but rare in others

Species	\ Ecological Region 1	2	3	4	5	6	7	8	9	10	Notes	Habitat
Crow Family												
Steller's Jay										x	Locally common permanent resident in Trans-Pecos mountains, rare visitor in Panhandle & Edwards Plateau.	Pine-oak & spruce-fir woodlands, higher elevations.
Blue Jay	x	x	x	x	x	x	x	x	x		Common permanent resident in eastern 1/2 of state, eastern 2/3 of Panhandle, decreasing westward.	Residential areas, oak woodlands, deciduous forest.
Green Jay						x					Common resident in Lower Rio Grande Valley, uncommon north to southern edge of Edwards Plateau.	Thorn forest, savannah, riparian woodlands.
Western Scrub Jay							x	x		x	Common resident in Edwards Plateau & much of Trans-Pecos, rare in Rolling Plains & South Plains.	Oak, juniper, pinyon pine woodlands.
Mexican Jay										x	Common resident in the Chisos mountains in Trans-Pecos.	Pine-oak juniper woodlands, at higher elevations.
American Crow	x	x	x	x	x	o	x	x	x		Common permanent resident in eastern 1/2 of state south to central coast. Rare in Trans-Pecos.	Woodland habitats, savannahs.
Tamaulipas Crow						x					Locally common winter resident in Lower Rio Grande Valley in Cameron County.	Riparian woodlands, dumps, farmland, urban areas.
Chihuahuan Raven							x	x	x	x	Common resident from Trans-Pecos & High Plains, Rolling Plains, west Edwards Plateau & South Texas.	Desert & dry thorn desert & thorn scrub.

Titmouse Family

Species	Ecological Region 1 2 3 4 5 6 7 8 9 10										Notes	Habitat
	1	2	3	4	5	6	7	8	9	10		
Titmouse Family												
Carolina Chickadee	x	x	x	x	x	o	x	x			Common permanent resident in eastern 2/3 of state into northern part of South Texas plains.	Deciduous & mixed woodlands, & riparian forests.
Mountain Chickadee										x	Common resident at high elevations in Trans-Pecos.	Montane coniferous forest.
Tufted Titmouse	x	x	x	x	x	x	x	x	o	x	Common resident in most of Texas, absent from Panhandle & South Plains.	Temperate woodlands, thorn forest, oak/juniper woods.
Verdin Family												
Verdin	x/o				x	x	x	x	x	x	Uncommon to common permanent resident from South Texas north through Trans-Pecos, Edwards Plateau & central coast.	Oak-juniper, thorn-scrub, desert.
Bushtit Family												
Bushtit							x	x	o	x	Uncommon to common permanent resident from Panhandle to Trans-Pecos & western Edwards Plateau.	Oak-juniper, pine woodlands, & thorn forest.
Nuthatch Family – Nuthatch Subfamily												
Red-breasted Nuthatch	x	x	x	x	o	x	x	x	x	x	Irregular to uncommon migrant & winter resident in nearly all parts of state.	Coniferous & mixed woodlands, deciduous forests.
White-breasted Nuthatch	x	x	x	o	x				x		Rare permanent resident in Trans-Pecos, Edwards Plateau & eastern 1/3 of state down to Houston, Texas.	Deciduous & mixed woodlands, pinyon-juniper forest.
Brown-headed Nuthatch	x										Rare/locally common permanent resident in the pine forests of east Texas south to upper coast.	Coniferous forest.
Creeper Family – Creeper Subfamily												
Brown Creeper	x	x	x	x	x	x	x	x	x		Rare & irregular to common migrant & winter resident throughout Texas east of Pecos River.	Coniferous forests & woodlands.

Table A.1
Birds of Texas

x - regular occurrence, abundant to uncommon o - more difficult to find, scarce to rare x/o - can be common in parts of the region, but rare in others

Wren Family

Species	Ecological Region 1	2	3	4	5	6	7	8	9	10	Notes	Habitat
Cactus Wren				o		x	x	x	x	x	Locally common permanent resident from south Texas, south plains, Trans-Pecos east to Edwards Plateau.	Thorn forests & deserts.
Rock Wren				o		x	x	x	x	x	Common summer resident in western 1/2 of state, Edwards Plateau, High Plains, Rolling Plains south to western South Texas.	Arroyos, cliffs, crags, slopes, & rocky canyons.
Canyon Wren				o	o	x	x	x	o	x	Uncommon to locally common permanent resident in western 1/2 of state, east to Edwards Plateau.	Crags, cliffs, canyons, & outcrops in arid regions.
Carolina Wren	x	x	x	x	x	x	x	x			Common permanent resident in eastern 2/3 of state west to north central Texas, Edwards Plateau, most South Texas.	Moist woodlands, thickets, tangles & undergrowth.
Bewick's Wren	x	x	x	x	x	x	x	x	x	x	Uncommon to common permanent resident in western 2/3 of state, rarer eastward.	Oak woodland, thorn forest, savannah, shrubby fields.
House Wren	x	x	x	x	x	o	x	x	x	x	Common migrant & uncommon winter resident throughout, rare summer resident in Panhandle.	Thickets, tangles & undergrowth, hedgerows, woods.
Winter Wren	x	x	x	x	x	o	o	o	o	o	Rare to uncommon migrant & winter resident throughout most of state, rare in Rolling Plains.	Thickets, tangles & undergrowth near rivers, swamps.
Sedge Wren	x	x	x	x	x	o	o				Common/locally abundant migrant & winter resident along coast, uncommon inland, rare in the west.	Low, wet marshes, grasslands, & estuaries.

Species	Ecological Region 1	2	3	4	5	6	7	8	9	10	Notes	Habitat
Marsh Wren	x	x	x	x	x	x	x	x	x	x	Common permanent resident of marshes along upper & central coast, rare migrant in west.	Cattail & brackish marshes, brackish marshes.
Kinglet Family												
Golden-crowned Kinglet	x	x	x	x	x	x	x	x	x	x	Uncommon to locally common migrant & winter resident throughout the state.	Coniferous forest, woodlands.
Ruby-crowned Kinglet	x	x	x	x	x	x	x	x	x	x	Common to abundant migrant & winter resident throughout the state.	Coniferous forests, woodlands, riparian forests.
Old World Warblers and Gnatcatcher Family												
Blue-gray Gnatcatcher	x	x	x	x	x	x	x	x	x	x	Rare to uncommon summer resident in most of state. Uncommon winter resident on coast to South Texas.	Broadleaf woodlands, thorn forest, open woods, & thickets.
Black-tailed Gnatcatcher						x				x	Rare to common permanent resident in Trans-Pecos south along Rio Grande to west 1/2 of South Texas.	Dry thorn forest, desert, desert scrub, dry washes, & mesquite.
Thrush Family												
Eastern Bluebird	x	x	x	x	x	x	x	x	x	x	Common summer resident in eastern 1/2 of state, rarer in west, migrant throughout.	Open country with scattered trees, farms, & roadsides.
Western Bluebird							o	o	o	x	Uncommon, local permanent resident in Trans-Pecos mountains, rare to common migrant & winter resident in western 1/3.	Open coniferous & broadleaf woodlands, savannahs.
Mountain Bluebird							o	x	x	x	Uncommon to common migrant & winter resident in western 2/3 of state, rare in Edwards Plateau in winter.	Open rangelands, meadows, hedgerows, deserts.
Veery	x	x	x	o	o	o					Rare to uncommon migrant in eastern 1/2 of state, common on upper coast in spring.	Moist forest, oak woodlands, riparian woodlands.

Table A.1
Birds of Texas

x - regular occurrence, abundant to uncommon   o - more difficult to find, scarce to rare   x/o - can be common in parts of the region, but rare in others

Species	Ecological Region 1	2	3	4	5	6	7	8	9	10	Notes	Habitat
Thrush Family												
Gray-cheeked Thrush	x	x	o	o	o						Rare/uncommon migrant in the eastern 1/2 of state, most common on coast.	Migrates through deciduous & mixed woodlands.
Swainson's Thrush	x	x	x	x	x	x	o	o	o		Uncommon to common migrant in eastern 1/2 of state, most common on coast.	Migrates through moist woodlands.
Hermit Thrush	x	x	x	x	x	x	x	x	x		Common migrant & winter resident throughout most of state, uncommon in Panhandle. Summers in Trans-Pecos.	Coniferous & mixed forest, riparian forest, woodlands.
Wood Thrush	x	x		x							Uncommon summer resident in forested eastern 1/2 of state, migrant in eastern 1/2 especially on coast.	Moist broadleaf woodlands & mixed forest.
American Robin	x	x	x	x	x	x	x	x	x		Common summer resident in northern 1/2 of state, common winter resident & migrant throughout.	Parkland, riparian forest, oak woodlands & forest.
Mimic Thrush Family												
Gray Catbird	x	x	x	x	x	x	x	x	x	x	Uncommon summer resident in northeast corner, common migrant in east, rare winter resident on coast.	Low dense thickets in deciduous woodlands, suburbs.
Northern Mockingbird	x	x	x	x	x	x	x	x	x	x	Common resident throughout the state.	Residential areas, agricultural areas, old fields, woods.
Brown Thrasher	x	x	x	x	x	o	o	o			Common to uncommon permanent resident & migrant.	Undergrowth, thickets & tangles in forests, old fields.

Species	Ecological Region 1	2	3	4	5	6	7	8	9	10	Notes	Habitat
Crissal Thrasher										x	Rare to locally common permanent resident in Trans-Pecos & western edge of Edwards Plateau.	Riparian thickets in deserts, pinyon-juniper.
Pipit Family												
American Pipit	x	x	x	x	x	x	x	x	x	x	Common migrant & winter resident in most of state, rare in northern Panhandle as winter resident.	Shortgrass prairie, plowed fields, mudflats, roadsides.
Waxwing Family												
Cedar Waxwing	x	x	x	x	x	x	x	x	x	x	Common to abundant winter resident nearly throughout, uncommon in Trans-Pecos, few breeders.	Open coniferous & deciduous woodlands, old fields.
Silky-flycatcher Family												
Phainopepla										x	Common permanent resident in Trans-Pecos, rare on western edge of Edwards Plateau, also rare in Lower Rio Grande Valley.	Riparian thickets, juniper-oak woodlands, desert scrub.
Shrike Family - Shrike Subfamily												
Loggerhead Shrike	x	x	x	x	x	x	x	x	x	x	Rare to common permanent resident/winter resident/migrant throughout, except for parts of South Texas plains.	Open woodlands, savannah, tallgrass prairie, farmland.
Starling Family - Starling Subfamily												
European Starling	x	x	x	x	x	x	x	x	x	x	Introduced species, uncommon to abundant resident throughout state.	Towns, farmland, savannah.
Vireo Family - Vireo Subfamily												
White-eyed Vireo	x	x	x	x	x	x	x	o	o	o	Uncommon/common migrant & summer resident throughout eastern 2/3 of state, uncommon Panhandle/Trans-Pecos.	Deciduous woodlands, edges, brambles, & undergrowth.
Bell's Vireo	o	o	o	o	o	x	x	o	o	x	Rare (east) to locally common (west) throughout, absent in west Panhandle, rare East Texas.	Deciduous woodlands, thorn forest, savannah, near water.
Black-capped Vireo						x	x			x	Local, rare to uncommon summer resident in Edwards Plateau & parts of Trans-Pecos. Rare migrant out of range in Texas.	Oak scrub & juniper woodlands, brushy hillsides, canyons.

Table A.1
Birds of Texas

x - regular occurrence, abundant to uncommon o - more difficult to find, scarce to rare x/o - can be common in parts of the region, but rare in others

Species	Ecological Region 1 2 3 4 5 6 7 8 9 10	Notes	Habitat
Vireo Family - Vireo Subfamily			
Solitary Vireo / Plumveous Vireo (west) / Blue-headed Vireo (east)	x x x x x x x x x x	Uncommon summer resident in Trans-Pecos, common migrant throughout, uncommon winter resident in eastern 1/2 of state.	Coniferous & mixed woodlands, riparian forest.
Yellow-throated Vireo	x x x x x x o o o	Uncommon to common summer resident/migrant in East Texas west to eastern Edwards Plateau, rare in western part.	Deciduous forest, oak woodlands, riparian forest.
Hutton's Vireo	o x	Locally common summer resident in Trans-Pecos mountains, very rare in Edwards Plateau, uncommon winter resident in Trans-Pecos.	Pine-oak & juniper woodlands.
Warbling Vireo	x x x o o o o o o x	Rare to uncommon summer resident in Trans-Pecos, East Texas & northeast Panhandle.	Mixed deciduous forest, riparian & oak woodlands.
Red-eyed Vireo	x x x x x x x o o	Uncommon to common summer resident in east 1/2 of state. Migrant throughout, rare in west.	Mixed forest & deciduous woodlands, riparian woods.
Wood-Warbler Family			
Blue-winged Warbler	x x x x x	Rare to locally common migrant in eastern 1/2 of state, more common on coast.	Deciduous scrub, oak & riparian woodlands.
Golden-winged Warbler	x x x x	Rare to locally common migrant in eastern 1/2 of state, more common on coast.	Deciduous scrub, oak & riparian woodlands.
Tennessee Warbler	x x x x	Common spring, uncommon fall migrant over eastern 1/3 of state, common on coast.	Coniferous & deciduous woodlands, oak & riparian forest; in migration, groves, brush.

Species	Ecological Region 1 2 3 4 5 6 7 8 9 10										Notes	Habitat
	1	2	3	4	5	6	7	8	9	10		
Orange-crowned Warbler	x	x	x	x	x	x	x	o	o	x	Common migrant & uncommon to locally common winter resident throughout except Panhandle, where it is rare.	Coniferous, deciduous & mixed woodlands, thickets.
Nashville Warbler	x	x	x	x	x	x	x	o	o	o	Common migrant except in Trans-Pecos & Panhandle where it is rare. Rare winter resident on coast.	Riparian, mixed & deciduous forest, bog forest.
Northern Parula	x	x	x	x		x	x				Common summer resident in East Texas, west to Dallas county to east Edwards Plateau. Common migrant in east, rare in west.	Riparian forest & oak woodlands with Spanish moss.
Yellow Warbler	x	x	x	x	x	x	x	x	x	x	Migrant throughout state, formerly rare summer resident in Trans-Pecos & along Rio Grande, rare winter resident.	Riparian thickets, second growth forest, hedgerows.
Chestnut-sided Warbler	x	x	x	x	x	x					Uncommon to locally common migrant in eastern $1/2$ of state, rare in western $1/2$.	Second growth woodlands, scrub & thickets.
Magnolia Warbler	x	x	x	x	x	x					Uncommon to locally common migrant in eastern $1/2$ of state, rare in western $1/2$.	Mixed-deciduous & coniferous forest, riparian woods.
Yellow-rumped Warbler	x	x	x	x	x	x	x	x	x	x	Common to abundant migrant & winter resident throughout state. Common summer resident at high elevations.	A variety of forested & open areas, coniferous/deciduous forests.
Townsend's Warbler									x	x	Uncommon to common migrant in western $1/3$ of state, rare in Lower Rio Grande Valley & coast.	Pine & oak forest.
Black-throated Green Warbler	x	x	x	x	x	x	x	o	o		Common migrant in eastern $1/2$ of state, rare in west. Uncommon winter resident in Lower Rio Grande Valley.	Coniferous & mixed forest.

x - regular occurrence, abundant to uncommon   o - more difficult to find, scarce to rare   x/o - can be common in parts of the region, but rare in others

Wood-Warbler Family

Species	Ecological Region 1 2 3 4 5 6 7 8 9 10	Notes	Habitat
Golden-cheeked Warbler	x (7)	Rare to locally common summer resident in Edwards Plateau & part of Cross Timbers, migrant in South Texas. Breeding range restricted to central Texas.	Oak-juniper in summer, pine-oak on wintering grounds.
Blackburnian Warbler	x x x (1 2 3)	Rare to uncommon migrant in eastern $\frac{1}{2}$ of state, more common on coast.	Coniferous & mixed forest, riparian & oak woodlands.
Yellow-throated Warbler	x x x (1 2 3) x (7)	Rare to common summer resident in eastern $\frac{1}{2}$ of state to Edwards Plateau. Rare winter resident in east & south.	Conifers, sycamores, cypress, riparian & oak woodlands.
Pine Warbler	x x x (1 2 3) o o o (5 6 7)	Common resident in pine forests of East Texas, Bastrop. Uncommon winter resident in east $\frac{1}{3}$.	Pine forest, riparian forest, oak woodlands.
Palm Warbler	x x x x (1 2 3 4)	Uncommon migrant in eastern $\frac{1}{2}$ of state. Uncommon winter resident on coast.	Marshes, swampy thickets & mangroves in migration.
Bay-breasted Warbler	x x x x (1 2 3 4)	Locally common spring migrant, uncommon in fall in eastern $\frac{1}{2}$ of state.	Coniferous forest, riparian & oak woodland, thorn forest.
Blackpoll Warbler	x x x x (1 2 3 4)	Uncommon spring migrant, rare in fall in eastern part of state mostly on coast.	Coniferous forest, various forest & scrubby sites.
Cerulean Warbler	x x x x (1 2 3 4)	Formerly a rare summer resident in northeast Texas, rare/uncommon spring migrant throughout.	Deciduous forest, riparian & oak woodlands.

Species	Ecological Region 1	2	3	4	5	6	7	8	9	10	Notes	Habitat
Black-and-white Warbler	x	x	x	x	x	x	x	x	x	x	Rare winter resident on coast, uncommon summer resident in east Texas to Edwards Plateau. Common migrant east 1/2.	Deciduous & mixed forest, riparian & oak woodlands.
American Redstart	x	x	x	x	x	x	o	o	o	o	Rare/uncommon summer resident in forested East Texas, migrant over eastern 1/3, rare west.	Deciduous forest, riparian & oak woodland.
Prothonotary Warbler	x	x	x	x	x						Uncommon/common summer resident in eastern Texas, west to Medina County. Rare in west.	Wooded swamps, riparian forests, mangroves.
Worm-eating Warbler	o	x	x	x	x						Very rare local summer resident in extreme east Texas. Uncommon migrant in eastern 1/3.	Deciduous forest, riparian forest, oak woodlands.
Swainson's Warbler	x	x	x	x							Uncommon/locally common summer resident in forested eastern 1/3 of Texas, uncommon migrant.	Canebrakes, riparian forest, swampy thickets, mangroves on wintering ground.
Ovenbird	x	x	x	x	x	x	x				Uncommon fall migrant, common in spring. Rare winter resident on coast & Lower Rio Grande Valley.	Deciduous forest, riparian & oak woodlands.
Northern Waterthrush	x	x	x	x	x	x	x	x		o	Uncommon & decreasing migrant in eastern 1/3 of state. Rare winter resident on coast, Lower Rio Grande Valley.	Swamps, bogs, ponds, rivers, mangroves, stagnant water.
Louisiana Waterthrush	x	x	x	x	x	x					Rare to uncommon summer resident in eastern 1/3 of state south to coastal plain. Uncommon migrant.	Streams, rivers, swales, ponds, riparian forest.
Kentucky Warbler	x	x	x	x							Uncommon to common summer resident in eastern 1/2 of state. Common migrant in east 1/2.	Moist, lowland forest.

Table A.1
Birds of Texas

x - regular occurrence, abundant to uncommon   o - more difficult to find, scarce to rare   x/o - can be common in parts of the region, but rare in others

Species	1	2	3	4	5	6	7	8	9	10	Notes	Habitat
Wood-Warbler Family												
Mourning Warbler	x	x	x	x	x		o			o	Common spring & fall migrant in eastern 1/3 of state, rare migrant in Trans-Pecos & Edwards Plateau.	Riparian forest, dense thickets, oak woodlands.
MacGillivray's Warbler	o					o	x	o		x	Uncommon migrant in western 1/2 of state, rare on lower coast.	Riparian forest, dense thickets, oak woodlands.
Common Yellowthroat	x	x	x	x	x	x	x	x	x	x	Common migrant throughout, uncommon summer resident/winter resident in various localities.	Marshes, streams, estuaries, wet meadows.
Hooded Warbler	x	x	x								Uncommon/common summer resident/migrant in forested eastern 1/3 of state, especially near coast.	Riparian forest, oak woodlands & dense thickets.
Wilson's Warbler	x	x	x	x	x	x	x	x	x	x	Uncommon to common migrant throughout, rare winter resident on coast to Lower Rio Grande Valley.	Riparian forest, oak woodlands & thickets, & thorn forest.
Canada Warbler	x	x	x	x							Common migrant in eastern 1/2 of state.	A wide variety of forests & thickets.
Yellow-breasted Chat	x	x	x	x	x	x	x	x	x	x	Locally common migrant/summer resident in most of the state, rare in High Plains, Rolling Plains & South Texas in summer.	Brushy pastures, dense thickets, riparian & thorn forest, oak-juniper woods.
Tanager Family												
Summer Tanager	x	x	x	x	x	x	o	o	o	x	Rare to common summer resident in much of the state, absent from most of High Plains, Rolling Plains, Lower Rio Grande Valley.	Mixed deciduous woodlands, riparian & oak forest.

Species	Ecological Region										Notes	Habitat
	1	2	3	4	5	6	7	8	9	10		
Scarlet Tanager	x	x	x								Uncommon to locally common spring migrant in eastern ½ of Texas, especially the upper coast.	Deciduous & mixed forest.
Cardinal Family												
Northern Cardinal	x	x	x	x	x	x	x	x	x	x	Common permanent resident in eastern ⅔ of state. Local in South Texas, Trans-Pecos, Panhandle & western Edwards Plateau.	Oak & riparian woodlands, mixed deciduous forest.
Pyrrhuloxia						x	x	o	o	x	Uncommon permanent resident in western Texas from Trans-Pecos through southern South Texas to Lower Rio Grande Valley.	Arid thorn forest, mesquite, thornscrub, desert scrub.
Rose-breasted Grosbeak	x	x	x	x							Uncommon to common migrant in eastern ½ of state, rare in west.	Deciduous forest, oak woodlands, savannahs, thorn forest.
Black-headed Grosbeak	o							o	x	x	Common summer resident in Trans-Pecos mountains, rare to uncommon migrant in High Plains & Edwards Plateau, winter resident on coast.	Open pine-oak, pinyon, pine & deciduous woodlands.
Blue Grosbeak	x	x	x	x	x	x	x	x	x	x	Rare to locally common summer resident throughout state. Common migrant throughout.	Brushy pastures, savannah, hedgerows, roadsides.
Lazuli Bunting						o	x	o	x	x	Rare spring transient nearly throughout Texas, casual in East Texas, rare summer resident in Panhandle & Trans-Pecos.	Willow thickets, hedgerows, savannah, thorn forest.
Indigo Bunting	x	x	x	x	x	x	o	o	o		Common to abundant summer resident/migrant in eastern ½ of state, uncommon in western ½.	Thornforest, brushy fields, savannah, thickets, pastures, brushy woodland edge.
Painted Bunting	x	x	x	x	x	x	x	x	x	x	Uncommon to common summer resident/migrant throughout the state. Rare winter resident in Lower Rio Grande Valley & coast.	Thornforest, riparian forest, brushy pastures & mesquite, savannahs.

Table A.1
Birds of Texas

x - regular occurrence, abundant to uncommon o - more difficult to find, scarce to rare x/o - can be common in parts of the region, but rare in others

Species	Ecological Region										Notes	Habitat
	1	2	3	4	5	6	7	8	9	10		
Cardinal Family												
Dickcissel	x	x	x	x	x	x	x	x	x	o	Uncommon to locally abundant summer resident/migrant east of Pecos River, rare in Trans-Pecos.	Agricultural fields, prairies, savannahs.
New World Sparrow Family												
Olive Sparrow		o/x				x					Common permanent resident in southern Texas, north to Goliad County, west to Uvalde County.	Thornforest, dense thickets & undergrowth.
Green-tailed Towhee						o	o	o		x	Rare summer resident in Trans-Pecos at higher elevations. Uncommon to common migrant/winter resident in western $1/2$.	Arid scrub thickets, thornforest, brushy pastures.
Eastern Towhee	x	x	x	x	o	o	o				Winter resident/migrant in eastern half of state to Bexar county.	Thickets & undergrowth of deciduous, riparian woodlands.
Spotted Towhee	x	x			x	x	x	x	x	x	Winter resident/migrant from Panhandle east to Travis County, south to Rio Grande & coast.	Streamside thickets, oak woodlands & thornforest.
Canyon Towhee						x	x	x	x	x	Rare to common resident in Trans-Pecos, Panhandle, South Plains, Edwards Plateau regions.	Arid scrub, brushy hillsides, wooded canyons.
Cassin's Sparrow						x	x	x	x	x	Rare to common summer resident in western $2/3$ of state east to Bastrop & south to Rio Grande.	Grasslands with scattered shrubs, thorn forest, mesquite.
Rufous-crowned Sparrow					x		x	x	x	x	Uncommon to common local resident in western $2/3$ of state, east to Edwards Plateau.	Rocky hillsides, steep slopes, arid scrub-oak-juniper.

Species	Ecological Region 1	2	3	4	5	6	7	8	9	10	Notes	Habitat
American Tree Sparrow								x	x		Rare to locally common winter resident in Panhandle, South Plains, north central Texas.	Weedy fields, prairies, marshes, overgrown pastures.
Chipping Sparrow	x	x	x	x	x	x	x	x	x	x	Common to locally abundant permanent resident in Trans-Pecos, Edwards Plateau & East Texas forests. Common winter resident/migrant throughout.	Woodland edges, grassy fields, open pine-oak woodlands.
Clay-colored Sparrow	x	x	x	x	x	x	x	x	x	x	Rare to common migrant throughout the state. Rare, irregular winter resident in east Trans-Pecos.	Brushy fields, groves, dry grasslands, dry thornforest.
Brewer's Sparrow								x	x		Uncommon to common migrant & winter resident in western 1/3 of state, especially Trans-Pecos.	Sagebrush flats, arid scrub, creosote deserts, thornscrub.
Field Sparrow	x	x	x	x	x	x	x	x	x	x	Common winter resident/migrant throughout state, uncommon to common permanent resident in Edwards Plateau, East Texas forests.	Open, brushy woodlands & old fields, savannahs.
Vesper Sparrow	x	x	x	x	x	x	x	x	x	x	Common winter resident/migrant throughout most of state, rarer in Panhandle.	Shortgrass prairie, arid scrub, savannahs, farmlands.
Lark Sparrow	x	x	x	x	x	x	x	x	x	x	Uncommon to locally common summer resident/migrant throughout state. Uncommon winter resident, rare in Panhandle.	Prairies, roadsides, open woodlands, mesas, savannahs.
Black-throated Sparrow						x	x			x	Common permanent resident in western 1/2 of state, Trans-Pecos to Edwards Plateau & South Texas. Less common in Panhandle.	Rocky slopes, desert scrub, thorn forest, juniper.
Lark Bunting	x	x	x			x	x	x	x	x	Uncommon to abundant migrant/winter resident in western 1/2 of state, irregular summer resident in Panhandle.	Agricultural fields, desert scrub, shortgrass prairie.

Table A.1
Birds of Texas

x - regular occurrence, abundant to uncommon   o - more difficult to find, scarce to rare   x/o - can be common in parts of the region, but rare in others

New World Sparrow Family

Species	\multicolumn{10}{c}{Ecological Region}	Notes	Habitat
	1	2	3	4	5	6	7	8	9	10		
Savannah Sparrow	x	x	x	x	x	x	x	x	x	x	Uncommon to abundant winter resident/migrant throughout the state.	Open habitats, grasslands, savannahs, pastures, fields.
Grasshopper Sparrow	x	x	x	x	x	x	x	x	x	x	Uncommon to common migrant throughout, winter resident in all but Panhandle, summer resident in all but East Texas, Trans-Pecos.	Pastures, grasslands, shortgrass prairies, fields, savannah.
Henslow's Sparrow	x	x									Rare to uncommon migrant & winter resident in eastern 1/2 of state to Travis County.	Weedy meadows, sedge marshes, wet meadows & fields.
Le Conte's Sparrow	x	x	x	x	x	x	x				Rare to locally uncommon migrant & local winter resident in eastern 1/2 of state.	Tallgrass prairies, rank fields, wet meadows, salt marshes.
Nelson's Sharp-tailed Sparrow	o	x	o	o							Migrant in eastern 1/3 of Texas, winter resident along coast.	Saltmarshes, lakeshores, spartina grass, wet grasslands.
Seaside Sparrow		x									Uncommon to common permanent resident in coastal marshes to Rio Grande.	Saltmarshes.
Fox Sparrow	x	x	x	x	x	x	x	x	x	x	Uncommon to common migrant & winter resident in eastern 1/2 of state, rare south of Edwards Plateau & west.	Undergrowth & thickets of deciduous, mixed forest.
Song Sparrow	x	x	x	x	x	x	x	x	x	x	Rare to common migrant & winter resident in most of Texas, rare from central coast to Rio Grande.	Streamside thickets, inland & coastal marshes, swamps.

Species	\multicolumn{10}{c}{Ecological Region}	Notes	Habitat
	1	2	3	4	5	6	7	8	9	10		
Lincoln's Sparrow	x	x	x	x	x	x	x	x	x	x	Uncommon to common migrant/winter resident in most of state.	Thickets, hedgerows, brushy fields, riparian woodlands.
Swamp Sparrow	x	x	x	x	x	x	x	x	x	x	Common migrant in eastern 1/2 of state, uncommon winter resident in eastern 1/2, rare in Panhandle.	Coastal/inland marshes, wet grasslands, brushy pastures.
White-throated Sparrow	x	x	x	x	x		x	x		o	Common to abundant migrant & winter resident in eastern 2/3 of state, uncommon in South Texas, Trans-Pecos, Panhandle.	Woodland undergrowth, thickets, brushy fields.
White-crowned Sparrow	x	x	x	x	x	x	x	x	x	x	Rare to abundant migrant & winter resident in all parts of state, local in East Texas.	Open woodlands, roadsides, brushy grasslands, brushy fields.
Harris' Sparrow	x	x	x	x	x	x	o	x		o	Common winter resident in central part of state, south to eastern Edwards Plateau & upper coast, rare west.	Open woodlands, brushlands, hedgerows, scrub, undergrowth.
Dark-eyed Junco	x	x	x	x	x	o	x	x	x	x	Uncommon to abundant migrant & winter resident throughout, less common on coast, rarer in south.	Open woodlands, farmlands, grasslands, oak-juniper.
McCown's Longspur	x	x	x	x	x	o	x	x	x	x	Rare & irregular to locally common migrant & winter resident in much of state, abundant in Panhandle.	Shortgrass prairie, plowed fields.
Lapland Longspur	x		x	x	x			x	x		Rare to locally common migrant & winter resident in northeastern 1/2, absent from Trans-Pecos, South Texas & coast.	Overgrazed pastures, shortgrass prairies, plowed fields.
Smith's Longspur			x	x	x						Rare to locally common migrant & winter resident in central parts of state, common north-central Texas.	Shortgrass prairie, overgrazed pastures, plowed fields.

Table A.1
Birds of Texas

x - regular occurrence, abundant to uncommon   o - more difficult to find, scarce to rare   x/o - can be common in parts of the region, but rare in others

Species	Ecological Region										Notes	Habitat
	1	2	3	4	5	6	7	8	9	10		
New World Sparrow Family												
Chestnut-collared Longspur	x	x		x	x	x	x	x	x	x	Rare & irregular to locally common migrant & winter resident in nearly all parts of the state.	Overgrazed pastures, shortgrass prairies, plowed fields.
Blackbird Family												
Bobolink	x	x	x		x						Rare to uncommon migrant in Panhandle & eastern 1/2 of state, especially the coast.	Hayfields, weedy meadows, tallgrass prairies, rice paddies.
Red-winged Blackbird	x	x	x	x	x	x	x	x	x	x	Uncommon to abundant permanent resident in Texas where appropriate habitat exists.	Thick vegetation of reedy marshes, brushy fields, hay fields.
Eastern Meadowlark	x	x	x	x	x	x	x	x	x	x	Uncommon to common permanent resident throughout the state except for west Panhandle & Trans-Pecos, migrant through most Texas.	Meadows, tallgrass prairie, grain & hay fields, savannah.
Western Meadowlark	x	x	x	x	x	x	x	x	x	x	Common summer resident in western 1/2 of state, winter resident & migrant throughout except forested east.	Fields & meadows, overgrazed pastures, savannah.
Yellow-headed Blackbird	x	x	x	x	x	x	x	x	x	x	Uncommon migrant in western 2/3 of state, rare summer resident in Panhandle, rare in winter.	Farmlands, reedy lakes & marshes, brushy pastures.
Rusty Blackbird	x	x	x	x							Rare to uncommon migrant & winter resident in eastern 1/2 of state, rare in west.	Wet woodlands, swamps, deciduous forests, marshes.
Brewer's Blackbird	x	x	x	x	x	x	x	x	x	x	Common to locally abundant migrant & winter resident in most of state, rare in forested parts of east.	Farm fields, prairies, pastures, feedlots, farmlands.

Species	Ecological Region 1	2	3	4	5	6	7	8	9	10	Notes	Habitat
Great-tailed Grackle	x	x	x	x	x	x	x	x	x	x	Common to abundant resident in most of eastern 2/3 of state, west to south Panhandle.	Marshes, agricultural areas, urban areas, roadsides.
Boat-tailed Grackle		x									Uncommon to abundant permanent resident along the upper & central coast to Nueces County.	Coastal saltwater marshes, brackish & freshwater marshes.
Common Grackle	x	x	x	x	x	x	x	x	x		Uncommon to common summer resident in eastern 1/2 of state west to High Plains & South Plains, rare Lower Rio Grande Valley.	Open fields, pastures, marshes, parks, suburbs.
Bronzed Cowbird	x			x	x					x	Common summer resident in South Texas, north to Edwards Plateau west to Trans-Pecos. Locally common in migration, spreading.	Open country, farmlands, brushy areas, urban areas.
Brown-headed Cowbird	x	x	x	x	x	x	x	x	x	x	Common permanent resident throughout the state. Numbers greater in winter. Brood parasite.	Prairie, open woodlands, farmlands, suburbs, city parks.
Orchard Oriole	x	x	x	x	x	x	x	x	x	x	Uncommon to locally common summer resident & migrant in many parts of state, uncommon in Panhandle, Trans-Pecos.	Streamside groves, open woodlands, orchards, pastures.
Hooded Oriole						x	x			x	Rare to locally common summer resident along Rio Grande from El Paso County to Lower Rio Grande Valley & south coast.	Riparian forest, palms, oak mottes, thorn forest.
Altamira Oriole						x					Uncommon permanent resident in Lower Rio Grande Valley.	Riparian & thorn forest, second growth, open woodlands.
Audubon's Oriole	x/o				x						Rare to uncommon permanent resident in South Texas north to Duval, Goliad, & Val Verde counties.	Thorn & riparian forest, pine-oak woodlands.

Table A.1
Birds of Texas

x - regular occurrence, abundant to uncommon o - more difficult to find, scarce to rare x/o - can be common in parts of the region, but rare in others

Species	| Ecological Region 1	2	3	4	5	6	7	8	9	10	Notes	Habitat
Blackbird Family												
Baltimore Oriole	x	x	x	x	x	x	x	x		o	Local summer resident in north Texas & east Panhandle. Migrant in eastern 1/2 of state.	Open woodlands, river groves, suburban shade trees.
Bullock's Oriole		x					x	x	x	x	Summer resident in western 1/2 of state east to Travis, south to coast & Rio Grande.	Deciduous & thorn forest, oak woodlands, second growth.
Scott's Oriole							x			x	Uncommon to common summer resident in Trans-Pecos & southern 1/2 of Edwards Plateau.	Desert scrub, oak chaparral, pinyon pine-oak scrub.
Finch Family												
Purple Finch	x	x	x	x	x						Uncommon & irregular winter visitor in eastern 1/2 of state, rare elsewhere.	Coniferous forest, pine-oak, open deciduous woodlands.
Cassin's Finch							o	o	o		Rare to uncommon & irregular winter visitor to High Plains, Rolling Plains, & Edwards Plateau.	Pine & pine-oak woodlands.
House Finch	x	x	x	x	x	x	x	x	x	x	Common permanent resident in western 1/2 of state, recently expanding in eastern portion.	Agricultural & urban areas, arid scrub, pine-oak.
Pine Siskin	x	x	x	x	x	x	x	x	x	x	Highly irregular winter resident/migrant throughout much of state, regular in Panhandle.	Conifers, mixed woods, weedy areas.
Lesser Goldfinch	x/o						x	x	x	o	Uncommon to common summer resident from Trans-Pecos, Edwards Plateau & southern Panhandle, irregular north-central Texas.	Arid scrub, oak-juniper, thorn forest, pine-oak woodlands.

Species	Ecological Region 1 2 3 4 5 6 7 8 9 10	Notes	Habitat
American Goldfinch	x x x x x x x x x x	Uncommon to locally abundant migrant & winter resident throughout, rare summer resident in extreme northeast.	Savannah, brushy pastures, prairies, thorn forest.
Evening Grosbeak	o o o o o o o o o o	Irregular winter visitor in most of state, absent most years, very rare to South Texas.	Mixed forest, coniferous forest.
Old World Sparrow Family			
House Sparrow	x x x x x x x x x x	Common introduced resident throughout the state, especially in cities & towns.	Urban areas, agricultural fields, feedlots, farms.

Numbered regions correspond to the Texas Ecoregions map on page 11.
Source: Information from this list was obtained from: *A Checklist of Texas Birds* (K. Bryan, T. Gallucci, G. Lasley, M. Lockwood, D. Riskind, TPW); *Checklist of the Birds of Texas* (Texas Ornithological Society); *A Field Guide: Birds of Texas* (J. Rappole and G. Blacklock); *Field Guide to the Birds of North America* (National Geographic Society); *The Birds of Texas* (J. Tveten); and personal communication with Mark Lockwood.

Table A.2
Hummingbirds of Texas

A list of the ten most commonly-occurring hummingbirds in Texas.

Common name	Scientific Name	Region Common 1	2	3	4	5	6	7	8	9	10	Identification Marks (Male)	Abundance
Anna's Hummingbird	*Calypte anna*	×									×	Rose-colored crown & gorget that extends onto neck; greenish coloration with gray underparts.	Uncommon spring & fall migrant in West Texas. Some birds overwinter on the coast & occasionally inland.
Black-chinned Hummingbird	*Archilochus alexandri*					×	×	×	×		×	Black chin with purple band across lower edge of throat; green back with whitish gray underparts.	Relatively common spring & summer resident in the western 1/2 of Texas. Could be a winter visitor on the coast.
Blue-throated Hummingbird	*Lampornis clemenciae*	×									×	Royal blue throat; broad white eye stripe, dark ear patch; large white patches on outer tail feathers.	Found mainly in Southwestern mountains of the U.S. Locally common in the mountains at Big Bend. Very rare in Davis Mts.
Broad-tailed Hummingbird	*Selasphorus platycercus*	×							×	×	×	Rose-colored gorget; green with grayish underparts & green crown; long, broad tail. Makes a distinctive sound in flight, described as an insect-like whirring or metallic buzzing.	Regularly seen in the Trans-Pecos. Breeds in the mountains. Occurs in small numbers in central Texas & the upper Texas Coast during migration.
Buff-bellied Hummingbird	*Amazilia yucatanensis*	×					×					Brilliant green head & upperparts; buffy belly & rusty tail; red bill with black tip. Female the same as male.	More numerous in the Lower Rio Grande Valley, where it breeds. A few inland records in central & southern Texas. Winter visitor to the coast.
Calliope Hummingbird	*Stellula calliope*	×							×		×	Magenta-streaked gorget; green back with whitish underparts; short squared tail; short bill.	Fairly regular August migrant in El Paso. May be seen in the Big Bend in August & September. Rare in other locations.

Common name	Scientific Name	Region Common 1	2	3	4	5	6	7	8	9	10	Identification Marks (Male)	Abundance
Lucifer Hummingbird	*Calothorax lucifer*										x	Pinkish-violet gorget elongated at sides; green back with white underparts & deeply forked tail; long downcurved bill.	Primarily a Mexican species. Enters the U.S. in the Big Bend Region & parts of the Southwest including Texas, New Mexico & Arizona. Locally common in the Big Bend. Fall wanderers have been reported in the Texas Hill Country & Rockport.
Magnificent Hummingbird	*Eugenes fulgens*										x	Brilliant green throat; glittering green back with purple crown; dark green & deeply notched tail.	Typically found in southeast Arizona & northwest New Mexico. When found in Texas it is isolated to certain places in the mountains of the Trans-Pecos.
Ruby-throated Hummingbird	*Archilochus colubris*	x	x	x	x	x						Ruby-colored gorget; green upper body with light gray underparts.	Relatively common spring & summer resident in the eastern 1/2 of Texas. Can be a rare winter visitor to the coast.
Rufous Hummingbird	*Selasphorus rufus*	x							x		x	Overall rust color with orange-red gorget & green crown; young males may show patches of green on back.	Common spring & fall migrant in West Texas. Some birds overwinter on the coast & occasionally inland.

Note: Numbered regions correspond to the Texas Ecoregion map on page 11.
Source: Information compiled from data collected through the Texas Hummingbird Roundup, a project of Texas Parks and Wildlife, Wildlife Diversity Program.

Table A.3

Mammals of Texas

A list of selected mammals found in Texas.

Common name	Scientific Name	Ecological Region 1 2 3 4 5 6 7 8 9 10	Habitat	Description
Opossums (Marsupials) – Order Didelphimorphia				
Virginia Opossum	*Didelphis virginiana*	x x x x x x x x x x	Deciduous woodlands, but also prairies, marshes, & farmlands. Den in hollow trees & logs, but also most any other cavity.	The size of a small dog, furred with long guard hairs & short, soft underfur, narrow face, & a longish, hairless tail.
Shrews and Moles – Order Insectivora				
Least Shrew	*Cryptotis parva*	x x x x x x x x	Grasslands, most foraging is done on the surface, but may also tunnel under damp leaves or loose soil.	Densely furred with a tiny tail, one of the smallest mammals. Snout is long & narrow, eyes are small & hidden.
Eastern Mole	*Scalopus aquaticus*	x x x x x x x x	Occurs in moist, sandy soil. Spends much of its life underground.	This plushly-furred mammal has large, shovel-like front paws with long claws. The tail is short, & eyes and ears are not visible.
Bats – Order Chiroptera				
Cave Myotis	*Myotis velifer*	x x x x x x x	Colonial, cave-dwelling bat. Inhabits cavities such as caves, buildings, rock crevices, & under bridges. Most abundant bat of the Edwards Plateau.	The Cave Myotis is the largest of the Myotis bats. The fur is a dull sepia, tipped in cream, with belly paler.
Eastern Pipistrelle	*Pipistrellus subflavus*	x x x x x x	Closely associated with woodlands, & tends to forage over waterways. Roosts in caves, crevices in cliffs, & buildings.	Small bat, pale yellowish brown back with tri-colored hairs. Retreats to caves, cliffs, & buildings.
Big Brown Bat	*Eptesicus fuscus*	x x x x x x x	Normally inhabits forest areas, roosts in crevices in buildings, caves, & crevices in rocks, under loose bark, & in the cavities of trees.	A medium-sized bat with shorter ears & wings. Pelage is rich chestnut brown.
Pallid Bat	*Antrozous pallidus*	x x x x x x	Rocky areas where it roosts in rock crevices, caves & mine tunnels, attics, under eaves, behind signs, in hollow trees, & in abandoned buildings. Forms small colonies.	A rather large bat, yellowish-brown with large (1") ears & relatively large, strong feet.
Brazilian Free-tailed Bat	*Tadarida brasiliensis*	x x x x x x x x x x	Can form very large colonies in roosts which are dark, dry, & have ample space. Roosts in a variety of areas such as under bridges, in attics, & in hollow trees.	A medium-sized reddish-brown bat whose tail is partly free of the uropotagium (membrane which extends between tail and legs).

Common name	Scientific Name	Ecological Region 1 2 3 4 5 6 7 8 9 10										Habitat	Description
		1	2	3	4	5	6	7	8	9	10		
Armadillos, Sloths, and Allies – Order Xenarthra													
Nine-banded Armadillo	*Dasypus novemcinctus*	x	x	x	x	x	x	x	x	x	x	Since these animals obtain food by probing for insects & other animal life in the ground, the hardness of the ground during the dry season is an important factor in their distribution.	A mammal the size of a small dog, sports a distinctive set of bony bands that resemble armor.
Hares and Rabbits – Order Lagomorpha													
Eastern Cottontail	*Sylvilagus floridanus*	x	x	x	x	x	x	x	x	x	x	Likes brushy areas, especially areas that are along streamsides, along country roads, edges of fields, & even suburban yards & gardens.	A large cottontail rabbit with relatively short ears & a reddish-brown to gray appearance.
Black-tailed Jackrabbit	*Lepus californicus*	x	x	x	x	x	x	x	x	x	x	Likes hot, dry, desert scrubland; rarely inhabits forested areas.	A large rabbit with long, black-tipped ears. Coloration is mostly buff, but sprinkled with black.
Rodents – Order Rodentia													
Spotted Ground Squirrel	*Spermophilus spilosoma*			x				x		x	x	Prefers dry, sandy areas, & areas also found in grassy parks, open pine forests, scattered brush, & occasionally rocky mesas.	Small ground squirrel marked on the gray to fawn-colored back with scattered white spots. Ears are tiny, and tail is short.
Thirteen-lined Ground Squirrel	*Spermophilus tridecemlineatus*			x	x		x	x		x		Typically inhabits shortgrass prairies, pastures, & along fencerows.	Small ground squirrel with 13 alternating dark/light stripes. Dark stripes have a row of dots running their length. Short tail.
Eastern Gray Squirrel	*Sciurus carolinensis*			x	x	x	x		x			Prefers dense hammocks of live oak & water oak, also in deep swamps of cypress, black gum, & magnolia.	Medium-sized squirrel with a long, furred tail. Back is yellow-rust, other areas grayish, underparts white.
Eastern Fox Squirrel	*Sciurus niger*			x	x	x	x	x	x		x	Adapted to a wide variety of forest habitats, including upland forests with mixed tree species.	A large tree squirrel with a long, furry tail. Back is rusty, feet cinnamon, tail cinnamon mixed with black.
Eastern Flying Squirrel	*Glaucomys volans*			x	x	x						Forested areas with available den sites, which are holes in stumps, or most any other dry cavity.	Exceedingly cute small arboreal squirrel with a flattened furry tail. Back is grayish, underparts white, large eyes. Often unwisely taken as pets.
Plains Pocket Gopher	*Geomys bursarius*						x			x	x	Sandy soils where the topsoil is 10 cm or more deep.	A thick, medium-small gopher. Eyes are tiny, ears rudimentary, & back is dark brown. Sports large, fur-lined cheek pouches.

Table A.3
Mammals of Texas

A list of selected mammals found in Texas.

Rodents – Order Rodentia

Common name	Scientific Name	1	2	3	4	5	6	7	8	9	10	Habitat	Description
Yellow-faced Pocket Gopher	*Cratogeomys castanops*						x	x		x	x	Deep, mellow soils that are relatively free from rocks. Burrows.	A rather large pocket gopher, it has a deep groove on the outer face of the upper incisors.
Hispid Pocket Mouse	*Chaetodipus hispidus*	x	x	x	x	x	x	x	x		x	Sandy soil with scattered to moderate stands of herbaceous vegetation.	Medium to large, large-footed pocket mouse. Tail sparsely furred.
American Beaver	*Castor canadensis*	x	x	x	x	x	x	x	x	x	x	Essentially aquatic, inhabiting ponds, streams, lakes, or rivers.	A large, aquatic rodent with a distinctive broad, flattened, scaled tail.
White-footed Mouse	*Peromyscus leucopus*	x	x	x	x	x	x	x	x	x	x	Woodland dwellers, denning under logs, hollow trees, in stumps, brush piles, burrows, & buildings.	A medium sized mouse, tail a little less than 1/2 body length, white feet, brownish-red back & white belly & sides.
Deer Mouse	*Peromyscus maniculatus*	x	x	x	x	x	x	x	x	x	x	Variety of habitats, including mixed forests, grasslands, & open deserts.	A small mouse, tail about 1/2 body length, distinctively dark above, light below. White belly & feet, brownish back.
Hispid Cotton Rat	*Sigmodon hispidus*	x	x	x	x	x	x	x	x	x	x	Tallgrass areas, including old fields, natural prairie, unmolested rights-of-way for roads & railroads, & other areas where the vegetation grows tall & which is not subject to flooding.	A medium to large rat with a grizzled brown pelage. Tail slightly shorter than body, slightly furred.
Eastern Woodrat	*Neotoma floridana*	x	x	x				x				Wide ranging animal, habitat includes swamplands, through forested uplands, & the arid plains.	A large rat with large, rounded ears & big, black eyes. Tail sparsely furred & dark above, white below. Back buffy gray, belly & feet creamy white.
Common Muskrat	*Ondatra zibethicus*	x		x	x					x	x	Found in creeks, rivers, lakes, drainage ditches, canals, & other marshy habitats.	A large, brownish, aquatic rodent, tail about as long as head & body. Tail sparsely furred, scaled.

Ecological Region

Common name	Scientific Name	1	2	3	4	5	6	7	8	9	10	Habitat	Description
Porcupine	*Erethizon dorsatum*						x	x	x	x	x	Adapted to a variety of habitats, including forested areas which have rocky areas, ridges, & slopes.	A large rodent with distinctive barbed quills. Generally brown to yellowish brown.
Carnivores – Order Carnivora													
Coyote	*Canis latrans*	x	x	x	x	x	x	x	x	x	x	Has an extensive range, including desert scrub, grassland, & forested areas.	A dog-like carnivore, similar to a red wolf & gray wolf but much smaller, more slender, & with a narrower snout.
Swift or Kit Fox	*Vulpes velox*							x	x	x	x	Open deserts or grasslands. They have also adapted to pasture, plowed fields, & fencerows.	Very small fox. Back buffy-yellow washed with black. Fluffy tail tipped in black.
Common Gray Fox	*Urocyon cinereoargenteus*	x	x	x	x	x	x	x	x	x	x	Wooded areas, particularly mixed hardwood forests.	A medium-sized fox with grayish back, red-brown legs, whitish belly. Black-tipped tail with black stripe above.
Ringtail	*Bassariscus astutus*	x	x	x	x	x	x	x	x	x	x	Variety of habitats, preference for rocky areas such as rock piles, stone fences, canyon walls, & talus slopes.	Cat-sized carnivore with raccoon-like rings on long tail. Eyes incompletely ringed in white, background of sooty gray.
Common Raccoon	*Procyon lotor*	x	x	x	x	x	x	x	x	x	x	Typically inhabits broadleaf woodlands, also in mixed pine forests of southeastern Texas. Seldom is very far from water.	Bulky, medium-sized carnivore with black mask & distinctive rings on shorter tail.
American Badger	*Taxidea taxus*	x	x	x	x	x	x	x	x	x	x	Occupies a variety of habitats. Most common in the prairie & desert sections of the West.	A broad & squat carnivore, relatively large & robust. Long front claws. Long pelage, grayish-yellow, with a distinctive stripe from the nose to back of the shoulders.
Western Spotted Skunk	*Spilogale gracilis*						x	x		x	x	Occupies a wide variety of habitats, often in close association with man, especially in rocky areas.	Small skunk, black with extensive white stripes & white spots. Tail is bushy & predominately white. Distinct white markings on face.
Eastern Spotted Skunk	*Spilogale putorius*	x	x	x	x	x				x	x	Wooded areas & tallgrass prairies, & prefers rocky canyons & outcrops when available.	Small & slender skunk, black with less extensive white stripes. Tail is mostly black, tipped with white. Less distinct white markings on face.

Table A.3
Mammals of Texas

A list of selected mammals found in Texas.

Carnivores – Order Carnivora

Common name	Scientific Name	Ecological Region 1 2 3 4 5 6 7 8 9 10										Habitat	Description
		1	2	3	4	5	6	7	8	9	10		
Striped Skunk	*Mephitis mephitis*	x	x	x	x	x	x	x	x	x	x	Woody or brushy areas & their associated farmlands.	Medium, robust skunk, two stripes originating from white patch on top of head extending down both sides of the back.
River Otter	*Lutra canadensis*	x	x	x	x	x		x	x			Largely aquatic, frequenting lakes & large streams.	Large, dark brown carnivore. Head broad & flattened, thick tail, small ears, webbed feet, streamlined body, adapted for aquatic life.
Mountain Lion	*Felis concolor*	x	x	x	x	x		x	x	x	x	Can occupy a variety of habitats, but prefers rocky, precipitous canyons, escarpments, rimrocks, & dense brush.	Large cat, tail longer than $\frac{1}{2}$ length of head & body, small, rounded ears with no tufts, unspotted, lithe body. Back & sides tawny, belly whitish.
Bobcat	*Lynx rufus*	x	x	x	x	x	x	x	x	x	x	Occupies a variety of habitats, but prefers rocky canyons or outcrops. May resort to thickets for protection & den sites.	A medium-sized cat about the size of a collie dog, short tail, reddish brown or grayish body with black & brownish red mottled markings. Ears slightly tufted.

Even-toed Ungulates – Order Artiodactyla

Common name	Scientific Name	1	2	3	4	5	6	7	8	9	10	Habitat	Description
White-tailed Deer	*Odocoileus virginianus*	x	x	x	x	x	x	x	x	x	x	Hardwood areas within their general range, also in areas which have a mixture of pines & hardwoods.	Relatively small deer, major points of antlers come off main beam, females usually antlerless. Tail rather long with white underneath.

Introduced, Exotic, or Feral Species

Common name	Scientific Name	1	2	3	4	5	6	7	8	9	10	Habitat	Description
Red Fox	*Vulpes vulpes*	x	x	x	x	x		x	x	x	x	Favors mixed wood uplands interspersed with farms & pastures. Dens in underground burrows, rock crevices, & other cavities.	Larger than the Swift Fox, thick bushy tail tipped in white. Forefeet & legs black up to elbow. Several color phases.
Norway Rat	*Rattus norvegicus*	x	x	x	x	x		x	x	x	x	Lives in close association with humans, mainly where vegetation is tall & rank.	Medium to large chunky rat. Smaller ears. Tail shorter than head and body length & sparsely furred.
Roof Rat	*Rattus rattus*	x	x	x	x	x	x	x	x	x	x	Lives in close association with humans. Frequents the attics, rafters, & crossbeams of buildings.	Medium-sized slender rat. Black or brown in color. Long, naked, scaly tail.

Common name	Scientific Name	Ecological Region 1 2 3 4 5 6 7 8 9 10											Habitat	Description
		1	2	3	4	5	6	7	8	9	10		

Introduced, Exotic, or Feral Species

Common name	Scientific Name	1	2	3	4	5	6	7	8	9	10	Habitat	Description
House Mouse	*Mus musculus*	x	x	x	x	x	x	x	x	x	x	Occurs as either a commensal or feral animal. May live in human habitations, or along waterways & in fields with dense vegetation.	A small mouse with a long, scaled tail. Feet buffy, back rusty red with black, belly buffy white. Relatively large ears.
Nutria	*Myocastor coypus*	x	x	x	x	x	x	x	x			Semiaquatic, living in marshes, swamps, & along the shores of rivers & lakes. Can live in either salt or fresh water.	A large aquatic rodent resembling a beaver, but with a long, rounded, ratlike tail. Females have mammae along each side of the back rather than on the belly.
Feral Pig	*Sus scrofa*	x	x		x	x	x	x				Prefers diverse forests with some openings, with a good litter layer to support food items. Will also inhabit marshes & grass-sedge flats in coastal areas.	Pigs released or escaped from domestic collections. Characteristics vary. Often black or brown with light grizzled hair, & a mane from the neck to the rump.

Note: Numbered regions correspond to the Texas Ecoregion Map on page 11.
Source: Much of this information was obtained from *The Mammals of Texas*, by W.B. Davis and D.J. Schmidly.

Table A.4
Amphibians and Reptiles of Texas

* Venomous Snakes   ** Threatened Species   *** Endangered Species   + Exotic Species

Common name	Scientific Name	Ecological Region 1 2 3 4 5 6 7 8 9 10	Habitat	Distribution
Toad Family				
Family Bufonidae				
Houston Toad***	*Bufo houstonensis*	x x _ _ _ _ _ _ _ _	Pine savannas, prairies, & sandy ridges.	From Harris to Bastrop counties.
Red-spotted Toad	*Bufo punctatus*	_ _ _ _ x x x x x x	Thrives in dry areas, desert & open grassland. Needs a permanent source of moisture.	Throughout western & west-central part.
Texas Toad	*Bufo speciosus*	_ _ x _ x x x x x x	Prefers dry areas & sandy soils in a variety of habitats.	All except east Texas & west Panhandle.
Gulf Coast Toad	*Bufo valliceps valliceps*	x x x x x x x _ _ _	Variety of moist areas, including ditches, backyards, & dump sites.	
East Texas Toad	*Bufo velatus*	x x _ _ _ _ _ _ _ _	Moist areas, including marshes, ditches, rain pools, & backyard gardens.	
Southwestern Woodhouse's Toad	*Bufo woodhousei australis*	_ _ _ _ _ _ _ _ x _	Variety of habitats, including canyons, river bottoms, irrigated fields, & backyard gardens. Prefers sandy areas.	
Woodhouse's Toad	*Bufo woodhousei woodhousei*	_ _ x x _ _ _ x x _	Variety of moist habitats, such as irrigation ditches, near streams, near rain pools, & in backyard gardens. Prefers sandy areas.	
Treefrogs and Relatives				
Family Hylidae				
Blanchard's Cricket Frog	*Acris crepitans blanchardi*	x x x x x x x x x x	Prefers shallow ponds with lots of vegetation.	All but far east Texas, west High Plains & extreme western edge of Texas.

Common name	Scientific Name	1	2	3	4	5	6	7	8	9	10	Habitat	Distribution
Cope's Gray Treefrog	*Hyla chrysoscelis*	x	x	x	x	x	x	x				Wooded areas along creeks & rivers with mature marginal trees.	Throughout eastern ¹/₂ of state.
Green Treefrog	*Hyla cinerea*	x	x	x			x					Prefers water with sandy banks & dense vegetation. Often seen around human habitations.	Throughout eastern ¹/₃ of state.
Squirrel Treefrog	*Hyla squirella*	x	x									Variety of habitats with sufficient moisture, insects, & hiding places.	From Corpus Christi Bay to Louisiana border.
Gray Treefrog	*Hyla versicolor*	x	x	x	x	x	x					Wooded areas along creeks & rivers where trees & shrubs hang over the water.	Eastern ¹/₂ of state, except lower Rio Grande.
Spotted Chorus Frog	*Pseudacris clarkii*	x	x	x	x	x	x	x	x			Marshy areas near waterways on the prairies.	
Northern Spring Peeper	*Pseudacris crucifer crucifer*	x	x	x								Moist, wooded areas with streams or ponds, in open marshy areas, or in swamps.	
Upland Chorus Frog	*Pseudacris triseriata feriarum*	x	x	x								Adapted to human habitation. Occupies dry grassy areas, river-bottom swamps, woodlands, cultivated fields, ponds, & streams.	Eastern ¹/₃ of the state.
Narrowmouth Toads	**Family Microhylidae**												
Eastern Narrowmouth Toad	*Gastrophryne carolinensis*	x	x	x	x							Requires ample moisture & cover.	
Great Plains Narrowmouth Toad	*Gastrophryne olivacea*	x	x	x	x	x	x	x	x		x	Moist areas in grasslands or woods with rodent burrows, which it may use for cover.	Found throughout most of state.

Table A.4
Amphibians and Reptiles of Texas

* Venomous Snakes   ** Threatened Species   *** Endangered Species   + Exotic Species

Common name	Scientific Name	Ecological Region 1 2 3 4 5 6 7 8 9 10	Habitat	Distribution
Spadefoot Toads	**Family Pelobatidae**			
Couch's Spadefoot	*Scaphiopus couchii*	x · · · x x x x x x	Shortgrass prairies & mesquite savannahs. Adapted to arid & semi-arid conditions.	Found in western ²⁄₃ of state.
Hurter's Spadefoot	*Scaphiopus holbrookii hurterii*	x x x x x · x · · ·	Sandy or gravelly soil in wooded areas or farmland. May also be found in arid or semi-arid areas.	Found in eastern ¹⁄₂ of state.
True Frogs	**Family Ranidae**			
Bullfrog	*Rana catesbeiana*	x x x x x x x x x x	Large areas of water with sufficient shallow areas for breeding. Found around lakes, ponds, cattle tanks, or slow-moving streams.	Throughout state, except mountains of west.
Bronze Frog	*Rana clamitans clamitans*	x x · · x · · · · ·	Needs a moist environment, stays near shallow water. Usually seen in the debris of fallen limbs & tree trunks near the water.	East & east-central Texas.
Pickerel Frog	*Rana palustris*	x x · · · · · · · ·	Moist areas, such as the coastal plains & floodplains along rivers. Also in meadows & woods away from water.	
Southern Leopard Frog	*Rana sphenocephala*	x x x x · x · · · ·	Prefers shallow water, but may be seen away from water if there is enough vegetation. Can live in brackish areas along the coast.	
Mole Salamanders	**Family Ambystomatidae**			
Barred Tiger Salamander	*Ambystoma tigrinum mavortium*	x · · · x x x x x ·	Adapted to a variety of habitats, but needs soil that can be burrowed in. May use burrows created by mammals or crawfish.	Occurs throughout state except eastern ¹⁄₃.
Eastern Tiger Salamander	*Ambystoma tigrinum tigrinum*	x x · · · · · · · ·	Occupies moist, wooded areas. May also be found in cultivated areas near ponds or streams. Needs soft soil for burrowing, & may use crawfish or mammal burrows.	Found in eastern ¹⁄₃ of state.

Common name	Scientific Name	Ecological Region										Habitat	Distribution
		1	2	3	4	5	6	7	8	9	10		
Snapping Turtles	**Family Chelydridae**												
Common Snapping Turtle	*Chelydra serpentina serpentina*	x	x	x	x	x	x	x	x	x	x	Prefers permanent sources of water & slow moving water, with soft, muddy bottoms & dense underwater vegetation.	All but west Trans-Pecos & Lower Rio Grande Valley.
Water Turtles/Box Turtles	**Family Emydidae**												
Texas Cooter	*Pseudemys texana*			x	x	x	x		x	x		Rivers, streams & pools. Must have underwater vegetation & sufficient basking sites.	Northwest central part of state.
Three-toed Box Turtle	*Terrapene carolina triunguis*	x	x	x								Woodlands & dense thickets. May also inhabit floodplains, meadows, & pastures with moisture.	Throughout eastern $1/3$ of state.
Ornate Box Turtle	*Terrapene ornata ornata*	x	x	x	x	x	x	x	x	x	x	Adapted to arid conditions. Found in grasslands, plains, & in pastures. Prefers sandy soil.	Thoughout state except far western edge.
Red-eared Slider	*Trachemys scripta elegans*	x	x	x	x	x	x	x	x	x	x	Quiet bodies of water with muddy bottoms & abundant underwater vegetation. May also be found in slow-moving water.	Throughout state except in far western part.
Mud and Musk Turtles	**Family Kinosternidae**												
Yellow Mud Turtle	*Kinosternon flavescens flavescens*		x	x	x	x	x	x	x	x	x	Quiet bodies of water with muddy bottoms & abundant underwater vegetation. May also be found in slow-moving water.	All except for eastern $1/3$.
Mississippi Mud Turtle	*Kinosternon subrubrum hippocrepis*	x	x	x	x							Tolerates brackish water. Prefers shallow, slow-moving water with soft bottoms & abundant vegetation.	Throughout eastern side of state.
Common Musk Turtle	*Sternotherus odoratus*	x	x	x	x				x	x		Found in almost any permanent body of water in its range. Also slow-moving water.	East Texas & most of the center of the state.
Tortoises	**Family Testudinidae**												
Texas Tortoise**	*Gopherus berlandieri*	x					x					Adapted to arid regions. Areas with sandy soil & sparse, low vegetation.	

Table A.4
Amphibians and Reptiles of Texas

* Venomous Snakes   ** Threatened Species   *** Endangered Species   + Exotic Species

Common name	Scientific Name	Ecological Region										Habitat	Distribution
		1	2	3	4	5	6	7	8	9	10		
Softshell Turtles	**Family Trionychidae**												
Midland Smooth Softshell	*Apalone muticus muticus*	x	x	x	x	x			x			Rivers & larger streams. Prefers a stronger current & sandy or muddy bottoms.	Eastern side of state, narrow band in High Plains.
Pallid Spiny Softshell	*Apalone spiniferus pallidus*	x	x	x	x	x		x	x			Rivers & larger streams. Prefers a stronger current & sandy or muddy bottoms.	Most of northern & eastern part of state.
Crocodilians	**Family Crocodylidae**												
American Alligator	*Alligator mississippiensis*	x	x	x	x		x					River swamps, lakes, & bayous. Can tolerate brackish water.	Throughout eastern & east-central & southern tip.
Anguid Lizards	**Family Anguidae**												
Texas Alligator Lizard	*Gerrhonotus liocephalus infernalis*							x			x	Terrestrial. Found on rocky hillsides with low-growing vegetation.	Edwards Plateau region & Big Bend.
Geckos	**Family Gekkonidae**												
Texas Banded Gecko	*Coleonyx brevis*							x	x		x	Terrestrial. Rocky desert areas & canyons near level ground. Shelters under rocks, under debris.	Throughout southwestern Texas.
Mediterranean Gecko+	*Hemidactylus turcicus*	x	x	x	x	x						Terrestrial. Common in human habitations. Shelters under palm fronds, in rough tree bark, & in rocky outcroppings.	Common in southern part of state.
Iguanid Lizards	**Familly Iguanidae**												
Green Anole	*Anolis carolinensis*	x	x	x		x						Arboreal. Found in trees, shrubs, vines, ground cover, fences, & walls. Requires some shade & moisture.	Common in moist eastern part of state & southern tip.
Texas Earless Lizard	*Cophosaurus texanus texanus*						x	x	x			Rock-dwelling. Dry rocky streambeds or broken rock around limestone cliffs.	Throughout north-central & west-central Texas.

Common name	Scientific Name	1	2	3	4	5	6	7	8	9	10	Habitat	Distribution
		Ecological Region											
Eastern Collared Lizard	*Crotaphytus collaris collaris*					x		x	x	x	x	Rock-dwelling. Most common in hilly areas, found in rock piles & basking on gentle slopes, gullies, or limestone ledges.	Throughout west & central regions to High Plains.
Northern Earless Lizard	*Holbrookia maculata maculata*								x	x		Ground-dwelling. Prefers sandy or gravelly soil.	Found in Panhandle.
Eastern Earless Lizard	*Holbrookia maculata perspicua*					x			x	x		Ground-dwelling. Prefers sandy or loamy soil.	Found in central part of north Texas.
Texas Horned Lizard**	*Phrynosoma cornutum*	x	x	x	x	x	x	x	x	x	x	Terrestrial. Prefers flat, open country with little ground cover. Can bury itself in sandy, loamy, or rocky soil.	Throughout Texas except most of east Texas.
Roundtail Horned Lizard	*Phrynosoma modestum*								x	x	x	Arid or semi-arid areas with scrubby vegetation & sandy or gravelly soil.	Most of eastern part of state & most of High Plains.
Texas Spiny Lizard	*Sceloporus olivaceus*	x	x	x	x	x	x	x	x	x		Arboreal. Favors mesquite trees. Common in wooded suburban areas.	In north-central, central & south Texas.
Crevice Spiny Lizard	*Sceloporus poinsettii*								x		x	Rock-dwelling. Adapted to arid & semi-arid areas, & inhabiting rocky canyons, limestone, & boulders.	In Edwards Plateau & Trans-Pecos.
Southern Prairie Lizard	*Sceloporus undulatus consobrinus*					x	x	x	x	x	x	Wide variety of habitats. Prefers rocky areas.	Found throughout western 1/2 of state.
Northern Fence Lizard	*Sceloporus undulatus hyacinthinus*	x	x	x	x	x						Variety of habitats, especially on fences, fallen logs, & stumps.	Found in eastern 1/2 of state, except Lower Rio Grande Valley.

Table A.4
Amphibians and Reptiles of Texas

* Venomous Snakes ** Threatened Species *** Endangered Species + Exotic Species

Common name	Scientific Name	Ecological Region 1 2 3 4 5 6 7 8 9 10	Habitat	Distribution
Iguanid Lizards	**Familly Iguanidae**			
Eastern Tree Lizard	*Urosaurus ornatus ornatus*	x x (regions 6, 7)	Mostly arboreal. Seen on fallen trees, fence posts, buildings, & rocks.	Central Texas & along Rio Grande, not to tip.
Desert Side-blotched Lizard	*Uta stansburiana stejnegeri*	x x (regions 8, 10)	Abundant in arid & semi-arid areas with sandy soil & large rocks for climbing.	In Trans-Pecos & eastern 1/2 of Panhandle.
Skinks	**Family Scincidae**			
Five-lined Skink	*Eumeces fasciatus*	x x x (regions 1, 2, 3)	Found with human habitations, particularly gardens & compost piles. Prefers a humid environment.	Found in eastern 1/2 of state.
Broadhead Skink	*Eumeces laticeps*	x x x (regions 1, 2, 3)	Moist, wooded areas. Also found in urban areas where there is debris or leaf litter for shelter.	Found in eastern portion of state.
Great Plains Skink	*Eumeces obsoletus*	x x x x x (regions 5, 6, 7, 8, 10)	Rocky grasslands with loose soil. Requires moist habitat. In arid regions is found close to water.	Found in western 2/3 of state.
Southern Prairie Skink	*Eumeces septentrionalis obtusirostris*	x x x x x x (regions 1, 2, 3, 6, 7, 8)	Requires a very moist environment with rocks for hiding & leaf litter or other vegetation.	Eastern 1/2 of state to Gulf, but not southeast corner.
Short-lined Skink	*Eumeces tetragrammus brevilineatus*	x x x x (regions 6, 7, 8, 10)	Terrestrial. Woody, rocky areas, usually at the base of hills & under rocks or leaf litter.	Throughout central Texas to west Texas.
Ground Skink	*Scincella lateralis*	x x x x x (regions 1, 2, 3, 4, 5)	May be found in gardens & urban areas. Prefers a humid environment, preferably in wooded area with abundant leaf litter.	Throughout eastern 1/2 of state to Rio Grande.

Common name	Scientific Name	Ecological Region 1 2 3 4 5 6 7 8 9 10										Habitat	Distribution
Whiptails	**Family Teiidae**												
Texas Spotted Whiptail	*Cnemidophorus gularis gularis*	x	x	x	x	x	x	x	x	x	x	Usually in the vicinity of a waterway. Occupies a variety of arid & semi-arid environments.	Found throughout most of the state, except east Texas, northern Panhandle & western Trans-Pecos.
Prairie-lined Racerunner	*Cnemidophorus sexlineatus viridis*	x	x	x	x	x	x	x				Sunny areas. May also be found on lowlands & hilly areas.	Occurs in wide swath down center of state.
Colorado Checkered Whiptail	*Cnemidophorus tesselatus*							x	x	x	x	Variety of habitats in association with rocky areas.	Occurs in Trans-Pecos & part of Panhandle.
Blind Snakes	**Family Leptotyphlopidae**												
Plains Blind Snake	*Leptotyphlops dulcis dulcis*	x	x	x	x	x	x	x	x			At the surface under leaf litter or decaying logs.	Occurs in wide swath down center of state.
Small Burrowing Snakes	**Family Colubridae**												
Flathead Snake	*Tantilla gracilis*	x	x	x	x	x	x	x	x			Burrows under loose, slightly damp soils. Inhabits deciduous woods & grass-brushland communities.	In eastern 2/3 of state, Edwards Plateau, High Plains, south Texas.
Texas Brown Snake	*Storeria dekayi texana*	x	x	x	x	x	x	x				Burrows beneath flat stones & underneath the porous surface of rotting woody debris.	Occurs in east, south, north-central part of Texas.
Texas Lined Snake	*Tropidoclonion lineatum texanum*	x	x	x	x	x	x					Grasslands. Under rocks on open prairie or along pasture-woodland edge.	Found in south & central part of state.
Ground Snake	*Sonora semiannulata*	x				x	x	x	x	x	x	In suburban areas, found around disturbed habitat such as dumps or vacant lots where debris is piled.	Found in eastern 2/3 of state to south tip.
Rough Earth Snake	*Virginia striatula*	x	x	x	x	x	x					Typically seen beneath boards & fallen siding around abandoned farms. Burrowing.	Found in eastern 2/3 of state.

Table A.4
Amphibians and Reptiles of Texas

* Venomous Snakes   ** Threatened Species   *** Endangered Species   + Exotic Species

Common name	Scientific Name	1	2	3	4	5	6	7	8	9	10	Habitat	Distribution
Garter and ribbon snakes													
Checkered Garter Snake	*Thamnophis marcianus marcianus*	x	x	x	x	x	x	x	x		x	Prefers grassy upland areas near water or in thorn brush of the lower coastal plain.	Found in western ²/₃ of the state.
Redstripe Ribbon Snake	*Thamnophis proximus rubrilineatus*					x		x				Found in association with water. Often seen basking on logs, rocks, or cypress knees.	Confined principally to Edwards Plateau.
Patchnose Snakes													
Texas Patchnose Snake	*Salvadora grahamiae lineata*	x				x	x					Common throughout the woodlands & farmlands of the central cross timbers. Seeks shelter beneath flat rocks, fallen branches, logs, or planks & siding around old farms.	From south Texas north to north-central Texas.
Green Snakes													
Rough Green Snake	*Opheodrys aestivus*	x	x	x	x	x		x	x			Arboreal. Prefers tightly-branched, leafy trees & shrubs along sun-edged pine & deciduous woods.	Occurs in eastern ²/₃ of state to south Texas.
Large Blotched Land Snakes													
Texas Rat Snake	*Elaphe obsoleta lindheimeri*	x	x	x	x	x	x		x	x		Abundant in deciduous woods & pastureland as well as a variety of other habitats.	Occurs in eastern ²/₃ of state.
Great Plains Rat Snake	*Elaphe guttata emoryi*	x	x	x	x	x	x	x	x		x	Variety of habitats, including grasslands, woodlands, deserts, & South Texas thorn brush.	Occurs throughout most of the state.
Prairie Kingsnake	*Lampropeltis calligaster calligaster*	x	x	x	x	x	x					Open grassland. Also found in rocky hillside pastures & riparian woodlands.	Occurs in central & north-central Texas.
Eastern Hognose Snake	*Heterodon platyrhinos*	x	x	x	x	x	x					Frequents deciduous or pine woods & forest grassland near water sources.	Found in eastern ¹/₂ of state.

Common name	Scientific Name	Ecological Region										Habitat	Distribution
		1	2	3	4	5	6	7	8	9	10		
Bullsnake	*Pituophis melanoleucus sayi*	x					x	x	x	x	x	Extremely varied range of open-terrain habitats, from sea level to at least 7,000 feet.	Found in western 2/3 of the state.
Speckled Kingsnakes													
Speckled Kingsnake	*Lampropeltis getulus holbrooki*	x	x	x		x			x	x		Damp, grassy pastures and shelter beneath piles of barrier beach driftwood & logs and stumps in forested bottomland.	East Texas & along upper Texas coast.
Whipsnakes/Racers/Indigos													
Eastern Coachwhip	*Masticophis flagellum flagellum*	x			x	x	x					Abundant around abandoned farms. Occurs in virtually every dry rural community.	Very common in eastern 1/3 of state.
Western Coachwhip	*Masticophis flagellum testaceus*	x	x	x		x	x	x	x	x	x	Almost every dry land, nonurban habitat in western Texas.	Found in western 2/3 of the state.
Eastern Yellowbelly Racer	*Coluber constrictor flaviventris*	x	x	x	x	x	x	x	x	x	x	Woodland-meadow interface. Also inhabits weed-grown fields, especially where there is abundant cover in the way of boards, tin roofing, & other debris.	Throughout central portion of state.
Aquatic Snakes													
Diamondback Water Snake	*Nerodia rhombifera rhombifera*	x	x	x	x	x	x	x	x	x		Almost any nonurban body of water. Will frequently use man-made debris around the edge as shelter.	Throughout eastern 3/4 of state.
Blotched Water Snake	*Nerodia erythrogaster transversa*	x	x	x	x	x	x	x	x			Lakes, bayous, ponds, rivers, & stock tanks.	Central & west central parts of Texas.
Graham's Crayfish Snake	*Regina grahamii*	x	x	x	x	x	x	x	x			Sloughs, rice field irrigation ditches, & muddy bottomland pastures.	Gulf Coastal Plain & headwaters of Edwards Plateau rivers. Not common.
Red and Black Banded Snakes													
Texas Longnose Snake	*Rhinocheilus lecontei tessellatus*	x				x	x	x	x	x	x	Burrows. Prefers dry, gravelly soils. Most often found near some moisture.	Occurs in western 2/3 of state.
Mexican Milk Snake	*Lampropeltis triangulum annulata*	x	x	x		x	x	x	x			Occupies both the semi-arid thorn brush of South Texas & the coastal barrier islands.	Primarily south Texas & coastal barrier islands.

Table A.4
Amphibians and Reptiles of Texas

* Venomous Snakes   ** Threatened Species   *** Endangered Species   + Exotic Species

Common name	Scientific Name	Ecological Region 1 2 3 4 5 6 7 8 9 10										Habitat	Distribution
Coral Snakes	**Family Elapidae**												
Texas Coral Snake*	*Micrurus fulvius tenere*	x	x	x	x	x	x	x				Prefers dry terrestrial areas, especially eastern pine forest, central oak-juniper brakes, & South Texas thorn brush. May be seen in suburban areas.	Southeastern 1/2 of state.
Moccasins	**Family Viperidae**												
Western Cottonmouth*	*Agkistrodon piscivorus leucostoma*	x	x	x	x	x		x	x			Woodlands or grasslands usually within 1/4 mile of a permanent body of water.	Eastern & central part of state.
Southern Copperhead*	*Agkistrodon contortrix contortrix*	x	x	x	x							Most common in mixed pasture & woodland, but also found in longleaf pine forests.	Eastern 1/4 of state.
Broad-banded Copperhead*	*Agkistrodon contortrix laticinctus*				x			x				Mesic upland woods on a thick carpet of oak leaves. Also abundant in bottomland on the eastern Edwards Plateau. Can be found in suburban residential areas.	Central portion of state.
Rattlesnakes													
Western Diamondback Rattlesnake*	*Crotalus atrox*	x	x	x	x	x	x	x	x	x	x	Variety of rural environments, especially where cover & small-mammal prey are available.	Most of state except east Texas.
Prairie Rattlesnake*	*Crotalus viridis viridis*								x	x	x	Widely distributed across the Great Plains.	Northwestern 1/3 of state.
Western Massasauga*	*Sistrurus catenatus tergeminus*	x	x				x	x				Occupies grassland areas often hidden below ground or in dense clumps of prickly pear or bunchgrass.	Diagonal strip from High Plains to Gulf Coast.

Note: Numbered regions correspond to the Texas Ecoregions map on page 11.

Source: Much of this information was obtained from the Texas Monthly Field Guide Series, *A Field Guide to Reptiles and Amphibians of Texas* (Judith Garrett and David Barker) and *A Field Guide to Texas Snakes* (Alan Tennant).

Table A.5
Native Plants of Texas

Please note that each two-page "spread" is divided into a top half (with plants' growing information) and a bottom half (with plants' ornamental and wildlife values). Numbered regions correspond to the Texas Ecoregion map on page 11.

Bald Cypress Family – Taxodiaceae

Species	Ecological Region 1 2 3 4 5 6 7 8 9 10	Habit Height	Flower	Fruit	Sun Exposure	Habitat	Soils and Moisture Regime
Bald cypress *Taxodium distichum*	x x x x x x x	Conifer 45'-100' Deciduous	Inconspicuous 5'-long drooping clusters of male cones. Female cones at branch tips. March-April	Cones, wrinkled, rounded, 1-inch in diameter. Sept.-Oct.	Full sun, part shade	Prefers moist soils in swamps, river bottoms, forests along streams.	Hydric-mesic. Seasonal poor drainage O.K. Sands, loams & clays.
Montezuma bald cypress *Taxodium mucronatum*	x	Conifer 45'-90' Deciduous	Inconspicuous 5'-long drooping clusters of male cones. Female cones at branch tips. Feb.-March	Cones, wrinkled, rounded, 1-inch in diameter. Sept.-Oct.	Full sun, part shade	Occurs on moist soils along swamps, river bottoms & resacas in extreme south Texas.	Hydric-mesic. Seasonal poor drainage O.K. Sands, loams & clays.

Cypress Family – Cupressaceae

Species	Ecological Region 1 2 3 4 5 6 7 8 9 10	Habit Height	Flower	Fruit	Sun Exposure	Habitat	Soils and Moisture Regime
Alligator juniper *Juniperus deppeana*	x	Conifer 15'-25' Evergreen	Inconspicuous staminate & pistillate, on separate trees. Jan.-March	Berry-like cones maturing in second year. Sept.-Dec.	Full sun	Prefers oak zones in mountainous regions in Trans-Pecos. Likes open rocky areas & foothills of Davis, Guadalupe, Chisos, Sierra Vieja, Chinati & Eagle mountains.	Well-drained, xeric. Sands, loams, clays. Limestone soils.
Arizona cypress *Cupressus arizonica*	x	Conifer 30'-75' Evergreen	Inconspicuous staminate & pistillate, on different twigs. April-May	Staminate cones, dry & woody. Sept.-Oct.	Full sun	Prefers high canyons, gravelly slopes or cuts on north exposure, especially in Chisos mountains from 3000'-8000'.	Well-drained, mesic, but tolerates arid conditions. Sands, loams & clays.

Species	Ornamental Value	Wildlife Value
Bald Cypress Family – Taxodiaceae		
Bald cypress *Taxodium distichum*	Large conifer with feathery, deciduous, needle-like leaves. Fast growing with reliable bronze fall color. Long-lived tree often used as ornamental. Spanish moss (good nesting material) festoons branches.	Excellent cover & nesting tree. Seeds eaten by many different kinds of birds, especially waterfowl & sandhill cranes. Squirrels & many other forms of wildlife eat seed cones. Good foraging substrate for insectivorous birds.
Montezuma bald cypress *Taxodium mucronatu*	Large majestic conifer with feathery, deciduous, needle-like leaves, straight trunk & enlarged base. Fast growing with reliable bronze fall color. Long-lived tree often used as ornamental. Spanish moss (good nesting material) festoons branches.	Excellent cover & nesting tree. Good foraging substrate for insectivorous birds. Seed cones eaten by many different kinds of wildlife. Small rodents & other small mammals relish them.
Cypress Family – Cupressaceae		
Alligator juniper *Juniperus deppeana*	The most abundant juniper in the Davis mountains. It is highly ornamental with distinctive checkered bark resembling the skin of an alligator's back. Has a long thick trunk. Branches don't grow to ground level. Fast growing & adaptable out of range.	Excellent protective cover & nesting tree. Leaves browsed by mule deer. Fruit eaten by gray fox, rock squirrels, wild turkey & other wildlife species.
Arizona cypress *Cupressus arizonica*	Highly ornamental & attractive evergreen with pretty grayish blue-green foliage. Widely used in landscapes as an ornamental. Fast growing, but rather short lived. Aromatic foliage & very attractive trunk. Not as pretty in areas with hot summers.	Arizona cypress provides excellent protective cover & is a good nesting tree for birds.

Table A.5
Native Plants of Texas

Please note that each two-page "spread" is divided into a top half (with plants' growing information) and a bottom half (with plants' ornamental and wildlife values). Numbered regions correspond to the Texas Ecoregion map on page 11.

Species	__ Ecological Region __ 1 2 3 4 5 6 7 8 9 10	Habit Height	Flower	Fruit	Sun Exposure	Habitat	Soils and Moisture Regime
Ashe juniper *Juniperus ashei*	x . . . . x x x . .	Conifer 10'-30' Evergreen	Inconspicuous. February	Cones, fleshy & berry-like. Aug.–Sept.	Full sun, part shade	Prefers rocky soils in canyons, ravines, arroyos, rimrock & breaks; on eroded slopes & flats.	Well-drained, xeric. Sands, loams & clays. Likes limestone soils.
Eastern red-cedar *Juniperus virginiana*	x x . x x x	Conifer 30'-60' Evergreen	Inconspicuous male catkins, female cones, appearing on separate trees. March–May	Cones, berry-like, bluish, sweet & resinous when ripe. Aug.–Dec.	Full sun, part shade, dappled shade	Prefers dry hillsides, old fields, pastures, areas along fence rows.	Well-drained, mesic. Tolerates dry land. Sands, loams & clays.
One-seed juniper *Juniperus monosperma*	. . . x x . . x x x	Conifer 15'-50' Evergreen	Inconspicuous, dioecious, male & female, very small. March–April	Cones, fleshy round dark blue to brownish on female tree. Sept.–Oct.	Full sun, part shade	Prefers steep slopes, broken ground about rim rock & breaks, eroded soils of arroyos & plains & in brushlands.	Well-drained, xeric. Sands, loams, clays, caliche-type & limestone soils.
Pinchot juniper *Juniperus pinchotii*	. . . . x . x x . .	Conifer 10'-25' Evergreen	Inconspicuous. February	Cones, red & berry-like, matures within a year. March	Full sun, part shade	Prefers dry hillsides & canyons of western Texas on open flats in sand & caprocked mesas.	Well-drained, mesic. Sands, loams & clays. Likes limestone or gypsum soils.
Rocky Mountain juniper *Juniperus scopulorum*	. . . . x x x	Conifer 20'-36' Evergreen	Inconspicuous, small yellowish male & female cones. April–May	Bluish berry-like fruit takes 2 years to ripen. Nov.–Dec.	Full sun, part shade	Prefers rocky areas in canyons & on breaks in Guadalupe Mountains of Trans-Pecos & Northern Plains.	Well-drained, xeric to mesic. Sands, loams, clays & caliche-type soils.

Species	Ornamental Value	Wildlife Value
Ashe juniper *Juniperus ashei*	Multi- or single-trunked thick evergreen tree with wonderfully shaggy bark. Leaves scale-like, dark green & aromatic. Female plant with large blue fruits. Dominant plant of the hill country.	Bark strips used as nest material by the Golden-cheeked warbler. Blue fruits a winter-time favorite of wildlife: bluebirds, robins, cedar waxwings, cardinals, finches & mammals. Good substrate for insectivorous birds. Larval host plant of Olive & Juniper hairstreak butterflies.
Eastern red-cedar *Juniperus virginiana*	Evergreen tree of variable shape, with scalelike or appressed leaves. Foliage is dense & aromatic. Often planted as an ornamental. Long lived & slow growing.	Dense-foliaged tree is excellent cover & nesting tree. Bluebirds, mockingbirds, robins, cedar waxwings, thrashers, warblers, finches & sparrows relish fruit, especially in winter. Opossums also eat fruit. Larval host plant to Olive hairstreak butterfly.
One-seed juniper *Juniperus monosperma*	Evergreen small tree with shrubby aspect, often with several small trunks forming low, open bush-like crown. Extremely cold hardy & drought tolerant. Will grow rapidly but needs pruning to get character. Only female plant has berries. Hates heat.	Excellent protective cover & nesting substrate. Blue-black fruit savored by quail, raccoons, rock squirrels & several song birds. Larval host plant for several species of hairstreak butterflies.
Pinchot juniper *Juniperus pinchotii*	Scraggly red-berried juniper good for reforesting burned out areas. Often forms thickets of excellent ground cover. Good for erosion control.	Several species of birds & small mammals dine on the berries. Makes an excellent place to build a nest or to escape from predators. Larval host plant of the Juniper hairstreak butterfly.
Rocky Mountain juniper *Juniperus scopulorum*	Large or shrubby evergreen with a short, stout trunk that branches out close to the ground. Has smooth, fibrous, shredding bark. Fruits take 2 years to ripen.	This is an excellent protective cover and nesting tree. Many species of birds & small mammals eat the berry-like fruit. Provides good food late in season. Larval host plant for the Olive hairstreak butterfly.

Table A.5
Native Plants of Texas

Please note that each two-page "spread" is divided into a top half (with plants' growing information) and a bottom half (with plants' ornamental and wildlife values). Numbered regions correspond to the Texas Ecoregion map on page 11.

Species	Ecological Region 1 2 3 4 5 6 7 8 9 10	Habit Height	Flower	Fruit	Sun Exposure	Habitat	Soils and Moisture Regime
Southern red-cedar *Juniperus silicicola*	x	Conifer 20'-30' Evergreen	Inconspicuous male & female cones. March-May	Cones, berry-like, bluish, small. Aug.-Dec.	Full sun, part shade	Prefers areas near water with shallow water table, mostly near the coast.	Mesic. Seasonal poor drainage O.K. Clays, acidic soils preferred.
Weeping juniper *Juniperus flaccida*	x	Conifer 20'-30' Evergreen	Inconspicuous, staminate & pistillate. April-May	Berry-like cones, mature in second season. Sept.-Oct.	Full sun, part shade	Prefers forested or open rocky slopes of the Chisos Mountains in the Trans-Pecos at elevations of 4000'-8000'.	Well-drained, mesic. Sands, loams, clays, acid or calcareous soils, also igneous.

Pine Family – Pinaceae

Species	Ecological Region 1 2 3 4 5 6 7 8 9 10	Habit Height	Flower	Fruit	Sun Exposure	Habitat	Soils and Moisture Regime
Blue Douglas fir *Pseudotsuga menziesii*	x	Conifer 15'-25' Evergreen	Inconspicuous, staminate & pistillate cones. May-July	Cones, ovoid & dark reddish brown. Aug.-Sept.	Full sun, part shade	Common in upper canyons & slopes of Guadalupe & Chisos Mountains from 6000'-8000'.	Well-drained, mesic. Sands, sandy loams, limestone or igneous soils.
Colorado pinyon pine *Pinus edulis*	x	Conifer 10'-20' Evergreen	Inconspicuous. April-May	Cones. Aug.-Sept.	Full sun	Prefers mountainous slopes in the Guadalupe Mountains.	Well-drained, xeric. Sands, loams & clays.

Species	Ornamental Value	Wildlife Value
Southern red-cedar *Juniperus silicicola*	Small evergreen tree with slender pendulous branches & usually single trunk. Fairly handsome with ornamental qualities, having scalelike or appressed leaves. Foliage is dense, cones are small & berry-like.	Dense-foliaged tree is excellent cover & nesting tree. Bluebirds, mockingbirds, robins, cedar waxwings, thrashers, warblers, finches & sparrows relish fruit, especially in winter. Small mammals also eat fruit. Larval host plant of Olive hairstreak butterfly.
Weeping juniper *Juniperus flaccida*	Evergreen shrub or tree with distinctive & highly attractive droopy branchlets which give the tree a wilted appearance. Trunk is also distinctive with reddish brown, deeply furrowed shredding bark. Highly ornamental & good accent plant. Slow growing.	This long-lived, winter-hardy tree provides excellent protective cover & good nesting sites for birds. Berry-like cones are eaten by a number of birds & small mammals.
Pine Family – Pinaceae		
Blue Douglas fir *Pseudotsuga menziesii*	Attractive evergreen with compact habit & palish blue-green leaves. Trees are straight & tall, leaves are linear & flat, elongate & pendulous. Branches can grow all the way to the ground. Requires more water than pinyon pine or junipers. Very ornamental.	Blue Douglas fir makes an excellent protective cover & nesting tree. Seeds are readily eaten by many species of small mammals, gamebirds, woodpeckers & jays.
Colorado pinyon pine *Pinus edulis*	Attractive conifer with rounded or pyramidal shape with leaves thickly covering twigs. Very drought tolerant. Has picturesque gnarled trunk. Makes an excellent accent plant. Fairly cold tolerant.	Colorado pinyon pine makes a good nesting & cover tree. Seeds are eaten by a number of species of small mammals, gamebirds, woodpeckers, jays, quail & turkey.

Table A.5
Native Plants of Texas

Please note that each two-page "spread" is divided into a top half (with plants' growing information) and a bottom half (with plants' ornamental and wildlife values). Numbered regions correspond to the Texas Ecoregion map on page 11.

Species	Ecological Region 1 2 3 4 5 6 7 8 9 10	Habit Height	Flower	Fruit	Sun Exposure	Habitat	Soils and Moisture Regime
Loblolly pine *Pinus taeda*	x x x	Conifer 60'-100' Evergreen	Inconspicuous, male & female cones. Feb.-March	Cones, medium-sized, 2"-6" long, light reddish brown, often armed with prickles. Sept.-Oct.	Full sun, some shade	Prefers gravelly uplands & bottom-lands of East Texas Pineywoods, Gulf Coast Prairies & Marshes & Oak Woods & Prairies, west to Bastrop.	Well-drained, mesic, but is more drought tolerant than long-leaf. Sands, sandy loams, acid soils preferred; but tolerates many other soil types. Also tolerates poor drainage.
Mexican pinyon pine *Pinus cembroides*	x (region 10)	Conifer 20'-50' Evergreen	Inconspicuous. April-May	Cones. Aug.-Sept.	Full sun	Prefers higher elevations from 4000'-8000' on rocky slopes of West Texas mountains.	Well-drained, xeric. Sands, loams & clays, likes limestone & caliche-like soils.
Remote pinyon pine *Pinus remota*	x (region 7)	Conifer 20'-30' Evergreen	Inconspicuous. February	Cones. Sept.-Oct.	Full sun, part shade	Prefers rocky mesas & dry limestone slopes of western Edwards Plateau.	Well-drained, xeric. Sands, loams & clays, likes limestone & caliche-like soils.
Rocky Mountain ponderosa pine *Pinus ponderosa v. scopulorum*	x (region 10)	Conifer 60'-70' Evergreen	Inconspicuous yellowish staminate & dark red pistillate. April-June	Cones, ovoid with seeds. Aug.-Sept.	Full sun	Prefers mountain slopes at higher elevations. Found in Davis, Guadalupe & Chisos Mountains at elevations above 3000'.	Well-drained, mesic. Sands, loams, clays & limestone soils.
Short-leaf pine *Pinus echinata*	x x	Conifer 80'-100' Evergreen	Inconspicuous, male & female cones. Feb.-March	Cones, mature in fall, persist on branches. Sept.-Oct.	Full sun, intolerant of shade	Prefers well-drained slopes, hills & flat woodlands, old fields & upland woods in East Texas.	Well-drained, mesic. Sands, loams, clays. Tolerates a variety of soils, but prefers acid soils.

Species	Ornamental Value	Wildlife Value
Loblolly pine *Pinus taeda*	Fast-growing, medium-coned pine with spreading branches & compact rounded crown. Also fire resistant. Highly drought tolerant. Most common pine in Eastern forests. Has good ornamental potential.	Provides excellent cover & nesting substrate for birds, & cavities for woodpeckers. Many birds & mammals eat the seeds exposed as 2-year old cones open, i.e., doves, woodpeckers, chickadees, titmice, sparrows, goldfinch, siskins. Larval host plant of Eastern Pine Elfin butterfly.
Mexican pinyon pine Pinus cembroides	Very attractive pine with gnarled trunk. Flexible blue-green needles are highly attractive. Makes a great accent plant. Not very heat tolerant, but fairly drought tolerant. Fairly slow growing.	Excellent nesting & cover tree throughout the year. Pinyon nuts are highly prized by both gamebirds like quail & turkey & others able to extract them, i.e., scrub jays, woodpeckers & finches. Ground squirrels, rock squirrels, & porcupines also love them.
Remote pinyon pine *Pinus remota*	Very attractive pine with pyramidal shape. Flexible blue-green needles are highly appealing. Makes a great accent plant. Very heat tolerant.	Excellent nesting & cover tree throughout the year. Pinyon nuts are highly prized by both gamebirds like quail & turkey & others able to extract them, i.e., scrub jays, woodpeckers & finches. Ground squirrels, rock squirrels, & porcupines also love them.
Rocky Mountain ponderosa pine *Pinus ponderosa v. scopulorum*	Magnificent evergreen with stout branches, thick, somewhat drooping but up-curved (at tip) branches. Crown is rounded or flat. Prefers cool micro-climate & a little extra moisture. Fire resistent. Can be used as shelter belt planting.	Excellent protective cover & nesting tree. Seeds of this pine are eaten by several species of birds & mammals including quail, porcupine, rock squirrels, etc. Also browsed by mule deer & mountain sheep. Excellent insect substrate for woodpeckers.
Short-leaf pine *Pinus echinata*	Small-coned pine, relatively fast growing, makes a good ornamental. Will reliably sprout from the base.	Provides excellent cover & nesting substrate for birds, & cavities for woodpeckers. Many birds & mammals eat the seeds exposed as 2-year old cones open, i.e., doves, woodpeckers, chickadees, titmice, sparrows, goldfinch, siskins. Larval host plant of Eastern Pine Elfin butterfly.

Table A.5
Native Plants of Texas

Please note that each two-page "spread" is divided into a top half (with plants' growing information) and a bottom half (with plants' ornamental and wildlife values). Numbered regions correspond to the Texas Ecoregion map on page 11.

Species	Ecological Region 1 2 3 4 5 6 7 8 9 10	Habit Height	Flower	Fruit	Sun Exposure	Habitat	Soils and Moisture Regime
Southwestern white pine (Limber pine) *Pinus strobiformis*	x (10)	Conifer 40'-60' Evergreen	Inconspicuous, red staminate cones & reddish purple pistillate scales. June	Cones, good crop every 3 years. Sept.-Oct.	Full sun	Found in small scattered stands, deep canyons, high ridges & rocky foothills at higher elevations in Davis & Guadaupe Mountains from 5000'-8000'.	Well-drained, xeric. Sands, loams, clays & limestone soils.

Grass Family – Poaceae

Species	Ecological Region 1 2 3 4 5 6 7 8 9 10	Habit Height	Flower	Fruit	Sun Exposure	Habitat	Soils and Moisture Regime
Alkali sacaton *Sporobolus airoides*	x x x (7 8 9) x (10)	Grass 2'-5' Warm-season perennial	Flowering spikelets greenish with yellow anthers, turning purplish. June-Nov.	Seeds. Sets seeds soon after flowering	Full sun, part shade	Prefers dry sandy or gravelly slopes, also occurs along saline or alkaline flats.	Well-drained, xeric. Sands, sandy loams, loams, clays & caliche-type soils.
Alkali sacaton *Sporobolus wrightii*	x x (6 7) x (10)	Grass 4'-6' Warm-season perennial	Flowering spikelets greenish yellow turning to gold. May-Dec.	Seeds. Sets seeds soon after flowering	Full sun, a little shade O.K.	Prefers moist clay flats on borders of alkaline or saline areas or on rocky slopes in West Texas.	Poor drainage O.K., mesic-hydric clay soils, either saline or alkaline.
Big bluestem *Andropogon gerardii*	x x x x x x x x x (1-9) x (10)	Grass 3'-6' Warm-season perennial bunch grass. Dormant in winter	Flowering spikelets of green to golden-tan in form of turkey foot. Aug.-Nov.	Seeds. Sets seed shortly after flowering	Full sun	Prefers moist soils of meadows & prairies in the eastern 1/2 of state.	Mesic; moderate moisture. Sands, loams & clays, acid or calcareous.
Big muhly *Muhlenbergia lindheimeri*	x x x (4 5 6)	Grass 2'-5' Warm-season perennial	Flowering spikelets silvery green to golden tan. July-Aug.	Seeds. Sept.-Nov.	Full sun, part shade	Prefers limestone uplands near streams.	Well-drained, mesic. Calcareous clays & limestone soils.

Species	Ornamental Value	Wildlife Value
Southwestern white pine (Limber pine) *Pinus strobiformis*	Highly attractive pine with bluish-green foliage & cones over 6" long. Branches are plume-like & droopy. Slow growing & long lived. Good erosion control planting.	Seeds from the cones are eaten by many species of small mammals, gamebirds & larger passerine birds. This makes an excellent protective cover & nesting tree. Good insect substrate for woodpeckers.
Grass Family – Poaceae		
Alkali sacaton *Sporobolus airoides*	Alkali sacaton is great in the proper habitat & under appropriate soil conditions. Strikingly attractive seed head with purplish or greenish spikelets.	This attractive grass provides fair grazing for wildlife. Grass parts are used as denning & nesting material. Seeds are eaten by a number of species of granivorous birds.
Alkali sacaton *Sporobolus wrightii*	Alkali sacaton is great in the proper habitat & under appropriate soil conditions. Strikingly attractive seed head to 12" long with golden spikelets. Forms dense clumps. Is good erosion control plant.	This attractive grass provides good forage for wildlife when actively growing & healthy. Grass parts are used as denning & nesting material. Seeds are eaten by a number of species of granivorous birds.
Big bluestem *Andropogon gerardi*	This big prairie perennial can be used as a meadow grass with wildflowers, a pocket tallgrass prairie, or a garden accent. Adds a dramatic component. Needs rich, deep soil with moisture present. Good erosion control. Best placed at bottom of slope.	Provides good cover & food for many species of wildlife. Grass parts used as nesting & denning material. Larval host plant of Delaware Skipper, Dusted Skipper, Bunchgrass Skipper, Large Wood Nymph, Cobweb, Clouded & Beard grass skippers.
Big muhly *Muhlenbergia lindheimeri*	This is a highly attractive bunch grass. Serves as a striking accent plant in any garden. Plant sports silvery golden plumes in the fall.	Big muhly is a good forage grass for wildlife. Birds readily eat the ripe seeds. Grass parts are used for nesting & denning material.

Table A.5
Native Plants of Texas

Please note that each two-page "spread" is divided into a top half (with plants' growing information) and a bottom half (with plants' ornamental and wildlife values). Numbered regions correspond to the Texas Ecoregion map on page 11.

Species	Ecological Region 1 2 3 4 5 6 7 8 9 10	Habit Height	Flower	Fruit	Sun Exposure	Habitat	Soils and Moisture Regime
Black grama *Bouteloua eriopoda*	x x x x x (6 7 8 9 10)	Grass 1'-2 1/2' Warm-season perennial	Spikelets, greenish turning yellowish, arranged down along stem. June-Oct.	Seeds. July-Nov.	Full sun	Prefers dry slopes & plains, often associated with shrubs & subshrubs.	Well-drained, xeric. Sands, loams & clays, likes limestone substrates.
Blue grama *Bouteloua gracilis*	x (5) x x x x x (6 7 8 9 10)	Grass 1/2'-3' Warm-season perennial	Spikelets, densely flowered with bluish cast. June-Oct.	Seeds. July-Nov.	Full sun, a little shade tolerated	Prefers open, grassy plains & rocky slopes in the High & Rolling Plains, also Edwards Plateau & Trans-Pecos.	Well-drained, xeric-mesic. Sandy loams, loams.
Broomsedge *Andropogon virginicus*	x x x (1 2 3)	Grass 3'-4' Warm-season perennial, dies back in winter	Flowering spikelets green to yellow gold. Sept.-Nov.	Seeds. Sets seed shortly after flowering	Part shade, dappled shade	Prefers loose moist soils of oak woods & prairies, also shaded banks along streams.	Mesic. Sands & sandy loams, loams.
Brownseed paspale *Paspalum plicatulum*	x x x (1 2 3) x x (4 5)	Grass 3'-5' Warm-season perennial	Flowering spikelets green turning dark brown. May-July	Seeds. June-Nov.	Full sun, part shade	Prefers open oak woodlands.	Mesic. Sands & sandy loams.
Buffalograss *Buchloe dactyloides*	x x x x x x x x x (1 2 3 4 5 6 7 8 9) x (10)	Grass 3"-12" Perennial-Turf grass	Flowering spikelets yellowish green. June-Nov. or whenever not dormant	Seeds. Sets seed shortly after flowering	Full sun	Prefers open areas in many kinds of soils, shortgrass prairies of Central & North Central Texas.	Xeric, well-drained. Sands, loams & clays.
Bullgrass *Muhlenbergia emersleyi*	x (10)	Grass 2'-4' Warm-season perennial	Flowering spikelets silvery pinkish purple. July-Nov.	Seeds. Sets seed shortly after flowering	Full sun, part shade	Prefers rocky mountain slopes, rock ledges, along canyos & arroyos at medium to high elevations.	Well-drained, xeric. Sands, loams & clays.

Species	Ornamental Value	Wildlife Value
Black grama *Bouteloua eriopoda*	Perennial warm-season grass with wiry stems from a knotty base. Grass stems often arch over. This is an attractive little grass found a lot in the rolling hills. Profits from protection from nearby shrubs which afford it a modicum of shade.	Black grama provides good grazing for wildlife. Sparrows & finches & various grosbeaks forage on the ripe seeds. Grass parts used as denning and nesting material.
Blue grama *Bouteloua gracilis*	This attractive sod-forming perennial grass has stout rhizomes & fine leaves. It is a good choice as a meadow grass as it leaves lots of space for the wildflowers. Can be mixed with Buffalo grass. Needs a little watering.	Provides good grazing for wildlife. Grains eaten by many species of sparrows & finches as well as other seed-eaters.
Broomsedge *Andropogon virginicus*	This beautiful grass is its most beautiful in the fall with its perky bushy head that looks like a broom. Takes on a lovely golden color.	Provides food & cover for many species of wild birds & mammals. Culms, leaves are used as nesting & denning material. Provides fair grazing for wildlife. Butterflies use grass as shelter on windy days. Larval host plant of Zabulon skipper.
Brownseed paspale *Paspalum plicatulum*	This bunch grass sets seed throughout much of the year.	Seeds provide fairly good forage for wildlife, both grazers & seed-eating birds. Parts of the grass are used as nesting & denning material.
Buffalograss *Buchloe dactyloides*	This is a wonderful turf grass. It takes a little longer to establish in caliche soils. Once established, it is very drought tolerant. It turns a soft golden brown when it goes dormant	Buffalograss provides fine nesting & denning materials, especially for lining bird's nests. Seeds of male flowers are eaten by small granivorous birds. Is the larval host plant of the Green skipper.
Bullgrass *Muhlenbergia emersleyi*	Coarse, clump-forming grass with elegant & showy purplish-silvery seed heads, usually open, sometimes contracted. Grows best on north-facing slopes. Good erosion control grass on steep mountain slopes.	Bullgrass is a valubable grass. Mule deer bed down in this grass. Provides good forage for all kinds of wildlife. Seeds are eaten by several species of granivorous birds & small mammals.

Table A.5
Native Plants of Texas

Please note that each two-page "spread" is divided into a top half (with plants' growing information) and a bottom half (with plants' ornamental and wildlife values). Numbered regions correspond to the Texas Ecoregion map on page 11.

Species	Ecological Region 1 2 3 4 5 6 7 8 9 10	Habit Height	Flower	Fruit	Sun Exposure	Habitat	Soils and Moisture Regime
Burrograss *Scleropogon brevifolius*	x x x x x x (5–10) x	Grass 4"-9" Sod-forming perennial	Flowering spikelets hairy, pink or white. July-Aug.	Seeds. July-Sept.	Full sun, a little shade O.K.	Prefers open, dry, rocky slopes & plains in central & western portions of state.	Well-drained, xeric. Sands, loams, clays, caliche-type & calcareous soils.
Bushy bluestem *Andropogon glomeratus*	x x x x x x x x x x	Grass 3'-4' Warm-season perennial	Flowering spikelets green to buffy gold. Sept.-Nov.	Seeds. Sets seed shortly after flowering	Full sun, part shade	Prefers low, moist sites.	Mesic, poor drainage O.K. Sands, sandy loams. Soils can be fairly sterile.
California cottontop *Digitaria californica*	x x x x x	Grass 1'-3' Warm-season perennial	Flowering spikelets greenish to whitish silver. July-Nov.	Seeds. Sets seed shortly after flowering	Full sun, part shade	Grows on wide variety of soil types in open grassy areas.	Well-drained, xeric to mesic. Sands, loams & clays.
Canada wildrye *Elymus canadensis*	x x x x x x x x x x	Grass 3'-5' Cool-season tufted perennial	Flowering spikelets green turning gold, with long awns. March-June	Seeds. May-Sept.	Full sun, part shade, dappled shade	Prefers shaded sites along fence rows, woods borders & moist ravines throughout state. Absent in southern part of South Texas.	Well-drained, mesic. Sands, loams & clays.
Cane bluestem *Bothriochloa barbinodes*	x x x x x x	Grass 3'-6' Perennial bunch grass	Flowering spikelets from whitish green to silver. April-Aug.	Seeds. May-Oct.	Full sun, a little shade O.K.	Prefers looser soils in the western 2/3 of the state. Grows in open areas & grasslands.	Well-drained, xeric. Sands, sandy loams, loams; likes limy soils.

Species	Ornamental Value	Wildlife Value
Burrograss *Scleropogon brevifolius*	Very aggressive but useful landscape grass. Blooms appear after heavy rains. Grass turns greenish after blooming with more rain. More drought tolerant than Buffalograss. Best to mow after blooming. Forms thick sod.	Provides poor grazing for wildlife, but it is a good lawn grass in dry areas. Fine leaves used to line bird's nests.
Bushy bluestem *Andropogon glomeratus*	Very attractive bunch grass for moist areas. Especially pretty in the fall. Tolerates poor drainage.	Provides food & cover for many species of wild birds & mammals. Culms, leaves are used as nesting & denning material. Larval host plant of several eastern skippers.
California cottontop *Digitaria californica*	An attractive tufted, leafy perennial grass with very pretty seed heads. This pretty grass can be a wonderful accent to the garden.	California cottontop provides good forage for wildlife. Many birds & small mammals eat the ripe seeds. Grass parts are used as nesting & denning material.
Canada wildrye *Elymus canadensis*	This tufted grass with attractive seed heads does best in shady areas with adequate moisture.	Provides good early food for many species of birds & small mammals that eat grain. Grass parts, leaves, stems, & spikelets used as nesting & denning material. Larval host plant for Zabulon skipper.
Cane bluestem *Bothriochloa barbinodes*	Very attractive accent plant or member of a pocket prairie or field of wildflowers.	Cane bluestem is an excellent forage grass for wildlife. Leaves are grazed, especially later on in the season. Grass parts used as nesting & denning material. Seeds eaten by granivorous birds & small mammals.

Table A.5
Native Plants of Texas

Please note that each two-page "spread" is divided into a top half (with plants' growing information) and a bottom half (with plants' ornamental and wildlife values). Numbered regions correspond to the Texas Ecoregion map on page 11.

Species	Ecological Region 1 2 3 4 5 6 7 8 9 10	Habit Height	Flower	Fruit	Sun Exposure	Habitat	Soils and Moisture Regime
Curly-mesquite *Hilaria berlangeri*	x x x x x x x (4–10)	Grass 4"–6" Warm-season perennial	Flowering spikelets greenish gray to silvery in fall. July–Nov.	Seeds. Aug.–Nov.	Full sun, a little shade O.K.	Prefers rocky slopes, dry hillsides & grassy or brushy plains.	Well-drained, xeric. Thin limestone soils, clays & caliche type soils. Also sands & loams.
Ear muhly *Muhlenbergia arenacea*	x x (8, 9)	Grass 4"–14" Low perennial	Flowering spikelets greenish-gray turning straw yellow. May–Nov.	Seeds. June–Nov.	Full sun, a little shade O.K.	Prefers sandy plains, valley flats, also along washes.	Well-drained, mesic-xeric. Sands, loams & limestone soils.
Eastern gammagrass *Tripsacum dactyloides*	x x x x (1–4) x (7)	Grass 3'–8' Warm-season perennial bunch grass	Flowering spikelets yellow & cornlike. July–Sept.	Seeds. April–Nov.	Full sun, part shade, dappled shade	Prefers low moist grassland sites in eastern portion of state.	Mesic, likes extra moisture. Seasonal poor drainage O.K. Sands, loams & clays.
False rhodesgrass *Trichloris crinata*	x (7) x (10)	Grass 2'–3' Warm-season perennial	Flowering spikelets turning silver white in color. May–Sept.	Seeds. Sets seeds soon after flowering	Full sun, part shade O.K.	Prefers heavy alluvial soils near streams.	Well-drained, mesic. Sands, loams & clays, calcareous substrate preferred.
Florida paspalum *Paspalum floridanum*	x x x x x (1–5)	Grass 3'–6' Warm-season perennial	Flowering spikelets green, arranged in two rows. Aug.–Nov.	Seeds. Sept.–Dec.	Full sun, part shade	Prefers grasslands, open woodlands & cutover woodlands in eastern Texas.	Moist. Seasonal poor drainage O.K. Sands, loams & clays.
Fluff grass *Erioneuron pulchellum*	x x x (8–10)	Grass 8"–10" Warm-season perennial	Flowering spikelets silvery white. June–Nov.	Seeds. Sets seed shortly after flowering	Full sun, a little shade O.K.	Prefers dry rocky slopes & desert flats with creosote bush in much of the Trans-Pecos.	Well-drained, xeric. Sands, loams & clays.

Species	Ornamental Value	Wildlife Value
Curly-mesquite *Hilaria berlangeri*	Curly-mesquite looks a bit like Buffalograss & can be used as a lawn grass, but it can be somewhat lumpy. It makes a better ground cover.	Seed heads are eaten by various granivorous birds. Grass parts are used as nesting & denning material by a variety of small wildlife species.
Ear muhly *Muhlenbergia arenacea*	Ear muhly forms extensive patches. This very delicate, elegant-looking grass can maintain itself in pure stands for several acres. It looks a lot like Burrowgrass when not in bloom. Requires low maintenance. Mow after blooming.	Provides only fair grazing for wildlife. Fine leaves used to line bird's nests.
Eastern gammagrass *Tripsacum dactyloides*	Forms very dense clump useful for buffer or areas of separation. Likes more shade & moisture than most grasses. Also dramatic accent plant. Can be grown in pure stands as pasture grass.	Good protective cover for small birds & mammals. Grass parts provide nesting & denning material. Provides very good forage for wildlife. Larval host plant to the Bunchgrass skipper.
False rhodesgrass *Trichloris crinata*	This absolutely gorgeous grass makes an excellent accent plant for any garden. It's very beautiful with its 2-inch fingers of white feathery seed heads above blue-green stems. Likes a little extra water. Blooms over long period of time.	Ripe seeds are eaten by several species of granivorous birds & small mammals. Grass parts are used as nesting & denning material.
Florida paspalum *Paspalum floridanum*	Perennial with interesting green flower head.	Provides fair forage for wildlife. Parts of plants used for nesting & denning material.
Fluff grass *Erioneuron pulchellum*	Fluff grass is a gorgeous short-tufted perennial grass with fluffy seed heads. This is another grass that is just beautiful after it has set seed & the sun hits it at the right angle.	Fluff grass is not considered especially palatable for livestock forage. Seed eating birds & small mammals do eat the ripe seeds, however; & grass parts are used as nesting & denning material.

Table A.5
Native Plants of Texas

Please note that each two-page "spread" is divided into a top half (with plants' growing information) and a bottom half (with plants' ornamental and wildlife values).
Numbered regions correspond to the Texas Ecoregion map on page 11.

Species	Ecological Region 1 2 3 4 5 6 7 8 9 10	Habit Height	Flower	Fruit	Sun Exposure	Habitat	Soils and Moisture Regime
Giant dropseed *Sporobolus giganteus*	x (9) x (10)	Grass 4'-7' Warm-season perennial	Flowering spikelets greenish with yellow turning pale & shiny. Aug.-Oct.	Seeds. Sets seed soon after flowering	Full sun, a little shade O.K.	Prefers open, sandy areas.	Well-drained, xeric. Sands & sandy loams.
Green sprangletop *Leptochloa dubia*	x x x x x x (3-8)	Grass 1'-3' Warm-season perennial	Flowering spikelets greenish turning yellowish. May-Nov.	Seeds. June-Nov.	Full sun, part shade	Prefers open areas on loose, rocky soils.	Well-drained, xeric-mesic. Sands, loams & clays, especially loose soils.
Gulf cordgrass *Spartina spartinae*	x x (6-7)	Grass, seaside 4'-7' Perennial, stout	Flowering spikelets greenish to straw-colored then tan. June-Sept.	Seeds. July-Nov.	Full sun	Prefers marshy areas, also coastal flats & brackish marshlands.	Hydric, tolerates wet soils. Sands, silts, muds.
Gulfdune paspalum *Paspalum monostachyum*	x (6)	Grass, seaside 1'-2 ½' Perennial, stout	Flowering spikelets greenish to straw then brown. May-Nov.	Seeds. June-Nov.	Full sun	Frequently on coastal dune formations, backshore dues & dune ridges.	Xeric, well-drained. Loose sands.
Hairy grama *Bouteloua hirsuta*	x x x x x x x x (3-10)	Grass 2'-4' Short-lived perennial	Spikelets, greenish to tan, then brown, arranged along stem. May-Sept.	Seeds. June-Nov.	Full sun, part shade	Grows in open grassy areas near woodland edges, along road-sides & fence rows.	Well-drained, xeric. Sands, clays & loams; likes limestone & caliche-like soils.
Hairy tridens *Erioneuron pilosus*	x x x x x x x x (3-10)	Grass 7"-10" Warm-season perennial	Flowering spikelets silvery white. April-July, sometimes to October	Seeds. Sets seed shortly after flowering	Full sun, a little shade O.K.	Prefers open range-land & pastures, along road right-of-ways; also frequent in grav-elly soils throughout Trans-Pecos.	Well-drained, xeric. Sands, loams & clays, prefers limestone substrates.

Species	Ornamental Value	Wildlife Value
Giant dropseed *Sporobolus giganteus*	Tall, robust clumped perennial grass with attractive flower heads adorned with 8 brown to purple-tinged spikelets. This is a plant of the dunes & grows especially well in Ward County.	Giant dropseed provides fair forage for wildlife. Seeds are eaten by various seed-eating birds & small mammals. Grass parts are used as denning & nesting material.
Green sprangletop *Leptochloa dubia*	This green tufted perennial with open seedhead grows in all regions but most common in western part of the state.	Green sprangletop is an excellent forage grass for all grazing wildlife. The seeds are eaten by several species of sparrows & finches. Grass parts are used as nesting & denning material.
Gulf cordgrass *Spartina spartinae*	This stout perennial with densely clumped stems has a stout spike-like flower head. It will form extensive meadows along coastal flats & other lowland areas. Can grow in soils that are submerged in salt water periodically.	This distinctive grass provides excellent food & cover for all sorts of marine & seashore critters, especially rails, shorebirds & beach rodents.
Gulfdune paspalum *Paspalum monostachyum*	This seaside paspale grass with smooth leaves & densely-flowered single branch prefers the backshore dunes & ridges. It tolerates salt air, loose soils & high winds.	This grass provides protective cover & forage for small seaside creatures.
Hairy grama *Bouteloua hirsuta*	This attractive tufted perennial has very perky looking seed heads like little combs that stand out from the stem.	Hairy grama is considered fair forage for wildlife. Birds & small mammals use the grass parts for nesting & denning material. Serves as a larval host plant for the Green skipper & the Orange roadside skipper.
Hairy tridens *Erioneuron pilosus*	Hairy tridens is an attractive short-tufted perennial grass. Very pretty when the seeds ripen & the flowerheads get fluffy looking.	Hairy tridens is not a terribly good forage grass for wildlife, but it does supply some seeds for granivorous birds & small mammals. Grass parts are used as nesting & denning material.

Table A.5
Native Plants of Texas

Please note that each two-page "spread" is divided into a top half (with plants' growing information) and a bottom half (with plants' ornamental and wildlife values).
Numbered regions correspond to the Texas Ecoregion map on page 11.

Species	Ecological Region 1 2 3 4 5 6 7 8 9 10	Habit Height	Flower	Fruit	Sun Exposure	Habitat	Soils and Moisture Regime
Hairyawn muhly *Muhlenbergia capillaris*	X X	Grass 1½'-3' Warm-season perennial, dormant in winter	Flowering spikelets delicate & green turning pink or coppery magenta. Aug.-Oct.	Seeds. Sets seed shortly after flowering	Full sun, part shade	Prefers prairies & openings in pine forests, also in Bastrop County.	Well-drained, fairly dry. Sands & sandy loams.
Hooded windmillgrass *Chloris cucullata*	X X X	Grass 1'-1½' Warm-season perennial	Flowering spikelets yellow green to straw then brown. May-June	Seeds. Aug.-Sept.	Full sun, part shade	Prefers pastures, lawns, parks & vacant lots.	Mesic. Sands, sandy loams of medium to coarse texture, acid to neutral.
Indian ricegrass *Oryzopsis hymenoides*	X X	Grass 1'-2' Perennial	Flowering spikelets greenish turning ivory colored. May-July	Seeds. June-Aug.	Full sun, part shade	Prefers dry sandy slopes. In the wild, found infrequently in western ½ of state.	Well-drained, xeric. Sands, loose; loams & clays also.
Indiangrass *Sorghastrum nutans*	X X X X X X	Grass 3'-8' Warm-season perennial bunch grass. Dormant in winter	Flowering spikelets a deep yellow. Oct.-Nov.	Seeds. Nov.-Dec.	Full sun, some shade O.K.	Prefers moist rich soils of tall-grass prairies of central & coastal Texas.	Mesic, likes moisture. Sands, loams & clays. Likes calcareous soils.
Inland sea-oats *Chasmanthium latifolium*	X X X X X X X X	Grass 2'-4' Warm-season perennial, dies back in winter	Flowering spikelets green to buffy tan. June-Oct.	Seeds. Sets seed shortly after flowering	Part shade, dappled shade, full shade	Prefers moist woodland soils, often along creek bottoms & near streamsides.	Mesic, seasonal poor drainage O.K. Sands, loams & clays.
Knotroot bristlegrass *Setaria geniculata*	X X X X X X X X X	Grass 2'-3' Bunch grass. Flowers year-round	Flowering spikelets a greenish yellow. Year-long	Seeds. Year-long	Full sun, part shade	Prefers moist areas along streams & ditches & lake borders.	Mesic, likes moisture, poor drainage O.K. Sands, loams & clays.

Species	Ornamental Value	Wildlife Value
Hairyawn muhly *Muhlenbergia capillaris*	Very beautiful feathery clumps are a great accent for garden. Perfect for a meadow garden with wildflowers.	Provides forage for seed-eating terrestrial birds & mammals, especially sparrows. Parts of plant are used as nesting & denning material.
Hooded windmillgrass *Chloris cuculata*	Attractive octopus-like flowering head.	Hooded windmillgrass provides fairly good forage for wildlife. Seeds are eaten by birds & small mammals. Grass parts used as nesting & denning material.
Indian ricegrass *Oryzopsis hymenoides*	Indian ricegrass is a great accent plant. This infrequently found grass is very elegant & worthy of cultivation. It is beautiful all year round, especially in fall & winter. Wiry, straw-colored stems, glaucous leaves & ivory seed heads please the eye.	Seeds are readily eaten by small mammals & granivorous birds. Grass parts are used as denning & nesting material.
Indiangrass *Sorghastrum nutans*	This gorgeous grass was major component of tallgrass prairie. Striking accent plant or member of pocket tallgrass prairie. Does well in a naturally moist rich swale area.	Fairly good grazing for wildlife when green. Seed-eating birds & small mammals eat ripe seeds. Stems, leaves used as nesting & denning material. Provides excellent protective cover for wildlife. Larval host plant of Pepper-and-salt skipper.
Inland sea-oats *Chasmanthium latifolium*	In moist soils in shaded areas, this beautiful grass makes a solid mat. Big drooping spikelets are especially fetching, esp. when turned to whitish gold in the fall. Great garden accent plant in shady moist areas.	Serves as excellent forage for wildlife especially birds & mammals. Many parts of the grass used as nesting & denning material. Larval host plant for Northern pearly eye, Pepper & salt skipper, Bell's roadside skipper & Bronzed roadside skipper.
Knotroot bristlegrass *Setaria geniculata*	This perky grass is the most widespread species of bristlegrass. Does well in a naturally moist rich swale area.	Fairly good grazing for wildlife when green. Seed-eating birds & small mammals eat ripe seeds, especially the Painted Bunting. Stems, leaves used as nesting & denning material.

Table A.5
Native Plants of Texas

Please note that each two-page "spread" is divided into a top half (with plants' growing information) and a bottom half (with plants' ornamental and wildlife values). Numbered regions correspond to the Texas Ecoregion map on page 11.

Species	Ecological Region 1 2 3 4 5 6 7 8 9 10	Habit Height	Flower	Fruit	Sun Exposure	Habitat	Soils and Moisture Regime
Little bluestem *Schizachyrium scoparium*	x x x x x x x x x x	Grass 2'-5' Warm-season perennial bunch grass. Dormant in winter	Flowering spikelets bluegreen to silvery gold. Aug.-Dec.	Seeds. Sept.-Dec.	Full sun, part shade	Prefers woods openings, rocky slopes of pastures & rangeland, along forest borders & prairies throughout Texas.	Well-drained, mesic. Sands, loams & clays.
Long-leaf squirrel-tail *Elymus longifolius*	x x x (7 8 9)	Grass 12" Warm-season perennial	Flowering spikelets yellowish-green. May-Sept.	Seeds. Sets seed shortly after flowering	Full sun, a little shade O.K.	Prefers dry, open often disturbed areas mainly in desert & montane areas in Franklin & Guadalupe mountains of West Texas.	Well-drained, xeric. Sands, loams & clays.
Longspike silver bluestem *Bothriochloa saccaroides v. longipaniculata*	x x x x (1 2 3 4) x (6)	Grass 2'-4' Warm-season perennial	Flowering spikelets green to silver. May-Oct.	Seeds. Sets seed shortly after flowering	Full sun, part shade	Prefers dryish open areas, woodland edges, along roadsides.	Xeric-mesic. Sands, sandy loams, loams & clays.
New Mexico little bluestem *Schizachyrium scoparium v. neomexicana*	x x x (8 9 10)	Grass 2'-5' Warm-season perennial bunch grass. Dormant in winter	Flowering spikelets blue-green to silvery gold. Aug.-Nov.	Seeds. Sept.-Dec.	Full sun, part shade	Prefers open rocky slopes in western part of the state.	Well-drained, xeric. Sands, loams & clays.
Pan American balsamscale *Elyonurus tripsacoides*	x (1) x (6)	Grass 1'-3' Warm-season, tufted perennial	Flowering spikelets greenish turning yellowish. May-Nov.	Seeds. Sets seed shortly after flowering	Full sun	Prefers coastal grasslands & woods openings	Xeric-mesic, well-drained. Sands & sandy loams.

Species	Ornamental Value	Wildlife Value
Little bluestem *Schizachyrium scoparium*	Most wide-ranging bunchgrass in the state, a dominant of the tallgrass prairie. Tolerant of a wide variety of moisture & drought. Little bluestem is a symphony of beautiful color changes through the year from blue-green to coppery gold in the fall.	Provides fairly good grazing for wildlife. Good cover grass, grass parts provide denning & nesting material for birds & mammals. Larval host plant for Dusted skipper, Delaware skipper, Dixie skipper, Cross-line skipper & Cobweb skipper.
Long-leaf squirrel-tail *Elymus longifolius*	Highly attractive & ornamental grass, very pleasing to the eye. Catches the light beautifully.	Squirrel-tail provides early forage until its mature seed heads develop making it hard to eat. Grass parts are used as nesting & denning material.
Longspike silver bluestem *Bothriochloa saccaroides v. longipaniculata*	This grass becomes increasingly beautiful as its seed head ripens & catches the sunlight, glowing silvery. This bunchgrass has a conspicuous basal cluster of leaves & stems.	This bunch grass is a fairly good forage grass for white-tailed deer. Parts of the grass are used as nesting & denning material by birds & small mammals. Many species of seed-eating birds eat the ripe seeds.
New Mexico little bluestem *Schizachyrium scoparium v. neomexicana*	Most wide-ranging bunchgrass in the state, a dominant of the tallgrass prairie. Tolerant of a wide variety of moisture & drought. Little bluestem is a symphony of beautiful color changes through the year from blue-green to coppery gold in the fall.	Provides fairly good grazing for wildlife. Good cover grass, grass parts provide denning & nesting material for birds & mammals. Larval host plant for Dusted skipper, Delaware skipper, Dixie skipper, Cross-line skipper & Cobweb skipper.
Pan American balsamscale *Elyonurus tripsacoides*	When the flower head appears, this is a very attractive grass.	When found in abundance, this tufted perennial grass can provide good forage for wildlife. Ripe seeds eaten by a few species of birds. Grass parts used as nesting & denning material.

Table A.5
Native Plants of Texas

Please note that each two-page "spread" is divided into a top half (with plants' growing information) and a bottom half (with plants' ornamental and wildlife values).
Numbered regions correspond to the Texas Ecoregion map on page 11.

Species	1	2	3	4	5	6	7	8	9	10	Habit Height	Flower	Fruit	Sun Exposure	Habitat	Soils and Moisture Regime
Pink pappasgrass *Pappophorum bicolor*	x					x	x	x		x	Grass 1/2'-2 1/2' Perennial	Flowering spikelets yellowish-pink turning to fluffy pinkish rose. April-Nov.	Seeds. April-Nov.	Full sun, part shade	Prefers grassy plains, moist road rights-of-way & open valleys.	Mesic. Sands, loams & clays.
Plains bristlegrass *Setaria macrostachya*	x					x					Grass 2'-4' Perennial	Flowering spikelets greenish to yellow. May-Nov.	Seeds. June-Nov.	Full sun, part shade	Prefers open grassy areas in southern portion of the state.	Well-drained, xeric to mesic. Sands, loams & clays.
Plains lovegrass *Eragrostis intermedia*			x	x	x	x	x	x		x	Grass 1 1/2'-3' Warm-season, tufted perennial	Flowering spikelets grayish-green turning reddish purple. June-Nov.	Seeds. Sets seed shortly after flowering	Full sun	Prefers sandy, clayey, rocky ground in open areas, also grows well in disturbed areas.	Well-drained, xeric. Sands & clays.
Prairie sandreed *Calamovilfa gigantea*								x	x	x	Grass 4'-7' Perennial	Flowering spikelets yellowish turning to tan, panicles 10"-12" long. June-Oct.	Seeds. Sets seed shortly after flowering	Full sun	Prefers open sandy hills & dunes.	Well-drained, xeric. Sands, sandy loams.
Purple muhly *Muhlenbergia rigida*										x	Grass 4'-5' Warm-season perennial	Flowering spikelets slightly purple in open flower heads. Sept.-Nov.	Seeds. Sets seed shortly after flowering	Full sun, a little shade O.K.	Prefers rocky mountain slopes at medium to high elevations.	Well-drained, xeric. Sands, loams & clays.
Purple triplasis *Triplasis purpurea*	x	x	x	x	x	x	x	x			Grass 2'-3' Warm-season perennial	Flowering spikelets greenish-tan to purplish. June-Sept.	Seeds. Aug.-Nov.	Full sun	Prefers open areas of loose sands.	Well-drained, xeric. Sands, sandy loams.
Purple-top grass *Tridens flavus*	x	x	x	x	x	x	x	x	x	x	Grass 2'-4' Warm-season perennial	Flowering spikelets yellow to purplish. June-Aug.	Seeds. Aug.-Nov.	Part shade, dappled shade	Prefers shade of open woods or along road-ways throughout the state.	Mesic, well-drained. Sands, sandy loams, clays.

Species	Ornamental Value	Wildlife Value
Pink pappasgrass *Pappophorum bicolor*	This is one of the truly beautiful grasses with its pink fluffy seed head that catches the sunlight.	Though it's not a good forage grass, it makes up for it in its beauty. A few birds eat the ripe seeds. Grass parts used for nesting & denning material.
Plains bristlegrass *Setaria macrostachya*	Tufted perennial grass with stiffly erect stems & densely flowered flowerheads.	Attractive seed heads provide lots of ripe seeds for granivorous sparrows, finches & buntings. Grass parts used as nesting & denning material Provides fair grazing for wildlife.
Plains lovegrass *Eragrostis intermedia*	This beautiful bunch grass has very elegant, delicate seed heads suffused with a reddish purple color when ripe. Grows well with other grasses & wildflowers in a prairie association or small pocket prairie.	Plains lovegrass provides fair grazing for wildlife. Small seed eating birds forage on the ripe seeds. Grass parts are used for denning & nesting material.
Prairie sandreed *Calamovilfa gigantea*	Highly ornamental dramatic accent grass. Has a stout creeping rhizome, large flower panicles & one-flowered spikelets. This grass has great value in controlling wind erosion in deep sands that development introduces.	Prairie sandreed provides good forage for many species of wildlife. Grass parts are used as denning & nesting material.
Purple muhly *Muhlenbergia rigida*	A robust perennial caespitose grass with a hard bulb enlargement underground at the end of the stem. Appear much-branched with open seed heads of dark purplish spikelets. When backlit by the sun this is a beautiful grass. Good erosion control grass.	Purple muhly is an excellent forage for wildlife. Ripe seeds are eaten by several kinds of seed-eating birds & small mammals. Grass parts are used as nesting & denning material.
Purple triplasis *Triplasis purpurea*	This diminutive attractive grass with the small purplish seed head prefers sandy areas.	Purple triplasis provides fairly good grazing & seed crop for granivorous birds & other kinds of wildlife.
Purple-top grass *Tridens flavus*	Tall, slender bunch grass with elegant purplish seed head. Very graceful appearance.	Purple-top grass provides fairly good grazing & forage for wildlife. Parts of the grass are used for nesting & denning material. Larval host plant for Cross-line skipper, Large wood nymph, Little Glassywing & Broad-winged skipper.

Table A.5
Native Plants of Texas

Please note that each two-page "spread" is divided into a top half (with plants' growing information) and a bottom half (with plants' ornamental and wildlife values). Numbered regions correspond to the Texas Ecoregion map on page 11.

Species	Ecological Region 1	2	3	4	5	6	7	8	9	10	Habit Height	Flower	Fruit	Sun Exposure	Habitat	Soils and Moisture Regime
Rio Grande lovegrass *Eragrostis palmeri*						x					Grass 1'-2 ½' Warm-season, tufted perennial	Flowering spikelets grayish-green turning purplish. Sept. Nov.	Seeds. Sets seed shortly after flowering	Full sun, part shade	Prefers open grassy areas in far south Texas.	Well-drained, xeric to mesic. Sands, loams & clays.
Sand big bluestem *Andropogon gerardi v. chrysocomus*				x	x		x	x	x	x	Grass 5'-8' Warm-season perennial bunch grass. Dormant in winter	Flowering spikelets darker & hairier turning yellowish. Aug.-Nov.	Seeds. Sets seed shortly after flowering	Full sun, part shade	Prefers open sandy soils in western portion of Texas.	Mesic-xeric, well-drained. Sands & sandy loams.
Sand dropseed *Sporobolus cryptandrus*		x	x	x	x	x	x	x	x	x	Grass 2'-5' Warm-season perennial	Flowering spikelets light brown to purplish tinged. May-Nov.	Seeds. Sets seed soon after flowering	Full sun, part shade	Prefers sandy soil, also very common along roadsides.	Well-drained, xeric. Sands & sandy loams.
Seep muhly *Muhlenbergia reverchonii*				x	x		x	x			Grass 1'-3' Warm-season perennial	Flowering spikelets green to golden tan. Aug.-Nov.	Seeds. Sept.-Dec.	Full sun, a little shade O.K.	Prefers rocky soils with limestone base often in seep areas.	Well-drained, mesic. Calcareous soils, clays, limestone based soils.
Showy chloris *Chloris virgata*		x	x	x	x	x	x	x	x	x	Grass 12" Annual	Flowering spikelets yellowish in finger-like arrangement. May-Sept.	Seeds. Sets seed shortly after flowering	Full sun, part shade	Prefers heavy sandy or gravelly soils of disturbed areas, along roadsides, lawns & parks.	Well-drained, mesic. Sands, heavy.
Showy chloris (Multi-flowered false-rhodesgrass) *Trichloris pluriflora*		x									Grass 2'-3' Warm-season perennial	Flowering spikelets tawny turning silvery white. July-Sept.	Seeds. Aug.-Oct.	Full sun	Prefers low areas.	Mesic, seasonal poor drainage O.K. Silts or clays.

Species	Ornamental Value	Wildlife Value
Rio Grande lovegrass *Eragrostis palmeri*	Attractive tufted perennial grass that grows only in the Rio Grande Valley. This species has a very pretty seed head.	Rio Grande lovegrass provides fair forage for wildlife. Some seed-eating birds dine on the ripe seeds. Grass parts are used as nesting & denning material.
Sand big bluestem *Andropogon gerardi v. chrysocomus*	This big prairie perennial can be used as a meadow grass with wild-flowers, a pocket tallgrass prairie or a garden accent in sandy areas. Adds a dramatic component. Needs sandy soils with moisture present. Good erosion control. Seed heads very hairy.	Provides good cover & food for many species of wildlife. Grass parts used as nesting & denning material. Larval host plant of Delaware Skipper, Dusted Skipper, Bunchgrass Skipper, Large Wood Nymph, Cobweb, Clouded & Beard grass skippers.
Sand dropseed *Sporobolus cryptandrus*	This erect tufted perennial grass with elegant flower head having light brown to purple-tinged spikelets. Prefers sands but does well in disturbed areas with other types of soils.	Reddish orange seeds are eaten by many granivorous birds. Provides only fair to poor grazing for larger wildlife. Grass parts used as denning & nesting material.
Seep muhly *Muhlenbergia reverchonii*	This is a very attractive delicate-headed grass with curly-cue leaves bunched at the base.	Seep muhly offers fair forage for small seed-eating birds. Leaves are used as nesting & denning material.
Showy chloris *Chloris virgata*	This grass is very attractive in shape & color. It can become weedy.	Showy chloris provides excellent forage during late summer for a variety of herbivores. Seeds are eaten by several species of granivorous birds. Grass parts are used as nesting & denning material.
Showy chloris (Multi-flowered false-rhodesgrass) *Trichloris pluriflora*	Highly ornamental grass with a very showy flower head. Especially striking when backlit by the sun. Makes an excellent accent plant for any garden	Provides cover for small animals. Ripe seeds eaten by granivorous birds & small rodents. Grass parts used as nesting & denning material.

Table A.5
Native Plants of Texas

Please note that each two-page "spread" is divided into a top half (with plants' growing information) and a bottom half (with plants' ornamental and wildlife values).
Numbered regions correspond to the Texas Ecoregion map on page 11.

Species	Ecological Region 1 2 3 4 5 6 7 8 9 10	Habit Height	Flower	Fruit	Sun Exposure	Habitat	Soils and Moisture Regime
Sideoats grama *Bouteloua curtipendula*	X X X X X X X X X X	Grass 2'-3' Warm-season perennial bunch grass. Dormant in winter	Spikelets, yellowish, arranged down along stem. May-Oct.	Seeds. June-Nov.	Full sun, part shade, dappled shade	Tolerates a variety of open places through-out state. Does well in disturbed areas. Not as common in eastern forests.	Well-drained, mesic-xeric. Sands, loams & clays, both limestone & igneous soils.
Slender grama *Bouteloua repens*	X	Grass ½'-2' Perennial	Flowering spikelets greenish to yellowish. April-Dec.	Seeds. May-Dec.	Full sun	Prefers open or brushy pastures & road rights-of-way, often found along streams & banks.	Well-drained, mesic to xeric. Sands, loams & clays.
Slim tridens *Tridens muticus v. elongatus*	X X X	Grass 1'-2' Warm-season perennial	Flowering spikelets greenish turning to tan. Aug.-Nov.	Seeds. Sept.-Nov.	Full sun, part shade	Prefers open clayey soils, but sometimes found on sandy sites.	Well-drained, xeric. Sands, sandy loams, gravelly clays.
Spike dropseed *Sporobolus contractus*	X X X	Grass 2'-3' Warm-season perennial	Flowering spikelets pale green in narrow-contract-ed panicle. July-Nov.	Seeds. Aug.-Nov.	Full sun	Prefers open sandy or gravelly sites, also slopes.	Well-drained, xeric-mesic. Sands, loams, clays, also calcareous soils.
Split-beard bluestem *Andropogon ternarius*	X X X X X	Grass 1½'-4' Warm-season perennial	Flowering spikelets green to silvery gold. Aug.-Nov.	Seeds. Sets seed shortly after flowering	Full sun, part shade	Prefers open areas & woodland edges, cut over woodland pastures.	Mesic, well-drained. Sands & sandy loams.
Sugarcane plumegrass *Erianthus giganteus*	X X X X X	Grass 6'-10' Warm-season perennial, dies back in winter	Flowering spikelets green turning peach. Sept.-Nov.	Seeds. Sets seed shortly after flowering	Full sun, part shade	Prefers moist areas near streams & lakes, swales, swamps & bogs.	Mesic-hydric, poor drainage O.K. Sands, loams & clays.

Species	Ornamental Value	Wildlife Value
Sideoats grama *Bouteloua curtipendula*	Our state grass is a strong perennial & works well as a garden accent. Competes well with short grasses but not tall-grass prairie grasses. Great choice for wildflower meadow garden.	Provides good grazing for wildlife & an abundance of bird seed for seed-eating birds of several varieties. Food available spring, summer & fall. Grass parts used as nesting & denning material. Larval host plant for Dotted skipper & Green skipper.
Slender grama *Bouteloua repens*	Tufted perennial grass with slender stems & perky seed heads. Good grass to mix with South Texas wildflowers.	Ripe seeds are eaten by several species of birds. Various parts of grass are used as nesting & denning material. Provides forage to a fair extent to grazers.
Slim tridens *Tridens muticus v. elongatus*	This slim tufted perennial grass is highly drought tolerant.	Slim tridens offers fair forage for birds & other wildlife. Grass parts are used as nesting & denning material. This grass is also grazed by mule deer.
Spike dropseed *Sporobolus contractus*	This tufted perennial grass frequently grows in sands, but also does well in calcareous soils. Has an attractive spike-like flower head.	Spike dropseed provides fair forage for wildlife. Sparrows & finches will eat the ripe seeds. Grass parts are used for denning & nesting material.
Split-beard bluestem *Andropogon ternarius*	This beautiful grass is its most beautiful in the autumn backlit by the sun. A good meadow grass planted with wildflowers.	Provides food & cover for many species of wild birds & mammals. Culms, leaves are used as nesting & denning material. Butterflies use grass as shelter on windy days. Larval host plant of several skippers.
Sugarcane plumegrass *Erianthus giganteus*	Excellent grass near a large water garden or near a small stream or lake. Seed heads are gorgeous, glowing a deep peach esp. when backlit by the sun.	While not an excellent forage grass for wildlife, it provides good cover for both terrestrial & small aquatic animals. Grass parts are used as nesting & denning material.

Table A.5
Native Plants of Texas

Please note that each two-page "spread" is divided into a top half (with plants' growing information) and a bottom half (with plants' ornamental and wildlife values). Numbered regions correspond to the Texas Ecoregion map on page 11.

Species	Ecological Region 1 2 3 4 5 6 7 8 9 10	Habit Height	Flower	Fruit	Sun Exposure	Habitat	Soils and Moisture Regime
Switchgrass *Panicum virgatum*	X X X X X X X X X X	Grass 3'-6' Warm-season perennial bunch grass	Flowering spikelets green turning rich gold. Aug.-Sept.	Seeds. Oct.-Nov.	Full sun, part shade	Prefers seasonally moist, open areas throughout Texas.	Moist. Seasonal poor drainage O.K. Sands, loams & clays.
Tall dropseed *Sporobolus asper*	X X X X X X X	Grass 3'-5' Warm-season perennial	Flowering spikelets light green to straw, in contracted panicles. Aug.-Oct.	Seeds. Sept.-Dec.	Full sun, some shade O.K.	Prefers open, rocky prairie sites, open meadows & woods.	Mesic, tolerates dry soils. Sands, loams, clays; likes limestone soils.
Tanglehead *Heteropogon contortus*	X X X X	Grass 3"-2 ½' Warm-season perennial	Flowering spikelets yellowish tan, turning brownish. March-Dec.	Seeds. Sets seed shortly after flowering	Full sun	Prefers grasslands of lower Texas Gulf Coast, also mountains of West Texas.	Mesic-xeric, well-drained. Sands & sandy loams.
Texas bluegrass *Poa arachnifera*	X X X X X X X X X	Grass 12"-2 ½' Cool season perennial	Flowering spikelets bluish-green to mauve. April-May	Seeds. May	Full sun, part shade	Grows in prairies & openings of woods.	Mesic. Sands, loams & clays.
Texas bristlegrass *Setaria texana*	X X	Grass 1 ½'-3' Perennial	Flowering spikelets greenish to greenish yellow. Year-long	Seeds. Year-long	Full sun, part shade	Prefers open grassy areas in South Texas & southern part of Edwards Plateau.	Well-drained, xeric to mesic. Sands, loams & clays.
Texas cupgrass *Eriochloa sericea*	X X X X X	Grass 3'-4' Perennial	Flowering spikelets green turning yellowish. March-Aug.	Seeds. April-Nov.	Full sun, some shade O.K.	Prefers prairies & grassy openings in scrub woodlands.	Well-drained, mesic. Sands, loams & clays; likes limestone soils.

Species	Ornamental Value	Wildlife Value
Switchgrass *Panicum virgatum*	Gorgeous tall-grass can be used as dramatic accent plant. Turns deep, rich golden color in fall. Has airy, filigreed seedhead. Can also be used in small pocket prairie. Does great in Houston, loves the extra water.	Provides fair grazing for wildlife, seeds sought after by seed-eating birds. Excellent sparrow food in winter. Provides good protective cover and nesting & denning material. Good place for butterflies to get out of the wind. Larval host plant for Delaware skipper.
Tall dropseed *Sporobolus asper*	There are many varieties of this species that are adapted to the various soils.	Provides good forage for seed-eating mammals & birds, also fair grazing for larger mammals. Grass parts used as nesting & denning material.
Tanglehead *Heteropogon contortus*	Tanglehead is a tuft-forming grass with curly sharp awns, making it an interesting looking grass.	While not excellent forage for wildlife, grass parts are used as nesting & denning material. A few birds will eat the ripe seeds.
Texas bluegrass *Poa arachnifera*	This is an absolutely beautiful grass, in both color & shape of flower head. Two color forms are blue-green and copper mauve.	Provides fair grazing for wildlife & seeds for sparrows & other granivorous birds & small mammals. Grass parts used as nesting & denning material.
Texas bristlegrass *Setaria texana*	Tufted perennial with erect stem & smaller flower head than plains bristlegrass. Leaves are dark green, spikelets are lime-green.	Texas bristlegrass provides only fair forage for grazing wildlife, but sparrows, finches & buntings forage on the ripe seeds.
Texas cupgrass *Eriochloa sericea*	Texas cupgrass can be used as a meadow grass with wildflowers or as a pocket prairie grass.	Texas cupgrass provides good cover & excellent forage for many species of wildlife. Grass parts are used as nesting & denning material by birds & small mammals.

Table A.5
Native Plants of Texas

Please note that each two-page "spread" is divided into a top half (with plants' growing information) and a bottom half (with plants' ornamental and wildlife values). Numbered regions correspond to the Texas Ecoregion map on page 11.

Species	1	2	3	4	5	6	7	8	9	10	Habit Height	Flower	Fruit	Sun Exposure	Habitat	Soils and Moisture Regime
Texas grama *Bouteloua rigidiseta*	x	x	x	x	x	x	x	x			Grass ½'-1½' Warm-season perennial	Flowering spikelets, perky & star-shaped, turns from green to silvery gold. April-Nov.	Seeds. May-Nov.	Full sun	Prefers grasslands, grassy woods openings, road rights-of-way & moist slopes.	Well-drained, xeric to mesic. Sands, loams & clays.
Tobossa grass *Hilaria mutica*					x	x	x	x	x	x	Grass 1'-2' Warm-season perennial	Flowering spikelets greenish to golden. April-Aug.	Seeds. Sets seed shortly after flowering	Full sun	Prefers dry rocky slopes, & on level plains & plateau.	Well-drained, xeric. Thin limestone soils, clays & caliche type soils.
Torrey muhly *Muhlenbergia torreyi*						x	x	x	x	x	Grass 6"-13" Warm-season perennial	Flowering spikelets yellowish coral in open flower heads. May-Oct.	Seeds. Sets seed shortly after flowering	Full sun, a little shade O.K.	Prefers dry, sandy mesas & valleys at lower elevations in the Trans-Pecos.	Well-drained, xeric. Sands & sandy loams.
Vine-mesquite *Panicum obtusum*			x	x	x	x	x	x	x	x	Grass 1'-2' Warm-season perennial	Flowering spikelets greenish. June-Oct.	Seeds. Sets seed soon after flowering	Full sun, part shade	Prefers clayey lowland pastures, swales & ditches that periodically dry out.	Mesic to xeric, periodic poor drainage O.K. Clays.
Western wheatgrass *Agropyron smithii*					x		x	x	x	x	Grass 1'-3' Cool-season perennial	Flowering spikelets bluish green. May-June then again Aug.-Sept.	Seeds. Sets seed shortly after flowering	Full sun, part shade	Prefers low, moist flats or flood plains, great in the High Plains region.	Moist, seasonal poor drainage O.K. Sands, loams & clays.
White tridens *Tridens albescens*	x	x	x	x	x	x	x	x	x	x	Grass 1½'-3' Perennial	Flowering spikelets greenish turning silvery white. March-Nov.	Seeds. April-Nov.	Full sun, part shade	Prefers clayey soils along ditches, in swales & areas that get abundance of drainage water.	Mesic. Clay loams & clays.

Species	Ornamental Value	Wildlife Value
Texas grama *Bouteloua rigidiseta*	Short, highly attractive tufted perennial grass with slender weak stems & very eye-catching flowering spikelets. When backlit, they catch the rays of the sun & glisten like little shooting stars.	A number of small birds will eat the ripe seeds. Perhaps not ever enough of it to provide much forage for the larger grazers.
Tobossa grass *Hilaria mutica*	Tobossa grass does very well in xeric conditions. It is a short clump-forming perennial with strong underground wiry stems.	Provides only fair to poor grazing for wildlife. Seeds are not plentiful but are eaten by various granivorous birds. Grass parts are used as nesting & denning material by a variety of small wildlife species.
Torrey muhly *Muhlenbergia torreyi*	This interesting grass dies out in the middle & forms a circle or ring of new growth. It is highly attractive as the ring breaks into separate clumps. Very distinctive looking, a conversation piece.	Torrey muhly makes excellent cover for small birds & mammals. Ripe seeds are eaten by several species of granivorous birds. Small rodents also eat the seeds. Parts are used as nesting & denning material.
Vine-mesquite *Panicum obtusum*	This warm-season perennial grass typically has erect stems from a knotty base. Narrow inflorescence, leaves bluish-green. Florets are distinctively rounded.	Vine-mesquite provides good grazing for wildlife. Seeds are eaten by several species of granivorous birds.
Western wheatgrass *Agropyron smithii*	Very handsome bluish-green grass that stays colorful all winter. Prefers cool summers. Needs a little watering in the summer. Can get aggressive with too much water though. Forms tight sod so not good to plant with wildflowers. Outcompetes weeds.	Western wheatgrass provides good protective cover for all sorts of animals. Grass parts are used as denning & nesting material. Many species of granivorous birds forage on the ripe seeds. Larval host plant for the Golden skipper.
White tridens *Tridens albescens*	Tufted perennial grass with attractive whitish seed heads with purplish tips. This pretty grass is good mixed in with other grasses & wildflowers.	White tridens provides fair grazing for wildlife. Seed-eating birds forage on the ripe seeds. Grass parts used as nesting & denning material.

Table A.5
Native Plants of Texas

Please note that each two-page "spread" is divided into a top half (with plants' growing information) and a bottom half (with plants' ornamental and wildlife values). Numbered regions correspond to the Texas Ecoregion map on page 11.

Species	1	2	3	4	5	6	7	8	9	10	Habit Height	Flower	Fruit	Sun Exposure	Habitat	Soils and Moisture Regime
Woolly brome *Bromus lanatipes*										x	Grass 1'-3' Warm-season perennial	Spikelets yellowish green, nodding at maturity. Aug.-Oct.	Seeds. Sept.-Oct.	Full sun, a little shade O.K.	Prefers mountain regions of the Trans-Pecos at higher elevations.	Well-drained, xeric. Igneous soils, sands & sandy loams.
Woolspike balsamscale *Elyonurus barbiculmis*										x	Grass 1'-2' Warm-season perennial	Flowering spikelets greenish to silvery white. June-Nov.	Seeds. Sets seed shortly after flowering	Full sun, a little shade O.K.	Prefers rocky slopes at elevations of 4000' & above on low rolling hills.	Well-drained, xeric. Sands & loams; prefers igneous soils.

Acanthus Family – Acanthaceae

Species	1	2	3	4	5	6	7	8	9	10	Habit Height	Flower	Fruit	Sun Exposure	Habitat	Soils and Moisture Regime
Flame acanthus *Anisacanthus insignis*										x	Shrub 2'-4' Deciduous	Showy pinkish-coral narrowly tubular flowers. June-Sept.	Capsule with seeds. Aug.-Nov.	Full sun, part sun, dappled shade	Prefers rich soils in thickets, also along aroyos, dry stream beds & canyons in West Texas from 3000'-5000'.	Mesic, well-drained. Sands, loams & clays, likes limestone soils.
Agarita *Berberis trifoliolata*	x				x	x	x	x		x	Shrub 3'-8' Evergreen	Showy yellow flowers. Feb.-March	Berries, red. May-July	Full sun, part shade	Prefers rocky slopes & flats of pastures, thickets & open woods.	Xeric, well-drained. Sands, loams or clays.
Red barbery *Berberis haematocarpa*										x	Shrub 3'-12' Evergreen	Showy racemes of yellow flowers. March-May	Berries, deep red. May-Aug.	Full sun, part shade	Prefers higher desert grasslands & canyons in West Texas from 4600'-7200' in elevation.	Well-drained, xeric. Sands, loams & clays.

Species	Ornamental Value	Wildlife Value
Woolly brome *Bromus lanatipes*	A clump-forming perennial grass which doesn't attain more than 3'. Leaf sheaths are woolly & spikelets are 5- to 9-flowered. They nod perkily at maturity.	This grass is fairly palatable to grazers. Grass parts used as nesting & denning material. Ripe seeds are eaten by several sparrows & finches as well as small mammals.
Woolspike balsamscale *Elyonurus barbiculmis*	This is a highly attractive erect perennial with long, hairy slender basal leaves with fragrant lemon odor. Roots are reddish in color.	This grass is not very palatable, but plays important role in grassland ecology. Seeds are eaten by several granivorous mammals & birds. Grass parts are used as nesting & denning material.
Acanthus Family – Acanthaceae		
Flame acanthus *Anisacanthus insignis*	Showy, profusely-blooming shrub with bright pinkish-coral blossoms that bloom steadily all summer. Shrub is irregularly branched. Very drought-tolerant once established.	Flowers attract myriads of butterflies, moths & other insects throughout the summer. Hummingbirds of various species feed on the nectar also. Leaves are browsed by mule deer & antelope. Larval host plant for crescentspot butterflies.
Barberry Family – Berberidaceae		
Agarita *Berberis trifoliolata*	Well-know striking evergreen shrub with the spiny blue-green trifoliate leaves. This plant makes a good hedge. Flowers bloom very early in the spring.	Early blooming golden yellow flowers offer very early nectar for all kinds of insects. Excellent cover & nesting place due to spiny leaves. Deer rarely browse this plant unless they are hungry. Birds & mammals of several species gorge on the ripe fruit.
Red barberry *Berberis haematocarpa*	Highly attractive spiny-leaved shrub with snappy red berries. Flowers are also highly attractive in the spring. Can be used as a ground cover. Or it can serve as a hedge.	Flowers attract many insects such as bees, butterflies, diurnal moths. Fruits are also sought after by many species of game & songbirds. Makes a good cover & nesting plant for small birds due to thorns.

Table A.5
Native Plants of Texas

Please note that each two-page "spread" is divided into a top half (with plants' growing information) and a bottom half (with plants' ornamental and wildlife values). Numbered regions correspond to the Texas Ecoregion map on page 11.

Bech Family – Fagaceae

Species	Ecological Region 1 2 3 4 5 6 7 8 9 10	Habit Height	Flower	Fruit	Sun Exposure	Habitat	Soils and Moisture Regime
Allegheny chinquapin *Castanea pumila*	x x	Shrub, large 15'-30' Deciduous	Showy white male catkins in clusters, female flowers inconspicuous on same tree, fragrant. March-June	Spike-like burs with nuts. Aug.-Sept.	Full sun, part shade	Prefers open woodlands & thickets in East Texas & Upper Texas Coast. Occurs on dryish, upland sandy soils.	Well-drained, mesic-xeric. Sands, sandy loams.
Havard shin-oak *Quercus havardii*	x x x	Shrub 2'-3' Deciduous	Inconspicuous male & female catkins. April-May	Acorns, large, produced each year. Sept.-Oct.	Full sun, part shade	Prefers sandy plains in the lower Panhandle.	Well-drained, xeric. Sands, deep.

Borage Family – Boraginaceae

Species	Ecological Region 1 2 3 4 5 6 7 8 9 10	Habit Height	Flower	Fruit	Sun Exposure	Habitat	Soils and Moisture Regime
Plume coldenia *Tiquilia greggii*	x	Shrub 1'-2' Deciduous	Hot pink, magenta to purple flowers nestled in whitish gray leaves. June-Oct.	Nutlets, dry & ovate. Aug.-Nov.	Full sun	Prefers limestone habitats of desertic mountains, slopes & flats, rocky hillsides & ravines from 2000'-4200'.	Well-drained, xeric. Prefers calcareous soils & limestone substrates.

Buddleia Family – Buddleiaceae

Species	Ecological Region 1 2 3 4 5 6 7 8 9 10	Habit Height	Flower	Fruit	Sun Exposure	Habitat	Soils and Moisture Regime
Butterfly bush *Buddleia marrubifolia*	x	Shrub 3'-5' Deciduous	Densely woolly-white flower clusters with yellow-orange blossoms. June-Oct.	Capsules with numerous small seeds. Aug.-Nov.	Full sun, part shade	Prefers limestone soils of the foothills & arroyos in desertic mountains of west Texas from 1800'-3800'.	Well-drained, xeric. Sands, loams & clays, especially limestone substrates.

Species	Ornamental Value	Wildlife Value
Beech Family – Fagaceae		
Allegheny chinquapin *Castanea pumila*	A large deciduous spreading shrub or small tree with simple, shiny green leaves with white hairy underside. Leaves are attractively scalloped on edges. Bark in distinctively furrowed. Mildly resistant to Chestnut blight.	Fragrant flowers attract a wide variety of insects. Catkins are also eaten by birds. Nuts are delicious & sweet & highly sought after by several species of gamebirds, woodpeckers & jays, as well as small mammals.
Havard shin-oak *Quercus havardii*	Low shrub which forms thickets in deep sands. Rather hard to get established. Leaves are muted green & leathery with furry undersides, quite variable in shape. Often grows to small tree. This is an Endangered species; acorns must not be collected.	Catkins are eaten by many species of birds in the spring. Acorns are eaten by javalina, prairie-chickens & quail. Not considered a very good browse plants. Leaves may be toxic to livestock.
Borage Family – Boraginaceae		
Plume coldenia *Tiquilia greggii*	Absolutely beautiful small gray-leaved shrub with several small magenta flowers peeking out from woolly spherical flower clusters. A great border plant. Good in small desert rock garden.	Flowers attract insects of several varieties. Nutlets are eaten by a few species of rodents & other small mammals.
Buddleia Family – Buddleiaceae		
Butterfly bush *Buddleia marrubifolia*	This is a gorgeous ornamental shrub with fuzzy, pale gray-green leaves & small orange-red lantana-like flowers. Not very cold tolerant. Blooms profusely for a long time.	Butterfly bush is highly attractive shrub that attracts myriads of butter-flies for much of the summer, as its name implies. Deer & antelope will browse readily on the leaves.

Please note that each two-page "spread" is divided into a top half (with plants' growing information) and a bottom half (with plants' ornamental and wildlife values). Numbered regions correspond to the Texas Ecoregion map on page 11.

Species	Ecological Region 1 2 3 4 5 6 7 8 9 10	Habit Height	Flower	Fruit	Sun Exposure	Habitat	Soils and Moisture Regime
Buddleya Family – Buddleiaceae							
Tepozan *Buddleja sessiliflora*	x (4)	Shrub 3'-7' Evergreen	Pretty greenish-yellow flowers borne in glomerules, fragrant. April-July	Capsules, small. June-Sept.	Full sun, part shade	Prefers sandbars & banks along resacas & in palm groves. Found only in Lower Rio Grande Valley.	Moist. Sand, sandy loams, clays. Prefers sand.
Caltrop Family – Zygophyllaceae							
Creosote bush *Larrea tridentata*	x (1)	Shrub 4'-10' Evergreen	Showy yellow flowers, 1/2" across. May-Sept., sometimes all year	Capsules, small & rounded, woolly with white to reddish hairs. July-Oct.	Full sun, part shade	Prefers alluvial hard pan soils of Chihuahuan Desert region.	Xeric, well-drained. Sands, loams & clays (hard pan).
Catalpa Family – Bignoniaceae							
Yellow trumpets *Tecoma stans*	x (1), x (5)	Shrub 3'-6' Deciduous	Showy yellow tubular flowers in clusters. April-Nov.	Capsules with winged seeds. June-Dec.	Full sun, part shade	Prefers rocky bluffs, slopes & canyons in desertic mountains of south Trans-Pecos form 2000'-5200' in elevation.	Well-drained, xeric. Sands, loams, prefers limestone substrates.
Citrus Family – Rutaceae							
Texas torchwood *Amyris texana*	x (1), x (4)	Shrub 3'-7' Evergreen	Panicles of greenish-white flowers, fragrant. Feb-June, also Sept.-Nov. depending on rains	Drupes, purple-black with one seed. June-Dec.	Full sun, part shade	Prefers brushy areas, locally abundant in chaparral.	Mesic-xeric, well-drained. Sands, loams & clays.

Species	Ornamental Value	Wildlife Value
Buddleya Family – Buddleiaceae		
Tepozan *Buddleja sessiliflora*	Attractive unarmed shrub with stems & young leaves covered with dense white pubescence (short fuzzy hairs). Leaves are entire with fine teeth on edges.	Several kinds of insects, especially butterflies, sip nectar from the nectar-laden flowers. White-tailed deer will browse on the leaves. For attracting butterflies, this plant is fantastic.
Caltrop Family – Zygophyllaceae		
Creosote bush *Larrea tridentata*	Dark green aromatic shrub with beautiful yellow flowers & unusual whitish fruits. Very drought-tolerant. There are no thorns & it can be pruned into desired shape. Light refreshing fragrance. Long lived. Other plants have a hard time growing underneath.	Insects of several varieties are attracted to the yellow flowers. This makes an excellent protective cover & nesting shrub. Leaves are consumed by various small mammals & antelope. Birds eat the flower buds.
Catalpa Family – Bignoniaceae		
Yellow trumpets *Tecoma stans*	Extremely ornamental shrub with showy yellow trumpet-shaped flowers. Attractive green compound leaves. Excellent plant for a rock garden or as an accent plant. Blooms off & on all season. Not too winter hardy, needs a protected area of garden.	Flowers attract myriads of insects. Excellent bee plant. Hummers will also come to these flowers. Leaves & flowers are browsed by several small animals. Seeds are eaten by a few small mammals. Larval host plant of Dogface butterfly.
Citrus Family – Rutaceae		
Texas torchwood *Amyris texana*	Much-branched aromatic rounded shrub with trifoliate leaves. Flowers are highly fragrant. The plant is winter-hardy to Houston.	Fragrant flowers attract many kinds of insects. White-tailed deer occasionally browse the leaves. Several species of birds are very fond of the fruit.

Table A.5
Native Plants of Texas

Please note that each two-page "spread" is divided into a top half (with plants' growing information) and a bottom half (with plants' ornamental and wildlife values).
Numbered regions correspond to the Texas Ecoregion map on page 11.

Elm Family – Ulmaceae

Species	Ecological Region 1 2 3 4 5 6 7 8 9 10	Habit Height	Flower	Fruit	Sun Exposure	Habitat	Soils and Moisture Regime
Granjeno *Celtis pallida*	x x x x	Shrub 10'-18' Evergreen	Inconspicuous greenish white flowers. Feb.-May	Drupes, yellow to orange, rounded. May-July	Full sun, part shade	Prefers mesas, foothills & thickets & brushlands.	Xeric, well-drained. Sands, loams & clays.

Ephedra Family – Ephedraceae

Species	Ecological Region 1 2 3 4 5 6 7 8 9 10	Habit Height	Flower	Fruit	Sun Exposure	Habitat	Soils and Moisture Regime
Joint-fir *Ephedra antisyphilitica*	x x x x x x	Shrub 3'-6' Evergreen	Greenish-yellow to reddish flowers. May-June	Males have tiny cones, females, red berries. July-Aug.	Full sun, part shade	Prefers gravelly or rocky soil on plains, hills, breaks, rimrock in arroyos, ravines & canyons.	Xeric, well-drained. Sands, loams, clays & caliche-type soils.
Torrey joint-fir *Ephedra torreyana*	x	Shrub 2'-3' Evergreen	Inconspicuous staminate spikes. April	Female cones, brownish with paired seeds. May-June	Full sun, part shade	Prefers gypseous & saline desertic habitats in sandy or rocky substrates at elevations of 2000'-6000'.	Xeric, well-drained. Sands, loams, clays; tolerates saline & gypseous soils.

Euphorbia Family – Euphorbiaceae

Species	Ecological Region 1 2 3 4 5 6 7 8 9 10	Habit Height	Flower	Fruit	Sun Exposure	Habitat	Soils and Moisture Regime
Candelilla *Euphorbia antisyphilitica*	x	Shrub 1'-3' Evergreen	Inconspicuous white & brown flowers. May-Oct.	Capsules. July-Nov.	Full sun, part shade	Prefers rocky or gravelly slopes, ridges & hills, usually on limestone substrates from 1100'-3800' in elevation.	Xeric, well-drained. Sands, loams & clays.

Figwort Family – Scrophulariaceae

Species	Ecological Region 1 2 3 4 5 6 7 8 9 10	Habit Height	Flower	Fruit	Sun Exposure	Habitat	Soils and Moisture Regime
Cenizo *Leucophyllum frutescens*	x x	Shrub 4'-8' Evergreen	Showy lavender to light purple flowers, almost bell-shaped. May-Oct.	Capsules. Sept.-Dec.	Full sun, a little shade O.K.	Prefers rocky limestone hills, bluffs, ravines, arroyos & brushlands.	Well-drained, xeric. Sands, loams & clays, likes limestone soils.

Species	Ornamental Value	Wildlife Value
Elm Family – Ulmaceae		
Granjeno *Celtis pallida*	Spiny, spreading, densely-branched shrub with deep green leaves having slightly scalloped edges. Very drought tolerant.	Flowers attract myriads of insects: bees, butterflies & diurnal moths. Fruits relished by all kind of critters: wrens, cardinals, pyrrhuloxias, mockingbirds, quail, raccoons, coyotes, rabbits. Leaves & stems browsed by deer. Larval host plant of Snout butterflies.
Ephedra Family – Ephedraceae		
Joint-fir *Ephedra antisyphilitica*	Interesting shrub with an erect or spreading habit. It can be hard to grow, but worth the work. Definitely keep it if you already have it on your property. Branches are evergreen with tiny scale leaves. Female plants have red berries. Don't overwater.	Birds will forage on the red berries. Deer love to browse on this plant so you might want to hide it under something thorny.
Torrey joint-fir *Ephedra torreyana*	Interesting slender-jointed shrub that forms clumps usually under another thorny tree or shrub. Sometimes hard to grow, but worth it. Branches are evergreen with tiny scale leaves. Female plants have red berries. Don't overwater.	Birds will forage on the red berries. Deer love to browse on this plant so you might want to hide it under something thorny. Berry-like cones eaten by quail & turkey.
Euphorbia Family – Euphorbiaceae		
Candelilla *Euphorbia antisyphilitica*	Forms grayish clumps of stems topped with unusual flowers. Stems are wand-like, fleshy or rubbery with waxy coating. This makes an interesting accent planting in a desert garden. Not cold hardy, but good in a pot.	Several species of insects are attracted to the flowers.
Figwort Family – Scrophulariaceae		
Cenizo *Leucophyllum frutescens*	Drought-hardy shrub with pretty gray leaves & long-blooming magenta to lavender flowers. The silvery-gray leaves lend a highly ornamental flair to this shrub.	The showy lavender flowers attract several kinds of insects. This dense shrub offers good cover & safe nesting site for birds. The leaves are not readily browsed by white-tailed deer. Larval host plant of the Theona Checkerspot.

Table A.5
Native Plants of Texas

Please note that each two-page "spread" is divided into a top half (with plants' growing information) and a bottom half (with plants' ornamental and wildlife values). Numbered regions correspond to the Texas Ecoregion map on page 11.

Species	Ecological Region 1 2 3 4 5 6 7 8 9 10	Habit Height	Flower	Fruit	Sun Exposure	Habitat	Soils and Moisture Regime
Violet silver-leaf *Leucophyllum candidum*	x (10)	Shrub 2'-3' Evergreen	Showy purple violet flowers. Sept.-Oct., sometimes in spring & summer after rains	Capsules, 2-valved with numerous seeds. Nov.-Dec.	Full sun, a little shade O.K.	Prefers rocky, gravelly limestone habitats.	Xeric, well-drained. Sands, loams & clays, rocky limestone soils preferred.
Frankenia Family – Frankeniaceae							
Brush holly *Xylosma flexuosa*	x (1) x (6)	Shrub 6'-10' Evergreen	Small white male & female flowers. Year-long	Berries, small & red with eight seeds. Year-long	Part shade, dappled shade	Prefers chaparral & brushy areas, also palm groves.	Mesic, poor drainage O.K. Sands, loams & clays.
Frankenia Family – Frankeniaceae							
Fourwing saltbush *Atriplex canescens*	x (1) x (6) x x (9,10)	Shrub 3'-8' Evergreen	Pretty spikes of female flowers on separate trees. April-Oct.	Showy four-winged bracted yellowish fruit. Aug.-Sept.	Full sun, part shade	Prefers grassy uplands to sandy deserts or salt or alkali flats.	Well-drained, xeric. Sands, loams & clays. Grows in limestone, caliche-type soils; tolerates saline soils.
Winter fat *Eurotia lanata*	x x x (8,9,10)	Shrub 1'-3' Persistent to Evergreen	Small greenish male & female flowers on same plant. April-Aug.	Showy fruit, silvery white dense furry tufts. Aug.-Oct.	Full sun, part shade	Prefers dry sub-alkaline soils of mesas & plains from 2000'-8000' in elevation in western Texas, the High Plains & Trans-Pecos.	Xeric, well-drained. Sands, loams, clays, caliche-type & lime-stone soils.

Species	Ornamental Value	Wildlife Value
Violet silver-leaf *Leucophyllum candidum*	Attractive dense gray-green shrub with beautiful purple violet flowers. Shrub is naturally dwarfed & needs no pruning.	Violet silver-leaf makes excellent protective cover & nesting shrub. Several kinds of insects are attracted to the flowers. The leaves are not browsed by mule deer or domestic livestock.
Frankenia Family – Frankeniaceae		
Brush holly *Xylosma flexuosa*	Slender, evergreen, thorny shrub or small tree with small white flowers & yellow & red berries. Highly ornamental shrub which blooms throughout the year.	Flowers full of nectar attracting an abundance of insects of many varieties. Fruits provide excellent food to birds & small mammals almost throughout the year.
Frankenia Family – Frankeniaceae		
Fourwing saltbush *Atriplex canescens*	An evergreen shrub with diffused branches, variable in shape. Female plants are more showy with their fall showy, yellow four-winged fruit covering the tree. This tree tolerates saline soils well and is quite drought tolerant.	This shrub is a valuable, palatable & nutritious food for wildlife. Fruit is eaten by scaled quail, porcupine, rock-squirrels, jack rabbits. Pollen from the flowers is sought after by bees & other many other kinds of insects.
Winter fat *Eurotia lanata*	Highly ornamental & gorgeous shrub in full fruit is backlit by the sun. Sports fuzzy pale bluish-green leaves & beautiful silvery white fruit. Good plant for erosion control. Highly drought-tolerant once established.	Plants only 1 year old bear highly nutritious seeds. Provides excellent forage for mule deer & elk, also for rabbits.

Table A.5
Native Plants of Texas

Please note that each two-page "spread" is divided into a top half (with plants' growing information) and a bottom half (with plants' ornamental and wildlife values). Numbered regions correspond to the Texas Ecoregion map on page 11.

Heath Family – Ericaceae

Species	1	2	3	4	5	6	7	8	9	10	Habit Height	Flower	Fruit	Sun Exposure	Habitat	Soils and Moisture Regime
Sweet-bells Leucothe (Fetter-bush) *Leucothoe racemosa*	x	x									Shrub 3'-12' Persistent	Showy racemes of pinkish urn-shaped flowers, all facing downward. April-June	Capsules with wingless seeds. Aug.-Sept.	Full sun	Prefers moist thickets & swamp forests, sunny lakeshores in East Texas, Upper Texas Coast.	Mesic-hydric. Sands, sandy loams, loams & clays, acid soils preferred.

Honeysuckle Family – Caprifoliaceae

Species	1	2	3	4	5	6	7	8	9	10	Habit Height	Flower	Fruit	Sun Exposure	Habitat	Soils and Moisture Regime
Coral-berry *Symphoricarpos orbiculata*	x	x	x	x		x					Shrub 1 1/2'-6' Deciduous	Showy, many-flowered greenish-white or pink, in terminal spikes. June-Aug.	Drupe, berry-like, pink to coral-red. Sept.-Oct.	Dappled shade, part shade	Prefers woods, thickets & streamside areas in eastern 1/3 of Texas.	Mesic, well-drained. Sands, loams & clays.
Maple-leaf viburnum (Arrow-wood) *Viburnum acerifolium*	x		x								Shrub 2'-6' Deciduous	Showy small white flowers in flattened flower clusters April-May	Drupes, red to purplish black, persistent. Aug.-Oct.	Part shade, dappled shade	Prefers moist woods & thickets of East Texas.	Well-drained, mesic. Sands, loams & clays. Likes acid soils.
Texas honeysuckle *Lonicera alba*					x	x		x		x	Shrub 4'-10' Deciduous	Showy white flowers. April-May	Berries, red. June-July	Full sun, part shade	Prefers rocky slopes, cliffs; also found in sandy soils, cedar brakes in Central, North Central Texas.	Well-drained, mesic. Sands, loams, & clays. Likes limestone soils.

Laurel Family – Lauraceae

Species	1	2	3	4	5	6	7	8	9	10	Habit Height	Flower	Fruit	Sun Exposure	Habitat	Soils and Moisture Regime
Sassafras *Sassafras albidum*	x										Shrub 15'-20' Deciduous	Showy yellow drooping clusters, before leaves sprout. March-April	Drupes, blue-black, lustrous. September	Full sun, part shade	Prefers sandy woods, old fields, on road cuts & along fence rows in eastern third of Texas.	Well-drained, mesic. Sands, loams & clays. Poor, dry upland soils tolerated.

Species	Ornamental Value	Wildlife Value
Heath Family – Ericaceae		
Sweet-bells Leucothoe (Fetter-bush) *Leucothoe racemosa*	Widely branching, erect shrub with racemes of pinkish white urn-shaped flowers. Leaves are simple, elliptic with finely toothed margins. Good understory tree for low woods & acid swamps. Quite ornamental.	This attractive shrub is NOT browsed by white-tailed deer.
Honeysuckle Family – Caprifoliaceae		
Coral-berry *Symphoricarpus orbiculata*	Hardy, slender erect thicket-forming shrub with brown shreddy bark & opposite oval-shaped leaves. Great erosion control plant. Highly ornamental.	Excellent cover shrub when bushy. Fruits are eaten by at least 12 species of birds including cardinals, bobwhite, quail, wild turkey bluebirds, robins, mockingbirds, thrashers & cedar waxwings.
Maple-leaf viburnum (Arrow-wood) *Viburnum acerifolium*	Thicket-forming shrubs with erect or ascending branches & attractive maple-like leaves. Quite ornamental with attractive flowers & fruits. Has excellent fall color of crimson to dark purple.	Flowers are popular with nectar-loving insects such as bees & butterflies. Fruits are relished by several species of birds. Foliage is browsed by white-tailed deer.
Texas honeysuckle *Lonicera alba*	This is a beautiful native honeysuckle. Flowers are showy in the spring & the red berries are beautiful while they last. Plant is drought tolerant in the Eastern Cross Timbers. This is not a difficult species to grow.	Flowers attract butterflies, bees & other insects. Translucent red fruits popular with bluebirds, cardinals, finches & sparrows, as well as neotropical migrants. Leaves browsed by white-tailed deer.
Laurel Family – Lauraceae		
Sassafras *Sassafras albidum*	Thinly branched, well-shaped aromatic shrub. Quite ornamental with variously shaped leaves. Leaves turn yellow, orange, & red in fall. Female plants put on better display. Not drought tolerant, good for East Texas only.	Blue black fruits are gobbled up by several species of birds, i.e., king birds, great-crested flycatchers, gray catbirds, brown thrashers, robins, bluebirds, vireos, warblers & sparrows. Larval host plant of Palamedes, Spicebush & Tiger swallowtail butterflies.

Table A.5
Native Plants of Texas

Please note that each two-page "spread" is divided into a top half (with plants' growing information) and a bottom half (with plants' ornamental and wildlife values). Numbered regions correspond to the Texas Ecoregion map on page 11.

Species	Ecological Region 1 2 3 4 5 6 7 8 9 10	Habit Height	Flower	Fruit	Sun Exposure	Habitat	Soils and Moisture Regime
Spicebush *Lindera benzoin*	x (7)	Shrub 10'-15' Deciduous	Small yellow-green flowers appear before leaves. March-April	Drupes, bright red. Aug.-Oct.	Part shade, dappled shade	Prefers rich wooded slopes & rocky areas along streams of the Edwards Plateau.	Well-drained, but moist. Loams, limestone & caliche-type soils.
Legume Family – Leguminosae							
Bee-brush *Aloysia gratissima*	x x x x (1-4) x x (5-6) x (8) x (10)	Shrub 4'-14' Persistent	Showy spikes of white flowers with yellow throats, very fragrant. March-Nov., especially after rains	Drupes, small with two nutlets. Aug.-Dec.	Full sun, part shade, dappled shade	Prefers rocky, gravelly limestone soils in chaparrals, thickets & arroyos. Found almost throughout Texas but may have been introduced in eastern portion of the state.	Moist, seasonal poor drainage O.K. Sands, loams, or clays.
Black dalea *Dalea frutescens*	x x (5-6) x x (7-8)	Shrub 1'-3' Deciduous	Showy magenta flowers. Aug.-Sept.	Leguminous pod. Oct.-Nov.	Full sun	Prefers dry limestone hills in brushy vegetation.	Well-drained, xeric. Sands, loams clays; likes limestone soils.
Canyon senna *Senna wislizenii*	x (10)	Shrub 4'-10' Deciduous	Showy golden yellow flowers in 6" clusters. May-July	Leguminous pods. July-Aug.	Full sun, part shade	Prefers igneous soils in Chihuahuan desert scrub habitats at elevations of 3000'-4000'.	Well-drained, xeric. Sands & loams, also clays, acid or calcareous.
Coralbean *Erythrina herbacea*	x x x (1-3)	Shrub 3'-6' Persistent	Showy coral red tubular flowers. May-Dec.	Pods with poisonous red seeds. Oct.-Dec.	Full sun, part shade	Prefers sandy woods on coastal plain, but will grow elsewhere.	Well-drained, mesic. Sands, loams & clays.

Species	Ornamental Value	Wildlife Value
Spicebush *Lindera benzoin*	Attractive, multi-trunked shrub that prefers rich soil or sandy gravel in the shade along streams. Leaves, twigs, bark & fruit contain nice aromatic oil. Red berry-like fruits are very ornamental.	Flowers attract several kinds of insects & are good early source of nectar. White-tailed deer & rabbits browse lightly on leaves. 24 species of birds feed on the red berries. Good cover & nesting site for birds. Larval host plant of Spicebush & Tiger swallowtail butterflies.
Legume Family – Leguminosae		
Bee-brush *Aloysia gratissima*	Thicket-forming, much branched, slender aromatic shrub. This fragrant ornamental blooms profusely & is easily transplanted. This is a bountiful honey plant, hence its common name. Good screen or hedge plant, but flowers poisonous to horses & mules.	Insects of all sorts are highly attracted to the fragrant white blossoms. Several species of birds are very fond of the fruit. The shrub makes a good cover & nesting site for small birds.
Black dalea *Dalea frutescens*	Attractive, bonsai-like shrub which is easy to maintain. Serves as a good low understory plant.	Flowers are an excellent nectar source for bees & many other kinds of insects. Good cover for small animals. Leaves are browsed by white-tailed deer & rabbits. Larval host plant of Dogface butterfly.
Canyon senna *Senna wislizenii*	This gorgeous shrub sports showy yellow flower clusters & has gracefully arching stems. It blooms all summer.	Flowers attract several varieties of insects, especially bees & butterflies. Shrub provides good protective cover. Seeds are eaten by a few small mammals.
Coralbean *Erythrina herbacea*	Striking shrub dies back in winter like a perennial in all areas but south Texas. Flamboyant summer flowers are highly ornamental. Seeds are also attractive, though extremely poisonous.	Elegant tubular flowers have copious nectar & are highly attractive to the Ruby-throated hummingbird. Seeds, though highly appealing visually, are poisonous and not eaten by wildlife.

Table A.5
Native Plants of Texas

Please note that each two-page "spread" is divided into a top half (with plants' growing information) and a bottom half (with plants' ornamental and wildlife values).
Numbered regions correspond to the Texas Ecoregion map on page 11.

Species	Ecological Region 1 2 3 4 5 6 7 8 9 10	Habit Height	Flower	Fruit	Sun Exposure	Habitat	Soils and Moisture Regime
Fairy duster *Calliandra conferta*	× × 7 ... 10 (× at 5,6,7 & 10)	Shrub ½'-3' Persistent	Showy reddish-purple globes with long stamens. March-May	Legumes, small gray to black in color. June-Aug.	Full sun, part shade	Prefers caliche & limestone hills & cuestas in brush country, also dry gravelly slopes & mesas.	Well-drained, xeric. Sands, loams & clays; likes limestone & caliche-type soils.
False indigo *Amorpha fruticosa*	× × × × × (1,2,3 & 5,6)	Shrub 5'-10' Deciduous	Showy purple flower spikes with yellow anthers. April-May	Pods, clustered, small & brown. July-Aug.	Full sun, part shade	Prefers low areas at the water's edge, along streams.	Mesic, seasonally poor drainage O.K. Sands, loams & clays.
Feather dalea *Dalea formosa*	× × × × × (6,7,8 & 9,10)	Shrub 1'-4' Deciduous	Showy magenta flowers with feathery appendage. April-Aug.	Flat leguminous pod covered with shaggy hair having 1 to 2 seeds. June-Oct.	Full sun, part shade	Prefers rocky hillsides & mesas at higher elevations in western Texas. Likes dry shallow soils, semi-arid limestone.	Well-drained, xeric. Sands, loams, clays, limestone & caliche-type soils.
Fragrant mimosa *Mimosa borealis*	× ... × (7 & 10)	Shrub 2'-6' Deciduous	Showy pink ball-like flowers, fragrant. April-July	Leguminous pod, clawed. June-Sept.	Full sun, part shade	Prefers brushy vegetation in Texas Hill Country and West Texas.	Well-drained, xeric. Sands, loams, clays, caliche-type & limestone soils.
Lead-plant amorpha *Amorpha canescens*	× × × × × (1,2,5 & 8,9)	Shrub 1'-4' Deciduous	Showy bluish-purple flowers on slender, dense racemes. June-July	Legume, brown with 1 brown seed. Aug.-Sept.	Full sun, part shade	Prefers sandy prairies & stream banks. In nature a disjunct population.	Well-drained, xeric-mesic. Sands & sandy loams.
Silver dalea *Dalea bicolor v. argyraea*	× (10)	Shrub 1'-3' Deciduous	Showy yellow & purple banner-type flowers on spikes, fragrant. July-Oct.	Leguminous pod, small, with seeds. Aug.-Nov.	Full sun	Prefers rocky, dry limestone hills and slopes, also found in outwash, gravelly areas.	Well-drained, xeric. Sands, loams & clays; likes limestone soils.

Species	Ornamental Value	Wildlife Value
Fairy duster *Calliandra conferta*	Low, densely-branched shrub with mimosa-like leaves & unusual reddish-purple flowers.	Flowers attract several kinds of insects, especially bees & butterflies. Hummingbirds are also attracted to these flowers, gleaning small insects along with the nectar. Good cover & nesting site. Foliage browsed by deer. Seeds eaten by quail.
False indigo *Amorpha fruticosa*	This moisture loving shrub is notable for its beautiful flowers, attractive leaves & airy form. Relatively fast growing.	Flowers are a good nectar source for bees, butterflies & other insects. Leaves are browsed by deer. Larval host plant for Dogface butterfly, Gray hairstreak, Silver-spotted skipper, Hoary edge skipper.
Feather dalea *Dalea formosa*	Small shrub with crooked branches jutting out at angles, thick dark compound leaves & flowers growing in clusters on short spikes. Attractive feathery gray white calyx surrounds magenta blossoms. Very colorful in full bloom. Drought tolerant.	Flowers attract myriads of insects of all varieties. Leaves are a palatable browse for deer.
Fragrant mimosa *Mimosa borealis*	Highly drought-tolerant, showy, long-blooming shrub. Looks very pretty in rock gardens. Makes a great accent shrub.	Pink flower puffs attract several kinds of insects. This is a good protective cover shrub with its small thorns. Leaves are browsed by mule deer.
Lead-plant amorpha *Amorpha canescens*	An erect, ascending shrub, leafed out to the base, with gray fuzzy compound leaves, bluish purple flowers & leguminous fruit. Has often been cultivated as an ornamental. Well-adapted to sandy or gravelly soils in sunny spots. Good soil cover.	Flowers attract several kinds of insects. Game species browse both on the leaves & the fruits.
Silver dalea *Dalea bicolor v. argyraea*	An erect shrub with compound leaves, attractive bicolored flowers, very attractive if done in a mass planting. Leaves are attractively fuzzy & appear silvery in angled light. Flowers are very fragrant.	Flowers are an excellent nectar source for bees & many other kinds of insects. Good cover for small animals. Young leaves are browsed by mule deer & jackrabbits. Leaves are toxic to some domestic livestock. Larval host plant of Sulphur butterflies.

Table A.5
Native Plants of Texas

Please note that each two-page "spread" is divided into a top half (with plants' growing information) and a bottom half (with plants' ornamental and wildlife values). Numbered regions correspond to the Texas Ecoregion map on page 11.

Species	1	2	3	4	5	6	7	8	9	10	Habit Height	Flower	Fruit	Sun Exposure	Habitat	Soils and Moisture Regime
						Ecological Region										
White-thorn acacia *Acacia constricta*	×					×			×	×	Shrub 9'-15' Deciduous	Showy yellow ball-like flowers, very fragrant. May-Aug. also following rains	Leguminous pods, reddish, 2"-4" long. July-Sept.	Full sun	Prefers desertic habitats at elevations from 1500'-6500'.	Well-drained, xeric. Sands or caliche soils.
Yellow sophora *Sophora tomentosa*	×					×					Shrub 6'-9' Evergreen	Showy, elongate racemes of yellow flowers. March-Oct.	Leguminous pods, necklace-like & densely hairy. July-Nov.	Full sun, part shade	Prefers sandy beaches & flatlands from Valley to Coastal Prairies.	Mesic-xeric, well-drained. Sands & loams. Tolerates saline soils.
Madder Family – Rubiaceae																
Buttonbush *Cephalanthus occidentalis*	×	×	×	×	×	×	×		×	×	Shrub 5'-20' Deciduous	Showy, creamy white round heads. June-Sept.	Capsule clusters, round & dark brown. Aug.-Nov.	Full sun, part shade	Prefers moist soils near swamps, ponds, along streams & stream margins.	Mesic-hydric. Moderate to high moisture. Seasonally poor drainage O.K. Sands, loams, clays. Likes limestone soils.
David's milkberry *Chiococca alba*						×					Shrub, vine-like Climber over shrubs Persistent	White to yellowish flowers, borne in racemes. Feb.-Sept.	Drupes, white, globose, very showy. May-Nov.	Part shade, dappled shade	Prefers loamy soils in thickets, brushy areas & palm groves in Cameron County.	Moist, poor drainage O.K. Sandy loams, loams & loamy clays.
Trompetillo *Bouvardia ternifolia*										×	Shrub 2'-4' Deciduous	Clusters of showy red tubular flowers. May-Nov.	Capsules. July-Dec.	Full sun, part shade	Prefers rocky habitats, usullly in mountains or canyons, 3500'-7300'.	Well-drained, xeric-mesic. Sands, loams & gravelly clays. Also igneous soils.

Species	Ornamental Value	Wildlife Value
White-thorn acacia *Acacia constricta*	Showy shrub with vivid yellow flowers that smell like roses. Profusely blooming with delicate foliage. Thorns are white & quite large, but thornless selection possible. Pods also a showy red color. Branches have purple cast & can be pruned to shape.	Excellent plant to attract insects of all varieties, especially bees & butterflies. Good honey plant. Occasionally browsed by game animals. Quail eat the seeds including Montezuma, Gambel's & Scaled quail. Jackrabbits also eat the leaves.
Yellow sophora *Sophora tomentosa*	Small rounded shrub with densely pubescent foliage, splashy yellow flowers & unusually furry seed pods shaped like a necklace. It makes a wonderful long-blooming accent plant. Leaves are a beautiful silvery green & feel like velvet. Seeds are poisonous.	Flowers attract a number of insects including butterflies, moths & bees. Foliage is not browsed by deer.

Madder Family – Rubiaceae

Species	Ornamental Value	Wildlife Value
Buttonbush *Cephalanthus occidentalis*	Shrub or small tree growing in low areas, often with swollen base. Leaves opposite & whorled, variously shaped. Bright yellow anthers around white flower balls create a halo effect. Highly ornamental. Suitable for bog or pond area.	Flowers attract hordes of bees, butterflies & other insects. Fruits are highly favored by more than 25 species of birds, including waterfowl, cardinals, finches, sparrows, etc.
David's milkberry *Chiococca alba*	An attractive scandent, unarmed smooth stemmed shrub that acts like a vine. It has simple opposite leaves & white flowers. Fruits are white rounded & very eye-catching. This plant makes a very nice ground cover.	Flowers attract several kinds of insects. Several species of birds thrive on the fruit. The shrub is a good place to hide from predators for small birds.
Trompetillo *Bouvardia ternifolia*	This is a gorgeous ornamental with brilliant clusters of bright red flowers suitable as a border palnt. It is also good in a pot or container in the winter to be put inside when the weather gets very cold.	Trompetillo is a premiere hummingbird plant. Leaves are also browsed by mule deer.

Table A.5
Native Plants of Texas

Please note that each two-page "spread" is divided into a top half (with plants' growing information) and a bottom half (with plants' ornamental and wildlife values). Numbered regions correspond to the Texas Ecoregion map on page 11.

Species	Ecological Region 1 2 3 4 5 6 7 8 9 10	Habit Height	Flower	Fruit	Sun Exposure	Habitat	Soils and Moisture Regime
Mallow Family – Malvaceae							
Rio Grande abutilon *Abutilon hypoleucum*	x (region 4)	Shrub 3'-4' Evergreen	Showy yellow to orange flowers. Year-long	Capsules, white & hairy turning dark brown with 3-9 heart-shaped seeds. Year-long	Part shade, dappled shade	Prefers woodlands & floodplains of the Rio Grande Valley.	Well-drained, yet moist. Sands & loams.
Rose pavonia *Pavonia lasiopetala*	x (3), x x (7 8)	Shrub 2'-5' Perennial	Showy pink flowers. May-Dec., sometimes all year	Capsules. July-Dec.	Full sun, part shade, dappled shade	Prefers rocky woods on Edwards Plateau & Rio Grande Plains.	Well-drained, mesic to xeric. Sands, loams & clays, likes limestone soils.
Turk's cap *Malvaviscus drummondii*	x x x x x (1 2 3 4 5 6)	Shrub 4'-9' Deciduous	Showy red flowers. May-Nov.	Berry-like fruit, red, flattened. Aug.-Sept.	Part shade, dappled shade, shade	Prefers moist woodlands, wood margins, streamsides, river edges in shady conditions. Low grounds.	Hydric-mesic, likes moisture. Sands, loams & clays. Likes limestone soils, tolerates gumbo.
Malpighia Family – Malpighiaceae							
Barbados cherry *Malpighia glabra*	x (2)	Shrub 5'-9' Evergreen	White to pale pink flowers. March-Dec.	Drupes, red & fleshy. May-Dec.	Full sun, part shade, dappled shade	Prefers thickets, brushlands & palm groves.	Mesic, well-drained. Sands, loams & clays.
Mint Family – Lamiaceae							
Autumn sage *Salvia greggii*	x x (5 6)	Shrub 2'-4' Persistent (almost evergreen)	Showy magenta red flowers, also comes in white, pink or coral. April-Dec.	Nutlets. June-Dec.	Full sun, part shade	Prefers rocky soils in central, south & west Texas.	Well-drained, mesic-xeric. Sands, loams & clays. Likes limestone soils, especially.

Species	Ornamental Value	Wildlife Value
Mallow Family – Malvaceae		
Rio Grande abutilon *Abutilon hypoleucum*	A large, thornless, softly rounded tropical shrub which blooms in the afternoon year-round. Attractive heart-shaped, lime-green leaves with velvety texture.	Myriads of insects are attracted to the copious pollen on the flowers. Leaves & stems are used as the larval host plant of the Laviana skipper.
Rose pavonia *Pavonia lasiopetala*	Very attractive flowering perennial shrub. Leaves are scalloped & velvety to the touch. Numerous flowers open every morning & close in the afternoon. Requires little care beyond occasional watering & pruning.	Lush pink flowers attract many species of butterflies & moths. Leaves are browsed by white-tailed deer.
Turk's cap *Malvaviscus drummondii*	A good ornamental for shady situations. Forms colonies in shady spots. Serves as good ground cover. Best pruned back after 2 years.	Attractive red flowers are very popular with hummingbirds. Butterflies, diurnal moths & other insects are also attracted to the flowers. The bland fruit is eaten by several species of birds & small mammals.
Malpighia Family – Malpighiaceae		
Barbados cherry *Malpighia glabra*	Erect shrub with many slender stems from the base. Leaves are simple & opposite, while flowers are pink, though sometimes white. Fruit is an attractive red color. This is a highly ornamental shrub.	Flowers attract an abundance of insects of all varieties. Several species of birds & small mammals eat the fruit. Raccoons & coyotes are especially fond of them. White-tailed deer browse the leaves. Larval host plant of Cassius Blue & White Patch butterflies.
Mint Family – Lamiaceae		
Autumn sage *Salvia greggii*	Aromatic showy shrub which blooms prolifically spring, summer & fall. Adaptable to other areas of the state where not native. Good as ground cover or hedge. Really needs good drainage.	Abundant flowers provide copious nectar which is attractive to bees & especially hummingbirds. Ruby-throats can't seem to get enough. Provides food over the long hot summer for them when other plants have waned.

Table A.5
Native Plants of Texas

Please note that each two-page "spread" is divided into a top half (with plants' growing information) and a bottom half (with plants' ornamental and wildlife values). Numbered regions correspond to the Texas Ecoregion map on page 11.

Species	Ecological Region 1 2 3 4 5 6 7 8 9 10	Habit Height	Flower	Fruit	Sun Exposure	Habitat	Soils and Moisture Regime
Mountain sage *Salvia regla*	x	Shrub 2'-6' Deciduous	Showy orange-red tubular flowers. June-Sept., mostly in fall	Calyx-tube with 4 nutlets nestled at the bottom. Aug.-Nov.	Part shade, dappled shade	Prefers rocky, wooded slopes & canyons of Chisos Mountains.	Well-drained, xeric-mesic. Sands, loams, clays, slightly acid to slightly alkaline.
Shrubby blue sage *Salvia ballotaeflora*	x x	Shrub 3'-6' Deciduous to Persistent	Bluish to purplish flowers. Jan.-Oct.	Fruiting calyx folded with 4 nutlets. March-Nov.	Full sun, part shade	Prefers rocky lime-stone canyons & slopes & hillsides from 1200'-2400'.	Well-drained, xeric. Sands, loams & clays, prefers limestone substrates.

Nightshade Family – Solanaceae

Species	Ecological Region 1 2 3 4 5 6 7 8 9 10	Habit Height	Flower	Fruit	Sun Exposure	Habitat	Soils and Moisture Regime
Carolina wolfberry *Lycium carolinianum*	x x	Shrub 3'-6' Evergreen with summer watering	Showy purple, egg-plant shaped flowers. April-Oct.	Red tomato-shaped fruit, 1/4"-1/2" in diameter. June-Nov.	Full sun, part shade	Occurs near ponds, ditches, marshes, on clay flats, salt flats or in gravelly soils on chaparral-covered hills in the Rio Grande Plains & on lower coastal marshes.	Moist, poor drainage O.K. Sands, loams, clays of gravelly texture.
Chile pequin *Capsicum annuum*	x x x x x	Shrub 1'-2' Deciduous	Small white perfect flowers with yellow anthers. March-Nov., sometimes year-round	Chili peppers, small & red. April-Dec.	Dappled shade, full shade	Prefers ledges along rivers, thickets & groves along arroyos.	Well-drained, mesic. Sands, loams & clays likes limestone soils.
Wolfberry *Lycium berlandieri*	x x x	Shrub 5'-7' Persistent to Evergreen	Showy blue to lavender flowers. Feb.-Oct.	Berries, bright red & many seeded. April-Dec.	Full sun, part shade	Prefers gravelly, rocky hills, limestone & alkali flats, arroyos & scrubland.	Xeric, well-drained. Sands, loams or clays.

Species	Ornamental Value	Wildlife Value
Mountain sage *Salvia regla*	Showy shrub of West Texas Mountains, highly suitable as ornamental. Mountain sage has glossy aromatic heart-shaped leaves & stays in bloom over long periods. Very drought tolerant once established although it does better if it is not put in direct sun.	The red tubular blooms of this species coincide with the timing of the migrating hummingbirds that pass through the west Texas mountains. Hummingbirds flock to this plant for its copious nectar.
Shrubby blue sage *Salvia ballotaeflora*	Highly aromatic, much-branched shrub with attractive leaves & bluish flowers.	Flowers attract many varieties of insects, especially bees. Nutlets are eaten by small rodents. Shrub provides excellent cover. Leaves are not heavily browsed by mule deer or other mammals.
Nightshade Family – Solanaceae		
Carolina wolfberry *Lycium carolinianum*	Medium-sized spiny erect to somewhat trailing shrub with thick fleshy grayish leaves & purple flowers. Red fruit is very attractive. If you don't water in summer, it will lose its leaves. Can be used as ground cover. Highly salt tolerant.	Flowers attract several kinds of insects. Red fruits are not only attractive to the eye they are relished by several species of birds, including Whooping cranes. White-tailed deer browse on the succulent leaves.
Chile pequin *Capsicum annuum*	Perky little shrub with electric red hot chili pepper berries. A pleasant airy understory shrub. Prefers moist soils. People use fruit as a very hot flavoring for foods.	Birds of several species are highly fond of the peppers. Plants are dispersed by birds.
Wolfberry *Lycium berlandieri*	Spiny, sparingly-branched shrub with semi-succulent leaves. Shrub is very attractive when in bloom & in fruit. Not native of Rolling Plains, but will grow there.	Flowers attract many insects while the leaves are browsed by white-tailed deer. Several species of birds & small mammals eat the fruit, including chachalacas in South Texas. Raccoon also love the fruit.

Table A.5
Native Plants of Texas

Please note that each two-page "spread" is divided into a top half (with plants' growing information) and a bottom half (with plants' ornamental and wildlife values). Numbered regions correspond to the Texas Ecoregion map on page 11.

Ocotillo Family – Fouquieriaceae

Species	Ecological Region 1 2 3 4 5 6 7 8 9 10	Habit Height	Flower	Fruit	Sun Exposure	Habitat	Soils and Moisture Regime
Ocotillo *Fouquieria splendens*	x (10)	Shrub 12'-25' Evergreen	Orange-red tubular flowers arranged in spikes. May-July	Capsules, ovoid, with numerous winged seeds. July-Sept.	Full sun, part shade	Prefers dry desert habitats throughout the Trans-Pecos.	Xeric, well-drained. Sands, sandy loams, either limestone or igneous based.

Olive Family – Oleaceae

Species	Ecological Region 1 2 3 4 5 6 7 8 9 10	Habit Height	Flower	Fruit	Sun Exposure	Habitat	Soils and Moisture Regime
Elbowbush *Forestiera pubescens*	x x (3,4) x (7)	Shrub 5'-10' Deciduous	Showy yellow bracts appear before leaves, early in spring. February	Berries, bluish-black (drupes). June-Oct.	Full sun, part shade, dappled shade	Prefers open pastures, brushy prairies, woodlands & thickets.	Well-drained soils, mesic to semi-dry. Sands, loams, & clays.

Palm Family – Palmae

Species	Ecological Region 1 2 3 4 5 6 7 8 9 10	Habit Height	Flower	Fruit	Sun Exposure	Habitat	Soils and Moisture Regime
Dwarf palmetto *Sabal minor*	x x (1,2) x (6)	Shrub 3'-5' Evergreen	Small, whitish flowers with yellow anthers on stalk (Spadix). May-June	Drupes, black, in drooping clusters. Sept.-Oct.	Full sun, part sun, dappled shade, shade	Prefers lowland swamps, river terraces & floodplains.	Mesic-hydric; poor drainage O.K. Sands, loams & clays.

Pokeweed Family – Phytolaccaceae

Species	Ecological Region 1 2 3 4 5 6 7 8 9 10	Habit Height	Flower	Fruit	Sun Exposure	Habitat	Soils and Moisture Regime
Snake-eyes *Phaulothamnus spinescens*	x (6)	Shrub 6'-10' Persistent to Evergreen	Inconspicuous male & female flowers, solitary or in racemes, on separate trees. Aug.-Sept.	Drupe, one-seeded, transparent looking like snake eyes. Sept.-Nov.	Part shade, dappled shade, shade	Prefers clayey soils in thickets & palm groves in southern-most Lower Rio Grande Valley.	Moist, poor drainage O.K. Sandy loams clays.

Species	Ornamental Value	Wildlife Value
Ocotillo Family – Fouquieriaceae		
Ocotillo *Fouquieria splendens*	Marvelously dramatic accent plant, resembling a coachwhip tipped in red & coated with green leaves during droughty periods. Has thorns. Can form a screen if planted close together.	This is a spectacular hummingbird plant. A special favorite of Lucifer hummingbirds. Nectar is also coveted by several varieties of insects, especially carpenter bees. Seeds eaten by granivorous birds & small mammals.
Olive Family – Oleaceae		
Elbowbush *Forestiera pubescens*	Straggling, irregularly shaped shrub. Though not beautiful, this is the first shrub to bloom in spring. Opposite softly fuzzy leaves & blue-black berries.	Yellow flowers appear early in spring providing early nectar source for bees, butterflies & other insects. Berries are eaten by several species of birds & small mammals. Leaves are browsed by white-tailed deer.
Palm Family – Palmae		
Dwarf palmetto *Sabal minor*	Highly dramatic accent plant for shady, moist location. Fairly drought resistant once it is established.	Excellent cover & nesting plant for small birds. Affords protection all year round. Flowers significant source of honey. Fruits eaten by several species of birds & small mammals.
Pokeweed Family – Phytolaccaceae		
Snake-eyes *Phaulothamnus spinescens*	Erect shrub with dense spiny branches & very unusual fruits that look like snake eyes. This species grows only in the southern-most tip of the state.	Snake-eyes is an excellent protective cover & nesting site for small birds. Fruits are eaten by several species of fruit-loving birds & small mammals. Deer occasionally browse the leaves. Warblers & long-billed thrashers are especially fond of the fruit.

Table A.5
Native Plants of Texas

Please note that each two-page "spread" is divided into a top half (with plants' growing information) and a bottom half (with plants' ornamental and wildlife values).
Numbered regions correspond to the Texas Ecoregion map on page 11.

Species	Ecological Region 1 2 3 4 5 6 7 8 9 10	Habit Height	Flower	Fruit	Sun Exposure	Habitat	Soils and Moisture Regime
Quassia Family – Simarubaceae							
Goat-bush *Castela texana*	x x x	Shrub 3'-10' Persistent to Evergreen	Showy red to orange axillary flowers. March-May	Drupes, bright red with one seed. June-Aug.	Full sun, part shade	Prefers gravelly hills, chaparral thickets, gulf shores & mesquite prairies.	Xeric, well-drained. Sands, loams & clays.
Rose Family – Rosaceae							
Apache-plume *Fallugia paradoxa*	x	Shrub 2'-10' Persistent to Evergreen	Fragile white rose-like flowers appearing with plumes. May-Dec.	Reddish-silver tinged achenes are plumose & borne in fluffy clusters. June-Dec.	Full sun, part shade	Prefers dry arroyos of deserts & foothills from 3000'-8000' in elevation.	Xeric, well-drained. Sands, loams & clays, prefers limestone base.
Oklahoma plum *Prunus gracilis*	x x x x x	Shrub, ornamental 2'-6' Deciduous	Showy white flowers, fragrant. March-April	Plums, red with oval stone. July-Aug.	Full sun, part shade, dappled shade	Prefers open hills & their woods from East Texas to Panhandle, along fencerows & edges of fields.	Well-drained, xeric to mesic. Sands.
Southern dewberry *Rubus trivialis*	x x x x x x	Shrub, vine-like Climber	Showy white flowers with five petals. Feb.-April	Dewberries. May-June	Full sun, part shade, dappled shade	Prefers low grounds, swampy areas at low elevations.	Mesic, tolerates poor drainage. Sands, loams & clays.

Species	Ornamental Value	Wildlife Value
Quassia Family – Simarubaceae		
Goat-bush *Castela texana*	Densely-branched spinose shrub with shiny green leaves, red-orange flowers & flashy red fruit. It has a very bitter bark.	Several kinds of insects are attracted to the flowers. White-tailed deer browse leaves & fruit. Several species of game & song birds also eat the fruits. It is frequently used as a nesting site by birds due to its protective thorns & dense branches.
Rose Family – Rosaceae		
Apache-plume *Fallugia paradoxa*	Straggling, clump-forming shrub with striking pink feathery plumes. Flowers & fruit give great color most of the year. Good erosion control plant. Very drought & heat tolerant. Also is winter hardy.	Flowers attract myriads of insects of all varieties. Makes a good protective cover & nesting shrub. Plumed achenes are used as nesting material by birds building cup nests. Leaves lightly browsed by mule deer.
Oklahoma plum *Prunus gracilis*	Beautiful thicket plant with ravishing spring white fragrant flowers that appear before the leaves.	Oklahoma plum flowers attract several kinds of insects, especially bees & butterflies. Several species of birds & small mammals relish the plums.
Southern dewberry *Rubus trivialis*	A weedy, trailing plant rooting at tips of canes & branches. Though this is not an overly attractive plant it has great wildlife value.	Flowers attract myriads of insects, while dewberries are great favorites of innumerable species of small birds & mammals. It also provides excellent cover for them as well.

Table A.5
Native Plants of Texas

Please note that each two-page "spread" is divided into a top half (with plants' growing information) and a bottom half (with plants' ornamental and wildlife values). Numbered regions correspond to the Texas Ecoregion map on page 11.

Species	Ecological Region 1 2 3 4 5 6 7 8 9 10	Habit Height	Flower	Fruit	Sun Exposure	Habitat	Soils and Moisture Regime
Rue Family – Rutaceae							
Star-leaf Mexican orange *Choisya dumosa*	x (10)	Shrub 1'-6' Persistent	Showy white flowers in cluster of 2 to 4, fragrant. June-Nov.	Follicles, green to brown. Aug.-Dec.	Full sun, part shade	Grows in pinyon belt of Davis & Guadalupe mountains on limestone & igneous formations. Prefers canyons & mountain slopes.	Well-drained, xeric-mesic. Sands, loams & limestone soils, will also grow on igneous soils.
Saltwort Family – Bataceae							
Seaside saltwort *Batis maritima*	x (1), x (6)	Shrub, seaside 1'-2' Evergreen	Small white male & female flowers, separate on same plant. June-Aug.	Fruit a fleshy yellow aggregate. Aug.-Oct.	Full sun	Prefers sandy beaches, mud flats & saline marshes.	Mesic, poor drainage O.K. Sands, sandy loams & clays.
Saxifrage Family – Saxifragaceae							
Buffalo current *Ribes odoratum*	x x x (8 9 10)	Shrub 4'-6' Deciduous	Showy golden yellow racemes of flowers. Feb.-May	Currents, yellow or black. June-Aug.	Full sun, part shade	Prefers cliffs, rocky slopes & sandy bluffs in western 1/2 of Texas.	Well-drained, xeric-mesic. Sands, loams, clays, limestone & caliche-type soils.
Virginia sweetspire *Itea virginica*	x x (1 2)	Shrub 4'-6' Deciduous	Showy white flowers in terminal raceme. April-June	Capsule, two-parted with dark brown seeds. Sept.-Oct.	Part shade, dappled shade	Prefers rich soils along swamps & streamsides.	Hydric, poor drainage O.K. Sands, loams, & clays, acid soils preferred.

Species	Ornamental Value	Wildlife Value
Rue Family – Rutaceae		
Star-leaf Mexican orange *Choisya dumosa*	Gorgeous low aromatic shrub, much branched with distinctive yellow-green palmate leaves in the shape of a star. Highly ornamental & quite a conversation piece.	Star-leaf provides good protective cover & nesting substrate for small birds. Flowers attract a wide assortment of insects.
Saltwort Family – Bataceae		
Seaside saltwort *Batis maritima*	Low, pale green shrub with creeping stems, thick succulent leaves & white flowers & fleshy yellow fruits. This species is highly salt tolerant & also tolerates seasonal poor drainage.	Fruits are eaten by several species of birds & small mammals. Colonial water birds will often establish a nesting site where this plant grows abundantly.
Saxifrage Family – Saxifragaceae		
Buffalo current *Ribes odoratum*	Highly ornamental shrub with parsley-shaped leaves, showy yellow flowers & excellent fruit. It has been widely introduced into cultivation & is relatively easy to grow.	Buffalo current provides excellent food for wildlife of all kinds. Insects of many varieties are attracted to the flowers and birds of all sorts flock to the berries. Foliage is browsed readily by mule deer.
Virginia sweetspire *Itea virginica*	Attractive understory shrub that does well in moist situations. Excellent erosion control. Flowers are showy, drooping white spires, & the leaves turn a bright red in the fall. It is highly tolerant of poor drainage. Need lots of water in the summer.	The flowers are an excellent nectar source for various kinds of insects. Shrub provides good cover for small animals.

Table A.5
Native Plants of Texas

Please note that each two-page "spread" is divided into a top half (with plants' growing information) and a bottom half (with plants' ornamental and wildlife values). Numbered regions correspond to the Texas Ecoregion map on page 11.

Staff Tree Family – Celastraceae

Strawberry Bush Family – Celastraceae

Sumac Family – Anacardiaceae

Species	Ecological Region 1 2 3 4 5 6 7 8 9 10	Habit Height	Flower	Fruit	Sun Exposure	Habitat	Soils and Moisture Regime
Plains greasebush *Foresellesia planitierum*	x x	Shrub 2'-3' Persistent to Evergreen	Showy, white, five-petalled flowers 1" across. March-July	Follicle, ovoid. Aug.-Sept.	Full sun, part shade	Prefers rocky calcareous slopes & breaks in western portion of the state, in the High Plains & Trans-Pecos.	Xeric, well-drained. Sands, loams, clays & caliche-type soils.
Strawberry bush *Euonymus americanus*	x x	Shrub 4'-6' Deciduous	Small greenish purple flowers. May-June	Capsule containing red fruits. Sept.-Nov.	Part shade, dappled shade, shade	Prefers muddy moist soils along streams & woods.	Mesic-hydric, likes moisture. Poor drainage O.K. Sands, sandy loams, clays & gumbos.
Fragrant sumac *Rhus aromatica*	x x x x x x x x	Shrub 3'-8' Deciduous	Inconspicuous yellow flowers appearing before leaves. Feb.-March	Berries, red. May-June	Full sun, part shade, dappled shade.	Prefers limestone outcrops, rocky slopes, prairies, & mesquite plains.	Well-drained, mesic. Sands, loams & clays. Likes limestone soils.
Little-leaf sumac *Rhus microphylla*	x x x x	Shrub 4'-15' Deciduous	Greenish-white in 2"-4" clusters. April-May	Drupes, reddish-orange & hairy. May-June	Full sun, part shade	Prefers dry rocky hillsides or gravelly mesas at altitude of 2000'-6000' In western 3/4 of Texas.	Well-drained, xeric. Sands, loams, clays, caliche-type & limestone soils.
Smooth sumac *Rhus glabra*	x x x x	Shrub 3'-10' Deciduous	Cluster of small white flowers. June-Aug.	Red, velvety berries in clusters. Sept.-Oct.	Full sun, part shade	Occurs on dry sandy hillsides & banks in East Texas to Bryan, Blackland Prairies & Rolling Plains.	Mesic-xeric, well-drained. Sands, loams & claims.

Species	Ornamental Value	Wildlife Value
Staff Tree Family – Celastraceae		
Plains greasebush *Forsellesia planitierum*	Irregularly-branched grayish-green spiny shrub very attractive in bloom, which it does profusely. Leaves are tiny & furry. Very cold & drought tolerant. Can't stand long, hot summers.	Myriads of insects are attracted to the flowers, it will just buzz with activity in the spring.
Strawberry Bush Family – Celastraceae		
Strawberry bush *Euonymus americanus*	Airy understory shrub with bright red fruits held for a long time through the fall. It prefers the shade & tolerates poor drainage. Drier areas are O.K., if it stays in the shade. Good for Houston.	Several species of birds favor the red fruits, including Eastern bluebirds, mockingbirds, thrashers, sparrows & warblers. Small terrestrial mammals such as rabbits, squirrels & raccoons also enjoy eating the fruit.
Sumac Family – Anacardiaceae		
Fragrant sumac *Rhus aromatica*	Aromatic shrub with pretty leaves & early flowers. Tends to form thickets & is irregularly branched.	Early flowers provide early nectar source for insects like bees, butterflies & moths. The red berries are one of the earliest summer fruits making it popular with several species of birds & small mammals. Larval host plant to Red-banded hairstreak.
Little-leaf sumac *Rhus microphylla*	Clump-forming, intricately branched shrub that can get very wide. It is important to space it accordingly from 8'-20' apart. Bright orange fruits are attractive & persistent. Very drought-tolerant shrub.	Bright orange fruits are highly sought after by several species of birds. Though they are sour, rock squirrels & other small mammals will eat them also. Leaves are sometimes browsed by mule & white-tailed deer, but not much.
Smooth sumac *Rhus glabra*	Thicket-forming shrub or sometimes small tree with lance-shaped compound leaves. Excellent for erosion control & beautiful red fall color. While it prefers sand, it will do well in other soil types. Outside its range it needs more water & lots of sun.	Flowers provide lots of nectar for butterflies & other insects. The fruit is eaten by cottontails, white-tailed deer & nearly 35 species of birds. Wild turkey & bobwhite also love fruits. Larval host plant of some species of hairstreaks.

Please note that each two-page "spread" is divided into a top half (with plants' growing information) and a bottom half (with plants' ornamental and wildlife values).
Numbered regions correspond to the Texas Ecoregion map on page 11.

Sunflower Family – Asteraceae

Species	Ecological Region 1 2 3 4 5 6 7 8 9 10	Habit Height	Flower	Fruit	Sun Exposure	Habitat	Soils and Moisture Regime
Baccharis *Baccharis halimifolia*	x x x	Shrub 6'-8' Deciduous	Showy, silvery white flowers, female tree especially. Sept.-Oct.	Achenes. Oct.-Nov.	Full sun	Colonizes disturbed soils. Prefers open sandy places in east, south east & north central Texas.	Mesic. Sands, & loams, prefers slightly acid soils.
Damianita *Chrysatinia mexicana*	x (region 7)	Shrub 1'-2' Evergreen	Showy yellow daisy-like flowers. May-Oct.	Achenes. July-Nov.	Full sun, part shade	Prefers rocky lime-stone outcrops of ridges, hills & moun-tains. Also thrives on igneous substrates from 1800'-7000'.	Well-drained, xeric. Prefers rocky lime-stone soils, also igneous soils. Sands, loams & clays O.K.
Fragrant boneset *Eupatorium odoratum*	x (region 1); x (region 5)	Shrub 2'-6' Deciduous to persistent	Showy flower heads, lilac to purple. Aug.-Oct.	Achenes. Sept.-Dec.	Part shade, dappled shade, shade	Prefers rocky clay soils along coast & in valley.	Mesic, poor drainage O.K. Sands, loams or clays.
Larch-leaf goldenweed *Ericameria laricifolia*	x (region 7)	Shrub 1'-3' Evergreen	Showy yellow flower heads. Aug.-Nov.	Achenes. Sept.-Dec.	Full sun, part shade	Prefers canyons & slopes of desertic mountains at eleva-tions of 4200'-5100'.	Xeric, well-drained. Sands, loams & clays.
Ox-eye daisy *Borrichia frutescens*	x (region 1); x (region 5)	Shrub, seaside 1'-4' Evergreen	Showy yellow composite flowers. Year-long	Achenes. Year-long	Full sun	Prefers salt marshes, sandy shores, sea beaches & saline prairies.	Mesic, poor drainage O.K. Sands, loams & clays.

Species	Ornamental Value	Wildlife Value
Sunflower Family – Asteraceae		
Baccharis *Baccharis halimifolia*	Female plants are gorgeous in full bloom which can last until Christmas. Easy to grow, tolerates poor soils. Good erosion control plant especially in disturbed areas.	Flowers are highly attractive to all kinds of insects: bees, butterflies, diurnal moths, etc. A good cover plant. Achenes eaten by seed-eating birds.
Damianita *Chrysatinia mexicana*	Highly ornamental aromatic shrub with profusely blooming daisy like flowers. Plant looks rather like a gnarled bonsai plant in dry habitats. Low-growing & long-blooming. Good as an undershrub in a rock garden	Flower attract several sorts of insects, especially bees. Achenes are eaten by several species of granivorous birds. Deer do not eat this shrub at all.
Fragrant boneset *Eupatorium odoratum*	Shrubby plant with erect or reclining branches. Can be used as a ground cover. Lilac flowers are very showy.	Lilac flowers provide abundant nectar to butterflies, bees & other insects when a lot of other plants are not in bloom. Leaves are frequently browsed by white-tailed deer. Ripe achenes are eaten by sparrows & finches.
Larch-leaf goldenweed *Ericameria laricifolia*	Much-branched, resinous aromatic shrub with yellow flowers & numerous small leaves emitting a tart lemony scent. Goldenweeds, as their name implies, turn golden in the fall.	Jackrabbits love to browse on this plant even though the leaves smell slightly like lemony turpentine when crushed. Achenes are eaten by several species of seed-eating birds. Insects are attracted to the flowers.
Ox-eye daisy *Borrichia frutescens*	Small, fleshy, pale green shrub with attractive bright yellow flowers. Plants tolerate salt & poor drainage conditions well.	Bees & butterflies are attracted to the flowers. Seed eating birds dine on the ripe achenes. Plants are also used for cover by small birds & mammals, especially rails.

Table A.5
Native Plants of Texas

Please note that each two-page "spread" is divided into a top half (with plants' growing information) and a bottom half (with plants' ornamental and wildlife values). Numbered regions correspond to the Texas Ecoregion map on page 11.

Species	Ecological Region 1	2	3	4	5	6	7	8	9	10	Habit Height	Flower	Fruit	Sun Exposure	Habitat	Soils and Moisture Regime
Rabbit-brush *Chrysothamnus nauseosus v graveolans*								x			Shrub 1'-9' Persistent to evergreen	Showy yellow flower clusters. Sept.-Oct.	Achenes, linear with copious, showy white or tawny wooly hairs. Oct.-Dec.	Full sun, part shade	Prefers draws on Rolling Plains in the Panhandle from 3000' and above elevation.	Xeric, well-drained. Sands and caliche soils.
Sand sage *Artemisia filifolia*								x	x	x	Shrub 3'-6' Persistent to evergreen	Small ray flowers. April-May, and again in Sept.-Oct.	Achenes. Sept.-Oct. and later	Full sun, part shade	Prefers dune areas, deep loose sands in Trans-Pecos & Plains country.	Well-drained, xeric. Sands, deep.
Skeleton-leaf golden-eye *Viguiera stenoloba*						x	x			x	Shrub 2'-4' Deciduous to evergreen	Showy yellow daisy-like flowers. May-Nov.	Achenes. July-Dec.	Full sun, part shade	Prefers limestone substrates in various habitats in west Texas.	Well-drained, xeric. Sands, loams, clays, especially limestone soils.

Vervain Family – Verbenaceae

Species	Ecological Region 1	2	3	4	5	6	7	8	9	10	Habit Height	Flower	Fruit	Sun Exposure	Habitat	Soils and Moisture Regime
American beauty-berry *Callicarpa americana*	x	x	x	x	x		x				Shrub 3'-9' Deciduous to evergreen	Small clusters of white or pink flowers at nodes. May-July	Berries, magenta, in clusters at nodes. Aug.-Nov.	Part shade, dappled shade	Prefers moist soils of canyons and bottom-lands, woods & thickets.	Well-drained, mesic. Sands, loams & clays. Likes rich soils.
Black mangrove *Avicennia germinans*	x					x					Shrub, seaside 3'-4' Evergreen	Showy creamy white flowers. July-Aug.	Capsule with one seed. Sept.-Oct.	Full sun	Prefers sandy or clay tidal flats & lagoons.	Mesic, poor drainage O.K. Sands, loams & clays.

Species	Ornamental Value	Wildlife Value
Rabbit-brush *Chrysothamnus nauseosus* v *graveolans*	Very showy, densely-branched western shrub forming a rounded clump, with deep root system. Prefers cool summers. Leaves are pungently aromatic. Good shrub for erosion control.	This is an excellent honey plant. Flowers attract several kinds of insects, especially bees & butterflies. Achenes are eaten by several species of seed-eating birds. Birds will also use the plumed achenes in nest construction. Mule deer browse foliage.
Sand sage *Artemisia filifolia*	Rounded freely branching aromatic shrub. This makes an excellent accent shrub or boundary planting or good for backdrop. Also serves as excellent erosion control plant.	Sand sage is excellent protective cover plant. Birds will eat the ripe achenes. Sparrows & finches are especially fond of them.
Skeleton-leaf golden-eye *Viguiera stenoloba*	Showy clumps of yellow flowers work well in desert garden. Flowers bloom for long periods. Very drought-tolerant & winter hardy.	Flowers attract many kinds of insects including butterflies, bees, diurnal moths & flies. Leaves are lightly browsed by mule deer during stress periods. Provides good protective cover & nesting substrate for small birds. Achenes eaten by seed-eating birds.
Vervain Family – Verbenaceae		
American beauty-berry *Callicarpa americana*	Open, much branched shrub with showy magenta berries. Has mounding form. Likes to be watered during dry periods.	Fruits are favored by several species of birds, i.e., bobwhite, mocking-birds, cardinals, thrashers, robins, finches & towhees. Raccoons, opossum & gray fox also relish berries.
Black mangrove *Avicennia germinans*	Shrub or small tree with leathery green leaves & attractive creamy white flowers. Highly tolerant of saline conditions as well as extremely poor drainage. Soils can even be permanently wet. Excellent erosion control plant.	Flowers attract a wide variety of insects, while the seeds are eaten by some species of birds & small mammals, especially rodents. Provides ample cover & nesting substrate along lower coastal areas for many species of colonial waterbirds.

Table A.5
Native Plants of Texas

Please note that each two-page "spread" is divided into a top half (with plants' growing information) and a bottom half (with plants' ornamental and wildlife values). Numbered regions correspond to the Texas Ecoregion map on page 11.

Species	1	2	3	4	5	6	7	8	9	10	Habit Height	Flower	Fruit	Sun Exposure	Habitat	Soils and Moisture Regime
Bushy lippia *Lippia alba*		x				x					Shrub 5'-7' Deciduous to persistent	Showy purple to violet flowers, sometimes pink & white. March-Oct.	Dry drupes with 2 nutlets. May-Nov.	Full sun, part shade	Prefers woods, river banks & resacas in southern Rio Grande Valley, Cameron & Hildago counties. Also on lower coast plains.	Moist soils. Sands, silts, loams & clays.
Lantana *Lantana horrida*	x	x	x	x	x	x					Shrub 3'-6' Deciduous	Showy yellow & orange heads made up of tiny florets. May to December (first frost)	Berries, green then dark blue-black. Sept.-Nov.	Full sun, part shade	Occurs in fields, thickets, swamps, rich sandy woods, scrub & gravelly hills.	Well-drained, xeric to mesic. Sands, loams & clays.
Redbrush lippia *Lippia graveolens*						x				x	Shrub 5'-7' Persistent	Showy yellowish white flowers with yellow centers. March-Dec.	Drupes, small 7 dry with 2 nutlets. May-Dec.	Full sun	Prefers dry, rocky hills, valleys, arroyos, chaparral & open desert scrub.	Well-drained, xeric. Sands, loams, gravelly clays; likes limestone caliche-like soils.
Beaked yucca *Yucca rostrata*										x	Succulent 6'-12' Evergreen	Showy panicles of white flowers on tall stalk. March-April	Capsules with seeds. Sept.-Oct.	Full sun	Prefers canyons & mountain slopes especially on limestone substrates in West Texas.	Well-drained xeric. Sands & loams; likes limestone soils.
Buckley yucca *Yucca constricta*	x	x				x				x	Succulent 2' leaves, 3'- 6' flower stalk Evergreen	Showy panicles of creamy-white flowers. April-June	Capsules. Sept.-Oct.	Full sun, part shade	Prefers brushy woods & grasslands.	Well-drained xeric. Sands, loams & clays; likes limestone soils.

Species	Ornamental Value	Wildlife Value
Bushy lippia *Lippia alba*	Much-branched aromatic shrub with opposite leaves & purple-violet flowers. This is a very ornamental plant & is widely cultivated.	Both butterflies & hummingbirds are attracted to these flowers. The ripe seeds are eaten by a number of bird species.
Lantana *Lantana horrida*	This showy shrub is planted has a long, profuse blooming season. It is planted almost throughout the state. It loves the hot weather. It's good to prune it back to the ground each winter.	Colorful, long-blooming flowers attract both butterflies & hummingbirds throughout the season. Northern cardinals & other species of birds eat the ripe fruit. Fairly deer resistant. Larval host plant of the Painted Lady.
Redbrush lippia *Lippia graveolens*	Slender, aromatic pubescent shrub with yellowish-white flowers & opposite leaves. Very drought tolerant once established.	Redbrush lippia is an excellent honey shrub. Myriads of insects are attracted to the nectar-laden flowers, especially bees & butterflies. Seeds are eaten by a number of species of birds.
Beaked yucca *Yucca rostrata*	Very tall yucca with massive trunk, good as accent plant & lovely when in bloom. These are the giant yuccas. Leaves have tips armed with healthy spines. Flowers are highly showy & also edible.	Elegant waxy flowers emit their fragrance at night attracting yucca moths which pollinate them. Flowers also attract other insects. They are edible & popular with mule deer. Seeds eaten by small mammals. Larval host plant to Yucca giant skipper.
Buckley yucca *Yucca constricta*	Very striking accent plant, lovely when in bloom. This plant is the most flower-like of all the yuccas. Leaves are dark green with white edges. Older leaves get threads. Tips are armed with healthy spines.	Elegant waxy flowers emit their fragrance at night attracting moths which pollinate them. Flowers are edible & popular with white-tailed deer. Larval host plant to Yucca giant skipper.

Table A.5
Native Plants of Texas

Please note that each two-page "spread" is divided into a top half (with plants' growing information) and a bottom half (with plants' ornamental and wildlife values). Numbered regions correspond to the Texas Ecoregion map on page 11.

Species	Ecological Region 1 2 3 4 5 6 7 8 9 10	Habit Height	Flower	Fruit	Sun Exposure	Habitat	Soils and Moisture Regime
Century plant *Agave americana*	x (1), x (6), x (10)	Succulent Leaves 2'-3', flower stalk 8'-9' Evergreen	Showy yellow flowers on tall bloom stalk, flowers only once. June-July	Capsules, brown & many seeded. Flowers only once in its lifetime	Full sun	Commonly on naturally occurring islands in Laguna Madre, escaped elsewhere.	Well-drained, xeric. Sands, loams & clays.
Faxon yucca *Yucca faxoniana*	x (10)	Succulent Leaves 1'-2' flower stalk 2'-6' Evergreen	Showy panicles of dense white flowers on tall stalk. March-April	Capsules, orange to brown turning to black, with seeds. June-July	Full sun	Prefers high desert plateaux, rimrock areas & mountain slopes & flats from 2700'-6700'.	Well-drained xeric. Sands & loams; likes limestone soils.
Huaco *Manfreda variegata*	x (1), x (6)	Succulent Leaves 2'-4', flower stalk 4'-12' Evergreen	Showy yellow to coral orange flowers, spicy fragrance. April-July	Capsules. July-Oct.	Full sun, part shade	Prefers prairies & chaparrals.	Mesic-xeric, well drained. Sands, loams & clays, acid or calcareous.
Narrow-leaf yucca *Yucca angustifolia*	x (5), x (8), x (9)	Succulent 1'-2' leaves, 2'-6' flower stalk Evergreen	Showy panicles of creamy-white flowers. June-July	Capsules. Sept.-Oct.	Full sun, part shade	Prefers rolling, well-drained grasslands & plains.	Well-drained xeric. Sands, loams & clays.
New Mexico century plant *Agave neomexicana*	x (10)	Succulent leaves 2'-3', flower stalk 8'-15' Evergreen	Showy yellowish panicles on tall scape. June-Aug. Blooms only once in its lifetime	Capsules, elliptical with seeds. Fruits only once in its lifetime	Full sun	Prefers rocky slopes & grasslands in Franklin Mountains in El Paso County, also in Guadalupe Mountains in Culberson County.	Well-drained, xeric. Sands & loams.

Species	Ornamental Value	Wildlife Value
Century plant *Agave americana*	Medium to large leaf-succulent with basal rosette of large attractive gray-green leaves. This is a naturalized plant that has escaped from cultivation. It is also widely cultivated for the beauty & shape of its spine-tipped leaves.	Plants live many years, bloom only once, then die (sending off pups on the side). Insects & hummingbirds are attracted to the flowers. Many birds & small mammals eat the ripe seeds.
Faxon yucca *Yucca faxoniana*	Very tall yucca with massive trunk, good as accent plant & lovely when in bloom. These are the giant yuccas. Leaves have tips armed with healthy spines. Flowers are highly showy & also edible. Can serve as excellent evergreen screen.	Elegant waxy flowers emit their fragrance at night attracting yucca moths which pollinate them. Flowers also attract other insects. They are edible & popular with mule deer. Seeds eaten by small mammals. Larval host plant to Yucca giant skipper.
Huaco *Manfreda variegata*	Green succulent rosette leaves with purplish-brown spots — very eye-catching. Makes an excellent accent plant for any garden. Spicy perfumed flowers are especially fragrant in the evening.	Fragrant flowers emit their perfume in the evening thus attracting many moths as pollinators. Finches, sparrows & other seed eating birds eat the ripe seeds as do several species of small rodents & other small mammals.
Narrow-leaf yucca *Yucca angustifolia*	Very winter-hardy attractive accent plant, magnificent when in bloom. This plant is the most flower-like of all the yuccas. Leaves are pale green edged with fine, curly white hairs. Tips are armed with healthy spines. Can tolerate shade.	Waxy white flowers emit their fragrance at night attracting moths which pollinate them. Flowers are edible & popular with white-tailed deer. Larval host plant to Yucca giant skipper & Strecker's giant skipper.
New Mexico century plant *Agave neomexicana*	An attractive stemless fiber plant with grayish basally clustered leaves forming almost globose rosettes. Cultivated mainly for the beauty of the basal rosette leaves.	When it finally blooms, flowers are highly attractive to insects & hummingbirds, as well as nectarivorous bats. Ripe seeds eaten by several species of small mammals & gamebirds.

Table A.5
Native Plants of Texas

Please note that each two-page "spread" is divided into a top half (with plants' growing information) and a bottom half (with plants' ornamental and wildlife values). Numbered regions correspond to the Texas Ecoregion map on page 11.

Species	Ecological Region 1 2 3 4 5 6 7 8 9 10	Habit Height	Flower	Fruit	Sun Exposure	Habitat	Soils and Moisture Regime
Pale-leaf yucca *Yucca pallida*	x (4)	Succulent 1' leaves, 2'-4' flower stalk Evergreen	Showy panicles of creamy-white flowers. May-June	Capsules. Aug.-Sept.	Full sun, part shade	Endemic to Blackland Prairies & adjacent limestone slopes.	Well-drained, xeric. Clays.
Plains yucca *Yucca campestris*	x (9)	Succulent 2' leaves, 3'-5' flower stalk Evergreen	Showy panicles of greenish-white flowers with pink tinge. April-June	Capsules, reddish-brown to gray. June-Aug.	Full sun	Prefers deep sands & dunes centered in Ward, Midland, Howard & Ector counties.	Well-drained, xeric. Sands.
Red yucca *Hesperaloe parviflora*	x x x (3,4,5) x (8)	Succulent Leaves 2'-3', flower stalk 5' Evergreen	Showy, coral to salmon pink flowers on tall stalk. May-Nov.	Capsules. Aug.-Dec.	Full sun, part shade, dappled shade	Prefers prairies, rocky slopes & mesquite groves.	Xeric, well-drained. Sands, loams & clays; likes limestone soils.
Rough agave *Agave scabra*	x (6)	Succulent Leaves 1'-2', flower stalk 4' Evergreen	Showy yellow flowers on tall bloom stalk. April-June	Capsule, brown, many-seeded. Flowers only once in its life-time	Full sun	Occurs on sandy & calcareous soils in extreme southwest Rio Grande Plains in Starr, Webb & Zapata counties.	Well-drained, xeric. Sands & clays, likes calcareous soils.
Sacahuista *Nolina texana*	x x (7,8) x (10)	Succulent 1½'-3' Evergreen	Showy whitish flowers. May-June	Capsules. Aug.-Nov.	Full sun, part shade	Prefers rocky soils & open areas on Edwards Plateau, Trans-Pecos & northern Rio Grande Plains.	Well-drained, xeric. Sands, loams & clays; likes limestone soils.

Species	Ornamental Value	Wildlife Value
Pale-leaf yucca *Yucca pallida*	Very striking accent plant, beautiful when in bloom. Leaves are a pale blue-green and only 1' tall. Tips are armed with healthy spines. Flower stalk not very tall.	Waxy white flowers emit their fragrance at night attracting moths which pollinate them. Flowers are edible & popular with white-tailed deer. Larval host plant to Yucca giant skipper.
Plains yucca *Yucca campestris*	Very striking accent plant, attractive when in bloom. This leaf succulent has solitary or numerous heads in thicket-like clumps. Plants may have stems or be stemless. Relatively unsymmetrical when mature.	Elegant waxy flowers emit their fragrance at night attracting moths which pollinate them. Flowers are edible & popular with mule deer. Seeds are eaten by small mammals & a few birds. Larval host plant to Yucca giant skipper.
Red yucca *Hesperaloe parviflora*	Very elegant succulent, used a lot in landscapes as an accent plant. Widely adaptable to various soils. Flowers bloom profusely & for a long time.	Ruby-throated & Black-chinned hummingbirds are highly attracted to flowers which provide copious nectar for long periods. White-tailed deer also love to eat the flowers.
Rough agave *Agave scabra*	Medium to large stemless plant with an open basal rosette of large grayish leaves with a rough surface.	Many species of insects are attracted to flower pollen & nectar. Hummingbirds also sip nectar from flowers. Many birds & small mammals dine on the ripe seeds.
Sacahuista *Nolina texana*	Relatively winter-hardy leaf succulent. Good accent plant on dry slopes. Large panicled flowers are hidden inside foliage.	Flowers attract several kinds of insects. The plant is toxic to livestock though. Serves as good protective cover for birds & small mammals. Larval host plant for Sandia & Atea hairstreak butterflies.

Table A.5
Native Plants of Texas

Please note that each two-page "spread" is divided into a top half (with plants' growing information) and a bottom half (with plants' ornamental and wildlife values). Numbered regions correspond to the Texas Ecoregion map on page 11.

Species	Ecological Region 1 2 3 4 5 6 7 8 9 10	Habit Height	Flower	Fruit	Sun Exposure	Habitat	Soils and Moisture Regime
Soaptree yucca *Yucca elata*	x (10)	Succulent 3'-4' leaves, 10'-18' flower stalk Evergreen	Showy panicles of creamy-white flowers. April-June	Capsules with seeds. Aug.-Sept.	Full sun	Prefers desert hills & grasslands, gypseous soils above 4000' elevation.	Well-drained xeric. Sands & loams; likes gypsum soils.
Spanish dagger *Yucca treculeana*	x (1), x x (6,7)	Succulent 5'-15' Evergreen	Showy, white & waxy flowers on tall flower stalk, fragrant at night. Feb.-April	Capsules. Sept.-Oct.	Full sun, part shade, dappled shade	Prefers tall chaparral or brushland.	Mesic, well-drained. Sands, loams, & clays.

Cactus Family – Cactaceae

Species	Ecological Region 1 2 3 4 5 6 7 8 9 10	Habit Height	Flower	Fruit	Sun Exposure	Habitat	Soils and Moisture Regime
Brown-spine prickly-pear cactus *Opuntia phaeacantha*	x (10)	Succulent 1'-5' Evergreen	Showy yellow or orange flowers. May-July	Tuna, purplish. Aug.-Sept.	Full sun	Prefers desert, grasslands & mountains. Very widespread species in west Texas.	Xeric, well-drained. Sands, loams & clays.
Prickly-pear cactus *Opuntia lindheimeri*	x (1), x x x x (6,7,8,9)	Succulent 1'-5' Evergreen	Showy yellow or orange to red flowers. May	Tuna, purplish. Sept.-Oct.	Full sun	Prefers open areas, woodlands, openings, pastures, disturbed & eroded soils O.K.	Xeric, well-drained. Sands, loams & clays.
Teddy-bear cholla *Opuntia imbricata*	x x x (7,8,9)	Succulent 3'-9' Evergreen	Showy hot pink flowers. May-June	Bright yellow tunas. Sept.-Oct.	Full sun, part shade	Prefers dry, rocky soils or sandy soils at elevations from 1200'-1800'.	Xeric, well-drained. Sands, caliche-like & limestone soils.

Species	Ornamental Value	Wildlife Value
Soaptree yucca *Yucca elata*	Very striking accent plant, lovely when in bloom. Forms a single or multi-trunked succulent. Leaves have tips armed with healthy spines. Flowers are highly showy & also edible.	Elegant waxy flowers emit their fragrance at night attracting yucca moths which pollinate them. Seeds eaten by small mammals. Flowers are edible & popular with mule deer. Larval host plant to Yucca giant skipper.
Spanish dagger *Yucca treculeana*	Dramatic accent plant with lush tropical-looking flowers. Hard to transplant old ones.	Moths pollinate fragrant white flowers by night. Good nesting shrub, well-protected. Flowers eaten by many species of mammals. Larval host plant for Strecker's giant skipper, Ursine giant skipper & Yucca giant skipper.
Cactus Family – Cactaceae		
Brown-spine prickly-pear cactus *Opuntia pheacantha*	Hardy succulent with attractive flowers & juicy rosy-purplish fruits. Makes a good barrier plant.	Flowers attract many kinds of insects, especially bees, moths, butter-flies, beetles, flies, etc. which are attracted to both nectar & pollen. Fruits & pads are highly sought after by several species of mammals which must brave the guard spines.
Prickly-pear cactus *Opuntia lindheimeri*	Hardy succulent with attractive flowers & juicy rosy-purplish fruits. Makes a good barrier plant.	Flowers attract many kinds of insects, especially bees, butterflies, beetles & flies, etc. which are attracted to both nectar & pollen. Fruits & pads are highly sought after by several species of mammals which must brave the guard spines.
Teddy-bear cholla *Opuntia imbricata*	Highly attractive, prickly shrub which is great from landscapes. It becomes tree-like in time. While it is a slow grower, it assumes a marvelous shape with time. If it rains, blooms are shiney. Plant is hard to handle because of spines.	Flowers are highly attractive to several kinds of insects, especially bees. Tunas are eaten by several species of birds. A spectacularly safe nesting tree, especially for Cactus Wren & Greater Roadrunner.

Table A.5
Native Plants of Texas

Please note that each two-page "spread" is divided into a top half (with plants' growing information) and a bottom half (with plants' ornamental and wildlife values). Numbered regions correspond to the Texas Ecoregion map on page 11.

Pineapple Family – Bromeliaceae

Species	Ecological Region 1 2 3 4 5 6 7 8 9 10	Habit Height	Flower	Fruit	Sun Exposure	Habitat	Soils and Moisture Regime
Texas false agave *Hechtia texensis*	x (10)	Succulent 2'-4' Evergreen	Small unisexual flowers on stalk. Feb.-May	Capsules, oval with oblong, narrowly winged seeds. May-Aug.	Full sun	Prefers canyons & rocky areas & limestone mesas, ridges & slopes especially in Big Bend area.	Well-drained, xeric. Prefers limestone soils.
Guapilla *Hechtia glomerata*	x (6)	Succulent 4"-6" Evergreen	Showy creamy white male & female flowers on separate plants. May-Aug.	Capsule, brown, many-seeded. July-Aug.	Full sun	Occurs on gravelly sites, sandstone formations & saline clays in Starr County.	Well-drained, xeric. Sands, sandy loams & clays.

Beech Family – Fagaceae

Species	Ecological Region 1 2 3 4 5 6 7 8 9 10	Habit Height	Flower	Fruit	Sun Exposure	Habitat	Soils and Moisture Regime
American beech *Fagus grandifolia*	x (1)	Tree, large 80'-100' Deciduous	Inconspicuous male & female flowers on same tree. April-May	Nut. Sept.-Nov.	Full sun, part shade	Grows in deep, rich, fertile soils along streams & woodlands of Pineywoods region.	Well-drained, mesic. Sandy loams, alluvial soils.
Arizona white oak *Quercus arizonica*	x (10)	Tree, small 20'-35' Deciduous	Inconspicuous staminate & pistillate catkins, yellowish. April-May	Acorns, every year. Sept.-Nov.	Full sun, part shade	Prefers some mountain ranges of the Trans-Pecos. High elevations in El Paso, Culberson & Brewster counties.	Well-drained, xeric to mesic. Loams, clays, various rocky soils.
Blackjack oak *Quercus marilandica*	x x x x x (1,2,3,4,5)	Tree, large 40'-60' Deciduous	Inconspicuous male & female catkins, red & greenish. April	Acorns, every 2 years. Nov.-Dec.	Full sun, part shade	Prefers upland forests of timber belt in East & Central Texas.	Well-drained, mesic-xeric. Sands, sandy loams, loams & clays. Tolerates dry, sandy, gravelly soils.

Species	Ornamental Value	Wildlife Value
Pineapple Family – Bromeliaceae		
Texas false agave *Hechtia texensis*	Highly ornamental succulent of Pineapple family with attractive yellowish-green leaves that turn reddish in the fall. The basal rosette of leaves make this plant a great accent plant in proper habitat.	Several small mammals eat the ripened seeds. Insects of many varieties are attracted to the small flowers.
Guapilla *Hechtia glomerata*	Sharply serrate linear basal rosette leaves with the habit of a yucca or agave, but in the pineapple family. Often forms dense colonies.	Flowers attract myriads of insects of all varieties. Spiny plant provides excellent cover for small mammals & birds. Seeds eaten by small mammals & birds.
Beech Family – Fagaceae		
American beech *Fagus grandifolia*	Handsome shade tree with beautiful shiny green leaves & smooth gray bark. Leaves turn copper gold in the fall.	Excellent cover & nesting tree. Prickly burrs contain sweet nuts relished by several kinds of game & songbirds, i.e. woodpeckers, titmice, nuthatches, jays & sparrows. Also eaten by raccoon, beaver, opossum & fox. Deer eat nuts & browse leaves.
Arizona white oak *Quercus arizonica*	At low elevations a tree, at high elevations a shrub with rounded top & spreading branches with firm, rigid evergreen leaves of bluish-green color.	Acorns & mast highly sought after by woodpeckers, gamebirds, jays & small mammals. Makes a good protective cover & nesting tree. Good substrate for insectivorous birds. Spring catkins eaten by various species of birds in the spring.
Blackjack oak *Quercus marilandica*	Beautiful shade tree often associated with Post oak. Leaves are dark green, distinctive & puppet-shaped. Slow-growing & hard to transplant. Can tolerate relatively poor conditions.	Provides dense canopy cover. Good nesting tree & substrate for insectivorous birds. Turkey & deer love acorns. Woodpeckers, jays, & doves eat & cache them. Smaller wildlife eat crushed ones. Larval host plant of Juvenal's, Horace's duskywings & White M hairstreak butterflies.

Native Plants of Texas

Please note that each two-page "spread" is divided into a top half (with plants' growing information) and a bottom half (with plants' ornamental and wildlife values). Numbered regions correspond to the Texas Ecoregion map on page 11.

Species	Ecological Region 1 2 3 4 5 6 7 8 9 10	Habit Height	Flower	Fruit	Sun Exposure	Habitat	Soils and Moisture Regime
Bluejack oak *Quercus incana*	x x x	Tree, small 30'-40' Deciduous	Inconspicuous male catkins & female flowers, red to yellowish green. April	Acorns, every second year. Sept.-Nov.	Full sun, part shade	Prefers dry, sandy uplands in timber belt of East & Central Texas.	Well-drained, xeric-mesic. Sands & sandy loams. Tolerates deep sugar sands.
Bur oak *Quercus macrocarpa*	x x x x x x x	Tree, large 60'-80' Deciduous	Inconspicuous male & female catkins, red & greenish. March-April	Acorns. Sept.-Oct.	Full sun, part shade	Prefers moist forests along streams & in fallow fields.	Well-drained, mesic. Sands, loams, and clays.
Chinquapin oak *Quercus muehlenbergii*	x x x x x x	Tree, large 40'-60' Deciduous	Inconspicuous catkins, male & female, cream to yellowish. March-June	Acorns. Sept.-Oct., every 2 years	Full sun, part shade	Prefers upland forested areas.	Well-drained, mesic. Loams, clays & lime stone soils.
Chisos red oak *Quercus gravesii*	x x	Tree, large 20'-40' Deciduous to Persistent	Insonspicuous staminate & pistillate catkins, reddish. April-May	Acorns. Aug.-Sept.	Full sun, part shade	Prefers mountains, canyons & arroyos in both igneous & limestone substrates in Davis, Guadalupe & Chisos mountains from 1200' to 7600' elevation.	Well-drained, mesic. Limestone & igneous soils; sands, loams & clays.
Emory oak *Quercus emoryi*	x x	Tree, large 30'-60' Persistent to Evergreen	Staminate & pistillate catkins on same tree, yellowish. March-April	Acorns, paired, sessile, every year. June-Sept.	Full sun, part shade	Prefers igneous mountainous regions & canyons in Trans-Pecos. Usually above 5000' in elevation.	Well-drained, mesic. Likes extra water. Likes deep soils, acid sands & loams, igneous soils.

Species	Ornamental Value	Wildlife Value
Bluejack oak *Quercus incana*	Very striking & decorative small oak tree. Leaves with white hoary undersides. Highly drought tolerant. Very interesting branching pattern. Trees often form dense thickets.	Wildlife feed on the acorns. The dense thickets that are formed provide excellent cover & nesting sites on otherwise barren sandy habitats.
Bur oak *Quercus macrocarpa*	Very graceful shade tree, widely adaptive, fast-growing for an oak. Attractive leaves, unusual acorn, drought resistant & long-lived.	Important source of food for several species of birds, woodpeckers, jays, game birds. Also sought after by mammals, white-tailed deer, squirrels & raccoons. Good substrate for insectivorous birds. Larval host plant for Sleepy & Juvenal's Duskywing butterflies.
Chinquapin oak *Quercus muehlenbergii*	Beautiful, fast-growing shade tree. Attractive leaf shape. Bronze autumn color.	Sweet, edible nuts favored by many species of birds & mammals, deer, raccoons, opossums & squirrels. Good nesting & cover tree. Good substrate for insectivorous birds. Larval host plant to Horace's Duskywing butterflies.
Chisos red oak *Quercus gravesii*	A small or large tree with roughly furrowed, hard, black bark & deciduous leaves that turn scarlet in the autumn.	The acorns are eaten by various species of ground squirrels & the foliage is sometimes browsed by mule deer. Acorns prized by jays, woodpeckers & gamebirds. Good protective cover & nesting tree. Birds eat catkins in sping. Good substrate for insectivorous birds.
Emory oak *Quercus emoryi*	A large shrub or tree to 60' depending on elevation with a black trunk, rounded shape & persistent holly-like leaves arranged in star-shaped clusters. Distinctive black bark like back of an armadillo. Does well in Alpine & Ft. Davis. Also Panhandle sands.	Emory oak acorns & mast are highly sought after by wildlife, both birds & mammals. Serves as an excellent protective cover & nesting tree. Good substrate for insectivorous birds. Birds eat the catkins in the spring.

Table A.5
Native Plants of Texas

Please note that each two-page "spread" is divided into a top half (with plants' growing information) and a bottom half (with plants' ornamental and wildlife values). Numbered regions correspond to the Texas Ecoregion map on page 11.

Species	Ecological Region 1 2 3 4 5 6 7 8 9 10	Habit Height	Flower	Fruit	Sun Exposure	Habitat	Soils and Moisture Regime
Gambel oak *Quercus gambelii*	x	Tree, small 15'-25'	Inconspicuous staminate & pistillate catkins. May	Acorns, every year. Sept.-Oct.	Full sun, part shade	Prefers high elevations, never found lower than 7,500'. Found in Chinati, Chisos, Davis & Guadalupe mountains.	Well-drained, mesic. Prefers alkaline or acid soils.
Gray oak *Quercus grisea*	x x	Tree, small 10'-50' Deciduous	Inconspicuous staminate & pistillate catkins on same tree. April	Acorns, every year. Sept.-Oct.	Full sun, part shade	Prefers mountainous areas, conyon slopes, wide areas in the Trans-Pecos to 7800' in Chisos, Chinati, Davis, Del Norte, Glass, Guadalupe, Hueco & Vieja mountains.	Well-drained, xeric. Igneous & limestone soils, prefers acid sands.
Lacey oak *Quercus glaucoides*	x x	Tree, small 20'-30' Deciduous	Inconspicuous male & female catkins, red & greenish. March-April	Acorns. Sept.-Oct.	Full sun, part shade	Likes deep soils; sands, loams, clays.	Well-drained, xeric. Sands, loams & clays. Loves thin limestone, caliche-type soils.
Mohr oak *Quercus mohriana*	x x x x	Tree, small 10'-20' Persistent to Evergreen	Inconspicuous male & female catkins, reddish. April-May	Acorns, reddish brown, every year. Sept.-Nov.	Full sun, part shade	Prefers limestone hills & mountains, also grasslands, igneous slopes in West & West Central Texas. Often shrubby, creating mottes in the Rolling Plains & western Edwards Plateau.	Well-drained, xeric. Sands, loams, hard limestone, exposed caliche-like soils.

Species	Ornamental Value	Wildlife Value
Gambel oak *Quercus gambelii*	An attractive small tree for highter elevations. Cannot tolerate long periods of high heat. Has variable habit & can form dense thickets. Young leaves are brownish gray & very attractively dissected.	Foliage is sometimes browsed by mule deer & porcupine. Sweet acorns are highly prized by birds of several species & also by small mammals. Good protective cover & nesting tree. Good substrate for insectivorous birds.
Gray oak *Quercus grisea*	Sometimes only a shrub on exposed slopes; a small tree on alluvial canyons. Has entire or toothed grayish-green leaves.	Leaves are browsed by mule deer, porcupine, while many species of ground squirrel, rodents & javalina feed on acorns. Gamebirds, jays & woodpeckers eat the acorns. Good cover & nest tree. Good substrate for insectivorous birds. Birds eat catkins.
Lacey oak *Quercus glaucoides*	A very attractive Texas oak of moderate size. May be multi-trunked. Has dusky blue to blue-gray deciduous leaves & fine golden fall color. Extremely drought tolerant. Can grow on thin, hard limestone rock specially on Edwards Plateau.	Excellent cover & nesting tree. Good substrate for insectivorous birds. Squirrels devour acorns & also nest in tree. Several species of birds also love acorns: turkey, quail, woodpeckers, doves & jays. White-tailed deer also love them.
Mohr oak *Quercus mohriana*	One of the few oaks of the midgrass to shortgrass prairies. A small, round-topped evergreen oak with dark green to gray green leaves with wavy edges & furry white underside. Forms thickets, is drought tolerant & fire resistant.	Mohr oak is an excellent nesting & protective cover for birds & small mammals. Catkins eaten by several species of birds. Acorns eaten & cached by several kinds of birds & mammals. Good substrate for insectivorous birds.

Table A.5
Native Plants of Texas

Please note that each two-page "spread" is divided into a top half (with plants' growing information) and a bottom half (with plants' ornamental and wildlife values). Numbered regions correspond to the Texas Ecoregion map on page 11.

Species	Ecological Region 1	2	3	4	5	6	7	8	9	10	Habit Height	Flower	Fruit	Sun Exposure	Habitat	Soils and Moisture Regime
Plateau liveoak *Quercus fusiformis*	x	x	x	x	x	x	x	x			Tree, large 30'-50' Evergreen	Inconspicuous male & female catkins, red & greenish. March-June	Acorns. Sept.-Oct.	Full sun, part shade	Prefers calcareous substrate, rocky limestone soils of the Hill Country.	Well-drained, xeric-mesic. Sands, loams, clays. Prefers limestone & caliche type soils. Will grow on any alkaline to slightly acid soil.
Post oak *Quercus stellata*	x	x	x	x	x	x	x	x			Tree, large 40'-50' Deciduous	Inconspicuous catkins, male & female, reddish. March-May	Acorns. Sept.-Nov.	Full sun, part shade	Prefers dryish uplands, also grows in moister areas in East Texas.	Well-drained, mesic. Sands, sandy loams, prefers acid soils. Also neutral clays.
Scaly-bark oak *Quercus sinuata v. breviloba*			x	x	x		x	x			Tree, small 12'-40' Deciduous	Inconspicuous male & female catkins, reddish. March	Acorns, every year. Sept.	Full sun, part shade	Prefers open wooded limestone hills at low elevations, also grows in grasslands.	Well-drained, xeric-mesic. Loam, clays. Likes limestone soils.
Shumard red oak *Quercus shumardii*	x	x	x	x	x						Tree, large 50'-100' Deciduous	Inconspicuous catkins, male & female, greenish. March-May	Acorns. Sept.-Oct., every 2 years	Full sun, part shade	Prefers moist forest & limestone upper woods.	Well-drained, mesic. Sands, loams & clays.
Southern live oak *Quercus virginiana*	x	x	x			x					Tree, large 40'-60' Evergreen	Inconspicuous male & female reddish green catkins on same tree. April-May	Acorns. Sept.-Oct.	Full sun, part shade	Prefers timberlands east of the Brazos in Gulf Coastal Prairies and south central Texas.	Well-drained, mesic. Sands, loams & clays. Prefers clay loams & gravelly clay loams.
Southern red oak *Quercus falcata*	x	x									Tree, large 60'-70' Deciduous	Inconspicuous male & female downy catkins, on the same tree. March-May	Acorns, rounded with shallow cup, ripening every fall. Sept.-Oct.	Full sun, part shade	Prefers upland sites in the forests of East Texas.	Well-drained, mesic. Sands, to sandy loams. Likes acid soils.

Species	Ornamental Value	Wildlife Value
Plateau liveoak *Quercus fusiformis*	Plateau liveoak is an excellent evergreen shade tree often found growing in mottes. Adapts to a variety of sites, but not extremely wet or dry ones.	Excellent cover & nesting tree. Acorns have high energy value & eaten by almost all forms of wildlife: deer, squirrels, fox, raccoons, game-birds, woodpeckers, & jays. Fine substrate for insectivorous birds. Larval host plant of 3 hairstreak species & duskywing butterflies.
Post oak *Quercus stellata*	Slow-growing oak with maltese-cross leaves. Widespread in Texas. Rugged shade tree good in otherwise inhospitable conditions. Winter silhouettes strikingly dramatic. Provides dense canopy cover. Dominant in sandy areas in north & east central Texas.	Good nesting & cover tree; fine substrate for insectivorous birds. Turkey & deer relish acorns as do doves, woodpeckers & jays. Smaller birds eat crushed ones that fall on ground. Larval host plant for Northern hairstreak, Horace's & Juvenal's duskywing butterflies.
Scaly-bark oak *Quercus sinuata v. breviloba*	A shaggy-barked multi-trunked tree which has many growth forms, responding to different habitat & moisture regimes. Can form dense thickets through suckering.	Excellent cover & nesting tree. Good substrate for insectivorous birds. Gamebirds, woodpeckers & jays eat or cache acorns. Also important food source for deer, small mammals & other wildlife. Larval host plant of duskywing & hairstreak butterflies.
Shumard red oak *Quercus shumardii*	Gorgeous shade tree with beautiful leaves. Red color in autumn. Fast-growing & disease resistant.	Acorns eaten by a number of birds & mammals. Good cover & nesting tree. Good substrate for insectivorous birds. Larval host plant for a few species of Duskywing butterflies.
Southern live oak *Quercus virginiana*	Gracious yet powerful shade tree usually festooned with Spanish moss. Long lived & resistant to salt spray. Often planted as orna-mental outside of natural range. May be susceptible to oak wilt.	Excellent cover & nest tree. Good substrate for insectivorous birds. Acorns relished by many species of small mammals (squirrels & raccoons), gamebirds & songbirds (woodpeckers & jays). Larval host plant of Horace's duskywing & Northern White M hairstreak butterflies.
Southern red oak *Quercus falcata*	Large shade tree with open, round-topped crown & stout branch-es. Deeply lobed leaves are attractive & produce showy red autumn color. Fast growing & long lived. Does not like clay soils.	Small acorns are eaten by several species of birds, woodpeckers, jays, game birds, etc. Deer, fox & squirrels also relish them. Good cover & nesting tree & good substrate for insectivorous birds. Larval host plant of Banded hairstreak & White M hairstreak butterflies.

Table A.5
Native Plants of Texas

Please note that each two-page "spread" is divided into a top half (with plants' growing information) and a bottom half (with plants' ornamental and wildlife values). Numbered regions correspond to the Texas Ecoregion map on page 11.

Species	Ecological Region 1 2 3 4 5 6 7 8 9 10	Habit Height	Flower	Fruit	Sun Exposure	Habitat	Soils and Moisture Regime
Swamp chestnut oak *Quercus michauxii*	x x	Tree, large 60'-80' Deciduous	Inconspicuous greenish male & female catkins. April-May	Acorns. Sept.-Oct.	Full sun, part shade	Prefers moist woods associated with major rivers & streams in East Texas.	Mesic-hydric. Sands, loams & clays; likes acid soils.
Vasey oak *Quercus pungens v. vaseyana*	x (7), x (10)	Tree, small 25'-30' Persistent to Evergreen	Inconspicuous male & female catkins, reddish on separate trees. March-May	Acorns, every year, solitary or in pairs. Sept.-Oct.	Full sun, part shade	Prefers dry limestone hills & canyon bluffs in desertic mountais, dry arroyos & along creek banks.	Well-drained, xeric. Sands, loams & clays. Likes limestone, caliche-type soils.
Water oak *Quercus nigra*	x x x	Tree, large 60'-80' Deciduous	Inconspicuous male catkins & female spikes. April-May	Acorns ripening every 2 years. Sept.-Oct.	Full sun, part shade	Occurs along streams & river bottoms, also moist upland woods in timber region of East Texas.	Mesic-hydric soils; poor drainage O.K. Sands, loams, clays, likes acid soils. Tolerates gumbo. Fast growing & easy to transplant.
Willow oak *Quercus phellos*	x x x	Tree, large 60'-100' Deciduous	Inconspicuous male hairy catkins & female clusters on same tree. March-May	Acorns, ripening every 2 years. Sept.-Oct.	Full sun, part shade	Grows in bottom-lands & floodplains associated with major rivers, streams & creeks throughout East Texas.	Mesic-hydric soils. Sands, loams & clays; tolerates poorly-drained hardpans.

Birch Family – Betulaceae

Species	Ecological Region 1 2 3 4 5 6 7 8 9 10	Habit Height	Flower	Fruit	Sun Exposure	Habitat	Soils and Moisture Regime
American hornbeam (Blue beech) *Carpinus caroliniana*	x x	Tree, small 15'-30' Deciduous	Inconspicuous male & female catkins on same tree. March-May	Nutlets, in clusters. Sept.-Oct.	Part shade, dappled shade, shade	Prefers rich bottom-lands, often along steams in moist woods.	Well-drained, mesic-hydric soils. Sands, loams & clays.

Species	Ornamental Value	Wildlife Value
Swamp chestnut oak *Quercus michauxii*	Attractive shade tree with simple shallowly toothed leaves, woolly on the bottom. This long-lived tree prefers moist soils. Grows well in Houston; tolerates gumbo soils.	Acorns are sought after by many species of wildlife especially wild turkey, quail, mourning dove, woodpeckers & jays. Good cover & nesting tree & good substrate for insectivorous birds. Larval host plant of Juvenal's & Horace's duskywing, Northern & White M hairstreak butterflies.
Vasey oak *Quercus pungens v. vaseyana*	A small very drought-tolerant evergreen oak. Sometimes a shrub. Forms small thickets. May be multi-trunked. Quite cold hardy. Leaves are pleasantly aromatic, lustrous with conspicuous veins.	Acorns are eaten by mule deer, raccoons, porcupines, & ground squirrels. Provides good nesting site & protective cover for birds. Jays & woodpeckers also eat them. Good substrate for insectivorous birds. Larval host plant to duskywing butterflies.
Water oak *Quercus nigra*	Medium to large-sized shade tree with a round top and dull blue-green leaves held until December. Grows on variety of sites, tolerates gumbo. Does well in Houston.	Sweet edible acorns favored by over 17 species of birds & also mammals, i.e. deer, raccoons, opossums & squirrels. Good nesting & cover tree. Good substrate for insectivorous birds. Larval host plant of Horace's Duskywing, White M & Northern hairstreak butterflies.
Willow oak *Quercus phellos*	A graceful, airy oak with attractive golden leaves in the fall. This fast-growing shade tree has lustrous foliage & a high-branching crown. Does not tolerate dry sites. Grows well in Houston.	Abundant acorns eaten by several species of wildlife that feed in bottomlands, i.e. squirrels, beaver & fox; jays, woodpeckers & wood duck. Good cover & nesting tree. Good substrate for insectivorous birds. Larval host plant of Horace's duskywing & White M hairstreak butterflies.

Birch Family – Betulaceae

American hornbeam (Blue beech) *Carpinus caroliniana*	Airy, graceful understory tree with simple, alternate leaves. Notable for its beautiful trunk which is smooth & sinewy. Very shade tolerant. Though it likes moisture, it doesn't tolerate flooding. Slow growing & short lived but pretty.	Nutlets are eaten by squirrels & other small mammals. Birds such as cardinals & finches also savor them. Larval host plant of Striped hairstreak, Red-spotted purple & Tiger swallowtail butterflies.

Native Plants of Texas

Please note that each two-page "spread" is divided into a top half (with plants' growing information) and a bottom half (with plants' ornamental and wildlife values). Numbered regions correspond to the Texas Ecoregion map on page 11.

Species	Ecological Region 1 2 3 4 5 6 7 8 9 10	Habit Height	Flower	Fruit	Sun Exposure	Habitat	Soils and Moisture Regime
River birch *Betula nigra*	x	Tree, large 25'-90' Deciduous	Inconspicuous catkins, male brown & female green on same tree. Feb.-March	Cones, cylinder-shaped with small winged seeds. April-June	Full sun, part shade	Occurs in wetlands near creeks, swamps & sloughs.	Mesic-hydric, poor drainage O.K. Sands, loams, or clays.

Borage Family – Boraginaceae

Species	Ecological Region 1 2 3 4 5 6 7 8 9 10	Habit Height	Flower	Fruit	Sun Exposure	Habitat	Soils and Moisture Regime
Anaqua *Ehretia anacua*	x x x	Tree, large 25'-45' Evergreen	Showy white clusters of flowers, fragrant. March-Nov. with the rains	Drupes, orange. April-June	Full sun, part shade, dappled shade	Prefers thickets, forests, palm groves & open woodlands along fence rows & in brushlands.	Well-drained, mesic. Sands, loams & clays.
Texas wild olive *Cordia boissieri*	x	Tree, small, ornamental 12'-24' Persistent to Evergreen	Showy white crinkly 2"-flowers with yellow spot in throat. Year-long	Drupe, fleshy egg-shaped, white turning to purple. Sept.-Nov.	Full sun, part shade	Occurs along road-sides, in pastures & on flat lands in poor, dry soil; also on hill-sides of the Lower Rio Grande Valley.	Well-drained, xeric. Sands, loams & clays; likes caliche-type soils.

Buckthorn Family – Rhamnaceae

Species	Ecological Region 1 2 3 4 5 6 7 8 9 10	Habit Height	Flower	Fruit	Sun Exposure	Habitat	Soils and Moisture Regime
Brasil *Condalia hookeri*	x x x	Tree, large 12'-30' Persistent to Evergreen	Inconspicuous yellowish flowers. March-April	Drupes, blue-black, sweet & fleshy. Sept.-Oct.	Full sun, part shade	Prefers dryish lime-stone hills, also locally found on Rio Grande plains.	Well-drained, mesic-xeric. Sands, loams, & clays.
Carolina buckthorn *Rhamnus caroliniana*	x x x x x	Tree, small 12'-20' Deciduous	Inconspicuous, small greenish-yellow flowers. May-June	Drupes, reddish brown. Aug.-Sept.	Full sun, part shade, shade	Prefers moist woods, fence rows, along creeks, heads of draws & canyon slopes.	Well-drained, mesic. Sands, loams & clays.

Species	Ornamental Value	Wildlife Value
River birch *Betula nigra*	Attractive ornamental tree with dark red-brown bark peeling off branches in papery sheets. Has graceful silhouette & good yellow fall color. Fast grower but short lived. Doesn't tolerate flooding, but likes moist soils. Does well in Houston.	Several species of small birds including chickadees & finches eat the ripe seeds. Twigs & buds are browsed by white-tailed deer. Beaver, rabbits & squirrels also eat various parts.
Borage Family – Boraginaceae		
Anaqua *Ehretia anacua*	Attractive rough-leafed tree with fragrant white flowers & bright orange juicy fruit. Very drought tolerant once established. Has a very dense crown. Often planted as an ornamental. Can be sensitive to frost. Good honey tree.	All sorts of insects gather nectar from the fragrant nectar-laden flowers. Fruits are eaten by numerous species of birds & small mammals.
Texas wild olive *Cordia boissieri*	An ornamental small tree with a narrow rounded crown & short trunk that creates deep shade underneath. This showy plant blooms all year. It is quite cold sensitive, but is fast growing. Once established, it is very drought tolerant.	Trumpet-shaped crinkly flowers attract several kinds of insects. The fruits are devoured by several species of birds & small mammals.
Buckthorn Family – Rhamnaceae		
Brasil *Condalia hookeri*	Can grow to be large shade tree in South Texas. Usually a small tree with spatulate lime green leaves. Flowers in spring, but fruits sporadically throughout late summer & fall. Has an attractive shape.	Continuously bears fruit that is sought after by many kinds of birds: robins, bluebirds, cardinals, towhees, sparrows, mockingbirds, finches, & gamebirds. Thorns make it a good cover & nesting tree. Flowers attract many insects. Larval host plant of Snout butterfly.
Carolina buckthorn *Rhamnus caroliniana*	Very attractive understory tree with pretty leaves & berries. Quite ornamental & adapted to a wide range of sites. Has good fall color & fruits borne over a long time.	When ripe, fruits are devoured by several species of birds, i.e. thrashers, robins, mockingbirds, cardinals, finches, etc. Flowers are good nectar source for bees, butterflies & other insects. Larval host plant for Gray hairstreak butterfly.

Table A.5
Native Plants of Texas

Please note that each two-page "spread" is divided into a top half (with plants' growing information) and a bottom half (with plants' ornamental and wildlife values). Numbered regions correspond to the Texas Ecoregion map on page 11.

Species	Ecological Region 1 2 3 4 5 6 7 8 9 10	Habit Height	Flower	Fruit	Sun Exposure	Habitat	Soils and Moisture Regime
Texas snakewood *Colubrina texensis*	x x x (6 7 8) x (10)	Tree, small 5'-15' Deciduous	Small greenish-yellow perfect flowers. April-May	Drupes, dark brown to black with 2-3 nutlets. June-Aug.	Full sun, part shade	Occurs in open areas, along hills in areas of local abundance.	Well-drained, xeric. Sands, loams, clays & limestone soils.
Caltrop Family – Zygophyl-laceae							
Guayacan *Guaiacum angustifolia*	x (1) x x (6 7) x (10)	Tree, small, ornamental 10'-20' Evergreen	Showy purple flowers with yellow anthers. March-April, off & on to Sept, depending on rains	Capsules, brown with 1-3 orange seeds. Aug.- Sept.	Full sun, part shade	Prefers brushy areas & open flats. Can be found on well-drained sites on the Coastal Bend.	Xeric, well-drained. Sands, loams & clays. Likes limestone soils.
Catalpa Family – Bignoniaceae							
Desert willow *Chilopsis linearis*	x x (6 7) x (10)	Tree, small, ornamental 10'-15' Deciduous	Showy pink-magenta trumpet shaped flowers. May-Sept.	Capsule with winged seeds. Aug.-Nov.	Full sun, part shade	Prefers dry washes & gravelly creek beds, arroyos & water courses.	Well-drained, mesic-xeric. Sands, loams & clays.
Citrus Family – Rutaceae							
Colima *Zanthoxylum fagara*	x (6) x (10)	Tree, small 10'-30' Evergreen	Small yellow-green flowers. Jan.-June	Follicle, rusty brown with one seed. Sept.-Dec.	Full sun, part shade	Prefers brushy areas or flats near coast.	Xeric, well-drained. Sands, loams or clays.
Hercules'-club *Zanthoxylum clava-herculis*	x x x x (2 3 4 5) x (10)	Tree, small 20'-40' Deciduous	Showy, greenish-yellow flat-topped flower clusters, distinctive odor. March-April	Capsule. Aug.-Sept.	Full sun	Prefers deep heavy soils on disturbed or abandoned cropland, along fence rows.	Well-drained, mesic. Sands, loams, acid or neutral.

Species	Ornamental Value	Wildlife Value
Texas snakewood *Colubrina texensis*	A thicket-forming small tree or shrub with light gray zig-zag twigs, urn-shaped fruit & grayish green leaves. Drought tolerant once established.	Texas snakewood makes a good protective cover & nesting tree. Several kinds of insects are attracted to the small nectar-laden flowers. Birds & small mammals will gladly eat the fruit.
Caltrop Family – Zygophyl-laceae		
Guayacan *Guaiacum angustifolia*	Highly attractive & unusual small tree with compact branches, tiny compound leaves & purple flower clusters. Tree has a very distinctive & eye-catching habit. Often grows in clumps with branches appearing thick, black & stubby.	The purple & yellow flowers attract several kinds of insects. Excellent honey plant. Good nest tree. Leaves are highly nutritious browse for white-tailed deer. Arils eaten by several species of birds & small mammals. Larval host plant of Gray & Lyside hairstreak butterflies.
Catalpa Family – Bignoniaceae		
Desert willow *Chilopsis linearis*	Fast-growing, lightly ornamental tree with attractive willow-like leaves & very showy tubular flowers. Can be quite winter hardy. Is a phreatophyte which will extend its roots deep down to the water table. Does not like to be overwatered in cultivation.	Both insects & hummingbirds are attracted to the flowers. Orioles & tanagers will also feed on the flowers. Various species of birds forage on the winged seeds.
Citrus Family – Rutaceae		
Colima *Zanthoxylum fagara*	Aromatic, very prickly small tree with compound leaves & small yellow-green flowers. Red berries can be very striking & decorative when plant is heavy with fruit.	Leaves are an important source of browse for white-tailed deer. Flowers attract several kinds of insects. Several species of passerine birds use it as a nesting & cover site. Berries are also eaten by birds.
Hercules'-club *Zanthoxylum clava-herculis*	Aromatic small tree with interesting trunk sporting warty protuberances. Intolerant of shade.	Birds eat the seeds which explains why so many have proliferated under telephone wires along fence lines. Larval host plant for the beautiful Giant swallowtail butterfly.

Table A.5
Native Plants of Texas

Please note that each two-page "spread" is divided into a top half (with plants' growing information) and a bottom half (with plants' ornamental and wildlife values). Numbered regions correspond to the Texas Ecoregion map on page 11.

Species	Ecological Region 1	2	3	4	5	6	7	8	9	10	Habit Height	Flower	Fruit	Sun Exposure	Habitat	Soils and Moisture Regime
Jopoy *Esenbeckia berlandieri v. runyonii*						x					Tree, small 10'-15' Evergreen	Showy white to greenish white flowers, in clusters, fragrant. March-April, again Sept-Oct.	Capsule, deeply lobed & woody. April-June, again in fall	Part shade, dappled shade	Prefers banks of resacas & streams in extreme South Texas, Cameron County.	Mesic, well-drained. Sands, loams & clays, alkaline soils preferred.
Lotebush *Ziziphus obtusifolia*		x				x	x			x	Tree, small 6'-10' Deciduous	Inconspicuous greenish yellow flowers. March-April	Drupe, black & fleshy. July-Sept.	Full sun, part shade	Prefers upland brushy areas & stream banks.	Well-drained, mesic-xeric. Sands, loams & clays.

Custard Apple Family – Annonaceae

Species	Ecological Region 1	2	3	4	5	6	7	8	9	10	Habit Height	Flower	Fruit	Sun Exposure	Habitat	Soils and Moisture Regime
Common paw paw *Asimina triloba*	x	x									Tree, small 20'-30' Deciduous	Exotic-looking maroon fleshy flowers. April-May	Paw paw. Sept.-Oct.	Full sun, part shade, dappled shade	Prefers deep rich soils of bottomlands & creek valleys in deep East & northeast Texas.	Mesic-hydric soils; prefers moist situations. Sands, sandy loams, loams & clays.

Cyrilla Family – Cyrillaceae

Species	Ecological Region 1	2	3	4	5	6	7	8	9	10	Habit Height	Flower	Fruit	Sun Exposure	Habitat	Soils and Moisture Regime
Titi *Cyrilla racemiflora*	x	x									Tree, small 10'-30' Persistent to Evergreen	Showy racemes of yellow-ish white flowers, fragrant. May	Capsules, egg-shaped with one to several small hard seeds. Aug.-Sept.	Full sun, part shade, dappled shade	Prefers wetland areas, swamps & bottom-lands of Pineywoods & Gulf Coast Prairies & Marshes. Also occurs on sandy ridges.	Hydric, poor drainage O.K. Sands, sandy loams, loams, acid soils preferred. Tolerates gumbo.

Species	Ornamental Value	Wildlife Value
Jopoy *Esenbeckia berlandieri v. runyonii*	Considered one of the rarest trees in Texas, this small attractive plant has dark glossy evergreen trifoliate leaves & is very ornamental. Has whitish bark with a rounded top look. Can be found in cultivation in Hidalgo, as well as Cameron counties.	Jopoy makes an excellent protective cover & nesting tree. Many kinds of insects are attracted to the fragrant flowers.
Lotebush *Ziziphus obtusifolia*	Rounded stout thorny shrub or small tree with grayish green leaves & black fleshy fruits. Becomes leafless during drought. Tolerates a variety of soil types.	Leaves are occasionally browsed by white-tailed deer. Flowers, though small, are very attractive to nectar-loving insects. Fruits are eaten by a number of small mammals & birds. Because of protective thorns, this is a good cover & nesting tree.
Custard Apple Family – Annonaceae		
Common paw paw *Asimina triloba*	Tropical-looking understory tree with large aromatic leaves. Leaves turn rich butter yellow in the fall. Prefers moist situations protected from the wind.	The luscious fruit is eaten by several kinds of wildlife, both birds & mammals. Fruits rarely stay on the tree long enough to get ripe. Larval host plant of the Zebra swallowtail butterfly.
Cyrilla Family – Cyrillaceae		
Titi *Cyrilla racemiflora*	Highly attractive almost evergreen tree which can form thickets. Great around shallow ponds & bog areas. Smooth cinnamon colored trunk with interesting flowers. Leaves reddish yellow in the fall.	Bees are highly attracted to the fragrant flowers. Fruits turn a mellow yellowish brown when ripe & seeds are eaten by small mammals & a few species of birds.

Table A.5
Native Plants of Texas

Please note that each two-page "spread" is divided into a top half (with plants' growing information) and a bottom half (with plants' ornamental and wildlife values). Numbered regions correspond to the Texas Ecoregion map on page 11.

Species	Ecological Region 1	2	3	4	5	6	7	8	9	10	Habit Height	Flower	Fruit	Sun Exposure	Habitat	Soils and Moisture Regime
Dogwood Family – Cornaceae																
Flowering dogwood *Cornus florida*	x	x									Tree, ornamental 25'-40' Deciduous	Showy white flowers (bracts). March-May	Berries, red. Aug.-Sept.	Dappled shade, part shade; can tolerate full sun. Very shade tolerant	Prefers moist woodlands & edges of thickets, also along streams.	Well-drained, mesic. Sands, sandy loams, loams, slightly acid soils.
Rough-leaf dogwood *Cornus drummondii*				x	x		x				Tree, small, ornamental 10'-20' Deciduous	Showy, creamy-white flower heads. May-Aug.	Drupes, white, globular. Aug.-Oct.	Part shade, dappled shade, shade	Prefers damp woodlands & thickets, occasionally found on dry hills in eastern half of Texas.	Mesic, likes fairly moist soils. Sandy loams, clays; likes limestone soils.
Ebony Family – Ebenaceae																
Common persimmon *Diospyros virginiana*	x	x	x	x	x			x			Tree, small 30'-40' Deciduous	Inconspicuous, male & female greenish yellow flowers on separate tree, fragrant. April-June	Berry (persimmon). Aug.-Feb.	Full sun, part shade	Prefers dryish woods, old fields & clearings, ditch banks in East Texas. Also mud bottomlands.	Well-drained, mesic. Sands, loams & clays. Thrives on almost any kind of soil.
Texas persimmon *Diospyros texana*		x	x	x	x					x	Tree, small 15'-40' Deciduous	Small greenish white flowers, fragrant. March	Fruit, small, round black & fleshy with lots of seeds. June-July	Full sun, part shade	Prefers limestone hills, shinnery oak dunes, breaks & rocky canyons, mesquite groves, areas along water courses.	Well-drained, xeric. Sands, loams & clays.

Species	Ornamental Value	Wildlife Value
Dogwood Family – Cornaceae		
Flowering dogwood *Cornus florida*	Medium-sized tree with graceful horizontal branches turning up at the tip. Single trunk is short & dark green leaves are opposite, simple, turning various shades of red in the fall. Spectacular in spring, striking in the fall. Good under shade trees.	Twenty-eight species of birds forage on the berries, from large game-birds to small songbirds. Squirrels & white-tailed deer also favor fruit. Larval host plant for Spring Azure butterfly.
Rough-leaf dogwood *Cornus drummondii*	Irregularly branched small spreading tree with smooth gray bark, opposite leaves & creamy-white flowers.	Dogwood flowers are a good nectar source for many species of insects. The white fruit is highly prized & eaten by at least 40 species of birds, including bobwhite, turkey, woodpeckers, doves & several species of songbirds.
Ebony Family – Ebenaceae		
Common persimmon *Diospyros virginiana*	Good understory tree or accent tree with drooping branches & conical crown. Good erosion control plant.	Fruit eaten by 16 species of birds, also by skunks, raccoons, opossums gray & fox squirrels. Leaves browsed by deer.
Texas persimmon *Diospyros texana*	Very attractive tree with smooth gnarled bark. Quite drought resistant once established.	Fragrant whitish flowers attract insects of many kinds. Ripe fruits eaten by several species of game & song birds. Mammals, especially javalina, relish the fruit. Leaves browsed by white-tailed deer. Larval host plant for Gray hairstreak & Henry's elfin butterflies.

Table A.5
Native Plants of Texas

Please note that each two-page "spread" is divided into a top half (with plants' growing information) and a bottom half (with plants' ornamental and wildlife values). Numbered regions correspond to the Texas Ecoregion map on page 11.

Elm Family – Ulmaceae

Species	Ecological Region 1 2 3 4 5 6 7 8 9 10										Habit Height	Flower	Fruit	Sun Exposure	Habitat	Soils and Moisture Regime
American elm *Ulmus americana*	x	x	x	x	x		x	x			Tree, large 40'-80' Deciduous	Inconspicuous red to green flowers. Feb.–April	Samara. March-June	Full sun, part shade	Prefers rich soils along streams & lowland areas.	Well-drained, mesic. Sands, loams & clays.
Cedar elm *Ulmus crassifolia*	x	x	x	x	x	x	x	x	x		Tree, large 30'-60' Deciduous	Inconspicuous greenish flowers. July-Sept.	Samara. Aug.–Oct.	Full sun, part shade	Prefers woodlands, ravines & open slopes.	Seasonal poor drainage O.K. Sands, loams & clays.
Net-leaf hackberry *Celtis reticulata*	x			x	x		x	x	x	x	Tree, large to medium 15'-30' Deciduous	Inconspicuous greenish flowers, small & perfect. May-June	Drupe, orange-red. Aug.-Sept.	Full sun, part shade	Prefers wooded limestone slopes. Mostly restricted to North Central, Central & parts of South Texas.	Well-drained, mesic-xeric. Sands, loams, & clays. Likes limestone & caliche-type soils.
Sugarberry *Celtis laevigata*	x	x	x	x	x	x	x	x	x		Tree, large 40'-60' Deciduous	Inconspicuous, small, greenish. May-June	Berry (drupe), orange-red to purplish-black. July-Aug.	Full sun, part shade	Rocky or alluvial soils along streams, in woodlands & thickets.	Well-drained, mesic to xeric; drought tolerant once established. Sands, loams, and clays. Prefers rich soils, but will tolerate wide range.
Winged elm *Ulmus alata*	x	x	x								Tree, large 30'-60' Deciduous	Inconspicuous, perfect, petalless flowers, red to yellow. Feb.-March	Samara, reddish, winged. May-Aug.	Full sun, part shade	Prefers woodlands, thickets & streamside areas, also fencerows & abandoned fields in East Texas Pineywoods, Oak Woods & Prairies, Blackland Prairies, & Upper Gulf Coast.	Well-drained, xeric-mesic. Sands & sandy loams, neutral to acid.

Species	Ornamental Value	Wildlife Value
Elm Family – Ulmaceae		
American elm *Ulmus americana*	Excellent shade tree turning yellow gold in autumn. Fast growing & handsome shape.	Seeds & buds eaten by gamebirds, woodpeckers, chickadees, robins, vireos, sparrows, orioles & finches. Good cover & nest tree with plenty of insects for insectivorous birds. Deer browse leaves; squirrels, foxes & rabbits eat seeds & buds. Long lived. Larval host plant to Comma, Question Mark, Mourning Cloak & Painted Lady butterflies.
Cedar elm *Ulmus crassifolia*	Good shade tree, each with a unique shape. Fast growing & long lived. Excellent yellow fall color.	Seeds & buds eaten by gamebirds, woodpeckers, chickadees, finches, sparrows & warblers. Good nesting & cover tree with lots of insects for insectivorous birds. Deer browse leaves; squirrels, foxes & rabbits eat seeds & buds. Larval host plant for Mourning Cloak & Question Mark.
Net-leaf hackberry *Celtis reticulata*	Can grow to be a shade tree with thickish rough-surfaced leaves with net-like veins on undersurface. Trees are strongly taprooted & extremely drought tolerant.	Fleshy fruits persist on this tree in the winter making it a valuable food source for all kinds of birds: robins, cedar waxwings, bluebirds, cardinals, finches & sparrows. Fine substrate for insectivorous birds. Larval host plant for Hackberry & Snout butterflies.
Sugarberry *Celtis laevigata*	Fast-growing shade tree adapted to most soils. Very drought tolerant. Yellow autumn color.	Fruit eaten by bluebirds, robins, cardinals, mockingbirds, cedar waxwings, thrashers, & sparrows. Good nest & cover tree, especially for neotropical migrants. Larval food plant for Question Mark, Mourning Cloak, Pale Emperor, Snout & Hackberry butterflies.
Winged elm *Ulmus alata*	Handsome shade tree with an open, round-topped crown, straight trunk & alternate simple coarsely toothed leaves. Beautiful yellow autumn color. Rapid growing & easy to transplant.	Excellent cover & nesting tree; also good substrate for insectivorous birds. Seeds eaten by gamebirds, songbirds & squirrels. Twigs & leaves browsed by deer, opossum & rabbits. Larval host plant of the Question Mark butterfly.

Table A.5
Native Plants of Texas

Please note that each two-page "spread" is divided into a top half (with plants' growing information) and a bottom half (with plants' ornamental and wildlife values). Numbered regions correspond to the Texas Ecoregion map on page 11.

Species	Ecological Region 1 2 3 4 5 6 7 8 9 10	Habit Height	Flower	Fruit	Sun Exposure	Habitat	Soils and Moisture Regime
Fig Family – Moraceae							
Bois d'arc *Maclura pomifera*	x x	Tree, small 30'-50' Evergreen	Inconspicuous male & female flowers on separate trees. April-June	Yellow-green drupelets aggregated into a small softball-sized ball. Sept.-Oct.	Full sun, part shade	Prefers rich soil in fields, woodlands, edges, fencerows, bottomlands, ravines & waste places.	Well-drained, mesic. Loams, clays.
Red mulberry *Morus rubra*	x x x x x x x x x	Tree, small 35'-40' Deciduous	Inconspicuous male & female greenish flowers. March-June	Mulberry (syncarp of aggregated red-black drupelets). April-Aug.	Full sun, part shade, dappled shade	Prefers rich soils along streams, creek bottoms & moist woodlands.	Well-drained, mesic. Sands, loams & clays.
Texas mulberry *Morus microphylla*	x x x x x x	Tree, small 10'-25' Deciduous	Small green to red inconspicuous ament-like spikes. March-April	Mulberries, red to black, 1-seeded drupes in syncarp. May-June	Full sun, part shade	Prefers canyons, limestone & igneous slopes in western ⅔ of Texas.	Well-drained, xeric. Sands, loams, clays, caliche-type & limestone soils.
Ginseng Family – Araliaceae							
Devil's walking-stick *Aralia spinosa*	x x	Tree, small 12'-30' Deciduous	Showy, large 1' clusters of small yellowish white flowers. July-Aug.	Drupes, wine-red to black & juicy with a single seed. Sept.-Oct.	Part shade, dappled shade, shade	Prefers rich moist soils along streams, woods & thickets, moist bottomlands of East Texas & Upper Texas Coast. Grows in Houston.	Mesic, likes moist soils. Sandy loams, loams.

Species	Ornamental Value	Wildlife Value
Fig Family – Moraceae		
Bois d'arc *Maclura pomifera*	Thorny tree with shiny bright green leaves & milky sap formerly used as living fence or hedge. "Osage oranges" are large & striking in appearance. Also good as understory tree. Good yellow fall color.	Excellent cover & nesting tree. Squirrels, foxes & bobwhite eat the seeds of the fruit.
Red mulberry *Morus rubra*	Handsome understory tree with polymorphic leaves, reddish black fruit & broad spreading crown.	Red mulberries are the prime source of spring fruit for neotropical migrant birds: 21 species devour them as soon as they ripen, including squirrels, raccoons, opossums & skunks. Larval host plant for Mourning Cloak butterfly.
Texas mulberry *Morus microphylla*	A small shaggy tree more often shrub with rough, sand-papery leaves & small fruits. Very drought tolerant once established.	Texas mulberry makes a good cover & nesting shrub. Several species of game & song birds, as well as opossum, raccoons & squirrels relish the ripe mulberries. Quail, mourning doves & cardinals are especially fond of them. Deer often browse the leaves.
Ginseng Family – Araliaceae		
Devil's walking-stick *Aralia spinosa*	Highly unusual understory tree with incredible twice pinnate leaves up to 4' long. Leaf stalks armed with small spines. Gorgeous bronze red & yellow fall color. Fast-growing, but rather short lived. Definite ornamental possibilities. Bizarre.	Flowers attract many insects, bees & butterflies. Fruits are relished by many species of birds & the leaves are browsed by deer. Definitely a conversation piece.

Table A.5
Native Plants of Texas

Please note that each two-page "spread" is divided into a top half (with plants' growing information) and a bottom half (with plants' ornamental and wildlife values). Numbered regions correspond to the Texas Ecoregion map on page 11.

Heath Family – Ericaceae

Species	Ecological Region 1 2 3 4 5 6 7 8 9 10	Habit Height	Flower	Fruit	Sun Exposure	Habitat	Soils and Moisture Regime
Farkleberry *Vaccinium arboreum*	x x x	Tree, small 15'-30' Persistent to Evergreen	Small drooping, urn-shaped white flowers. May-June	Berries, blue. Sept.-Oct.	Part shade, dappled shade	Prefers open mixed woods, dry sterile hillsides or pimple mounds in bottom-land woods. Found in East Texas west to Bastrop & Nueces counties.	Well-drained, mesic. Sands & sandy loams.
Texas madrone *Arbutus xalapensis*	x x	Tree, medium 20'-30' Evergreen	Small white to pinkish urn-shaped flowers. Feb.-April	Berries, bright red. Sept.-Oct.	Part shade	Prefers wooded, rocky canyons & limestone bluffs.	Well-drained, mesic. Sands, loams & clays. Likes limestone, caliche-like soils.

Holly Family – Aquifoliaceae

Species	Ecological Region 1 2 3 4 5 6 7 8 9 10	Habit Height	Flower	Fruit	Sun Exposure	Habitat	Soils and Moisture Regime
American holly *Ilex opaca*	x x x	Tree, ornamental 15'-25' Evergreen	Inconspicuous male & female greenish flowers on separate trees. March-April	Red berries on female tree, persist through winter. Sept.-Dec.	Full sun, part shade, dappled shade, shade	Prefers moist woods; hammocks along streams, upper river bottoms; can tolerate drier soils on hill-sides. Found in East Texas west to Wilson County, Gulf Coast Prairies, Oak Woodlands & Prairies.	Well-drained, mesic. Sands & loams, acidic soils.

Species	Ornamental Value	Wildlife Value
Heath Family – Ericaceae		
Farkleberry *Vaccinium arboreum*	Attractive irregular shrub to small tree with shiny smooth dark green leaves. Good understory tree. Tree has good red fall color fading to deep purple.	The small blue berries which ripen in the fall are devoured by several species of resident & wintering birds. Berries also sought after by various small mammals, i.e., squirrels, rabbits, etc. Larval host plant to Henry's elfin & Striped hairstreak butterflies.
Texas madrone *Arbutus xalapensis*	Absolutely gorgeous multi-trunked ornamental tree with papery thin peeling bark. Soft cream-colored spring bark turns reddish in summer. Attractive urn-shaped flowers set off nicely from dark green leathery leaves. Can be hard to grow, but worth it.	Flowers attract several kinds of insects. Berries are sought after by several species of birds & small mammals, also by white-tailed deer.
Holly Family – Aquifoliaceae		
American holly *Ilex opaca*	Slow-growing, long-lived understory leaves with narrow bushy triangular crown & Christmas holly evergreen leaves & brilliant red berries on female trees. This is a handsome ornamental all year round, also useful as a screening plant.	Excellent cover & nesting tree. Red berries are relished by several species of birds: robins, cedar waxwings, thrashers, towhees, etc. Small mammals also eat berries as winter food. Larval host plant for Henry's Elfin butterfly.

Table A.5
Native Plants of Texas

Please note that each two-page "spread" is divided into a top half (with plants' growing information) and a bottom half (with plants' ornamental and wildlife values). Numbered regions correspond to the Texas Ecoregion map on page 11.

Species	Ecological Region 1 2 3 4 5 6 7 8 9 10	Habit Height	Flower	Fruit	Sun Exposure	Habitat	Soils and Moisture Regime
Common winterberry *Ilex verticillata*	x x	Tree, ornamental 15'-25' Deciduous	Inconspicuous male & female greenish flowers on separate trees. April-June	Red berries on female tree, persist through winter. Sept.-Oct. ripens.	Full sun, part shade	Prefers wet woods; hammocks along streams, swamps, pond margins, river banks. Found in East Texas, & Upper Texas Coast.	Mesic-hydric. Seasonal poor drainage O.K. Sandy loams & clays.
Deciduous Holly *Ilex decidua*	x x x x x x x	Tree, small 10'-30' Deciduous	Inconspicuous male & female flowers on separate trees. March-May	Drupes, orange-red on female tree. Sept.-Feb	Full sun, part shade	Prefers moist areas near streams & woodlands.	Well-drained, mesic. Seasonal poor drainage O.K. Sands, loams & clays.
Yaupon *Ilex vomitoria*	x x x x x	Tree, small 15'-25' Evergreen	Inconspicuous male & female creamy white flowers on separate trees. April	Drupes, (berry-like fruits) red on female tree. Sept.-Dec.	Full sun, part shade, dappled shade, shade	Prefers low woods, hammocks & sandy pinelands along streams, East Texas Pineywoods, Gulf Coast, eastern Edwards Plateau and Oak Woods & Prairies.	Well-drained, mesic. Seasonal poor drainage O.K. Sands, loams & clays.

Honeysuckle Family – Caprifoliaceae

Species	Ecological Region 1 2 3 4 5 6 7 8 9 10	Habit Height	Flower	Fruit	Sun Exposure	Habitat	Soils and Moisture Regime
American elderberry *Sambucus canadensis*	x x x x x x	Tree, small, ornamental 15'-30' Persistent	Showy white 4"-8" flower clusters. June-Sept.	Berries, blue-black. Sept.-Nov.	Full sun, part shade	Prefers wet soils in low places especially along streams & swamp edges.	Hydric-mesic. Tolerates poor drainage. Sands, loams & gravelly clays.

Species	Ornamental Value	Wildlife Value
Common winterberry *Ilex verticillata*	This ornamental holly is most beautiful early November on through the winter when bright red berries cover the limbs, hence its name. Tolerates wet soils. Grows in gumbo; good for Houston.	Excellent cover & nesting tree. Flowers attract several kinds of insects. Red berries are relished by several species of birds. Good food source for them in the winter. Larval host plant for Henry's Elfin butterfly.
Deciduous Holly *Ilex decidua*	Good understory tree or accent tree with spreading open crown, often with inclined trunk. Female trees have red berries held over winter, very ornamental.	Fruits are eaten by several species of birds, bobwhite, doves, robins, cedar waxwings, bluebirds, jays & mockingbirds. Squirrels, opossums, rabbits & fox eat berries too. Flower nectar & pollen attract several insects. Good nest tree.
Yaupon *Ilex vomitoria*	Good understory tree or accent tree with a "branchy" appearance. Female trees have red berries held over winter, very ornamental. Shiny dark evergreen leaves attractive. Adaptable, grows in sun or shade, dry or moist soils of various types.	Fruits are eaten by several species of birds, bobwhite, doves, robins, cedar waxwings, bluebirds, jays & mockingbirds. Squirrels, opossum, rabbits & fox eat berries too. Flower nectar & pollen attract many insects. Good nest tree. Larval host plant of Henry's Elfin.

Honeysuckle Family – Caprifoliaceae

Species	Ornamental Value	Wildlife Value
American elderberry *Sambucus canadensis*	Attractive erect shrub with white flower pompoms which prefers moist conditions in alluvial soils. Has attractive pinnate leaves. It loves extra water & will grow fast if well supplied. Can stand a certain amount of drought, though.	Flowers are an excellent source of nectar for bees, butterflies, diurnal moths & other insects. Fruits are eaten by several species of birds, including gamebirds & songbirds. Small mammals also relish the ripe fruit. Leaves are browsed by deer.

Table A.5
Native Plants of Texas

Please note that each two-page "spread" is divided into a top half (with plants' growing information) and a bottom half (with plants' ornamental and wildlife values). Numbered regions correspond to the Texas Ecoregion map on page 11.

Species	Ecological Region 1 2 3 4 5 6 7 8 9 10	Habit/Height	Flower	Fruit	Sun Exposure	Habitat	Soils and Moisture Regime
Blue elderberry *Sambucus caerulea*	X (10)	Tree, small 10'-12' Deciduous	Showy yellowish-white flowers in cymes. April-Aug.	Sweet, juicy blue berries. Aug.-Sept.	Full sun, part shade	Prefers moist areas in canyons, streamsides, talus slopes, at the bases of cliffs at 7000' elevation plus.	Well-drained, mesic. Sands, loams, clays, limestone soils.
Rusty black-haw viburnum *Viburnum rufidulum*	X (1,2,3), X (4,5), X (7,8), X (10)	Tree, small, ornamental 20'-30' Deciduous	Showy creamy-white clusters of flowers. March-May	Berries, bluish-black (drupes) Sept.-Oct.	Full sun, part shade	Prefers moist soils along streamsides, in open woods & thickets.	Well-drained, mesic. Sands, loams & clays, especially limestone soils.

Horse-chestnut Family – Hippocastanaceae

Species	Ecological Region 1 2 3 4 5 6 7 8 9 10	Habit/Height	Flower	Fruit	Sun Exposure	Habitat	Soils and Moisture Regime
Red buckeye *Aesculus pavia*	X (1,2,3,4), X (7,8)	Tree, small, ornamental 10'-35' Deciduous, early	Showy red/yellow tubular flowers in clusters. March	Capsule, round & leathery. September	Part shade, dappled shade, shade	Prefers moist soils in forests, along streams, thickets & rocky hills.	Well-drained, mesic. Moderate moisture. Sands, loams & clays.
Texas buckeye *Aesculus glabra v. arguta*	X (1), X (3,4,5), X (7)	Tree, small, ornamental 15'-40' Deciduous	Showy yellowish-green panicles of tubular flowers. March-May	Capsule, round & leathery. Sept.-Oct.	Part shade, dappled shade, shade	Prefers moist, rich soils in woodlands, along river banks. Prefers northern exposures.	Well-drained, mesic. Moderate moisture. Sands, loams & clays.

Legume Family – Leguminosae

Species	Ecological Region 1 2 3 4 5 6 7 8 9 10	Habit/Height	Flower	Fruit	Sun Exposure	Habitat	Soils and Moisture Regime
Black-brush acacia *Acacia rigidula*	X (1), X (6,7), X (10)	Tree, small, ornamental 10'-15' Deciduous	Showy creamy-white racemes, fragrant. April-May	Leguminous pod, reddish brown, with dark green seeds. Aug.-Sept.	Full sun, part shade	Prefers open or brushy areas, roadsides & pastures.	Xeric, well-drained. Sands, loams & clays.

Species	Ornamental Value	Wildlife Value
Blue elderberry *Sambucus caerulea*	This very rare plant is only found above 7000'. It has beautiful flowers & sweet edible fruit. Good for eroison control. Grows rapidly, sprouts from base.	Flowers attract myriads of insects. Sweet fruit is highly sought after by 12 species of birds & several small mammals. Foliage browsed by mule deer. Gambel's & Scaled quail are especially fond of the berries. So is the Ring-necked pheasant.
Rusty black-haw viburnum *Viburnum rufidulum*	Small, single-trunked ornamental with broad crown. Attractive as understory tree, also beautiful in the open. Leaves very glossy, turning red, mauve or orange in fall. Slow growing, staying shrub size for a long time.	Flowers are good nectar source for bees, butterflies & other insects. Fruits relished by several kinds of birds & small mammals. Robins, cedar waxwings, cardinals, bluebirds & mockingbirds love fruit, as do squirrels, opossums, raccoons & rabbits.

Horse-chestnut Family – Hippocastanaceae

Species	Ornamental Value	Wildlife Value
Red buckeye *Aesculus pavia*	Showy small tree or shrub with rounded crown, distinctive flower clusters & attractive palmate leaves. Blooms very early; loses leaves early. Good understory tree.	The scarlet tubular flowers are visited by hummingbirds. Butterflies are also attracted to the nectar. Seeds are poisonous, however, & not eaten by wildlife.
Texas buckeye *Aesculus glabra v. arguta*	Showy small tree or shrub with rounded crown. Has distinctive flower clusters & attractive pointy palmate leaves. Good understory tree.	The yellowish-green tubular flowers are attractive to insects. Good protective cover shrub. White-tailed deer will not browse the leaves of this tree. Seeds are poisonous, however, & not eaten by wildlife.

Legume Family – Leguminosae

Species	Ornamental Value	Wildlife Value
Black-brush acacia *Acacia rigidula*	Attractive, stiff thorny shrub that is gorgeous when in bloom. Relatively slow-growing, but worth the wait. And it is longer lived than many other acacias. Can form thickets. If you prune the trunks, it will become a graceful tree. Good erosion control.	Flowers attract myriads of bees, butterflies, diurnal moths & other insects in the spring. Excellent honey plant. Seeds are eaten by bobwhite quail. Leaves & beans are browsed by white-tailed deer.

Table A.5
Native Plants of Texas

Please note that each two-page "spread" is divided into a top half (with plants' growing information) and a bottom half (with plants' ornamental and wildlife values). Numbered regions correspond to the Texas Ecoregion map on page 11.

Species	Ecological Region 1 2 3 4 5 6 7 8 9 10	Habit Height	Flower	Fruit	Sun Exposure	Habitat	Soils and Moisture Regime
Common Honey-locust *Gleditsia triacanthos*	× × × × × × × (1,2,3,4,5,6,7)	Tree, large 50'-100' Deciduous	Inconspicuous male & female perfect or imperfect flowers. May-June	Legume. Sept.-Oct.	Full sun, part shade	Prefers rich deep soils of eastern ⅓ of Texas.	Needs moisture; mesic. Loams & clay.
Eastern redbud *Cercis canadensis* v. *canadensis*	× × × × (1,2,3,4)	Tree, ornamental 10'-40' Deciduous	Showy magenta pea-like flowers, before leaves. March	Legumes, brownish-red, in clusters. September	Full sun, part shade, dappled shade	Prefers forested sandy areas, upland woods, woodland edges & along stream banks in eastern Texas.	Well-drained, mesic; moderate moisture. Sands, loams & heavy black clays.
Eve's necklace *Sophora affinis*	× × × (4,5,7)	Tree, small 15'-30' Deciduous	Showy clusters of pinkish-white flowers. May	Legume black in color, looks like necklace, because of constrictions between seeds. September	Full sun, part shade, dappled shade	Prefers fields, woodlands, occurs along rights-of-way of central & northeast Texas.	Well-drained, mesic. Sands, loams & clays.
Goldenball leadtree *Leucaena retusa*	× × × (7,8,10)	Tree, small, ornamental 12'-25' Deciduous	Showy yellow flower balls, very fragrant. April-Oct.	Leguminous pod, linear. Sept.-Nov.	Full sun, part shade	Prefers dry rocky canyons on rocky soils.	Well-drained, xeric. Sands, loams & clays; prefers limestone, caliche-type soils.
Great leadtree (Tepaguaje) *Leucaena pulverulenta*	× (6)	Tree, large 30'-55' Deciduous	Showy, white balls, fragrant. March-July	Legume, strap-shaped with seeds traversely arranged. Sept.-Dec.	Full sun, part shade, dappled shade	Prefers rich soils along streams & resacas in extreme southern Rio Grande Plain.	Moist soils, poor drainage O.K. Sands, loams & clays.

Species	Ornamental Value	Wildlife Value
Common Honey-locust *Gleditsia triacanthos*	Heavily thorned tree with pretty leaves.	Good protective cover & nesting tree. Sweet pulp of young pods eaten by deer, fox & gray squirrels, rabbits & deer. Bees & butterflies attracted to nectar. Good honey tree. Larval host plant for Silver- spotted skipper.
Eastern redbud *Cercis canadensis v. canadensis*	Highly ornamental & showy small tree with spreading, flat or rounded crown. Good understory tree or accent plant. Fast growing, usually with single trunk.	Beautiful magenta flowers are copious early nectar source for butter-flies, moths, bees, etc. Seeds are eaten by a number of species of birds; foliage browsed by white-tailed deer. Larval host plant to Henry's Elfin butterfly.
Eve's necklace *Sophora affinis*	Ornamental understory tree with pretty compound leaves & showy pink flower clusters. Fast growing.	Ring-tailed cats are known to eat the fruits & the foliage is browsed by white-tailed deer. The seeds are poisonous for most. Nectar of flowers attracts various bees, diurnal moths & butterflies.
Goldenball leadtree *Leucaena retusa*	Airy ornamental with bright green twice compound leaves with profusely blooming yellow ball-like blossoms. Flaking bark is cinnamon-colored & very attractive. Tree blooms from spring until fall. Sun-loving flowers are well able to grow underneath.	Excellent cover & nesting tree. Insects of many varieties are attracted to the copious nectar of the fragrant flowers. White-tailed deer browse the leaves.
Great leadtree (Tepaguaje) *Leucaena pulverulenta*	Small tree with smooth gray bark & rounded crown. Leaves appear light & feathery. Flowers are white & fragrant, shaped like small balls. Tree is often planted as a good yard tree. Very ornamental in appearance.	Myriads of insects are attracted to the fragrant flowers. Several species of birds use this tree as a protective cover & nesting tree.

Table A.5
Native Plants of Texas

Please note that each two-page "spread" is divided into a top half (with plants' growing information) and a bottom half (with plants' ornamental and wildlife values). Numbered regions correspond to the Texas Ecoregion map on page 11.

Species	Ecological Region 1 2 3 4 5 6 7 8 9 10	Habit Height	Flower	Fruit	Sun Exposure	Habitat	Soils and Moisture Regime
Gregg acacia *Acacia greggii*	x x x x	Tree, small, ornamental 5'-9' Deciduous	Showy creamy-yellow spikes with exerted stamens. April-Oct., shorter bloom time further north	Legume, light brown to reddish, persistent. July-Dec.	Full sun, part shade	Prefers chaparral & brushy areas in Rio Grande Plains, Trans-Pecos & parts of Rolling Plains.	Well-drained, xeric. Sands, loams, clays, caliche type & limestone soils.
Guajillo *Acacia berlandieri*	x x x	Tree, small, ornamental 9'-15' Deciduous to Persistent	Showy creamy-white globose flowers, fragrant. Feb.-April, also Nov.-March in Valley	Legume, large, curved with 5-10 seeds April-June	Full sun, part shade	Prefers limestone & caliche cuestas on dry brushy hillsides.	Well-drained, xeric. Sands, loams & clays, gravelly limestone & caliche-type soils.
Honey mesquite *Prosopis glandulosa*	x x x x x x x x x	Tree, large 20-30' Deciduous	Showy creamy yellow elongated spike-like racemes. May-Sept.	Legumes in loose clusters. Aug.-Sept.	Full sun, part shade	Tolerates wide range of situations, open fields, edges of woodlands, etc.	Well-drained, xeric. Sands, loams & clays.
Huisache *Acacia farnesiana*	x x x x x	Tree, small, ornamental 15'-30' Deciduous	Showy, yellow round heads, fragrant. Feb.-March	Legume, brownish-black. Aug.-Sept.	Full sun	Prefers open areas, fields, pastures & fence rows.	Moderately well-drained. Seasonal poor drainage O.K. Sands, loams & clays.
Mexican poinciana *Caesalpinia mexicana*	x x	Tree, small, ornamental 10'-20' Persistent to Evergreen	Showy bright yellow racemes of flowers, fragrant. Feb.-Sept. & after rains	Legume, greenish brown. May-Nov.	Full sun, part shade	Prefers chaparral & woodlands along creeks & canyons.	Well-drained, xeric. Sands, loams & clays, likes limestone, caliche-like soils.

Species	Ornamental Value	Wildlife Value
Gregg acacia *Acacia greggii*	Thorny, thicket-forming, round-topped shrub or small tree with delicate compound leaves & creamy yellow flowers. Can form impenetrable thickets in shrub form.	Gregg acacia furnishes cover & shelter for small animals. Flowers attract myriads of insects. Seeds are eaten by bobwhite & scaled quail. White-tailed deer browse foliage. Pollen important bee food. Good honey plant.
Guajillo *Acacia berlandieri*	Spreading small ornamental tree or shrub with gray to whitish branches & delicate fern-like leaves. When in bloom, tree is covered with deliciously fragrant creamy-white puffs of flowers. Spines are small.	Fragrant flowers attract myriads of nectar-loving insects. Leaves & branches browsed by white-tailed deer. This makes an excellent honey plant. Also serves well as a good protective cover & nesting site for the birds.
Honey mesquite *Prosopis glandulosa*	Attractive tree with crooked, drooping branches, feathery leaves & rounded crown. Fast growing & often shrubby, forming thickets. Fixes nitrogen in the soil.	Good nectar plant for bees & other insects. Many species of wildlife like quail, bobwhite, doves depend on it for food & shelter from the sun. Squirrels, coyotes, skunks, rabbits & deer eat pods. Larval host plant for Long-tailed skipper & Reickert's blue butterflies.
Huisache *Acacia farnesiana*	Medium-sized tree to shrub; densely branched & armed with long paired, straight spines. Rapid growth rate. Profusely flowering in early spring. In southern Texas starts flowering in late December. Very fragrant. Fairly drought tolerant.	Provides quick shade in spring. Good cover & nesting tree especially for White-winged doves. Good nurse tree to other plants. Small mammals eat the pods. Excellent pollen & nectar source for bees & other insects. Larval host plant for Marine Blue butterfly.
Mexican poinciana *Caesalpinia mexicana*	An introduced ornamental that becomes established along fence rows, blooming off & on throughout the year. Bright yellow showy flowers are stunning. This can be a highly attractive accent plant for any yard.	Fragrant flowers are a special favorite of the carpenter & bumble bees. Other insects are also attracted to the nectar. Birds use the shrub as a nesting site.

Table A.5
Native Plants of Texas

Please note that each two-page "spread" is divided into a top half (with plants' growing information) and a bottom half (with plants' ornamental and wildlife values). Numbered regions correspond to the Texas Ecoregion map on page 11.

Species	Ecological Region 1 2 3 4 5 6 7 8 9 10	Habit Height	Flower	Fruit	Sun Exposure	Habitat	Soils and Moisture Regime
Mexican redbud *Cercis canadensis v. mexicana*	x x _ _ _ _ x x _ _	Tree, small, ornamental 10'-30' Deciduous	Showy magenta pea-like flowers. March, before leaves	Legumes, brownish-red, in clusters. September	Full sun, part shade, dappled shade	Prefers thinner calcareous, rocky soils of Edwards Plateau & North Central Texas.	Well-drained, mesic; but less moisture than eastern variety. Sands, loams & clays; likes limestone soils.
New Mexico locust *Robinia neomexicana*	_ _ _ _ _ _ _ _ _ x	Tree, small, ornamental 10'-25' Deciduous	Showy rose-colored flower clusters. April-Aug.	Legumes with seeds. Sept.-Oct.	Full sun, part shade	Found only in the Guadalupe mountains at 5000'-8000' in pine-oak & ponderosa pine-Douglas fir associations. Prefers moist soils along streams.	Well-drained, mesic. Sands, loams & clays.
Retama *Parkinsonia aculeata*	x _ _ _ _ _ x x _ x	Tree, small, ornamental 9'-30' Deciduous	Showy yellow flowers, fragrant. April-July	Leguminous, linear orange to brown, with greenish brown seeds. Aug.-Oct.	Full sun, part shade	Prefers low, poorly drained areas, also on a variety of other sites.	Mesic, poor drainage O.K. Sands, loams & clays.
Roemer's acacia *Acacia roemeriana*	_ _ _ _ _ _ x x _ x	Tree, small, ornamental 5'-10' Deciduous	Showy creamy-white flower balls. April-Aug.	Legume, brown. July-Sept.	Full sun, part shade	Prefers chaparral & brushy areas on limestone soils, gravelly bluffs & banks.	Well-drained, xeric. Sands, loams, clays & limestone soils.
Screwbean mesquite *Prosopis pubescens*	_ _ _ _ _ _ _ _ _ x	Tree, small, ornamental 10'-30' Deciduous	Showy cream or greenish-white cylindrical spikes. May-June	Legumes shaped like corkscrew, hairy at first. July-Aug.	Full sun, part shade	Prefers arroyos, washes & larger tributaries & deltas along Rio Grande in West Texas.	Well-drained, mesic. Sands & loams.

Species	Ornamental Value	Wildlife Value
Mexican redbud *Cercis canadensis* v. *mexicana*	Highly ornamental & showy small tree with spreading, flat or rounded crown. Good understory tree or accent plant. Fast growing, usually with single trunk. Leaves have distinctive kidney shape & are shinier than other subspecies of Redbud.	Beautiful magenta flowers are copious early nectar source for butterflies, moths, bees, etc. Seeds are eaten by a number of species of birds; foliage browsed by white-tailed deer. Larval host plant to Henry's Elfin butterfly.
New Mexico locust *Robinia neomexicana*	Can be used as an understory ornamental tree. This spiny small tree will form thickets. It has very attractive compound leaves & gorgeous rose-colored flowers. Good erosion control plant.	Flowers attract several varieties of insects. Leaves are browsed by mule deer. Fruit is eaten by Gambel's quail, mountain sheep, mule deer, porcupines & ground squirrels.
Retama *Parkinsonia aculeata*	A thorny, green-barked shrub with graceful drooping branches & rounded crown. Flowers are a fragrant bright yellow. Leaves are small & delicate, giving tree a light airy appearance. Almost always in bloom. Tolerates salt. Can become weedy.	Flower nectar attracts myriads of insects. Deer occasionally browse the leaves. Pods are also eaten. Seeds are relished by doves, bobwhite quail & other species of birds & small mammals. Good nesting site & cover tree for several bird species.
Roemer's acacia *Acacia roemeriana*	Round-topped, spiny shrub with many spreading branches, bipinnately compound leaves & creamy white ball-like flowers.	Roemer's acacia provides good protective cover & nesting sites for birds. Nectar-laden flowers attract many kinds of insects, especially bees & butterflies.
Screwbean mesquite *Prosopsis pubescens*	Screwbean mesquite is absolutely dazzling when it's in bloom. Blossoms vary in color from a rich yellowy cream to white. Foliage is lacy & thorns are small. Grows only where water table is near to the surface or where lots of run-off is available.	Fragrant flowers attract myriads of insects. Many mammals will eat the seeds of the screwbeans. Roadrunners, Gambel's & Montezuma quail are especially fond of them.

Table A.5
Native Plants of Texas

Please note that each two-page "spread" is divided into a top half (with plants' growing information) and a bottom half (with plants' ornamental and wildlife values). Numbered regions correspond to the Texas Ecoregion map on page 11.

Species	Ecological Region 1	2	3	4	5	6	7	8	9	10	Habit Height	Flower	Fruit	Sun Exposure	Habitat	Soils and Moisture Regime
Tenaza (Ape's ear-ring) *Pithecellobium pallens*		X				X					Tree, small 4'-18' Deciduous	Showy cream-colored spikes, fragrant. May-Aug., also after rains	Legume, reddish brown with blackish seeds. July-Oct.	Full sun, part shade	Prefers alluvial soils of stream bottoms or the edges of water holes in Coastal Prairies & South Texas marshes.	Well-drained, yet moist. Loams & clay loams.
Texas ebony *Pithecellobium ebano*		X				X					Tree, large 25'-30' Evergreen	Showy white spikes, fragrant. May-Oct.	Leguminous pod, brown with red seeds persistent on tree. July-Dec.	Full sun, part shade	Prefers low woods in coastal part of Rio Grande Valley & Plains.	Mesic, well-drained. Sands, loams & clays, grows in caliche-type soils.
Texas kidneywood *Eysenhardtia texana*		X				X	X			X	Tree, small, ornamental 6'-15' Deciduous	Showy racemes of white flowers, fragrant. April-Nov., especially after rains	Pods, small & linear. July-Sept.	Full sun, part shade	Prefers chaparral & brushy areas on calcareous soils.	Xeric, well-drained. Sands, loams & clays.
Texas mountain-laurel *Sophora secundiflora*						X	X			X	Tree, small 6'-30' Evergreen	Showy, lavender-purple flower clusters, fragrant. March-April	Leguminous pod, brown with red toxic seeds. Oct.-Dec.	Full sun, part shade, dappled shade	Prefers brushy vegetation & caliche cuestas in Edwards Plateau, also on gravelly hills in South Texas, West Texas & Coastal Bend.	Well-drained, xeric. Sands, loams & clays.
Texas paloverde *Cercidium texanum*		X				X					Tree, small 15'-25' Deciduous	Showy, bright yellow flower clusters. March-April, also after rains to September	Leguminous pod, dark brown with 1-4 seeds. Aug.-Dec.	Full sun, part shade	Prefers open or brushy areas, flats & gently rolling slopes.	Xeric, well-drained. Sands, sandy loams, loams & clays. Like alkaline soils.

Species	Ornamental Value	Wildlife Value
Tenaza (Ape's ear-ring) *Pithecellobium pallens*	Spiny small tree with loosely spaced, airy compound leaves. When in bloom, the entire tree is covered in fragrant clusters of white globe-shaped flowers. Fairly fast growing but not overly drought tolerant.	Bees, butterflies & myriads of other insects are attracted to the fragrant flowers.
Texas ebony *Pithecellobium ebano*	A medium-sized tree with a rounded very dense dark crown & dark bark. Zig-zag branches are spiny. Very beautiful tree which is extremely drought-tolerant. Good canopy tree in Valley.	Many species of birds use the tree as a nest site, especially white-winged doves, due to dense foliage & thorns. Several kinds of insects are attracted to the flowers. Good substrate for insectivorous birds. Larval host plant for Cassius Blue, Coyote & Orange giant skipper butterflies.
Texas kidneywood *Eysenhardtia texana*	Irregularly-shaped spineless shrub with aromatic compound leaves giving the shrub an airy appearance. Flowers can be profuse. Quick growing & very drought tolerant.	Sweet-scented flowers attract myriads of insects: bees, butterflies, diurnal moths. Leaves are heavily browsed by deer. Seeds occasionally consumed by birds. Larval host plant for the Dogface butterfly.
Texas mountain-laurel *Sophora secundiflora*	Attractive evergreen tree with shiny dark green leathery compound leaves & showy purple flowers that smell a bit like grape Kool- Aid™. Has excellent ornamental potential. Fairly drought-tolerant and can be grown from seed. Seeds very toxic.	Fragrant flower clusters attract much insect activity in the spring. Leaves are only browsed by white-tailed deer when they are very hungry. Seeds are avoided. This is a good cover & nesting tree, however.
Texas paloverde *Cercidium texanum*	Fairly small, green-barked, spiny ornamental tree with asymmetrical yellow flowers. Well adapted to arid environments. It will shed its leaves during drought conditions. Puts down deep taproot to soak up water.	Flower nectar attracts myriads of bees, butterflies & other insects. White-tailed deer occasionally browse the leaves. Seeds are eaten by several species of birds & small mammals. This makes an excellent nesting tree for birds.

Table A.5
Native Plants of Texas

Please note that each two-page "spread" is divided into a top half (with plants' growing information) and a bottom half (with plants' ornamental and wildlife values). Numbered regions correspond to the Texas Ecoregion map on page 11.

Species	Ecological Region 1 2 3 4 5 6 7 8 9 10	Habit Height	Flower	Fruit	Sun Exposure	Habitat	Soils and Moisture Regime
Texas redbud *Cercis canadensis* v. *texana*	x x x x x	Tree, small, ornamental 10'-30' Deciduous	Showy magenta pea-like flowers. March, before leaves	Legumes, brownish-red, in clusters. September	Full sun, part shade, dappled shade	Prefers thinner calcareous, rocky soils of Edwards Plateau & North Central Texas.	Well-drained, mesic; but less moisture than Eastern variety. Sands, loams & clays; likes limestone soils.
Wherry mimosa *Mimosa wherryiana*	x	Tree, small, ornamental 2'-7' Deciduous	Showy creamy yellow globes, fragrant. May-Sept.	Legume, small with sharp slender prickles on margin & dark brown seeds. July-Nov.	Full sun, part shade	Prefers caliche & gravelly hills in Starr & Zapata counties in the Lower Rio Grande Valley.	Xeric, well-drained. Sands, loams, clays & caliche-like soils.
Wright acacia *Acacia wrightii*	x x x x	Tree, small, ornamental 20'-30' Evergreen	Showy creamy-yellow flowers in fuzzy cylindrical spikes. March-May, and after rains	Legume, broad, light brownish green with dark brown seeds. May-Aug.	Full sun, part shade	Prefers chaparral & woodlands along creeks & canyons.	Well-drained, xeric. Sands, loams & clays, likes limestone, caliche-type soils.

Linden Family – Tiliaceae

Species	Ecological Region 1 2 3 4 5 6 7 8 9 10	Habit Height	Flower	Fruit	Sun Exposure	Habitat	Soils and Moisture Regime
Carolina basswood *Tilia caroliniana*	x x x x	Tree, large 40'-80' Deciduous	Showy clusters of white, 5-petaled flowers, highly fragrant. April-June	Nutlets. May-Aug.	Full sun, slight shade	Prefers deep rich soils of open woodlands along forested streams & lowlands in East or Central Texas, also part of Upper Texas Coast.	Well-drained, mesic. Sands, loams & clays.

Species	Ornamental Value	Wildlife Value
Texas redbud *Cercis canadensis* v. *texana*	Highly ornamental & showy small tree with spreading, flat or rounded crown. Good understory tree or accent plant. Fast growing, usually with single trunk. Leaves have distinctive kidney shape & are shinier than other subspecies of redbud.	Beautiful magenta flowers are copious early nectar source for butterflies, moths, bees, etc. Seeds are eaten by a number of species of birds; foliage browsed by white-tailed deer. Larval host plant to Henry's Elfin butterfly.
Wherry mimosa *Mimosa wherryiana*	Absolutely beautiful, rare, ornamental shrub or tree with slender zig-zag twigs & blackish gray bark. This plant is very sensitive to the cold. When in bloom, the flowers are very fragrant & eye-catching. Foliage is feathery & thorns are not vicious.	Wherry mimosa is an excellent honey plant. Bees, flies, moths & butterflies are highly attracted to the flowers. This plant provides good protective cover & a nesting site for birds.
Wright acacia *Acacia wrightii*	Spiny shrub or small tree with wide spreading branches & irregular crown. Attractive light yellow bottlebrush-like flowers. Delicate foliage gives light shade, allowing other wildflowers to grow underneath. Fairly cold hardy for an acacia.	Pollen produced by flowers an important food source for bees. Makes an excellent honey tree. Good protective cover & nesting site for birds. Larval host plant for the Marine blue butterfly.
Linden Family – Tiliaceae		
Carolina basswood *Tilia caroliniana*	Large, often leaning shade tree with narrow irregularly rounded crown, attractive lopsided heart-shaped leaves & copious highly fragrant blooms. You can smell the tree almost before you see it. You can also hear all the buzzing from bees. Fast grower.	Fragrant flowers literally drip with nectar & attract all kinds of nectar-loving insects. Excellent honey tree. Fruit is eaten by several species of birds & small mammals. Good cover & nesting tree.

Table A.5
Native Plants of Texas

Please note that each two-page "spread" is divided into a top half (with plants' growing information) and a bottom half (with plants' ornamental and wildlife values). Numbered regions correspond to the Texas Ecoregion map on page 11.

Species	Ecological Region 1 2 3 4 5 6 7 8 9 10	Habit Height	Flower	Fruit	Sun Exposure	Habitat	Soils and Moisture Regime
Magnolia Family – Magnoliaceae							
Sweet bay *Magnolia virginiana*	x x	Tree, ornamental 20'-50' Persistent to almost evergreen	Showy white flowers, fragrant. April-July	Capsules, reddish, woody & cone-like with bright red flattened seeds. Aug.-Sept.	Full sun, part sun, dappled shade	Prefers moist soils of swamps & woodlands.	Mesic-hydric, poor drainage O.K. Sands, sandy loams & loams, acid soils preferred.
Maple Family – Aceraceae							
Big-toothed maple *Acer grandidentatum*	x x	Tree, small, ornamental 20'-50' Deciduous	Small & yellow, in few-flowered clusters. April-May	Samara, double-winged rose-colored. September	Full sun, part shade	Prefers moist canyons of Edwards Plateau & mountains of Trans-Pecos.	Mesic, likes moist soils. Sands, loams & clays. Likes limestone soils.
Drummond red maple *Acer rubrum v. drummondii*	x x x	Tree, small, ornamental 90'-100' Deciduous	Showy bright red clusters, before leaves. February	Samara with 2 wings. March-June	Full sun, part shade	Prefers wet areas on sandy lands, swamps & alluvial forest. Also found on drier ridges throughout Pineywoods in East Texas.	Mesic-hydric, poor drainage O.K. Sands, loams, & clays. Likes acid soils.
Olive Family – Oleaceae							
Fragrant ash *Fraxinus cuspidata*	x	Tree, medium to small 15'-25' Deciduous	Panicles, 3"-4", of male and female cream-colored flowers, fragrant. June	Samara. July	Full sun, part shade	Prefers rocky canyon slopes in Trans-Pecos, gravelly hillsides from 4000'.	Well-drained, xeric-mesic. Sands, loams, clays; likes limestone, caliche-like soils, also slightly acidic igneous soils.

Species	Ornamental Value	Wildlife Value
Magnolia Family – Magnoliaceae		
Sweet bay *Magnolia virginiana*	Semi-evergreen ornamental tree with leaves bright & glossy green on top & silky white underneath. Beautiful, fragrant flowers very showy. Other plantings can grow underneath. Tolerates Houston gumbo.	Moths & beetles are attracted to the lemon-scented flowers.
Maple Family – Aceraceae		
Big-toothed maple *Acer grandidentatum*	One of the most beautiful ornamental trees in Texas with its beautifully shaped leaves & exquisite fall color. Grows quickly & does very well under cultivation.	White-tailed deer browse the foliage. Samaras used as food by many species of birds & small mammals. In the spring, many species of birds eat the young flowers. Good nesting & cover tree. Excellent substrate for insectivorous birds.
Drummond red maple *Acer rubrum* v. *drummondii*	Large shade tree with simple distinctively-shaped leaves which turn red in the fall. Popular ornamental & shade tree, as they are beautiful both spring & fall. Relatively short lived with shallow root system. Does well in Houston.	Many kinds of birds feed on the winged seeds, i.e. woodpeckers, cardinals, finches, robins, cedar waxwings, warblers, & sparrows, also squirrels & rabbits. Good cover & nesting tree. Good substrate for insectivorous birds. Foliage browsed by deer.
Olive Family – Oleaceae		
Fragrant ash *Fraxinus cuspidata*	Very ornamental small to medium-sized tree that looks a bit like the East Texas Fringe tree. Quite drought tolerant, but grows faster with additional water.	Good cover & nesting tree. Cardinals, pyrrhuloxias, finches, red-winged blackbirds relish ripe seeds in samaras. Foliage browsed by rabbits & mule deer. Larval host plant of swallowtail butterflies.

Table A.5
Native Plants of Texas

Please note that each two-page "spread" is divided into a top half (with plants' growing information) and a bottom half (with plants' ornamental and wildlife values). Numbered regions correspond to the Texas Ecoregion map on page 11.

Species	Ecological Region 1 2 3 4 5 6 7 8 9 10	Habit Height	Flower	Fruit	Sun Exposure	Habitat	Soils and Moisture Regime
Fresno *Fraxinus berlandieriana*	x ... x x	Tree, large 30'-40' Deciduous	Panicles of male & female greenish purple & green. March-June	Samara. June-Aug.	Full sun, part shade	Grows along wooded streams, in canyons of the Edwards Plateau & Rio Grande Valley.	Well-drained, but moist soils. Sands, loams, clays; likes limestone, caliche-like soils.
Fringe Tree *Chionanthus virginica*	x x	Tree, ornamental 15'-20' Deciduous	Showy white flowers in loose hanging clusters with subtle fragrance. April	Drupes, dark blue, in grape-like clusters. Aug.-Sept.	Full sun, partial shade, dappled shade	Prefers moist woods & thickets throughout Pineywoods of East Texas west to Brazos County.	Well-drained, mesic. Sands, loams & clays, prefers acid soils.
Green ash *Fraxinus pensylvanica*	x x x x x x x	Tree, large 30'-80' Deciduous	Inconspicuous male & female yellowish catkins & spikes. April-May	Samara. Sept.-Oct.	Full sun, part shade	Alluvial woods & swamps along rivers & streams, swales & depressions in prairies.	Needs moisture; poor drainage O.K. Acid sands, sandy loams & heavy limestone clays.
Gregg ash *Fraxinus greggi*	x ... x	Tree, medium to small 15'-25' Deciduous	Perfect, male or female or both can occur on same or different trees. March-May	Samara. July-Sept.	Full sun, part shade	Prefers dry rocky hillsides & arroyo banks in Trans-Pecos, also dry creek beds & washes from 4000'-7000'.	Well-drained, xeric. Limestone & caliche soils.
Texas ash *Fraxinus texensis*	x x x x x	Tree, small 30'-45' Deciduous	Small male flowers, female flowers in clusters, purplish. Feb.-March	Samara. Aug.-Sept.	Full sun, part shade	Prefers canyons, bluffs, rocky slopes, open woodlands, near lakes in Edwards Plateau & Western Cross Timbers.	Well-drained, xeric-mesic. Sands, loams & clays. Likes limestone soils.

Species	Ornamental Value	Wildlife Value
Fresno *Fraxinus berlandieriana*	Spreading, round-topped tree. Fairly fast growing & long lived.	Good cover & nesting tree. Cardinals, pyrrhuloxias, finches, red-winged blackbirds relish seeds. Foliage browsed by cottontails & white-tailed deer. Larval host plant for Two-tailed tiger swallowtail & Tiger swallow-tail butterflies.
Fringe Tree *Chionanthus virginica*	Highly ornamental tree which is breathtaking when in bloom. Males plants have more spectacular flowers. Leaves are dark green & glossy & turn yellow in the autumn.	Flowers are excellent nectar source for butterflies, moths, & bees. Fruit is relished by many species of birds including woodpeckers, bluejays, mockingbirds & cardinals.
Green ash *Fraxinus pensylvanica*	Fairly fast-growing & long-lived shade tree. Brilliant yellow autumn color.	Excellent cover and nesting tree. Cardinals, finches, red-winged blackbirds relish fruit. Foliage browsed by cottontails & white-tailed deer. Larval host plant for Two-tailed tiger swallowtail & Tiger swallow-tail butterflies.
Gregg ash *Fraxinus greggi*	Small to medium-sized tree with trifoliate compound leaves & smooth iron gray bark. Quite ornamental & very drought tolerant. Can form thickets or clumps.	Good cover & nesting tree. Birds are very fond of the seeds contained in the samaras. Excellent mule deer browse.
Texas ash *Fraxinus texensis*	Short-trunked medium-sized tree with contorted branches. Has beautiful reddish-yellow fall color. Long lived & healthy & very drought tolerant. Flowers & fruit quite decorative.	Good substrate for insectivorous birds. Fine nesting & cover tree. Several species of birds relish both flowers & fruits, especially finches, cardinals & grosbeaks. Foliage browsed by rabbits, porcupine & white-tailed deer.

Table A.5
Native Plants of Texas

Please note that each two-page "spread" is divided into a top half (with plants' growing information) and a bottom half (with plants' ornamental and wildlife values). Numbered regions correspond to the Texas Ecoregion map on page 11.

Species	1	2	3	4	5	6	7	8	9	10	Habit Height	Flower	Fruit	Sun Exposure	Habitat	Soils and Moisture Regime
Velvet ash *Fraxinus velutina*										x	Tree, large 30'-50' Deciduous	Furry panicles. April-June or March-May depending on altitude	Samara. September	Full sun, part shade	Prefers areas around arroyos where water is available. Occurs along rivers, streams, dry streambeds & narrow canyons.	Well-drained, mesic. Sands, loams, clays, caliche & limestone soils.
White ash *Fraxinus americana*	x	x	x		x	x	x				Tree, large 60'-70' Deciduous	Inconspicuous male & female flower clusters. April-May	Samara. Aug.-Sept.	Full sun, part shade	Grows in deep, rich moist soils on slopes & stream bottoms in eastern 1/3 of Texas.	Needs moisture, but good drainage. Sands, loams & clays.
Palm Family – Arecaceae																
Sabal palm *Sabal texana*							x				Tree, large 30'-50' Evergreen	Showy white & fragrant, 7'-8' stalks. March-April	Berry, dark purple to black with one seed. May-June	Full sun, part shade	Last native remnants on the flatlands of the Lower Rio Grande Valley.	Moist soils, poor drainage O.K. Sands, loams & clays.
Rose Family – Rosaceae																
Black cherry *Prunus serotina* v. *serotina*	x	x	x								Tree, small, ornamental 60'-100' Deciduous	Showy racemes of white perfect flowers, fragrant. March-April	Cherries, small purple black, sweet or tart. June-Oct.	Full sun, part shade	Prefers eastern woodlands, thickets, fencerows & areas along roadsides.	Well-drained, mesic. Sands, loams & clays.
Cherry-laurel *Prunus caroliniana*	x	x									Tree, ornamental 20'-30' Evergreen	Showy creamy white elongated spike-like racemes. March-April	Berries, blue-black. Aug.-Sept.	Full sun, part shade, dappled shade	Prefers well-drained, deep moist bottom-land soils in fields, woodlands & creek bottoms.	Well-drained, mesic. Sands, loams & clay loams.

Species	Ornamental Value	Wildlife Value
Velvet ash *Fraxinus velutina*	This is an excellent landscape plant, easily reared from seed. Grows rapidly & is not susceptible to borers. Very ornamental. Prefers north side of hillsides.	Good cover & nesting tree. Birds are very fond of the seeds contained in the samaras. Excellent mule deer browse. Leaves browsed by other herbivores.
White ash *Fraxinus americana*	Beautiful shade tree with compound leaves turning delicate shades of pink, orange & purple in fall. Trees in open condition have short trunk & round top, in the forest, long trunk & narrow crown.	Excellent cover & nesting tree. Seeds are eaten by several species of birds, i.e., wood duck, bobwhite, sapsuckers, cedar waxwings, finches, cardinals & sparrows. Deer browse leaves. Larval host plant for Mourning cloak, Two-tailed & Tiger swallowtail butterflies.
Palm Family – Arecaceae		
Sabal palm *Sabal texana*	Majestic native palm with dramatic fan-shaped leaves forming a dense rounded crown. Slow growing, but cold hardy to Lake Livingston. Has an enormous root system. There are no thorns on leaves. Very ornamental.	Excellent cover & nesting site for birds. Insects are attracted to the flowers. Many species of South Texas birds forage on the ripe fruit.
Rose Family – Rosaceae		
Black cherry *Prunus serotina v. serotina*	Attractive ornamental with decorative flowers, copious fruits, shiny green leaves & grayish brown horizontally striped bark. Easy to grow. Other varieties available for all regions of Texas except South Texas.	Copious fruits are eagerly devoured by a wide variety of wildlife including 33 kinds of birds, raccoons, opossums, squirrels & rabbits. Foliage is not browsed by deer. Larval host plant to some Hairstreak butterfly species.
Cherry-laurel *Prunus caroliniana*	Attractive tree with shiny green simple evergreen leaves with finely serrated edges. Fast growing, but somewhat short lived; is easy to train into a hedge or can grow to handsome shade tree.	Good nectar plant for bees & other insects in the spring. Birds love the black berries which persist throughout the winter. Sometimes the berries ferment making robins & cedar waxwings tipsy. Larval host plant for a few species of butterflies.

Table A.5
Native Plants of Texas

Please note that each two-page "spread" is divided into a top half (with plants' growing information) and a bottom half (with plants' ornamental and wildlife values). Numbered regions correspond to the Texas Ecoregion map on page 11.

Species	Ecological Region 1	2	3	4	5	6	7	8	9	10	Habit Height	Flower	Fruit	Sun Exposure	Habitat	Soils and Moisture Regime
Chickasaw plum *Prunus angustifolia*	x	x	x		x				x		Tree, small, ornamental 10'-25' Deciduous	Showy white flowers in 2-4 flowered umbels, fragrant. March-April	Plums, red or yellow. May-July	Full sun, part shade	Prefers old fields, edges of woods, roadsides & fencerows.	Well-drained, xeric to mesic. Sands.
Chisos rosewood *Vauquelinia angustifolia*										x	Tree, small, ornamental 10'-30' Deciduous	Showy white flowers in clusters, fragrant. June-Aug.	Follicle, densely hairy. Aug.-Oct.	Full sun, part shade	Found scattered in canyons & along rocky slopes & chaparral in Chisos, Dead Horse mountains in the Trans-Pecos from 5300'-6500'.	Well-drained, xeric-mesic. Acid sands, loams, also clays.
Cockspur hawthorn *Crataegus crus-galli*	x			x	x		x				Tree, small, ornamental 10'-25' Deciduous	Showy, white perfect flowers. May-June	Pome (apple-like fruit), dull red in color. Oct.-Nov.	Full sun, part shade	Prefers limestone bluffs, hilltops, woods & thickets & fence rows in East Texas.	Well-drained, mesic; moderate moisture; will tolerate dry conditions. Sands, loams & clays.
Common chokecherry *Prunus virginiana*	x			x				x	x	x	Tree, small, ornamental 15'-30' Deciduous	Showy, short dense racemes of white flowers, fragrant. April-July	Chokecherries luscious scarlet to purple black. July-Sept.	Full sun, part shade, dappled shade	Prefers open woods, rocky slopes, bluffs, rimrock, breaks & seepage areas.	Well-drained, mesic. Sands, loams, clays & limestone soils.
Green hawthorn *Crataegus viridis*	x	x	x		x		x				Tree, small, ornamental 20'-35' Deciduous	Showy, white perfect flowers. March-April	Pome (apple-like fruit), orange or red in color. Sept.-Nov.	Full sun, part shade	Prefers low, wet alluvial woods, also sandy fields in East Texas & Upper Texas Coast.	Medium to high moisture. Seasonal poor drainage O.K. Sands, loams & clays.

Species	Ornamental Value	Wildlife Value
Chickasaw plum *Prunus angustifolia*	Twiggy, thicket-forming shrub or small tree with short trunk. Good for shelter belt planting. White flowers are highly attractive and fragrant.	Chickasaw plum is a good protective cover & nesting tree. Fragrant white flowers attract many kinds of insects. Plums are sought after by many birds & small mammals.
Chisos rosewood *Vauquelinia angustifolia*	Small ornamental evergreen tree with narrow toothed leaves & many small greenish-white flower clusters. Can be used as a dense screen. Is fairly cold hardy. Does not appreciate very hot summers.	Fruits are eaten by birds if other fruits are not available. Best as a protective cover & nesting tree. Leaves are browsed by mule deer.
Cockspur hawthorn *Crataegus crus-galli*	Most widespread hawthorn with strongly horizontal branches, large thorns & beautiful flowers in the spring. Has shiny leathery leaves & reddish-brown fissured bark.	Good protective cover & nesting tree. Flowers provide abundant nectar. Fruits are highly sought after by many species of birds & mammals including skunks, squirrels & fox. Larval host plant for some Hairstreak butterflies.
Common chokecherry *Prunus virginiana*	Large ornamental understory shrub to small tree with erect or horizontal branches, racemes of white fragrant flowers, red to black chokecherries. This is a good erosion control plant.	Flowers attract hordes of insects of all kinds. Fruit eaten by at least 40 species of birds. Leaves browsed by cotton-tail & deer. Larval host plant for Tiger swallowtail, Striped hairstreak, Coral hairstreak, Red-spotted purple & Spring azure butterflies.
Green hawthorn *Crataegus viridis*	Medium-sized tree forming a broad rounded crown, serrated dark green shiny leaves, with bark that shreds into small scales. Often thornless.	Beautiful white flowers with yellow stamens attract bees & butterflies. Red orange haws disappear quickly, highly prized by several species of birds & mammals. Good cover & nesting tree. Larval host plant for some Hairstreak butterflies.

Table A.5
Native Plants of Texas

Please note that each two-page "spread" is divided into a top half (with plants' growing information) and a bottom half (with plants' ornamental and wildlife values). Numbered regions correspond to the Texas Ecoregion map on page 11.

Species	Ecological Region 1 2 3 4 5 6 7 8 9 10										Habit Height	Flower	Fruit	Sun Exposure	Habitat	Soils and Moisture Regime
Mexican plum *Prunus mexicana*	x	x	x	x			x				Tree, small, ornamental 15′-35′ Deciduous	Showy, white perfect flowers, fragrant. Feb.-April	Plum, red-purple. Sept.-Oct.	Full sun, part shade	Prefers river or creek bottoms, hardwood slopes hillsides, & prairies.	Well-drained, mesic. Sands, loams & clays.
Mountain mahogany *Cercocarpus montanus v. argenteus*							x			x	Tree, small, ornamental 8′-15′ Persistent to evergreen	White to yellowish flowers. March-June	Brown, leathery fruit, tipped with long white plume. May-Nov.	Full sun, part shade	Prefers rocky slopes & canyons of Edwards Plateau & rocky bluffs of Trans-Pecos.	Well-drained, mesic-xeric. Sands, loams & clays. Likes limestone, caliche-like soils.
Munson plum *Prunus munsoniana*				x	x		x				Tree, small, ornamental 15′-25′ Deciduous	Showy, white perfect flowers, fragrant. March	Plum, red or yellow with white dots. Sept.-Oct.	Full sun, part shade	Prefers limestone ledges & slopes; also grassy thickets.	Well-drained, mesic. Sands, loams & clay (especially those with high limestone content.)
Murray plum *Prunus murrayana*										x	Tree, small 12′-15′ Deciduous	Simple 1-5 flowered umbel of white-petalled flowers. March-April	This plant has not yet flowered in cultivation.	Full sun, part shade	Prefers canyons & rocky slopes of Jeff Davis, Brewster counties, in Davis, Eagle & Del Norte mountains.	Well-drained mesic. Acid sands, sandy loams. Likes igneous soils.
Parsley hawthorn *Crataegus marshallii*	x	x				x					Tree, ornamental 10′-25′ Deciduous	Showy white flowers. March	Red haws. Sept.-Oct.	Full sun, dappled shade, part shade	Prefers sandy wood-lands & pastures. Found mostly along fencelines & wood-land edges in East Texas.	Well-drained, mesic. Sands & sandy loams, acid. Also tolerates calcareous soils.
Prairie crabapple *Pyrus ioensis*						x			x		Tree, small, ornamental 10′-30′ Deciduous	Showy white or salmon pink-petalled blossoms. Feb.-April	Crab apple (pome). Aug.-Oct.	Full sun, part shade	Prefers stream banks & heads of canyons, limestone slopes & draws.	Well-drained, mesic. Sands, loams, clays & limestone soils.

Species	Ornamental Value	Wildlife Value
Mexican plum *Prunus mexicana*	Medium sized, single-trunked ornamental tree with broad crown & satiny silver bark with dark fissures. Excellent accent plant with heavenly fragrance when in bloom.	Early spring clouds of white flowers are wonderful nectar source, attracting bees, butterflies & diurnal moths. Gamebirds, songbirds & several species of mammals feast on the ripe plums. Larval host plant for Tiger swallowtail butterfly.
Mountain mahogany *Cercocarpus montanus v. argenteus*	An attractive, small ornamental tree. Pretty dark green leaves with dense white wool underneath & stunning fruit give it a very special look. Most beautiful in fall. Especially striking when backlit by the sun. Fairly slow growing.	Good cover & nesting tree. The plumes of the fruit used as nesting material. Leaves are browsed by white-tailed & mule deer.
Munson plum *Prunus munsoniana*	Thicket-forming ornamental shrub or small round-topped tree with bright lustrous green leaves & smooth thin bark.	Spring flowers with copious nectar attract butterflies, bees & other insects. Plums are relished by several species of birds & small mammals.
Murray plum *Prunus murrayana*	Small tree or shrub in protected situations. Is very intricately branched with small white flower clusters. This is a rare plant that could have excellent ornamental value. More work needs to be done on this species. New populations need to be found.	There are also excellent wildlife possibilities for this plant. Flowers attract insects. Mule deer will browse the leaves.
Parsley hawthorn *Crataegus marshallii*	Beautiful blossoms add a touch of ethereal beauty to this understory tree. Usually with several trunks & flaky gray bark revealing an orange layer underneath. Fruits are a shiny bright red color.	Beautiful white blossoms attract nectar lovers. Red haws are gone in a flash as they are highly prized by many species of birds, also by mammals. Large thorns make it a good protective cover & nest tree. Larval host plant of the Gray Hairstreak butterfly.
Prairie crabapple *Pyrus ioensis*	While Prairie crabapple is not native to the High Plains, it would grow well there with proper treatment. It has lovely flowers in the spring & would make a nice accent plant. In the wild the tree is rare.	All kinds of insects are attracted to the spring blossoms, especially bees & butterflies. Approximately 20 species of wildlife, both birds & small mammals, enjoy the small crab apples.

Please note that each two-page "spread" is divided into a top half (with plants' growing information) and a bottom half (with plants' ornamental and wildlife values). Numbered regions correspond to the Texas Ecoregion map on page 11.

Species	Ecological Region 1 2 3 4 5 6 7 8 9 10	Habit Height	Flower	Fruit	Sun Exposure	Habitat	Soils and Moisture Regime
Red chokecherry *Pyrus arbutifolia*	× × _ _ _ _ _ _ _ _	Tree, small, ornamental 8'-12' Deciduous	Showy, white to pink flowers. March-May	Pome (apple-like fruit). Sept.-Oct.	Full sun, part shade	Prefers wet woods & swamps of East Texas, Upper Texas Coast.	Mesic-hydric, seasonal poor drainage O.K. Sands, loams & clays.
Reverchon hawthorn *Crataegus reverchonii*	_ _ _ × × _ × _ _ _	Tree, small, ornamental 10'-25' Deciduous	Showy white flowers, fragrant. May-Aug.	Pomes, red, roundish & shiny. Sept.-Oct.	Full sun, part shade	Prefers thickets & open woods in north central Texas.	Well-drained, mesic. Sands, neutral to slightly acid; clays & limestone soils.
Silver-leaf mountain mahogany *Cercocarpus montanus* v. *argenteus*	_ _ _ _ _ _ × × × ×	Tree, small 12'-15' Persistent to Evergreen	White to yellowish flowers. March-April; further north June-July	Fruit, slim, leathery, brown & plume-tipped. May-Nov.	Full sun, part shade	Prefers rocky slopes & canyons in Edwards Plateau, Trans-Pecos & Panhandle.	Well-drained, xeric. Sands, loams & clays, & caliche type soils, alkaline to neutral.
Southwestern black cherry *Prunus serotina* v. *rufula*	_ _ _ _ _ _ _ _ _ ×	Tree, small 25'-50' Deciduous	Showy racemes of creamy white flowers. March-April	Cherries, small & black, ripen individually. July-Oct.	Full sun, part shade	Prefers areas near streams, found in canyons & other protected areas.	Well-drained, mesic. Deep sands, loams & clays.
Utah serviceberry *Amelanchier utahensis*	_ _ _ _ _ _ _ _ _ ×	Tree, small, ornamental 16'-25' Deciduous	Showy white to pink flowers. April, May or June, depending on rains	Berries (pomes), bluish-black. Aug.-Sept.	Full sun, part shade	Prefers dry canyons & slopes & mountain sides at 7000', in Guadalupe mountains, Culberson County.	Well-drained, mesic. Sands, loams & clays.

Species	Ornamental Value	Wildlife Value
Red chokecherry *Pyrus arbutifolia*	Ornamental shrub to small tree with good fall color, turning bright red. Flowers are also quite showy in the spring.	The fruit is a highly valuable wildlife food in the fall & winter & is eaten by at least 13 species of birds including quail, pheasant, turkey, robins & cedar waxwings. Beautiful flowers attract several varieties of insects: bees, butterflies & moths.
Reverchon hawthorn *Crataegus reverchonii*	Highly attractive small tree with glistening tan flakey bark with lovely white flowers. Good accent plant.	Fragrant flowers offer copious nectar to bees & butterflies, & juicy fruit favored by several species of birds & small mammals. Thorns make this an excellent protective cover & nest tree. Larval host plant of a few hairstreak butterflies.
Silver-leaf mountain mahogany *Cercocarpus montanus* *v. argenteus*	A small persistent to evergreen tree with dark green leathery leaves with dense woolly-white undersides. Very ornamental. Is most beautiful in the late summer & fall when feather-like fruits mature. Slow to moderate grower; drought tolerant.	While birds may use silky plumed fruit to line nests, not much fruit is eaten. White-tailed deer browse on leaves with enthusiasm.
Southwestern black cherry *Prunus serotina* *v. rufula*	Very ornamental overstory tree with attractive bark, pretty leaves & showy flowers & fruit. Has fruit in all stages of ripening on same raceme.	Very important wildlife food source. Flowers attract several species of insects. Ripe cherries eaten by several species of birds & small mammals, especially rodents, ground squirrels, rabbits. Foliage browsed by deer & rabbits. Good nest & cover tree.
Utah serviceberry *Amelanchier utahensis*	This extremely showy ornamental with the white to pink flowers & pretty leaves makes an excellent accent plant in the right habitat.	The showy flowers attract myriads of insects of many varieties. Birds & gound squirrels are highly fond of the ripe fruit. Mule deer readily browse the leaves.

Table A.5
Native Plants of Texas

Please note that each two-page "spread" is divided into a top half (with plants' growing information) and a bottom half (with plants' ornamental and wildlife values). Numbered regions correspond to the Texas Ecoregion map on page 11.

Sapodilla Family – Sapotaceae

Species	Ecological Region (1–10)	Habit / Height	Flower	Fruit	Sun Exposure	Habitat	Soils and Moisture Regime
Chittamwood *Bumelia lanuginosa v. oblongifolia*	1, 2, 3, 4, 5, 6, 7, 8, 10	Tree, large 30'-80' Persistent	White perfect flowers, fragrant. June-July	Berries, blue-black. Sept.-Oct.	Full sun, part shade	Mostly uplands, sometimes bottom-lands, woodlands, edges & fencerows. This subspecies occurs on eastern half of Rolling Plains.	Well-drained, mesic. Sandy loams, loams, and clays. Tolerates gumbo.
Coma (Saffron plum) *Bumelia celastrina*	1, 7	Tree, small 15'-25' Persistent to Evergreen	Small green & white flowers, fragrant. May-Nov.	Berries, blue-black. April-June	Full sun, part shade	Prefers open brushy flats or gently rolling slopes, or along resacas, gravelly hills, thickets & salt marshes in South Texas.	Xeric, well-drained. Sands, sandy loams or clays. Prefers alkaline soils.
Woolly-bucket bumelia *Bumelia lanuginosa*	1, 2, 3, 4, 5, 6, 7, 8, 10	Tree, large 40'-80' Persistent	White perfect flowers, fragrant. June-July	Berries, blue-black. Sept.-Oct.	Full sun, part shade	Mostly uplands, sometimes bottom-lands, woodlands, edges & fencerows.	Well-drained, mesic. Sandy loams, loams, & clays. Tolerates gumbo.

Soapberry Family – Sapindaceae

Species	Ecological Region (1–10)	Habit / Height	Flower	Fruit	Sun Exposure	Habitat	Soils and Moisture Regime
Mexican buckeye *Ungnadia speciosa*	1, 2, 3, 4, 5, 7, 10	Tree, small, ornamental 15'-30' Deciduous	Showy clusters of pink-magenta flowers cloak branches before leaves come out. Fragrant. March-May	Capsules (tripar-tite leathery "buckeyes"), brown-black. Oct.-Nov.	Full sun, part shade	Prefers rocky areas in canyons, slopes & ridges & along fencerows.	Well-drained, mesic. Sands, loams & clays.

Species	Ornamental Value	Wildlife Value
Sapodilla Family – Sapotaceae		
Chittamwood *Bumelia lanuginosa v. oblongifolia*	Large shade tree with simple green leaves with white woolly under-surface.	Several species of birds feed on the fruit, including cardinals, finches, robins, cedar waxwings, warblers, & vireos. Good cover & nesting tree due to protective thorns. Good substrate for insectivorous birds.
Coma (Saffron plum) *Bumelia celastrina*	Spiny small tree with simple leaves, greenish-white flowers & fleshy blue-black fruits. Can also be a shrub.	Flowers attract several kinds of insects, while fleshy fruits are eaten by many species of birds. In South Texas, the chachalacas love them. Raccoons & coyotes also relish them. Provides excellent cover & is a great nesting tree for many bird species.
Woolly-bucket bumelia *Bumelia lanuginosa*	Large shade tree with simple green leaves with white woolly under-surface.	Several species of birds feed on the fruit, including cardinals, finches, robins, cedar waxwings, warblers, & vireos. Good cover & nesting tree due to protective thorns. Good substrate for insectivorous birds.
Soapberry Family – Sapindaceae		
Mexican buckeye *Ungnadia speciosa*	Showy, small, shrubby often multi-trunked ornamental with irregular shape. Spectacular pink blossoms in spring. Good understory tree, prefers at least $1/2$ a day in sun. Has pretty yellow fall color also.	Splashy pink flowers are a good nectar source for bees, butterflies, diurnal moths. Good honey plant. Sweet seeds eaten by a few species of birds & mammals, though poisonous to humans. Larval host plant for Henry's Elfin butterfly.

Table A.5
Native Plants of Texas

Please note that each two-page "spread" is divided into a top half (with plants' growing information) and a bottom half (with plants' ornamental and wildlife values). Numbered regions correspond to the Texas Ecoregion map on page 11.

Species	1	2	3	4	5	6	7	8	9	10	Habit Height	Flower	Fruit	Sun Exposure	Habitat	Soils and Moisture Regime
Western soapberry *Sapindus drummondii*	x	x	x	x	x	x	x	x	x	x	Tree, large 15'-50' Deciduous	Clusters of small white flowers. May-June	Round, amber, wrinkled berry-like fruit with 1 seed. Sept.-Oct.	Full sun, part shade	Prefers moist soils along streams & fencerows, scattered throughout Texas.	Well-drained, mesic. Sands, loams & clays, likes limestone soils.
Staff Tree Family – Celastraceae																
Desert yaupon *Schaefferia cuneifolia*						x				x	Tree, small, ornamental 3'-6' Evergreen	Small greenish flowers. Feb.-Sept.	Red to orange showy berries (drupes). July-Nov.	Full sun, part shade	Prefers rocky hillsides, chaparral or xeric sites near coast.	Xeric, well-drained. Sands, loams, clays.
Styrax Family – Styracaceae																
Big-leaf snowbell *Styrax americana*	x										Tree, ornamental 12'-15' Deciduous	Showy, elegantly shaped white flowers. May-June	Drupes, round & pea-sized. Sept.-Oct.	Part shade, dappled shade	Prefers moist soils of the Big Thicket, in moist woods & river bottoms.	Mesic-hydric, tolerates poor drainage. Sands, sandy loams, prefers acid soils.
Sumac Family – Anacardiaceae																
Flameleaf sumac *Rhus copallina*	x	x	x	x		x	x				Tree, small 15'-25' Deciduous	Male & female flowers, small greenish white, on separate trees. July-Aug.	Drupes, small red, in clusters, remain after leaves fall. Sept.-Nov.	Full sun, part shade, dappled shade	Prefers fence rows, fields & bottomlands in East & East Central Texas. Tolerates rocky areas.	Well-drained, mesic. Sands, loams & clays.
Lance-leaf sumac *Rhus lanceolata*			x	x			x			x	Tree, small 10'-20' Deciduous	Male & female flowers, small greenish white, on separate trees. June	Drupes, small red, in clusters, remain after leaves fall. Sept.-Dec.	Full sun, part shade	Occurs on limestone & in calcareous soils, woodlands & roadside edges, along fencerows. Tolerates disturbed soils.	Well-drained, mesic. Sands, sandy loams, neutral clays, likes limestone soils.

Species	Ornamental Value	Wildlife Value
Western soapberry *Sapindus drummondii*	Fine-looking shade tree with dependable yellow fall foliage. Translucent amber fruits have white seeds which are poisonous to us. Moderately fast growing; also tolerates poor sites. Forms thickets but does not live long.	Fruit highly prized by many kinds of birds that are not affected by poison. Bluebirds, robins, cedar waxwings devour them. Small flowers provide nectar to various insects. Good nest & cover tree. Substrate to insectivores. Larval host plant to Soapberry hairstreak butterfly.

Staff Tree Family – Celastraceae

Species	Ornamental Value	Wildlife Value
Desert yaupon *Schaefleria cuneifolia*	Densely-branched, rigid ornamental shrub with beautiful red berries on female plant. Twigs are somewhat spiny.	Leaves are frequently browsed by white-tailed deer & fruits are a favorite of several species of birds & small mammals. Quail, wrens, coyotes & woodrats are especially fond of them. Birds use tree as nesting & cover site.

Styrax Family – Styracaceae

Species	Ornamental Value	Wildlife Value
Big-leaf snowbell *Styrax americana*	Beautiful small white flowering ornamental tree, similar to Two-winged Silver-bell. Does well in Houston.	White flowers attract many kinds of insects, especially bees & butterflies. Fruit is especially favored by the wood duck. Also eaten by other species of birds.

Sumac Family – Anacardiaceae

Species	Ornamental Value	Wildlife Value
Flameleaf sumac *Rhus copallina*	A small, commonly clump-forming shrub or small tree with elegant compound leaves & showy red fruit clusters. Only trees with female flowers have fruit. Beautiful red color in the fall. Fast growing.	Fruit is eaten by at least 21 species of birds, Flowers attract numerous insects in spring, good nectar source for bees & butterflies. Larval host plant for Red-banded hairstreak butterfly.
Lance-leaf sumac *Rhus lanceolata*	Sometimes thicket-forming small tree with elegant compound leaves & showy red fruit clusters. Only trees with female flowers have fruit. Beautiful red color in the fall. Fast growing with a very attractive shape.	Fruit is eaten by more than 20 species of birds, favored by quail & turkey. Flowers attract numerous insects in spring, good nectar source for bees & butterflies. Leaves browsed by deer. Larval host plant for Red-banded hairstreak butterfly.

Table A.5
Native Plants of Texas

Please note that each two-page "spread" is divided into a top half (with plants' growing information) and a bottom half (with plants' ornamental and wildlife values). Numbered regions correspond to the Texas Ecoregion map on page 11.

Species	Ecological Region 1 2 3 4 5 6 7 8 9 10	Habit Height	Flower	Fruit	Sun Exposure	Habitat	Soils and Moisture Regime
Sweetleaf Family – Symplocaceae							
Sweetleaf *Symplocos tinctoria*	x x	Tree, ornamental 30'-50' Persistent to Evergreen	Showy clusters of yellow flowers, fragrant. Feb.-May	Drupes, blue-gray to orange brown. Sept.-Oct.	Full sun, part shade	Prefers low moist grounds of river bottoms & bay flats.	Mesic-hydric, tolerates poor drainage. Sands & sandy loams, acid soils preferred.
Sycamore Family – Platanaceae							
Sycamore *Platanus occidentalis*	x x x x x x x	Tree, large 100'-150' Deciduous	Inconspicuous male & female globose heads reddish, greenish. April-May	Round seed head. Sept.-Oct.	Full sun, part shade	Rich bottomland soils along streams & creek bottoms.	Well-drained, mesic. Sands, sandy loams, & clays.
Tupelo Family – Nyssaceae							
Black gum *Nyssa sylvatica*	x x x	Tree, large 80'-100' Deciduous	Inconspicuous male & female greenish flowers, sometimes on same or different trees. April-June	Drupes, blue-black. Sept.-Oct.	Full sun, part shade	Rich bottomland soils in East Texas. Pineywoods, along streams & creek bottoms, or moist open woods in sandy soils.	Mesic-hydric. Likes moisture. Poor drainage O.K. Sands, sandy loams, & clays. Likes acid soils.
Vervain Family – Verbenaceae							
Berlandier fiddlewood *Citharexylum berlandieri*	x (region 6)	Tree, small, ornamental 5'-20' Persistent	Pretty white flowers, fragrant. Feb.-Aug.	Drupes, yellow to red with two seeds. April-Oct.	Full sun, part shade	Occurs in thickets on flats & brushy habitats in Cameron & Willacy counties in extreme south Texas.	Well-drained, xeric. Clay or clay loam soils.

Species	Ornamental Value	Wildlife Value
Sweetleaf Family – Symplocaceae		
Sweetleaf *Symplocos tinctoria*	Semi-evergreen small tree with slender upright branches & beautiful bright yellow flower clusters. Leaves are thick, leathery & lustrous.	Flowers attract many different kinds of insects. The leaves are sweet & greedily eaten by several herbivorous species of wildlife. Seeds from the fruit are eaten by Eastern phoebe & many other species of birds. Larval host plant of King's hairstreak butterfly.
Sycamore Family – Platanaceae		
Sycamore *Platanus occidentalis*	Majestic shade tree. Fast growing with pretty leaves and bark.	Globose fruit with seeds eaten by a variety of birds & mammals, including muskrat. Goldfinches, purple & house finches are especially fond of fruit. Good substrate for insectivorous birds.
Tupelo Family – Nyssaceae		
Black gum *Nyssa sylvatica*	Tall shade tree with short, crooked branches & narrow, flat-topped crown. Has gorgeous, early red fall color. Does well in gumbo. Good tree for Houston area.	Dark fruits provide an early source of food for a variety of birds & mammals. Favored by bluebirds, catbirds, mockingbirds, robins, summer tanagers & finches. Good substrate for insectivorous birds. Foliage browsed by deer. Bees attracted to flowers.
Vervain Family – Verbenaceae		
Berlandier fiddlewood *Citharexylum berlandieri*	A crooked shrub to small gnarled tree with small fragrant white flowers borne on racemes. Yellow to red berries are very stunning when plant is in fruit.	Many small insects are attracted to the fragrant flowers for their nectar. Several species of South Texas fruit-eating birds relish the ripe berries.

Table A.5
Native Plants of Texas

Please note that each two-page "spread" is divided into a top half (with plants' growing information) and a bottom half (with plants' ornamental and wildlife values). Numbered regions correspond to the Texas Ecoregion map on page 11.

Species	1	2	3	4	5	6	7	8	9	10	Habit Height	Flower	Fruit	Sun Exposure	Habitat	Soils and Moisture Regime
						Ecological Region										
Wright's lippia *Aloysia wrightii*							x	x		x	Tree, small ornamental 3'-6' Deciduous	Small, crowded white spikes. April-May	Calyx, 2-segmented with 2 nutlets. June-Aug.	Full sun	Prefers rocky slopes, banks, ledges, arroyos, gullies, limestone hills, mesa slopes, & desert scrub from 2000'-6000'.	Well-drained, xeric. Sands, loams, clays, caliche-like limestone soils.
Walnut Family – Juglandaceae																
Black hickory *Carya texana*	x	x	x	x	x	x	x				Tree, large 30'-80' Deciduous	Inconspicuous catkins, male & female, reddish on same tree. March	Nut. Oct.-Nov.	Full sun, part shade	Prefers dry, sandy uplands or rocky slopes throughout the eastern portion of the state, often associated with Post & Blackjack oaks. West to Gillespie & Bexar counties.	Well-drained, mesic. Sands, loams & clays.
Little walnut *Juglans microcarpa*					x		x			x	Tree, small 10'-30' Deciduous	Inconspicuous male & female flowers, greenish, on same trees. March-April	Walnut, small. Sept.-Oct.	Full sun, part shade	Prefers rocky areas near streams, arroyos & rocky ravines in Central, South & West Texas.	Well-drained, mesic. Loams, clays. Likes rocky limestone soils.
Pecan *Carya illinoensis*	x	x	x	x	x	x	x	x			Tree, large 50'-60' Deciduous	Inconspicuous catkins, male & female, yellowish on same tree. March-May	Nut. Sept.-Oct.	Full sun, part shade	Prefers rich bottom-lands.	Well-drained, mesic. Sands, loams, or clays.

Species	Ornamental Value	Wildlife Value
Wright's lippia *Aloysia wrightii*	A small slender-branched hairy aromatic shrub with profusely flowering white flower spikes.	Wright's aloysia is an excellent honey plant. Flowers attract myriads of insects, bees & butterflies, especially. Birds will eat the ripe nutlets.
Walnut Family – Juglandaceae		
Black hickory *Carya texana*	This medium to large-sized shade tree is the most wide-ranging hickory in Texas. It occasionally grows to 100' tall, has crooked branches & either a narrow or spreading crown depending on amount of sun. Leaves are compound & alternate.	Texas hickory is a good substrate for insectivorous birds. Excellent cover & nesting tree. Nuts are fairly sweet, but hard to crack. Gamebirds, quail & turkey, eat them from the ground after shells have softened. Larval host plant for Banded hairstreak butterfly.
Little walnut *Juglans microcarpa*	A main-trunked small tree with a long tap root. Often hybridizes with Arizona walnut. Quite disease resistant.	Produces small walnuts with high-quality meat eaten by rock squirrels & other small mammals. Gamebirds & songbirds also favor nuts. Good nesting & cover tree. Larval host plant of the Banded hairstreak butterfly.
Pecan *Carya illinoenensis*	Beautiful shade tree with elegant compound leaves. Prefers deep, rich soils but will grow in thinner soils. Sometimes turns yellow in fall.	Sweet edible nuts valuable for all kinds of wildlife, birds & mammals alike including woodpeckers, jays, sparrows, fox squirrel, gray squirrel, opossum, & raccoons. Good substrate for insectivorous birds. Larval host plant for Gray hairstreak butterfly.

Table A.5
Native Plants of Texas

Please note that each two-page "spread" is divided into a top half (with plants' growing information) and a bottom half (with plants' ornamental and wildlife values). Numbered regions correspond to the Texas Ecoregion map on page 11.

Species	Ecological Region 1 2 3 4 5 6 7 8 9 10	Habit Height	Flower	Fruit	Sun Exposure	Habitat	Soils and Moisture Regime
Shagbark hickory *Carya ovata*	x x	Tree, large 60'-100' Deciduous	Inconspicuous green male catkins & female spikes on same trees. March-June	Hickory. Sept.-Oct.	Full sun, part shade	Prefers rich wood-lands, bottoms & slopes, often near streams & swamps.	Well-drained, mesic. Sands, loams & clays.
Wax myrtle Family – Myricaceae							
Wax myrtle *Myrica cerifera*	x x x	Tree, small, or shrub 6'-12' Evergreen	Inconspicuous whitish flowers. March-April	Berries, globose, waxy. Nov.-Dec.	Full sun, part shade, dappled shade	Prefers moist or dry soils of Pineywoods & hardwoods. Woodlands & grass-lands in East Texas, Gulf Coast Prairies & Marshes.	Mesic, poor drainage O.K.; can tolerate drier substrate. Sands, loams & clays.
Willow family – Salicaceae							
Black willow *Salix nigra*	x x x x x x x x	Tree, large 35'-80' Deciduous	Male & female creamy yellow catkins, on separate trees. April-May	Capsules, light brown. May-June	Full sun, part shade	Prefers alluvial soils along streams.	Hydric-mesic, poor drainage O.K. Sand, loams & clays.
Eastern cottonwood *Populus deltoides*	x x x x x x	Tree, large 40'-100' Deciduous	Inconspicuous male & female catkins red & brown. March-June	Brown female capsules with cottony seeds. May-June	Full sun, part shade	Rich bottomland soils along streams.	Well-drained, mesic. Sands, loams, & clays.
Meseta cottonwood *Populus fremontii* v. *mesetae*	x	Tree, large 30'-60' Deciduous	Inconspicuous male & female catkins red & yellow. March-June	Brown female capsules with cottony seeds. May-June	Full sun, part shade	Prefers moist soils along streams or water holes from sea level to 7000'.	Well-drained, mesic. Likes rocky or deep alluvial soils: sands, loams clays & caliche.

Species	Ornamental Value	Wildlife Value
Shagbark hickory *Carya ovata*	Tall shade tree with oblong crown & shaggy bark. Slow growing, but long lived. Leaves are compound with serrated edges. Next to pecan, this tree has tastiest nuts. Very shade tolerant when young. Sometimes subject to insect damage.	Game birds such as turkey, bobwhite quail love the nuts as do many kinds of mammals. Several other birds, i.e., jays, woodpeckers & doves will eat the nuts too. Good cover & nesting tree. Good substrate for insectivorous birds.
Wax myrtle Family – Myricaceae		
Wax myrtle *Myrica cerifera*	Softly shaped, low-growing evergreen shrub or small tree. Is fast growing & has aromatic leaves & distinctive waxy pale bluish berries. If left unpruned, it is naturally shrubby looking. Tolerates poor drainage.	Dense growth provides excellent cover & nesting sites. Over 40 species of birds eat the waxy berries, cedar waxwings, robins, cardinals, mockingbirds, warblers, towhees, & sparrows. Eaten by bobwhite, quail & turkey, too. Larval host plant for Red-banded hairstreak butterfly.
Willow family – Salicaceae		
Black willow *Salix nigra*	Occurs throughout Texas where there's standing water. A rapid-grower that is often multitrunked & has irregular crown. Very airy, very graceful light green leaves & brown-black fissured bark. Not a strong tree, sometimes subject to breakage. Good fall color.	Young shoots browsed by white-tailed deer. Catkins eaten by several species of birds. Silky-haired seeds used as nesting material. Larval host plant of Mourning cloak & Viceroy butterflies.
Eastern cottonwood *Populus deltoides*	Very large shade tree with fluttery green leaves. Fast growing with excellent fall color. Easy to establish.	Foliage, bark, seeds & leaves important to wildlife especially deer & rabbits. Seeds eaten by many birds, especially grosbeaks & cardinals . Cottony seeds used to line nests. Larval host plant for Mourning Cloak, Red-spotted Purple, Viceroy & Tiger Swallowtail butterflies.
Meseta cottonwood *Populus fremontii* v. *mesetae*	This is the most common poplar in Presidio, Brewster & Jeff Davis counties. Has excellent fall color. Some cities don't allow this tree because of its copious "cotton" fallout in the spring.	Foliage, bark, seeds & leaves important to wildlife especially deer & rabbits. Seeds eaten by many birds, especially pyrrloxias & cardinals . Cottony seeds used to line nests. Foliage is browsed by mule deer. Larval host plant of swallowtail butterflies.

Table A.5
Native Plants of Texas

Please note that each two-page "spread" is divided into a top half (with plants' growing information) and a bottom half (with plants' ornamental and wildlife values). Numbered regions correspond to the Texas Ecoregion map on page 11.

Species	Ecological Region 1 2 3 4 5 6 7 8 9 10	Habit Height	Flower	Fruit	Sun Exposure	Habitat	Soils and Moisture Regime
Peach-leaf willow *Salix amygdaloides*	x x x x	Tree, large 30'-40' Deciduous	Male & female creamy yellowish-green catkins, on separate trees. April-May	Capsules, borne on catkins reddish-yellow with numerous seeds. May-June	Full sun, part shade	Prefers areas around water ways whether wet or dry, ponds or any other water-holding depression.	Well-drained but moist. Sand, loams & clays; limestone soils.
Plains cottonwood *Populus sargentii*	x x x x	Tree, large 50'-60' Deciduous	Inconspicuous, yellow male & female catkins. March-June	Capsule with oblong seeds. June-Aug.	Full sun, part shade	Prefers sandy alluvial soils along rivers & streams, near stock tanks & along road-side banks.	Well-drained, mesic. Sands, sandy loams.
Quaking aspen *Populus tremuloides*	x	Tree, large 20'-40' Deciduous	Droopy male & female catkins. April-May	Capsules green to brown with light brown seeds. May-June	Full sun, part shade	Confined to highest mountains in the Trans-Pecos. Prefers ravines & talus slopes above 7000'.	Well-drained, mesic. Sands, loams, caliche & limestone soils, also igneous soils.
Rio Grande cottonwood (Alamo) *Populus wislizenii*	x	Tree, large 50'-90' Deciduous	Staminate & pistillate catkins. March-July	Capsules, egg-shaped with light brown seeds covered with silky hairs. May-Aug.	Full sun, part shade	Prefers areas along river, streams & irrigation canals in valleys & canyons.	Well-drained, mesic. Likes deep or rocky alluvial soils; sands, loams, clays; caliche-type soils.

Witch hazel Family – Hamamelidaceae

Species	Ecological Region 1 2 3 4 5 6 7 8 9 10	Habit Height	Flower	Fruit	Sun Exposure	Habitat	Soils and Moisture Regime
Sweetgum *Liquidamber styraciflua*	x x	Tree, large 60'-100' Deciduous	Inconspicuous male & female greenish flowers on same tree. March-May	Capsules, arranged in spiny globe. Sept.-Nov.	Full sun, part shade	Grows in low wet areas on acid sands, flooded river bottoms, also in drier upland hills.	Needs moisture, mesic. Sands, loams & clay loams.

Species	Ornamental Value	Wildlife Value
Peach-leaf willow *Salix amygdaloides*	A striking willow with yellow twigs, green peach-leaf shaped leaves that are attractively silvery white underneath. Tree has drooping branches. Rapid growing but not long lived.	Catkins provide food & nesting material for many forms of wildlife. Good substrate for insectivorous birds. Allows light underneath the tree for other things to grow. Larval host plant for Mourning Cloak butterfly.
Plains cottonwood *Populus sargentii*	Plains cottonwood provides good shade. Branches are erect & spreading to form a broad crown. Attractive shiny yellowish green leaves flutter in the wind.	Good nesting & cover tree for birds. Foliage is browsed by deer & cotton-tail rabbit. The seeds are eaten by several species of birds.
Quaking aspen *Populus tremuloides*	For only those high altitude areas in the Trans-Pecos. Very ornamental. Leaves flutter nervously in the breeze. Has excellent golden yellow fall color, smooth whitish bark reminiscent of beeches in the east.	Catkins & seeds are eaten by a number of species of game & songbirds, especially quail. Twigs, bark & buds are heavily browsed by mule deer, rabbits, squirrels & porcupines.
Rio Grande cottonwood (Alamo) *Populus wislizenii*	Good overstory, shade producing tree with thick trunk. Rapid grower on moist sites, but fairly short lived. Some cities don't allow them because of voluminous "snow" fall in spring.	Leaves occasionally browsed by wildlife. Good protective cover & nesting tree. Cottony catkins used as nest-lining material. A few birds eat the seeds.

Witch hazel Family – Hamamelidaceae

Species	Ornamental Value	Wildlife Value
Sweetgum *Liquidamber styraciflua*	Beautiful tall shade tree with symmetrical pyramidal crown & striking star-shaped leaves. Leaves turn gorgeous colors in the fall, from gold to bright scarlet then to deep crimson. Fast growing & long lived. Highly ornamental.	Good protective cover & nesting tree. At least 25 species of birds feed upon the fruit as do beaver, gray & fox squirrels. Birds include mallards, doves, finches, juncoes, sparrows, towhees, chickadees, titmice & siskins.

Table A.5
Native Plants of Texas

Please note that each two-page "spread" is divided into a top half (with plants' growing information) and a bottom half (with plants' ornamental and wildlife values). Numbered regions correspond to the Texas Ecoregion map on page 11.

Buttercup Family – Ranunculaceae

Species	Ecological Region 1 2 3 4 5 6 7 8 9 10										Habit Height	Flower	Fruit	Sun Exposure	Habitat	Soils and Moisture Regime
	1	2	3	4	5	6	7	8	9	10						
Blue jasmine *Clematis crispa*	x	x	x								Vine Climber to 10' Deciduous	Showy lavender bell-shaped flowers with flared edges. March-June.	Achenes. Aug.-Sept.	Part shade, dappled shade	Prefers moist soils in low woods.	Mesic-hydric. Poor drainage O.K. Sands, loams & clays. Will tolerate gumbo.
Old man's beard *Clematis drummondii*			x	x	x	x	x	x		x	Vine Climber Deciduous	Creamy white to palest yellow flowers. March-Sept.	Achenes, slender & plumose. Aug.-Oct.	Full sun, part shade	Prefers dryish soils, dry washes & rocky canyons, roadsides, fencerows & thickets.	Xeric, well-drained, drought-tolerant. Sands, loams & clays, likes limestone soils.
Purple leatherflower *Clematis pitcheri*	x	x	x	x	x	x	x	x			Vine Climber, high Deciduous	Showy, purple nodding urn-shaped flowers. June-Aug.	Achenes, leathery. Sept.-Oct.	Part shade, dappled shade, shade	Prefers thickets, woodland borders, likes moist low ground.	Mesic, prefers moist soils. Sands, loams, clays; likes limestone soils.

Catalpa Family – Bignoniaceae

Species	1	2	3	4	5	6	7	8	9	10	Habit Height	Flower	Fruit	Sun Exposure	Habitat	Soils and Moisture Regime
Cross-vine *Bignonia capreolata*	x	x	x								Vine Climber to 50' Persistent	Showy, tubular flowers, red on outside, yellow on inside. March-April.	Capsule with winged seeds. Aug.-Sept.	Full sun, part shade, dappled shade, shade	Prefers cool moist soils of woodlands, pinelands, also creek bottoms.	Moderate to high moisture. Seasonal poor drainage O.K. Sands, loams & clays.
Trumpet-creeper *Campsis radicans*	x	x	x	x	x						Vine Climbs to the sky Persistent	Showy orange tubular flowers in dense clusters. June-Sept.	Capsule with winged seeds. Sept.-Nov.	Full sun, part shade	Tolerates a variety of soils throughout eastern half of Texas.	Mesic; moderate moisture; poor drainage O.K. Sands, loams & clays.

Species	Ornamental Value	Wildlife Value
Buttercup Family – Ranunculaceae		
Blue jasmine *Clematis crispa*	Very elegant flowers. Works well on a lattice but does not climb high. Can sprawl over low structures such as planter boxes or patio pots.	Lavender blue flowers attract many kinds of insects including butterflies. Several species of birds eat the ripe achenes.
Old man's beard *Clematis drummondii*	A vigorous climber that will drape other trees & shrubs. Especially beautiful in late summer & fall when the feathery achenes are backlit by the sun, they glisten. This can be a very ornamental vine.	Old man's beard serves as an excellent protective cover & nesting site. Achenes are eaten by many species of birds. Larval host plant of the Fatal metalmark butterfly.
Purple leatherflower *Clematis pitcheri*	This high climbing vine with the elegant leaves & lovely flowers will clamber over a trellis, trees, or shrubs. This species is fairly cold hardy.	This vine provides good cover for small birds. A thick clump is an excellent place to hide from predators. Achenes eaten by a few species of birds.
Catalpa Family – Bignoniaceae		
Cross-vine *Bignonia capreolata*	Beautiful flowering vine clinging to bricks, stones & fences as well as other shrubs & trees. Profuse flowers when in bloom. Tolerates pollution well.	Striking orange & yellow tubular flowers are highly attractive to butterflies & especially the Ruby-throated hummingbird. Bloom time coincides with migration when other sources of nectar are scarce, helping this little mite on the way.
Trumpet-creeper *Campsis radicans*	Striking vine adapted to nearly every soil type. Excellent for hiding ugly structures. Sometimes can do too well & needs to be cut back.	This is premier plant to attract hummingbirds. Both Ruby-throat & Black-chinned hummers are highly fond of it. Copious nectar sustains these beauties. The plant is also an excellent nectar source for the larger butterflies.

Table A.5
Native Plants of Texas

Please note that each two-page "spread" is divided into a top half (with plants' growing information) and a bottom half (with plants' ornamental and wildlife values). Numbered regions correspond to the Texas Ecoregion map on page 11.

Cucumber Family – Curcurbitaceae

Species	1	2	3	4	5	6	7	8	9	10	Habit Height	Flower	Fruit	Sun Exposure	Habitat	Soils and Moisture Regime
Globe-berry *Ibervillea lindheimeri*	x	x	x			x					Vine Climber Deciduous	Small greenish yellow flowers. April-July	Orange to bright red globular fruit. Aug.-Oct.	Full sun, part shade	Prefers dryish soils in open woodlands or thickets, among brush, along fence rows. Tolerates rocky soils.	Xeric-mesic, well-drained. Sands, loams & clays.

Figwort Family – Scrophulariaceae

Species	1	2	3	4	5	6	7	8	9	10	Habit Height	Flower	Fruit	Sun Exposure	Habitat	Soils and Moisture Regime
Snapdragon vine *Maurandya antirrhiniflora*	x	x	x	x	x	x	x			x	Vine Climber to 3' Perennial	Showy purple flowers. March-Sept.	Capsule, round. Sept.-Dec.	Full sun, part shade	Prefers limestone hills & bluffs, also dunes, shrubs & boulders.	Mesic, well-drained. Sands, loams, clays.
Pepper-vine *Ampelopsis arborea*	x	x	x	x	x	x					Vine Climber Deciduous	Inconspicuous greenish-white flowers. June-Aug.	Berries, bluish-purple. Sept.-Oct.	Part shade, dappled shade, shade	Prefers rich woodlands & bottomlands, edges of swamps, fence rows & waste places.	Mesic, likes soils to be moist. Sands, loams & clays.
Canyon grape *Vitis arizonica*									x	x	Vine Climber Deciduous	Inconspicuous whitish flowers. May-June	Grapes, blue-black. July-Aug.	Full sun, part shade	Prefers ravines & gulches at altitudes of 2000'-7000' in western portion of the state.	Xeric-mesic, well-drained. Sands, loams, clays; likes limestone soils.
Gray-leaf grape *Vitis cinerea*	x	x	x	x		x					Vine Climber Deciduous	Inconspicuous whitish-green flowers. May-June	Grapes, blue-purple to black. Aug.-Nov.	Full sun, part shade, dappled shade	Prefers moist alluvial soils along streams, thickets & bottomlands.	Mesic, moist soils. Sands, loams & clays.

Species	Ornamental Value	Wildlife Value
Cucumber Family – Curcurbitaceae		
Globe-berry *Ibervillea lindheimeri*	Drought-tolerant & salt-tolerant climber with interestingly shaped leaves & decorative colorful fruit.	Many species of birds, both gallinaceous & large song birds eat this fruit when it is ripe. Insects are attracted to the floral nectar.
Figwort Family – Scrophulariaceae		
Snapdragon vine *Maurandya antirrhiniflora*	Elegant, delicate-leafed climber & ground cover. Fast grower; tolerates salt. Looks great in a pot. Leaves have excellent fall color.	Fruits are a favorite with many species of birds. Flowers are a good nectar source for many kinds of insects, especially butterflies. Lush clumps provide good cover. Larval host plant of Buckeye butterfly.
Peppervine *Ampelopsis arborea*	This vigorous vine with the beautiful compound dissected leaves which are dark green on top & pale underneath can sometimes be too successful in a small garden. It is very attractive, however, if kept under control.	Bluish-purple berries provide a great source of food for many game-birds & songbirds alike. Bobwhite, flickers, brown thrashers & hermit thrushes love them. Small mammals also relish them. Excellent browse for white-tailed deer.
Canyon grape *Vitis arizonica*	Very drought-tolerant climbing vine. Does not like excess moisture. It is also very cold-hardy. Good plant for erosion control. Not really native of the Rolling Plains but will grow well here.	Birds such as doves, several quail, woodpeckers, kingbirds, jays, flycatchers, mockingbirds, pyrruloxias, thrashers, thrushes, finches & sparrows dine voraciously on the fruit. Grapes are also a favorite of fox, skunk & coyotes. Also eaten by mule deer.
Gray-leaf grape *Vitis cinerea*	High climbing vine which can reach a large size. Leaves are large with attractive gray hairs on the under-surface. Bears lots of juicy grapes.	The ripe grapes are highly favored by several species of gamebirds & songbirds. Squirrels, opossums, raccoons, & foxes also partake of them.

Table A.5
Native Plants of Texas

Please note that each two-page "spread" is divided into a top half (with plants' growing information) and a bottom half (with plants' ornamental and wildlife values). Numbered regions correspond to the Texas Ecoregion map on page 11.

Species	Ecological Region (marked)	Habit / Height	Flower	Fruit	Sun Exposure	Habitat	Soils and Moisture Regime
Heart-leaf ampelopsis *Ampelopsis cordata*	1, 2, 3, 4, 5, 6, 7, 9	Vine High climber Deciduous	Inconspicuous greenish flowers. May–June	Berries, bluish-purple. Aug.–Nov.	Part shade, dappled shade, shade	Prefers rich woodlands & bottomlands along rivers & streams.	Well-drained, but moist. Sands, loams & clays; likes limestone, caliche-type soils.
Hiedra creeper *Parthenocissus vitacea*	7, 8, 9	Vine Climber & ground cover Deciduous	Inconspicuous greenish flowers. May–July	Berries, blue-black. Sept.–Nov.	Full sun	Prefers woods, thickets & on banks in West Texas.	Well-drained, mesic. Sands, loams, clays.
Muscadine grape *Vitis rotundafolia*	1, 2	Vine Climber, to 40' Deciduous	Inconspicuous white flowers. May–June	Grapes, purple-bronze. Sept.–Oct.	Part shade, dappled shade	Prefers forests & woods of East Texas.	Mesic, well-drained. Sands, loams & clays.
Mustang grape *Vitis mustangensis*	1, 2, 3, 5, 6, 7	Vine Climber Deciduous	Inconspicuous greenish flowers. April–May	Grapes, purple-black. Aug.–Sept.	Full sun, part shade, dappled shade	Prefers steam bottoms, thickets, fence rows, woodland edges & sandy areas.	Mesic, well-drained. Sands, loams, clays; likes limestone soils.
Panhandle grape *Vitis acerifolia*	4, 7, 8	Vine Climber Deciduous	Inconspicuous whitish flowers. May–June	Grapes, blue-purple to black, sweet. July–Aug.	Full sun, part shade	Prefers low, open woods in stream bottoms, dunes & rocky slopes in Panhandle.	Well-drained, mesic. Sands, loams & clays, also limestone & caliche-like soils.
Thicket creeper *Parthenocissus inserta*	8, 9, 10	Vine Climber & ground cover Deciduous	Inconspicuous greenish flowers. May–July	Berries, blue-black. Sept.–Nov.	Full sun	Prefers woods, thickets & on banks in West Texas.	Well-drained, mesic. Sands, loams, clays.

Species	Ornamental Value	Wildlife Value
Heart-leaf ampelopsis *Ampelopsis cordata*	Vine with pretty heart-shaped leaves & bluish-purple fruit. Very fast growing climber.	A number of species of birds consume the fruit, including cardinals, bobwhite, woodpeckers, brown thrashers, hermit thrushes, finches & sparrows.
Hiedra creeper *Parthenocissus vitacea*	Very attractive vine with lush green palmate leaves, thicker & skinnier. Vigorous climber well able to cloak walls, columns, etc. by fastening on to masonry. Also good ground cover. Striking red-orange fall color. Drought tolerant, prefers full sun.	Many species of birds compete for the blue-black berries including woodpeckers, kingbirds, flycatchers, cardinals, mockingbirds, bluebirds, warblers & sparrows.
Muscadine grape *Vitis rotundafolia*	Vigorous climbing vine with attractive orbicular leaves & luscious fruit. Grapes make good jelly.	The ripe grapes are eaten by several species of game & songbirds, as well as by mammals such as gray fox, white-tailed deer, skunks, rabbits, opossums & raccoons.
Mustang grape *Vitis mustangensis*	Highly vigorous climber. May need to be cut back. Can grow over trellises, fences, arbors & trees.	Birds such as mourning doves, gallinaceous birds, woodpeckers, kingbirds, blue jays, flycatchers, mockingbirds, cardinals, thrashers, thrushes, finches & sparrows dine voraciously on the fruit. Grapes are also a favorite of many mammals.
Panhandle grape *Vitis acerifolia*	Stocky, erect, much-branched vine that climbs rarely, but loves to cover rockers & shrubs with pretty light grayish green leaves with cobwebby appearance. Fruits ripen early & are very edible.	The ripe grapes are highly favored by several species of gamebirds & songbirds. Rock squirrels, raccoons, & foxes also partake of them.
Thicket creeper *Parthenocissus inserta*	Very attractive vine with lush green palmate leaves, thicker & skinnier. Vigorous climber well able to cloak walls, columns, etc. by fastening on to masonry. Also good ground cover. Striking red-orange fall color. Drought tolerant, prefers full sun.	Many species of birds compete for the blue-black berries including woodpeckers, kingbirds, flycatchers, cardinals, mockingbirds, bluebirds, warblers & sparrows.

Table A.5
Native Plants of Texas

Please note that each two-page "spread" is divided into a top half (with plants' growing information) and a bottom half (with plants' ornamental and wildlife values). Numbered regions correspond to the Texas Ecoregion map on page 11.

Species	1	2	3	4	5	6	7	8	9	10	Habit / Height	Flower	Fruit	Sun Exposure	Habitat	Soils and Moisture Regime
Virginia creeper *Parthenocissus quinquefolia*	x	x	x	x	x	x		x			Vine Climber & ground cover Deciduous	Inconspicuous greenish flowers. May–June	Berries, blue-black. Sept.–Nov.	Full sun, part shade, dappled shade	Prefers rich soils of woodlands & thickets & rocky banks in eastern half of Texas.	Well-drained, mesic. Sands, loams, clays. Tolerates gumbo soils.
Honeysuckle Family – Caprifoliaceae																
Coral honeysuckle *Lonicera sempervirens*	x	x	x	x	x						Vine Climber to 40' Persistent	Showy orange red tubular flowers in clusters. March–Dec.	Berries, red. April–Jan.	Full sun, part shade	Prefers moist fertile soils of East Texas, woods & thickets.	Mesic-hydric soils; poor drainage O.K. Sands, loams & clays.
Logania Family – Loganaceae																
Carolina jessamine *Gelsemium sempervirens*	x	x	x								Vine Climber to 50' Evergreen	Showy yellow tubular flowers in clusters, fragrant. Jan.–April	Capsule, flattened, elliptic with numerous dull brown narrowly winged seeds. Sept.–Oct.	Full sun, part shade, dappled shade	Prefers woodlands in East Texas.	Mesic. Sands, sandy loams, loams, clays.
Milkweed Family – Asclepiadace																
Vine milkweed *Sarcostemma cynanchoides v. hartwegii*					x	x	x	x	x	x	Vine Climber to 3' Deciduous	Attractive whitish green flowers, sometimes purple & pinkish. July–Aug.	Follicles, paired & spindle-shaped with silk haired seeds. Aug.–Oct.	Full sun, part shade	Prefers sandy hills, canyon breaks, usually climbing shrubs & fences, likes rocky soils.	Well-drained, xeric. Sands especially, sandy loams, clays & calilche-type soils in western half of Texas.
Climbing milkweed vine *Sarcostemma cynanchoides v. cynanchoides*					x	x	x	x	x	x	Vine High climber Deciduous	Showy pinkish white to purple flowers. April–Aug.	Follicles. July–Oct.	Full sun, part shade	Prefers loose or rocky soils; climbs shrubs & small trees.	Mesic, well-drained. Sands, loams & clays; likes limestone & caliche-like soils.

Species	Ornamental Value	Wildlife Value
Virginia creeper *Parthenocissus quinquefolia*	Very attractive vine with lush green palmate leaves. Vigorous climber well able to cloak walls, columns, etc. by fastening on to masonry. Also good ground cover. Striking red-orange fall color.	Many species of birds compete for the blue-black berries including woodpeckers, kingbirds, great-crested flycatchers, titmice, cardinals, mockingbirds, bluebirds, warblers & sparrows.
Honeysuckle Family – Caprifoliaceae		
Coral honeysuckle *Lonicera sempervirens*	A beautiful everblooming vine that grows well & is well-behaved. Likes morning sun & afternoon dappled shade. Needs extra water when getting established, but not later.	Ruby-throated & Black-chinned hummers are attracted to this vine spring, summer & fall, especially during migration. Orioles also sip nectar, as do butterflies. Fruit-eating birds relish the succulent red berries in the fall. Larval host plant of Spring Azure butterfly.
Logania Family – Loganaceae		
Carolina jessamine *Gelsemium sempervirens*	Highly ornamental climbing vine with opposite leaves & gorgeous yellow flowers. Plant sometimes forms rich carpets on the ground. Parts of this plant are poisonous. Often planted in areas where it is not native. Used as a screen or to cover walls.	Cascades of yellow flowers attract myriads of insects. Provides good cover & hiding places for small birds. Seeds are eaten by the bobwhite quail & leaves are eaten by the marsh rabbit.
Milkweed Family – Asclepiadace		
Vine milkweed *Sarcostemma cynanchoides* v. *hartwegii*	A climbing vine with trailing or twining stems, growing to about 3'. It has many branches & unusual complex flowers. Leaves grow in pairs with clusters of 20 whitish green flowers, pinker or purple-tinged farther west. Very ornamental & showy.	Flowers attract many pollinating insects. Stems & leaves serve as larval host plant of many milkweed butterflies like Queen & Monarch. Ripe seeds foraged by birds, & used in nest construction.
Climbing milkweed vine *Sarcostemma cynanchoides* v. *cynanchoides*	Attractive climbing vine of the Milkweed Family with intricate flowers.	Flowers attract several larger insects. Silky-haired seeds used as nesting material. Flattened seeds also eaten by a few birds. Larval host plant of Monarch & Queen butterflies.

Please note that each two-page "spread" is divided into a top half (with plants' growing information) and a bottom half (with plants' ornamental and wildlife values). Numbered regions correspond to the Texas Ecoregion map on page 11.

Species	Ecological Region 1 2 3 4 5 6 7 8 9 10										Habit Height	Flower	Fruit	Sun Exposure	Habitat	Soils and Moisture Regime
Soft twine vine *Sarcostemma torreyi*										x	Vine High climber Deciduous	Showy cream-colored flowers with purple spot in umbels. May-Aug.	Follicles, long & pointed with comose seeds. Aug.-Nov.	Full sun, part shade	Prefers dry hillsides & gravelly soils in scrubby woodland associations of Chisos mountain foothills at elevations of less than 3500'.	Well-drained, xeric-mesic. Sands, loams & clays; likes rocky soils.
Moonseed Family – Menespermaceae																
Carolina moonseed *Cocculus carolinus*		x	x	x	x		x				Vine Climber to 15' Evergreen	Inconspicuous greenish flowers. July-Aug.	Conspicuous brilliant red berries (drupes). Sept.-Oct.	Full sun, part shade	Prefers rich moist soils of woods & thickets.	Well-drained, mesic. Sands, loams & clays. Tolerates gumbo soils of Houston.
Correhuela *Cocculus diversifolius*						x					Vine Climber Persistent	White male & female flowers, borne in racemes. Feb.-Sept.	Drupes, blue-black. May-Nov.	Part shade, dappled shade	Prefers brushy areas on a variety of soil types in the Lower Rio Grande Valley.	Well-drained, mesic. Sands, loams & clays, likes caliche-type soils.
Passionflower Family – Passifloraceae																
May-pop *Passiflora incarnata*	x	x	x								Vine Climber to 6', also ground cover Dormant in winter	Showy pink-purple flower. April-Sept.	Ovoid fruit with seeds. June-Oct.	Full sun, part shade, dappled shade	Grows in old fields, along roadsides & streams & woodland edges in Eastern 1/3 of Texas.	Well-drained, mesic. Sands, loams & clays.
Yellow passionvine *Passiflora lutea*	x	x				x	x				Vine Climber to 3' Deciduous	Showy whitish-yellow flowers. May-Sept.	Fleshy globose fruit. Aug.-Nov.	Part shade, dappled shade, shade	Prefers shady, low moist woods.	Mesic, likes moist soils. Sands, sandy loams; likes limestone soils.

Species	Ornamental Value	Wildlife Value
Soft twine vine *Sarcostemma torreyi*	Attractive climbing vine with large heart-shaped leaves & curious warty fruit pods in the Milkweed Family. Flowers are highly intricate as others in the milkweed family.	Flowers attract several larger insects. Silky-haired seeds used as nesting material. Flattened seeds also eaten by a few birds & small mammals. Larval host plant of Monarch & Queen butterflies.
Moonseed Family – Menespermaceae		
Carolina moonseed *Cocculus carolinus*	Relatively fast growing, slender twining vine that prefers full sun & some kind of support. Leaves are attractively shaped & fruits are highly ornamental. Will grow over shrubs & small trees.	Dense clusters of brilliant red fruit are relished by bluebirds, mocking-birds, cardinals, robins, warblers & sparrows.
Correhuela *Cocculus diversifolius*	An attractive woody climbing, twining vine with simple, variably-shaped leaves, white flowers & blue-black fruit. Twines on fences & other plants.	Several kinds of insects are attracted to the flowers. While the fruit will make people sick, birds will eat them when they are ripe. White-tailed deer browse the leaves occasionally.
Passionflower Family – Passifloraceae		
May-pop *Passiflora incarnata*	This healthy climber is graced with an unbelievable intricate & eye-catching flower. It uses its tendrils for climbing & is often found sprawling over the ground, thus serving as excellent ground cover.	These beautiful vines are larval food plants for the Zebra long-wing, Gulf Fritillary & Julia butterflies. Several species of birds dine on the ripened fruits.
Yellow passionvine *Passiflora lutea*	Delicate looking vine with interestingly shaped leaves & complex flowers. Prefers moist & shady areas.	Flowers attract several kinds of insects, especially butterflies. Birds & small mammals partake of the fruit. Larval host plant of the Julia, Mexican & Gulf fritillaries, as well as Zebra & Crimson-patch longwing butterflies.

Table A.5
Native Plants of Texas

Please note that each two-page "spread" is divided into a top half (with plants' growing information) and a bottom half (with plants' ornamental and wildlife values). Numbered regions correspond to the Texas Ecoregion map on page 11.

Species	Ecological Region 1	2	3	4	5	6	7	8	9	10	Habit / Height	Flower	Fruit	Sun Exposure	Habitat	Soils and Moisture Regime
Pipevine Family – Aristolochiaceae																
Marsh's pipevine *Aristolochia marshii*						x					Vine Climber Persistent, but dies back	Bizarre reddish-purple pipe-shaped flowers. Feb.-June	Capsules. May-Aug.	Part shade, dappled shade	Prefers alluvial soils along rivers & resacas in the Rio Grande Valley.	Mesic, poor drainage O.K. Sands, silts & clays.
Pipevine *Aristolochia serpentaria*	x		x	x							Vine Weak climber Deciduous	Showy, purple & yellow, amazingly shaped flower. April-June	Capsules with many seeds. Aug.	Full sun, part shade	Prefers moist bottomland woods, also along rivers.	Well-drained, mesic. Sandy loams, loams & clays.
Woolly pipevine *Aristolochia tomentosa*	x		x	x							Vine Climber to 50' Perennial	Bizarre dark purple & greenish yellow flower. March-May	Pods. June-Aug.	Part shade, dappled shade	Prefers deep soils along streams & river bottoms.	Well-drained, mesic. Sands, sandy loams, loams.
Rose Family – Rosaceae																
Prairie rose *Rosa setigera*	x		x	x	x						Vine Climber from 9'-15' Deciduous	Showy rose-pink flowers. May	Rosehips, red. July-Aug.	Full sun, part shade	Prefers openings & post oak woodlands.	Well-drained, mesic. Sands, loams & clays, especially calcareous soils.
Smilax Family – Smilacaceae																
Laurel greenbriar *Smilax laurifolia*	x	x									Vine Climber from 5'-15' Evergreen	Inconspicuous greenish-white flowers. July-Aug.	Drupes, black & berry-like. Oct.-Nov.	Part shade, dappled shade, shade	Prefers swamps & wet woods in East Texas & Upper Texas Coast.	Mesic-hydric, poor drainage O.K. Sands, sandy loams, acid soils prefered.

Species	Ornamental Value	Wildlife Value
Pipevine Family – Aristolochiaceae		
Marsh's pipevine *Aristolochia marshii*	Herbaceous twining vine with slender stems & triangular lobed leaves & unusual pipe-shaped flowers.	This unusual vine is the larval host plant for the Polydamus swallowtail butterfly.
Pipevine *Aristolochia serpentria*	Vine with very unusual flower with ascending spreading habit. Plant is good ground cover.	The leaves & stems of this vine are used as a larval host plant for the Pipevine swallowtail butterfly.
Woolly pipevine *Aristolochia tomentosa*	High climber with large handsome heart-shaped leaves & unusual flower which is slow to come into bloom. Flower looks like a Dutchman's pipe or a strange bird. Best when planted next to other shrubs so that it can use them as support.	Woolly pipevine stems & leaves are the larval host plant of the Pipevine swallowtail butterfly.
Rose Family – Rosaceae		
Prairie rose *Rosa setigera*	Luscious rose-red blossoms gradually fade to white, leaving all shades in between in a tapestry of pinks. Shiny leaves turn reddish in the fall. This vine has no thorns. Fruits are bright red & highly decorative.	Several species of birds devour the red fruits including cardinals, mockingbirds, bluebirds, woodpeckers, great-crested flycatchers, catbirds & thrashers.
Smilax Family – Smilacaceae		
Laurel greenbriar *Smilax laurifolia*	Thorny vine with attractive leaves of pale green color setting upright on the stem. Good protective screening plant. Keep away from human traffic areas.	At lease five species of birds eat the fruit, as do small mammals. Excellent protective cover plant. Tubers are also eaten by mammals.

Table A.5
Native Plants of Texas

Please note that each two-page "spread" is divided into a top half (with plants' growing information) and a bottom half (with plants' ornamental and wildlife values). Numbered regions correspond to the Texas Ecoregion map on page 11.

Species	1	2	3	4	5	6	7	8	9	10	Habit Height	Flower	Fruit	Sun Exposure	Habitat	Soils and Moisture Regime
Soapberry Family – Sapindaceae																
Serjania *Serjania brachycarpa*					x						Vine Climber Persistent	Small yellow flowers in panicles; male & female flowers on separate plants. Feb.-Nov.	Samaras bearing seeds. March-Dec.	Full sun, part shade, dappled shade	Frequently found on loamy soils near the Rio Grande flood plain.	Mesic-hydric, poor drainage O.K. Sands, loams & clays.
Amaryllis Family – Amaryllidaceae																
Spider lily *Hymenocallis liriosme*	x	x									Wildflower 1'-2' Perennial	Showy white flowers with long narrow petal-like segments, fragrant. May-July	Capsule, tri-partite. July-Sept.	Full sun, part shade, dappled shade	Prefers periodically inundated bottom-lands, marshes, along stream banks or in ditches in various soils.	Poor drainage O.K. Even tolerates standing water. Sands, loams & clays, acid or calcareous.
Buttercup Family – Ranunculaceae																
Prairie larkspur *Delphinium carolinianum*	x	x	x		x						Wildflower 1 ½'-3' Perennial	Showy blue to white spurred flowers on 6" spikes. April-May	Follicle with numerous brown seeds. June-July	Full sun, part shade	Prefers open woods, fields, meadows & prairies, also grows along roadsides of Northeast Texas & the Edwards Plateau.	Well-drained, mesic. Sands, loams, clays; tolerates calcareous or acid soils.
Wild columbine *Aquilegia canadensis*	x	x			x						Wildflower 1'-3' Perennial	Showy red & yellow tubular flowers. March-May	Follicle with seeds. May-July	Part shade, dappled shade, full shade	Prefers moist, shaded canyons growing in & around rock of cliff faces & boulders.	Well-drained, mesic. likes moisture. Sands & loams; likes limestone based soils.

Species	Ornamental Value	Wildlife Value
Soapberry Family – Sapindaceae		
Serjania *Serjania brachycarpa*	Slender, somewhat hairy scandent vine with woody base, no thorns & compound leaves. Forms a dense mantle that can cover shrubs & small trees.	This dense vine provides excellent protective cover for small birds. Insects are attracted to the flowers. Several species of birds dine on the ripe seeds.
Amaryllis Family – Amaryllidaceae		
Spider lily *Hymenocallis liriosme*	Very striking white flower, each blossom about 7" across. Flowers are very fragrant. Flowers often grow in clumps. Very good plant for a bog garden. Grows well in Houston gumbo.	Several varieties of insects are attracted to these very fragrant flowers.
Buttercup Family – Ranunculaceae		
Prairie larkspur *Delphinium carolinianum*	Attractive wildflowers for a pocket prairie or meadow garden. This species come in various color varieties from white to pale blue to dark blue.	Prairie largespur attracts several varieties of insects that forage on the nectar. Bees are especially fond of these flowers.
Wild columbine *Aquilegia canadensis*	A hill country native that grows well in gardens where the soils are rich in organic matter & well drained. Likes shade & extra moisture.	Wild columbine is a wonderful hummingbird plant. Flowers also attract other varieties of insects.

Table A.5
Native Plants of Texas

Please note that each two-page "spread" is divided into a top half (with plants' growing information) and a bottom half (with plants' ornamental and wildlife values). Numbered regions correspond to the Texas Ecoregion map on page 11.

Species	Ecological Region 1 2 3 4 5 6 7 8 9 10	Habit Height	Flower	Fruit	Sun Exposure	Habitat	Soils and Moisture Regime
Yellow columbine *Aquilegia longissima*	x (10)	Wildflower 1'-3' Perennial	Showy yellow flowers with long spurs. May	Follicle with seeds. July	Dappled shade, shade	Grows near rocky crevices in the Trans-Pecos.	Well-drained, mesic. Sands, loams, limestone or igneous soils.

Campanula Family – Campanulaceae

Species	Ecological Region 1 2 3 4 5 6 7 8 9 10	Habit Height	Flower	Fruit	Sun Exposure	Habitat	Soils and Moisture Regime
Cardinal flower *Lobelia cardinalis*	x x x x x x x x x x (1–10)	Wildflower 6"-6' Perennial	Showy red tubular flowers, fragrant. May-Oct.	Capsules with seeds. June-Nov.	Full sun, part shade, dappled shade	Prefers moist soils in open places along streams, meadows & along roadsides; also about ponds & springs, & near swamps where the shade is not too dense.	Moist soils, poor drainage O.K. Sands, loams, clays & limestone based soils.

Evening-primrose Family – Onagraceae

Species	Ecological Region 1 2 3 4 5 6 7 8 9 10	Habit Height	Flower	Fruit	Sun Exposure	Habitat	Soils and Moisture Regime
Missouri evening-primrose *Oenothera macrocarpa*	x x (7, 8)	Wildflower 1' Perennial	Showy, fluttery yellow flowers. April-June	Capsule with numerous seeds. June-Aug.	Full sun	Grows on dry, thin, rocky exposed calcareous soils on hillsides, slopes, on prairies & cliffs in Edwards Plateau, Blackland Prairies, High Plains & Rolling Plains.	Well-drained, xeric. Sands, limestone & caliche-type soils.
Square-bud evening-primrose *Calylophus drummondianus*	x x x x x x x x (1,2,3,4,6,7,8,9)	Wildflower 1'-1 1/2' Perennial	Showy yellow flowers with black center. March-July	Capsule with seeds. May-Nov.	Full sun, part shade	Grows on sandy or rocky soils in open fields, prairies, meadows throughout most of the state.	Well-drained, xeric. Sands, loams, clays, limestone-based & caliche-type soils.

Species	Ornamental Value	Wildlife Value
Yellow columbine *Aquilegia longissima*	This native of the Trans-Pecos will grow in other areas of Texas such as the Edwards Plateau in proper shady, moist, well-drained habitat. The lemon yellow flowers with the spectacular long spurs are very elegant to behold.	Even though the flowers are yellow, hummingbirds will sip nectar from this plant. Insects are also attracted to the flowers.
Campanula Family – Campanulaceae		
Cardinal flower *Lobelia cardinalis*	Cardinal flower cannot be equalled for sheer visual impact, planted in dense stands in a shady part of the garden. In peak bloom they create an incredible spectacle. Bright scarlet flowers are clustered on racemes as long as 18".	Cardinal flower is a premiere hummingbird plant & will not fail to draw in any Ruby-throats passing through your area.
Evening-primrose Family – Onagraceae		
Missouri evening-primrose *Oenothera macrocarpa*	Missouri primrose has large fluttery yellow petals which open in the evening. Plants are great in a rock garden. Spent flowers turn pinkish coral.	Missouri primrose flowers are pollinated by nocturnal moths.
Square-bud evening-primrose *Calylophus drummon-dianus*	Showy, upright, bushy clumps of yellow flowers. Leaves are narrow with spiny-toothed margins. Habit is sometimes sprawling or reclining with flowers remaining open throughout the day. Good in a rock garden as it needs excellent drainage to thrive.	A wide array of diurnal insects are attracted to the flowers which are open throughout the day.

Table A.5
Native Plants of Texas

Please note that each two-page "spread" is divided into a top half (with plants' growing information) and a bottom half (with plants' ornamental and wildlife values). Numbered regions correspond to the Texas Ecoregion map on page 11.

Figwort Family – Scrophulariaceae

Species	Ecological Region 1 2 3 4 5 6 7 8 9 10	Habit Height	Flower	Fruit	Sun Exposure	Habitat	Soils and Moisture Regime
Wild foxglove *Penstemon cobaea*	x x x x x x	Wildflower 1'-2 ½' Perennial	Showy large tubular pale violet flowers with nectar guides. April-May	Capsules with seeds. June-July	Full sun, part shade	Prefers open areas, meadows, prairies, pastures & roadside areas.	Well-drained, mesic. Sands, loams, clays & limestone outcrops.
Gulf Coast penstemon *Penstemon tenuis*	x x	Wildflower 1'-2' Perennial	Showy pale pink to purple flowers. March-May	Capsules, ovoid with numerous seeds. May-July	Full sun, part shade, dappled shade	Prefers poorly drained soils of the Gulf Prairies & Marshes.	Poor drainage O.K. Sands, loams & clays.
Havard penstemon *Penstemon havardii*	x	Wildflower 2'-6' Perennial	Brilliant red tubular flowers on tall stalk. April-June	Capsule, ovoid with numerous seeds. June-Aug.	Full sun, part shade	Grows on limestone soils in the mountains of the Trans-Pecos. Very common in Brewster County.	Well-drained. Sands, loams, clays & limestone-based soils.
Indian paintbrush *Castilleja indivisa*	x x x x x x	Wildflower 6"-12" Annual	Showy orange to red bracts. March-May	Capsules with seeds. May-July	Full sun, a little shade O.K.	Prefers fields, meadows, prairies & roadside areas in eastern portion of the state including the Coastal plains.	Mesic, well-drained. Sands, loams & clays.
Pink plains penstemon *Penstemon ambiguus*	x x	Wildflower 1'-4' Perennial	Showy pale pink flowers. May-Oct.	Capsule with seeds. July-Nov.	Full sun, part shade	Grows in open areas, prairies, meadows & fields in High Plains, Rolling Plains & the Trans-Pecos.	Well-drained, xeric. Sands, but will also grow in heavier soils.

Species	Ornamental Value	Wildlife Value
Figwort Family – Scrophulariaceae		
Wild foxglove *Penstemon cobaea*	In full boom, gorgeous flowers open, covering ²/₃ of the flower stalk. This is a beautiful choice for a wildflower meadow or pocket prairie. It loves limestone soils.	Wild foxglove is highly attractive to bees, especially the larger varieties such as bumblebees & carpenter bees who eagerly forage for the nectar & the pollen. Larval host plant of the Dotted checkerspot butterfly.
Gulf Coast penstemon *Penstemon tenuis*	This penstemon does well on gumbo soils of the Houston area. Creates masses of beautiful color in the spring which may last for several weeks. They respond to extra watering in the summer to prolong bloom time.	A wide array of insects are attracted to the flowers, including bees & syrphid flies.
Havard penstemon *Penstemon havardii*	This beautiful endemic penstemon can grow very tall. Very drought-tolerant, it's probably best to cut it back after it has bloomed. This plant has excellent landscaping potential.	Havard penstemon is a premier hummingbird plant. Sometimes it will bloom again in the fall which is good for migrant hummers returning to their wintering ground.
Indian paintbrush *Castilleja indivisa*	Indian paintbrush is an excellent choice for a pocket prairie or meadow garden. Grows very well when planted with native grasses. Looks great when interspersed among masses of bluebonnets & showy evening primrose.	Insects of several varieties are attracted to the small flowers. Hummingbirds will also feed from them, attracted to the red-orange bracts that surround them. Larval host plant of the Buckeye butterfly.
Pink plains penstemon *Penstemon ambiguus*	Pink plains penstemon produces masses of color for long periods of time in the summer until the first frost. While the plant prefers sandy habitats, it will also grow in loams & clays.	Pink plains penstemon attracts a wide variety of insects that forage on the nectar. Clumps of them offer cover & hiding places for small creatures.

Table A.5
Native Plants of Texas

Please note that each two-page "spread" is divided into a top half (with plants' growing information) and a bottom half (with plants' ornamental and wildlife values). Numbered regions correspond to the Texas Ecoregion map on page 11.

Species	1	2	3	4	5	6	7	8	9	10	Habit Height	Flower	Fruit	Sun Exposure	Habitat	Soils and Moisture Regime
Flax Family – Linaceae																
Blue flax *Linum lewisii*									x	x	Wildflower 1'-2' Annual	Showy blue flowers with 5 petals. April-Oct.	Capsule with flat oily seeds. June-Nov.	Full sun, part shade	Grows in sandy rocky soils on slopes in Panhandle & Trans-Pecos.	Well-drained, xeric. Sands, loams, clays, limestone-based & caliche-type soils.
Four o'clock Family – Nyctaginaceae																
Heart's delight *Abronia ameliae*						x					Wildflower 8"-24" Perennial	Showy deep pink flowers in 3" heads, very fragrant. March-June	Anthocarp with seeds. March-June	Full sun, part shade	Grows in sandy areas in live oak woods, along roadsides from the Rio Grande Plains north to the Panhandle.	Well-drained, xeric. Sands, deep.
Gentian Family – Gentianaceae																
Mountain pink *Centaurium beyrichii*								x	x	x	Wildflower 4"-12" Annual	Showy pink bouquets of flowers. May-July	Seeds, light brown. July-Sept.	Full sun, part shade	Prefers dry, barren, open areas, also prairies & rocky slopes.	Well-drained, xeric. Sands, gravelly limestone or granitic soils.
Texas bluebells *Eustoma grandiflora*	x	x	x	x	x	x	x				Wildflower 1'-2' Annual	Showy blue-purple flowers. June-Oct.	Capsule with seeds. Aug.-Nov.	Full sun, part shade	Prefers damp prairies, pond edges, open fields & banks along streams throughout much of Texas.	Mesic, seasonal poor drainage O.K. Sands, loams & clays.
Iris Family – Iridaceae																
Herbertia *Herbertia lahue*	x	x				x					Wildflower 4"-12"	Showy purple flowers. March-May	Capsules with seeds. May-July	Full sun, part shade	Prefers open grasslands & meadows.	Well-drained, mesic. Sands, loams & clays.

Species	Ornamental Value	Wildlife Value
Flax Family – Linaceae		
Blue flax *Linum lewisii*	Blue flax appreciates well-drained soils & produces a profusion of beautiful blue flowers. Does well in a meadow garden or pocket prairie.	Blue flax attracts bees, butterflies & other small insects.
Four o'clock Family – Nyctaginaceae		
Heart's delight *Abronia ameliae*	Highly ornamental wildflower that does well in a garden or planned landscape.	Heart's delight is highly attractive to butterflies & especially moths. Insects are attracted by the highly fragrant perfume.
Gentian Family – Gentianaceae		
Mountain pink *Centaurium beyrichii*	This is such a beautiful plant, it's worth the trouble to plant the tiny seeds. Prefers rocky disturbed sites subject to run-off. It grows in the shape of an inverted cone.	Mountain pink has many insect visitors foraging for nectar, especially small bees, butterflies, diurnal moths & bee-mimic flies.
Texas bluebells *Eustoma grandiflora*	Texas Bluebell, otherwise known as Bluebell Gentian is a showy wildflower that responds favorably to good soils, extra water & a little fertilizer. Leaves are pale greenish blue & very attractive also. Cut flowers can last a week in water.	Texas bluebell is very attractive to several kinds of insects, especially bees & butterflies.
Iris Family – Iridaceae		
Herbertia *Herbertia lahue*	Pretty, delicately colored flowers growing from a roundish bulb usually forming large colonies. When in large numbers it forms areas of solid blue.	Bees are attracted to these delicate lavender flowers.

Table A.5
Native Plants of Texas

Please note that each two-page "spread" is divided into a top half (with plants' growing information) and a bottom half (with plants' ornamental and wildlife values). Numbered regions correspond to the Texas Ecoregion map on page 11.

Species	Ecological Region 1 2 3 4 5 6 7 8 9 10										Habit Height	Flower	Fruit	Sun Exposure	Habitat	Soils and Moisture Regime
Prairie celestial *Nemastylis geminiflora*			x	x	x		x				Perennial Wildflower 5"-10" Perennial	Showy lavender-blue to white flowers. March-May	Capsules with angular brown seeds. March-May	Full sun, part shade, dappled shade	Prefers clay & limestone soils from South to North Central Texas, including the Edwards Plateau.	Well-drained, mesic. Sands, clays, especially limestone soils.
Legume Family – Leguminosae																
Big Bend lupine *Lupinus havardii*	x										Wildflower 2'-4' Annual	Showy blue & white flowers. Jan.-June	Leguminous pod with seeds. March-Aug.	Full sun, a small amount of shade O.K.	Grows on open gravelly flats near the Chisos Mountains also the rolling limestone hills from the mouth of the Pecos River to Del Rio in the Trans-Pecos.	Well-drained, xeric. Sands & loams & gravelly limestone-based soils.
Hoary pea *Tephrosia lindheimeri*		x				x	x				Wildflower 9"-10" Perennial	Showy magenta flowers in 4" clusters. April-Oct.	Leguminous pod with seeds. June-Nov.	Full sun, part shade	Grows in open areas, prairies, plains, brushlands & chaparral.	Well-drained, xeric. Sands & loams.
Partridge pea *Chamaecrista fasciculata*	x	x	x	x	x	x					Wildflower 6"-12" Annual	Showy yellow flowers. June-Oct.	Legume with seeds. Aug.-Nov.	Full sun, part shade	Prefers sandy soils in old fields, open woodlands & pastures in eastern 1/2 of the state & coastal plains.	Mesic, well-drained. Sands, loams & clays.

Species	Ornamental Value	Wildlife Value
Prairie celestial *Nemastylis geminiflora*	Prairie celestials are an ethereally beautiful flower that will grace any wildflower meadow garden. They grow well in grassy areas & are often found in colonies.	Bees of various kinds are attracted to the flowers.
Legume Family – Leguminosae		
Big Bend lupine *Lupinus havardii*	With good rains, Big Bend bluebonnet can create an incredible sea of blue in the desert landscape extending from the river bottoms to the top of the mountains.	Insects, especially bees gather nectar from the flowers. Mule deer love to browse the foliage of this plant.
Hoary pea *Tephrosia lindheimeri*	Hoary pea makes an excellent showy ground cover. It will also climb a trellis. Once established it's an easy plant to care for. The gray-green leaves are especially attractive.	Insects such as bees & small butterflies are attracted to the flowers. The ripe seeds are eaten by several species of birds & small mammals. The plant's leaves are poisonous to livestock however.
Partridge pea *Chamaecrista fasciculata*	Partridge pea offers bright yellow splashes of color from June to October. Flowers open early in the morning, often closing up later in the day. Good border plant. Also does well in unattended natural areas.	Partridge pea attracts bees, butterflies and ants. Ripe seeds are eaten by a number of species of gamebirds as well as songbirds. Larval host plant for Cloudless giant sulphur, Orange sulphur & Sleepy orange butterflies.

Table A.5
Native Plants of Texas

Please note that each two-page "spread" is divided into a top half (with plants' growing information) and a bottom half (with plants' ornamental and wildlife values). Numbered regions correspond to the Texas Ecoregion map on page 11.

Species	Ecological Region 1 2 3 4 5 6 7 8 9 10	Habit Height	Flower	Fruit	Sun Exposure	Habitat	Soils and Moisture Regime
Texas bluebonnet *Lupinus texensis*	x x x x x x x x	Wildflower 8"–16" Annual	Showy blue and white pea-like flowers in racemes, fragrant. March–May	Legume. May–July	Full sun, a little shade O.K.	Prefers open fields, meadows & prairies, also roadside areas throughout much of the state from Corpus Christi to Abilene.	Well-drained, mesic to xeric. Sands, loams, clays & limestone soils; really likes calcareous soils.
Lily Family – Liliaceae							
Lila de los llanos *Anthericum chandleri*	x x	Wildflower 1'–3' Perennial	Pretty pale orange flowers. May–Nov.	Capsule with seeds. July–Dec.	Full sun, part shade, dappled shade	Grows in prairies & chaparral in the Lower Rio Grande Valley & along the southern coast.	Well-drained. Sands, loams & clays.
Wild hyacinth *Camassia scilloides*	x x x x	Wildflower 6"–2' Perennial	Showy lavender flowers on 6" spikes, fragrant. March–May	Capsule, 3-valved with roundish black shiny seeds. March–May	Full sun, part shade, dappled shade	Prefers sandy or rocky soils in meadows, fields prairies & open woods from Central Texas northward, also Edwards Plateau.	Well-drained, mesic. Sands, loams, clays & limestone soils.

Species	Ornamental Value	Wildlife Value
Texas bluebonnet *Lupinus texensis*	Our state flower, this Texas endemic cloaks meadows, prairies & roadsides come spring in an ocean of blue. An incredible sight that dazzles all newcomers to the state. Bluebonnets take a little work to get established & depend on the fall rains.	Bluebonnets are attended by bees & other insects who forage on the nectar & pollinate the plants. Plants let the bees know a particular flower has been pollinated by turning from white to dark red at the center of the banner. Larval host plant of hairstreak & elfin butterflies.
Lily Family – Liliaceae		
Lila de los llanos *Anthericum chandleri*	*Anthericum* sports yellow to pale orange flowers on slender elegant stems. Plant does well in slightly shady conditions & can bloom for a long period of time.	Flowers attract an assortment of insects.
Wild hyacinth *Camassia scilloides*	Delicate lavender spikes do best on a gentle slope where there is good drainage. Does well in shady areas especially where the soils are drier.	Bees & butterflies are attracted by the fragrant flowers & forage avidly for nectar.

Table A.5
Native Plants of Texas

Please note that each two-page "spread" is divided into a top half (with plants' growing information) and a bottom half (with plants' ornamental and wildlife values).
Numbered regions correspond to the Texas Ecoregion map on page 11.

Mallow Family – Malvaceae

Species	Ecological Region (1 2 3 4 5 6 7 8 9 10)	Habit / Height	Flower	Fruit	Sun Exposure	Habitat	Soils and Moisture Regime
Copper-mallow *Sphaeralcea angustifolia*	5, 8, 9, 10	Wildflower 1'-6' Perennial	Showy coral orange flowers on spikes. Feb.-Nov.	Capsules with seeds. April-Dec.	Full sun, part shade	Grows on sandy or rocky soils, usually on limestone or gypsum in brushlands, plains, rangelands, slopes & hillsides in High Plains, Rolling Plains, Edwards Plateau & Trans-Pecos.	Well-drained, xeric. Sands, loams & clays, either gypseous or calcareous soils.
Halbert-leaf Rose-mallow *Hibiscus militaris*	1, 2, 3	Wildflower 3'-8' Perennial	Showy white or pink flowers. May-Oct.	Capsules, smooth with several seeds in each section. July-Nov.	Full sun, part shade	Prefers freshwater marshes & shallow water areas in East & North Central Texas.	Poor drainage O.K.; mesic to hydric. Sands, clays & loams.
Heartleaf hibiscus *Hibiscus cardiophyllus*	3, 6, 7	Wildflower 3'-8' Perennial	Showy red flowers. Year-long	Capsule, multi-valved, with seeds. Year-long	Full sun, part shade, dappled shade	Grows in chaparral & brush country, also in canyons in Corpus Christi, south to Rio Grande Plains west to Val Verde County.	Well-drained, xeric. Sands, loams, clays & caliche-type soils.
Winecup *Callirhoe involucrata*	1, 2, 3, 4, 5, 6, 7, 10	Wildflower 6"-12" Perennial	Showy deep magenta to wine-red flowers. March-May	Capsules. May-July	Full sun, part shade, dappled shade	Prefers open woods, prairies, meadows & fields.	Well-drained, mesic. Sands, loams, clays or gravelly soils, either calcareous or acid-based.

Species	Ornamental Value	Wildlife Value
Mallow Family – Malvaceae		
Copper-mallow *Sphaeralcea angustifolia*	Copper mallow performs very well in cultivation. Columns of pale orange blossoms are set off by attractive soft grayish-green foliage. Blooms for a long period of time weather permitting. Fairly drought-tolerant.	Copper mallow is readily browsed by Mule deer & other herbivores. Bees, butterflies & other nectar & pollen loving insects are attracted to the flowers. Ripe seeds are eaten by seed-eating birds & small mammals. Larval host plant of Common checkered skipper butterfly.
Halbert-leaf Rose-mallow *Hibiscus militaris*	This spectacular flower can grow to almost 6' tall. Once established it provides lots of showy blooms throughout the summer & into the fall.	Insects are attracted to the flowers for the abundant pollen & nectar.
Heartleaf hibiscus *Hibiscus cardiophyllus*	Highly ornamental hibiscus that is quite drought-tolerant. If you plant it on clay, it must be well drained. The color of the flower varies from deep red to rose to orangy-red. Not cold hardy.	Pollen attracts many kinds of bees, beetles & other small insects.
Winecup *Callirhoe involucrata*	Beautiful wine-colored wildflowers that can grace any wildflower meadow garden. These plants tend to sprawl & have trailing stems. They can even clamber over small shrubs. They respond to extra watering by blooming for a much longer of period of time.	Winecup is visited by bees which gather pollen from the flowers.

Table A.5
Native Plants of Texas

Please note that each two-page "spread" is divided into a top half (with plants' growing information) and a bottom half (with plants' ornamental and wildlife values). Numbered regions correspond to the Texas Ecoregion map on page 11.

Species	\u00201	2	3	4	5	6	7	8	9	10	Habit Height	Flower	Fruit	Sun Exposure	Habitat	Soils and Moisture Regime
Milkweed Family – Asclepiadaceae																
Butterfly-weed *Asclepias tuberosa*	x	x	x		x						Wildflower 1'-2'	Showy orange complex flowers. April-Sept.	Follicle with comose seeds. June-Nov.	Full sun, part shade, dappled shade	Prefers prairies, meadows, open woods & thickets in Eastern Texas & west to Hill Country.	Well-drained, mesic. Sands, loams, clays & limestone soils.
Mint Family – Lamiaceae																
Cedar sage *Salvia roemeriana*								x		x	Wildflower 1'-2' Perennial	Showy red tubular flowers. March-July	Nutlets. May-Sept.	Part shade, dappled shade, full shade	Prefers rocky, shaded woods, canyon edges, bases of limestone outcrops in Edwards Plateau & Trans-Pecos	Well-drained, mesic. Sands, loams, clays & limestone-based soils.
False dragon-head *Physostegia intermedia*	x	x			x						Wildflower 4'-5' Perennial	Showy pink to pale purple flowers. April-June	Schizocarp with 4 nutlets. June-Aug.	Full sun, part shade, dappled shade	Prefers moist to wet areas, growing along aquatic ditches, in swamps, marshes & bottomlands in East & Southeast Texas.	Poor drainage O.K. Sands, loams & clays.
Horsemint *Monarda citriodora*	x	x	x	x	x	x	x	x	x	x	Wildflower 1'-1 ½' Annual	Showy purple tripartite spikes. April-June	Schizocarp with 4 brown nutlets. June-Aug.	Full sun, part shade	Prefers slopes, prairies & meadows throughout Texas.	Well-drained, xeric-mesic. Sands, loams & clays.
Mealy sage *Salvia farinacea*		x	x	x	x	x	x			x	Wildflower 1'-2' Perennial	Showy dark blue flowers in spikes. April-Dec.	Nutlets. June-Dec.	Full sun, part shade	Prefers dry calcareous soils of the Edwards Plateau, Trans-Pecos, High Plains, Rolling Plains & elsewhere throughout the state.	Well-drained, xeric. Sands, loams & clays, especial limestone & caliche-type soils.

Species	Ornamental Value	Wildlife Value
Milkweed Family – Asclepiadaceae		
Butterfly-weed *Asclepias tuberosa*	With its splashy orange, complex flowers, this is our most striking milkweed. It is very drought-tolerant once it is established & lives for a very long time. Has a big taproot.	This milkweed is a larval host plant for Milkweed butterflies such as the Monarch & the Queen. The female lays her eggs on the stems & leaves of the plant. Caterpillars feed on the milky sap sequestering the secondary compounds making them poisonous.
Mint Family – Lamiaceae		
Cedar sage *Salvia roemeriana*	Cedar sage with its showy red tubular flowers & soft kidney-shaped leaves does supremely well in a shady garden. It makes a great ground cover, growing well in an Ashe juniper association.	Black-chinned & Ruby-throated hummingbirds sip nectar from these plants which offer nectar when they first arrive from their wintering grounds. Plants are also popular in the Trans-Pecos to several other species of hummingbirds.
False dragon-head *Physostegia intermedia*	False dragon-head prefers damp areas & does very well in a water garden. They are highly showy when in bloom.	False dragon-head attracts a wide assortment of insects, especially bees.
Horsemint *Monarda citriodora*	Aromatic meadow wildflower that is easy to grow. Flowers continue to bloom right through the summer. Does really well planted with Indian blanket among species of native grasses.	Horsemint attracts butterflies, bees & a wide variety of other insects who forage on the nectar.
Mealy sage *Salvia farinacea*	Mealy sage likes to grow on thin limestone soils best & prefers habitats in full sun. Does well in mass plantings & is commonly available in native plant nurseries.	Mealy sage is always attended by a multitude of bees who forage on the nectar. Hummingbirds will also sip nectar from the tubular flowers.

Table A.5
Native Plants of Texas

Please note that each two-page "spread" is divided into a top half (with plants' growing information) and a bottom half (with plants' ornamental and wildlife values). Numbered regions correspond to the Texas Ecoregion map on page 11.

Species	Ecological Region 1 2 3 4 5 6 7 8 9 10	Habit Height	Flower	Fruit	Sun Exposure	Habitat	Soils and Moisture Regime
Obedient plant *Physostegia pulchella*	x	Wildflower 1'-3' Perennial	Showy magenta or deep reddish-purple flowers. May-June	Fruiting calyx. July-Nov.	Full sun, part shade, dappled shade	Prefers wet soils of bottomland hardwood forest, also along streams in East Texas.	Mesic, seasonal poor drainage O.K. Sands & clays.
Scarlet sage *Salvia coccinea*	x x x x x x	Wildflower 2'-4' Perennial	Showy red tubular flowers. May-Dec.	Calyx with nutlets. June-Dec.	Full sun, part shade, dappled shade	Prefers sandy soils in thickets, chaparral, on edges of open woods from East to South Texas.	Mesic, seasonal poor drainage O.K. Sands, loams, clays & caliche-type soils.

Mustard Family – Brassicaceae

Species	Ecological Region 1 2 3 4 5 6 7 8 9 10	Habit Height	Flower	Fruit	Sun Exposure	Habitat	Soils and Moisture Regime
Mountain peppergrass *Lepidium montanum*	x x x x	Wildflower 1'-2' Biennial	Showy white flowers. March-June	Silicles. May-Aug.	Full sun, part shade	Grows in sandy, calcareous or saline soils in open areas, deserts, brushlands, rangelands & openings on cedar slopes in Panhandle & southwest Texas	Well-drained, xeric. Sands, loams, limestone-based & caliche-type soils.

Nightshade Family – Solanaceae

Species	Ecological Region 1 2 3 4 5 6 7 8 9 10	Habit Height	Flower	Fruit	Sun Exposure	Habitat	Soils and Moisture Regime
Purple groundcherry *Physalis lobata*	x x x	Wildflower 2"-6" Perennial	Showy blue-lavender flowers. March-Dec.	Berry, roundish. May-Dec.	Full sun, part shade	Grows in a wide variety of habitats in the western 1/2 of the state.	Well-drained, xeric. Sands, loams, clays, limestone-based soils.

Species	Ornamental Value	Wildlife Value
Obedient plant *Phystostegia pulchella*	Very showy wildflower that is widely cultivated. It spreads by rhizomes to form large colonies. It loves areas along wet depressions & streams. Interestingly, it is fairly drought tolerant once established & will grow in a garden away from flowing water.	Obedient plant, also called beautiful false dragon-head, attracts many insects, especially the larger bees.
Scarlet sage *Salvia coccinea*	Scarlet sage can thrive in any part of the state. It is not very cold hardy, however. Oddly, it looks better if planted in dry, shady areas with poor soil. In rich soils with lots of water it gets very tall, coarse & slightly unattractive.	Scarlet sage is another excellent hummingbird plant & will draw in the hummingbirds of your area, including any migrants passing through in spring & fall. Bees & other insects are also attracted to the nectar, despite the red flower color.
Mustard Family – Brassicaceae		
Mountain peppergrass *Lepidium montanum*	These low dense plants are spectacular when in bloom. Works well with clumps placed near rocks or used as a border. It prefers full sun with well-drained soils. Flowers are open only in the morning.	Bees, butterflies & other small nectar-loving insects attend the mounds of white flowers in the morning. Larval host plant of the Checkered white butterfly.
Nightshade Family – Solanaceae		
Purple groundcherry *Physalis lobata*	These attractive clumps of blue-lavender flowers can form thick luxuriant carpets of green and blue blanketing the ground. Makes a good ground cover for a perennial bed.	Bees, butterflies & other insects are attracted to the flowers.

Table A.5
Native Plants of Texas

Please note that each two-page "spread" is divided into a top half (with plants' growing information) and a bottom half (with plants' ornamental and wildlife values). Numbered regions correspond to the Texas Ecoregion map on page 11.

Species	Ecological Region 1 2 3 4 5 6 7 8 9 10	Habit Height	Flower	Fruit	Sun Exposure	Habitat	Soils and Moisture Regime
Parsley Family – Apiaceae							
Eryngo *Eryngium leavenworthii*	x x x x x x x x x x	Wildflower 1'-2' Annual	Unusual magenta thistle-like flowers. Aug.-Sept.	Schizocarp with 2 mericarps. Oct.-Nov.	Full sun, part shade	Grows in open areas on plains & prairies throughout most of the state.	Well-drained, xeric. Sands, loams, clays, limestone-based & caliche-like soils.
Phlox Family – Polemoniaceae							
Drummond phlox *Phlox drummondii*	x x x x x x	Wildflower 6"-20" Annual	Showy red or magenta flowers about 1" across. March-June	Seeds, 1 to several. May-Aug.	Full sun, part shade, dappled shade	Prefers grasslands, open meadows, & woodlands in neutral to acid soils.	Well-drained, mesic. Sands, sandy loams, acid to neutral.
Louisiana phlox *Phlox divaricata*	x x	Wildflower 4"-18" Perennial	Showy lavender to white flowers about 1" across. March-May	Seeds, 1 to several. May-July	Full sun, part shade, dappled shade	Prefers humus-rich woodland soils in East Texas.	Well-drained, mesic. Sands, loams & clays.
Rio Grande phlox *Phlox glabriflora*	x x	Wildflower 9"-10" Annual	Showy deep pink flowers with white centers. May-June	Capsules with seeds. July-Aug.	Full sun, part shade	Grows in open sandy areas in the Coastal Bend area & Lower Rio Grande Valley.	Well-drained, xeric. Sands, deep.
Scarlet standing-cypress *Ipomopsis aggregata*	x	Wildflower 3'-5' Annual	Showy red tubular flowers with yellow splotches. Aug.-Oct.	Capsule with seeds. Oct.-Nov.	Full sun, part shade	Grows in igneous soils on dry rocky slopes in the Trans-Pecos especially in the Davis Mountains above 4000'.	Well-drained, xeric. Sands & loams, likes igneous soils.

Species	Ornamental Value	Wildlife Value
Parsley Family – Apiaceae		
Eryngo *Eryngium leavenworthii*	Very distinctive prickly plant with curious spiny bracts & fuzzy magenta flowers. This is a good plant for a meadow garden in a place that does not get much people traffic. Makes a great colorful display & is always a conversation piece.	Several species of insects are attracted to the small flowers. Makes a good protective cover plant when found close together. Seed eating birds forage on the ripe mericarps.
Phlox Family – Polemoniaceae		
Drummond phlox *Phlox drummondii*	Drummond phlox has five recognized subspecies, each of which is highly attractive in a garden. The plant is very easy to grow & provides splashes of beautiful red to magenta to pink spring color depending on the subspecies you purchase.	Drummond phlox attracts myriads of insects in the spring that forage for nectar.
Louisiana phlox *Phlox divaricata*	Louisiana phlox add highly attractive splash of lavender pink color to a garden. They definitely appreciate an extra dash of water & deep soils. They sometimes come in blue.	Louisiana phlox attracts myriads of insects in the spring that forage for nectar.
Rio Grande phlox *Phlox glabriflora*	These gorgeous vivid flowers form lush mounds for a little over one month's time in late spring. The species needs deep sands with excellent drainage. Provides incredible splashes of color for your garden.	Insects of a wide variety are attracted to the flowers.
Scarlet standing-cypress *Ipomopsis aggregata*	This spectacular flower with red tubular flowers & elegantly dissected leaves thrives in high desert habitats. Rosettes are present throughout most of the winter.	This is a popular plant with the many hummingbirds of the area which zip from flower to flower sipping nectar & pollinating the plant.

Table A.5
Native Plants of Texas

Please note that each two-page "spread" is divided into a top half (with plants' growing information) and a bottom half (with plants' ornamental and wildlife values). Numbered regions correspond to the Texas Ecoregion map on page 11.

Species	Ecological Region 1	2	3	4	5	6	7	8	9	10	Habit Height	Flower	Fruit	Sun Exposure	Habitat	Soils and Moisture Regime
Standing cypress *Ipomopsis rubra*	x	x	x	x	x			x			Wildflower 2'-6' Biennial	Showy red-orange tubular flowers. May-June	Seeds elongate, swelling when wet. July-Aug.	Full sun, part shade, dappled shade	Prefers rocky or sandy ground in fields or along edges of woods in Edwards Plateau, Cross Timbers, Oak Woods & Prairies & East Texas. Also Pineywoods.	Well-drained, mesic. Sands, loams & gravelly soils.
Poppy Family – Papaveraceae																
Crested prickly-poppy *Argemone polyanthemos*							x	x	x		Wildflower 1'-4' Perennial	Splashy white crepe-like flowers with yellow center. April-Oct.	Capsule with seeds. June-Nov.	Full sun, part shade	Grows sandy or gravelly soils on prairies, foothills & mesa in northwest portion of Texas. Occurs in Marathon Basin.	Well-drained, xeric. Sands, loams, clays, especially gravelly soils.
Mexican gold poppy *Eschscholzia mexicana*										x	Wildflower 1/2'-1' Annual	Gorgeous golden flowers. March-May	Capsule, ribbed with 2 valves & many seeds. March-May	Full sun, small amount of shade O.K.	Grows on limestone slopes of the Franklin Mountains in El Paso also found near the city of Lajitas.	Well-drained, xeric. Sands, loams & limestone-based soils.
Red prickly-poppy *Argemone sanguinea*						x					Wildflower 1'-3' Annual	Showy pinkish red flowers. Year-long	Capsules. Year-long	Full sun, part shade	Grows in open areas, meadows, fields, along roadsides, waste places in South Texas.	Well-drained. Sands, loams & clays; a variety of soils.
White prickly-poppy *Argemone albiflora v. texana*	x	x	x	x	x	x				x	Wildflower 1'-2' Annual	Showy crepe-paper-like white flowers. March-June	Capsules with seeds. May-Aug.	Full sun, part shade, dappled shade	Grows in open fields, meadows, prairies, along roadsides throughout most of Texas.	Well-drained, xeric. Sands, loams, clays, limestone-based & caliche-type soils.

Species	Ornamental Value	Wildlife Value
Standing cypress *Ipomopsis rubra*	With splashy red-orange flowers & elegantly divided threadlike leaves, standing cypress is a spectacular plant. It does not flower the first year seeds are planted but forms a low attractive basal rosette.	Standing cypress is a wonderful hummingbird plant. Exerted yellow anthers & red tubular flowers attract any hummer in the area. Hummer's heads get yellow with pollen as they zip from flower to flower.
Poppy Family – Papaveraceae		
Crested prickly-poppy *Argemone polyanthemos*	This is a very showy, very prickly poppy. Though not vicious, stems & leaves have numerous conspicuous prickles. This is a long-term bloomer with flowers coming out from April to October.	Bees, butterflies & especially beetles are attracted to the pollen of this flower.
Mexican gold poppy *Eschscholzia mexicana*	These incredibly beautiful golden poppies make a magnificent sight when in full bloom. Lacy blue-green foliage sets off the orange-gold flowers. Grows well on rocky limestone slopes.	Myriads of insects such as bees & butterflies are attracted to the flowers.
Red prickly-poppy *Argemone sanguinea*	Colorful poppy with big gorgeous deep red to pinkish lavender flowers. Plants like a little extra water & don't appreciate competition. Does well on disturbed soils.	Poppies attract bees, beetles, bugs & other small insects that forage on the pollen.
White prickly-poppy *Argemone albiflora* v. *texana*	White prickly-poppy is a very striking white flowered plant with plenty of prickles on the stems & leaves. A highly drought-tolerant plant, it will look good when everything else is brown. It prefers full sun to shady areas.	Several varieties of insects forage on the pollen & nectar of this plant, especially bees & beetles. Deer don't browse this plant due to the prickles.

Table A.5
Native Plants of Texas

Please note that each two-page "spread" is divided into a top half (with plants' growing information) and a bottom half (with plants' ornamental and wildlife values). Numbered regions correspond to the Texas Ecoregion map on page 11.

Sunflower Family – Asteraceae

Species	1	2	3	4	5	6	7	8	9	10	Habit Height	Flower	Fruit	Sun Exposure	Habitat	Soils and Moisture Regime
Blackfoot daisy *Melampodium leucanthum*								x	x	x	Wildflower 6"–12" Perennial	Showy white clumps of daisy-like flowers, fragrant. Mar.–Nov.	Achenes. May–Dec.	Full sun, part shade	Prefers limestone & calcareous soils in open, dry rocky areas in Edwards Plateau, Trans-Pecos, High Plains & Rolling Plains.	Well-drained, xeric. Sands, limestone-based or caliche-type soils.
Brown-eyed Susan *Rudbeckia hirta*	x	x	x	x	x		x	x			Wildflower 1'–2' Annual	Showy yellow ray flowers with dark brown centers. May–Sept.	Achenes. July–Nov.	Full sun, part shade, dappled shade	Prefers open prairies, grasslands & woodland meadows in the eastern ²⁄₃ of the state.	Well-drained, mesic. Sands, loams & clays.
Chocolate daisy *Berlandiera lyrata*									x	x	Wildflower 1'–3'	Showy yellow daisy-like flowers with maroon centers. April–June	Achenes. June–Aug.	Full sun, part shade	Grows on dry rocky limestone soils, open areas, along roadsides.	Well-drained, xeric. Sands, loams, clays, limestone-based, caliche-type soils.
Desert marigold *Baileya multiradiata*							x		x		Wildflower 1'–1 1/2' Perennial, short-lived	Splashy yellow daisy-like flowers. Year-long	Achenes. Year-long	Full sun, part shade	Grows in flat desert areas in the Trans-Pecos & western portion of the Edwards Plateau.	Well-drained, xeric. Sands, loams, clays & caliche-type soils.
Engelmann daisy *Engelmannia pinnatifida*	x	x	x	x	x	x	x		x	x	Wildflower 1'–3' Perennial	Showy yellow daisy-like flowers. Feb.–Nov.	Achenes. April–Dec.	Full sun, part shade, dappled shade	Grows in opens fields, meadows, along roadsides throughout much of the state.	Well-drained, xeric to mesic. Sands, loams & clays; neutral to calcareous soils.

Species	Ornamental Value	Wildlife Value
Sunflower Family – Asteraceae		
Blackfoot daisy *Melampodium leucanthum*	Blackfoot daisy does very well in a rock garden providing showy clumps of white daisy-like flowers. Continues to bloom throughout the season especially after rains. Slightly cold-sensitive.	Blackfoot daisy attracts bees, butterflies & other small insects who gather the nectar. Ripe seed heads provide food for small seed-eating birds.
Brown-eyed Susan *Rudbeckia hirta*	Brown-eyed Susans provide a lush splash of color in your meadow garden or pocket prairie. It does especially well if the rains are good or with a little extra watering. It will grow well in both partially shady areas & the sun.	Bees, butterflies & many other kinds of insects forage for nectar from these flowers all summer. In the fall when the flowers have good to seed, numerous seed-eating bircs forage on the ripe achenes.
Chocolate daisy *Berlandiera lyrata*	Sometimes called Brooch flower, this yellow dark-eyed daisy-like wildflower does well in a meadow garden. It's also striking as an accent plant. Very drought-tolerant, it prefers well-drained soils.	Bees, butterflies & other insects are attracted to the flowers.
Desert marigold *Baileya multiradiata*	Spectacular golden long-blooming wildflower that grows in striking clumps. Leaves are a soft woolly gray-green color set off the blossoms beautifully. This hardy drought-tolerant species will bloom for the entire year weather permitting.	A wide variety of insects, especially bees & butterflies are attracted to these flowers. Foliage can be toxic to some forms of livestock, especially sheep. Not heavily browsed by Mule deer.
Englemann daisy *Englemannia pinnatifida*	Lemon-yellow flowers blanket the fields & roadsides especially in the spring. With a little extra water in your garden, these flowers will prolong bloom-time through the summer.	Englemann daisy attracts a multitude of bees, butterflies & other insects which forage on the nectar. Seed-eating birds such as sparrows, buntings & finches dine on the ripe achenes in the fall.

Table A.5
Native Plants of Texas

Please note that each two-page "spread" is divided into a top half (with plants' growing information) and a bottom half (with plants' ornamental and wildlife values). Numbered regions correspond to the Texas Ecoregion map on page 11.

Species	Ecological Region 1 2 3 4 5 6 7 8 9 10	Habit Height	Flower	Fruit	Sun Exposure	Habitat	Soils and Moisture Regime
Giant goldenrod *Solidago canadensis*	x (1–10)	Wildflower 2'-7' Perennial	Showy yellow flowers in pyramidal heads. Sept.-Nov.	Achenes. Oct.-Nov.	Full sun, part shade	Prefers open fields, meadows, prairies & moist soils near streams.	Mesic, poor drainage O.K. Sands, loams & clays, also caliche-type soils.
Golden wave *Coreopsis tinctoria*	x (1–7)	Wildflower 1'-4' Annual	Showy yellow daisy-like flowers with brown centers. March-June or later depending on rains	Achenes. May-Aug.	Full sun, part shade	Prefers seasonally moist soils in the eastern portion of the state, but grows throughout.	Mesic, seasonal poor drainage O.K. Sands, loams, clays; either calcareous or acid.
Golden-eye *Viguiera dentata*	x (4, 5, 7, 10)	Wildflower 3'-6'	Showy yellow daisy-like flowers. October	Achenes. November	Full sun, part shade	Prefers dry caliche soils of the Texas Hill Country & chalky cuestas of North Central Texas, Blackland Prairies & to a less extent in the Trans-Pecos.	Well-drained mesic. Sands, loams, clays & limestone soils.
Green-eyes *Berlandiera texana*	x (1, 8, 9)	Wildflower 1'-4' Perennial	Showy yellow daisy-like flowers with green centers. April-Nov.	Achenes. June-Dec.	Full sun, part shade, dappled shade	Grows along woodland edges, on hillsides & along riverbanks from Corpus Christi to the High Plains.	Well-drained, xeric to mesic. Sands, loams & limestone-based & caliche-type soils.
Greenthread *Thelesperma filifolium*	x (1, 2, 4, 5, 6, 7, 8, 9)	Wildflower 1'-1 1/2' Annual	Showy yellow daisy-like flowers. Feb.-Dec.	Achenes. April-Dec.	Full sun, some shade O.K.	Prefers dry, calcareous soils on prairies throughout Texas. Rare in East Texas & Trans-Pecos.	Well-drained, xeric. Sands, loams, clays & limestone-based soils.

Species	Ornamental Value	Wildlife Value
Giant goldenrod *Solidago canadensis*	Goldenrod is spectacular in the autumn. Its large pyramidal flower clusters infuse golden color into wildflower meadows.	Bees & butterflies gather pollen from goldenrod in the fall.
Golden wave *Coreopsis tinctoria*	Great profusions of this golden yellow flower blanket roadsides & meadows, like undulating waves of a golden ocean.	Golden wave attracts a wide variety of insects, especially bees & butterflies who sip nectar from the disk flowers. Ripe achenes are sought after by many species of seed-eating birds, especially the Painted Bunting.
Golden-eye *Viguiera dentata*	This open busy perennial thrives at sunny edges of woods & tends to grow in large colonies. Extremely drought tolerant, it can be absolutely magnificent in full bloom.	Golden-eye provides a great deal of nectar to bees & butterflies foraging in the fall. Ripe achenes are relished by several species of small seed-eating birds. Also provides good protective cover. Larval host plant of the Bordered patch butterfly.
Green-eyes *Berlandiera texana*	A very-long-lived perennial flower with showy yellow flowers. Starts blooming in the spring, but also during the summer & then again in the fall. Is responsive to a little extra watering, though it is drought-tolerant once established.	Bees, butterflies & other nectar-loving insects are attracted to the flowers. The ripe achenes are devoured by many species of seed-eating birds.
Greenthread *Thelesperma filifolium*	Looking much like Golden-wave, this attractive, daisy-like flower grows in large masses of golden yellow over large expanses of prairie habitats. This plant prefers lots of sun & excellent drainage for best results.	Greenthread attracts nectar-loving insects of all varieties, especially bees & butterflies. Ripe achenes, after flowers have good to seed, are highly sought after by several species of granivorous birds like the Painted Bunting. Larval host plant of Dwarf Yellow butterfly.

Table A.5
Native Plants of Texas

Please note that each two-page "spread" is divided into a top half (with plants' growing information) and a bottom half (with plants' ornamental and wildlife values). Numbered regions correspond to the Texas Ecoregion map on page 11.

Species	1	2	3	4	5	6	7	8	9	10	Habit Height	Flower	Fruit	Sun Exposure	Habitat	Soils and Moisture Regime
Heath aster *Aster ericoides*	x	x	x	x	x	x	x	x	x	x	Wildflower 4"-30" Perennial	Showy pale bluish-white flowers. Oct.-Nov.	Achenes. Nov.-Dec.	Full sun, part shade	Prefers open situations throughout much of north central & southeast Texas, including the Plains country & parts of East, South & West Texas.	Well-drained, mesic. Sands, loams & clays.
Huisache-daisy *Amblyolepis setigera*				x	x	x	x	x	x	x	Wildflower 6"-18" Annual	Showy golden yellow daisy-like flowers. April-June	Achenes. June-Aug.	Full sun, part shade	Grows in fields, meadows, prairies throughout the western portion of the state.	Well-drained, xeric. Sands, loams, caliche-type soils.
Indian blanket *Gaillardia pulchella*	x	x	x	x	x	x	x	x	x	x	Wildflower 1' Annual	Showy yellow & red daisy-like flowers. March-Oct.	Achenes. May-Nov.	Full sun, part shade	Prefers open grassy areas, prairies, meadows, also disturbed areas in a variety of soils.	Well-drained, xeric-mesic. Sands, loams & clays.
Kansas gayfeather *Liatris pycnostachya*	x		x								Wildflower 2'-5' Perennial	Showy purple to pale lavender flowers in solitary spikes. Aug.-Oct.	Achenes, cylindrical, ribbed & tapered at base. Oct.-Nov.	Full sun, a little shade O.K.	Prefers sandy, acid bogs in East Texas; also open prairie habitats.	Well-drained sandy or rocky soils. Sands & loams.
Lance-leaf coreopsis *Coreopsis lanceolata*	x	x									Wildflower 8"-48" Perennial	Ray flowers splashy yellow, disk flowers deep yellow. March-May	Achene, black, flattened & winged. May-July	Full sun, part shade, dappled shade	Prefers open flat woods & fields in East & South East Texas.	Well-drained, mesic. Sands, clays & loams.

Species	Ornamental Value	Wildlife Value
Heath aster *Aster ericoides*	This profusely blooming fall aster grows into a much-branched erect or reclining or arching plant. The numerous flowers provide an extravagant fall show. Narrowly lanceolate leaves are attractively elegant.	Heath aster provides abundant fall nectar for bees, butterflies & other insects foraging in the late fall. Many seed-eating birds dine on the ripe achenes. Its shrubby aspect provides good cover for small sparrows & finches. Larval host plant of Pearly crescentspot butterfly.
Huisache-daisy *Amblyolepis setigera*	Huisache-daisy is a few-branched attractive yellow-flowered plant with a two-toned daisy-like flower. Looks great in a meadow where it will bloom profusely for over two months.	Bees, butterflies & other small insects are attracted to flowers. Ripe achenes are eaten by many species of small seed-eating birds.
Indian blanket *Gaillardia pulchella*	This is a marvelously easy wildflower to grow & it comes in various coloration patterns from mainly yellow to mostly reddish. Blooms most of the season from spring to late fall & provides lots of color to a wildflower meadow.	Indian blanket attracts bees, butterflies & several other varieties of small insects who forage on the nectar. Ripe seed heads are favorites with many species of seed-eating passerines like the Painted Bunting.
Kansas gayfeather *Liatris pycnostachya*	Very splashy fall flowers that grows well in rock garden or in a pocket prairie or wildflower meadow mixed in with grasses.	Gayfeather is highly sought after by bees, butterflies & other small insects for its abundant nectar in the fall.
Lance-leaf coreopsis *Coreopsis lanceolata*	Lance-leaf coreopsis is a very showy wildflower that grows very easily & provides a wonderful splash of color for the garden. It is widely found in cultivation.	Growing in healthy clumps, these flowers provide abundant nectar for butterflies & bees. Ripe seed heads are eaten by several species of granivorous birds.

Table A.5
Native Plants of Texas

Please note that each two-page "spread" is divided into a top half (with plants' growing information) and a bottom half (with plants' ornamental and wildlife values). Numbered regions correspond to the Texas Ecoregion map on page 11.

Species	Ecological Region 1 2 3 4 5 6 7 8 9 10	Habit Height	Flower	Fruit	Sun Exposure	Habitat	Soils and Moisture Regime
Late boneset *Eupatorium serotinum*	x x x x x	Wildflower 2'-5' Perennial	Showy off-white flower heads. Sept.–Nov.	Achenes. Nov.–Jan.	Full sun, part shade	Prefers open places, woodland edges, near ponds.	Mesic, likes moisture. Sands, loams & clays.
Limoncillo *Pectis angustifolia*	· · · · · · x x · x	Wildflower 6"–10" Annual	Petite yellow daisy-like flowers. June–Oct.	Achenes. Aug.–Nov.	Full sun, part shade	Grows on dry calcareous soils of uplands in Edwards Plateau west to Trans-Pecos.	Well-drained, xeric. Sands, loams, gravelly caliche-type soils.
Maximilian sunflower *Helianthus maximiliani*	· · x x x x x x · x	Wildflower 4'-6' Perennial	Showy bright yellow flowers. Aug.–Oct.	Achenes. Nov.–Dec.	Full sun, part shade	Prefers seasonally moist ditches & depressions in grasslands, prairies & meadows in Edwards Plateau, North & South East Texas.	Well-drained, xeric; tolerates seasonally poor drainage. Sands, loams, clays & limestone-based soils.
Mexican hat *Ratibida columnifera*	x x x x x x x x x x	Wildflower 2'-3' Perennial	Showy, variably-colored flowers, yellow to orange to brown with tall seedhead. May–Dec.	Achenes. July–Dec.	Full sun, part shade	Grows in open fields, meadows, fields, prairies, along roadsides in western $\frac{2}{3}$ of the state.	Well-drained, xeric. Sands, loams, clays, limestone-based & caliche-type soils.
Paperflower *Psilostrophe tagetina*	· · · · · x x x x x	Wildflower 1'-1 1/2' Annual or short-lived Perennial	Showy yellow daisy-like flowers. Feb.–Oct.	Achenes. April–Nov.	Full sun, some shade O.K.	Grows in various soils in plains, rangelands, along hillsides & on slopes.	Well-drained, xeric. Sands, loams & clays.
Parralena *Dysodia pentachaeta*	x · · · · · x x x x	Wildflower 4"–10" Annual	Small yellow mini-daisies. March–Nov.	Achenes. May–Dec.	Full sun, part shade	Grows on dry loose soils in open areas in central & western portion of the state.	Well-drained, xeric. Sands, loams, clays, limestone-based soils.

Species	Ornamental Value	Wildlife Value
Late boneset *Eupatorium serotinum*	This late blooming shrubby wildflower with opposite leaves and much-branched, flat-topped terminal flower clusters, often forms colonies.	Masses of off-white flowers is an excellent nectar source for migrating monarch butterflies & other late foraging insects. Plants provide good protection for butterflies on windy days. Many species of sparrows & finches eat the ripe achenes in winter.
Limoncillo *Pectis angustifolia*	Attractive clumps of petite daisy-like flowers & narrow highly aromatic leaves. Lemoncillo forms low-growing little mats in a rock garden. Good for borders along walkways or walls. Also good in mass plantings. Smells heavenly.	Bees, butterflies & other small nectar-loving insects are attracted to the flowers. Deer do not browse the foliage of this plant. Ripe achenes are eaten by small seed-eating birds.
Maximilian sunflower *Helianthus maximiliani*	With its bright yellow flowers, Maximilian sunflower is gorgeous in the fall. Does very well growing among native grasses in a pocket prairie. Occurs in colonies on both dry & moist ground.	Maximilian sunflower provides copious nectar to butterflies & bees in the fall.
Mexican hat *Ratibida columnifera*	Mexican hat varies a lot in both size & color depending on conditions. In gardens, it sometimes does better for longer with a little shade. It does not like standing water, so make sure soils are well-drained.	Mexican hat attracts bees, butterflies & other nectar-loving insects. Ripe achenes are eaten by many species of seed-eating birds.
Paperflower *Psilostrophe tagetina*	Herbage is attractive coated with dense, woolly coating of soft hairs which allows it to survive the extremely hot dry conditions of its desert habitat. Flowers are thick & showy for long periods of time. Even cut flowers don't loose their color.	Bees, butterflies & other small insects forage for nectar from the flowers. Foliage can be toxic to livestock. Mule deer do not browse this plant.
Parralena *Dyssodia pentachaeta*	There are many species & varieties of this plant that are adapted to various parts of the state. They are all aromatic, have petite perky yellow flowers & are great for rock gardens.	Small bees, butterflies & other insects are attracted to the flowers. Mule deer will only feed on this when very hungry. Livestock will also ignore this plant as potential forage.

Table A.5
Native Plants of Texas

Please note that each two-page "spread" is divided into a top half (with plants' growing information) and a bottom half (with plants' ornamental and wildlife values). Numbered regions correspond to the Texas Ecoregion map on page 11.

Species	Ecological Region 1 2 3 4 5 6 7 8 9 10	Habit Height	Flower	Fruit	Sun Exposure	Habitat	Soils and Moisture Regime
Purple coneflower *Echinacea angustifolia*	x x x x	Wildflower 1'-2' Perennial	Showy pink to lavender flowers with narrow petals. April-May	Achenes. June-Aug.	Full sun, part shade	Prefers rocky open woods & prairies in North Texas, West Texas & the Edwards Plateau.	Well-drained, mesic-xeric. Sands, loams & clays.
Red gaillardia *Gaillardia amblyodon*	x x x x x x x x	Wildflower 1' Annual	Showy red daisy-like flowers. March-Nov.	Achenes. May-Nov.	Full sun, part shade	Prefers open grassy areas, prairies, meadows, also disturbed areas in a variety of soils.	Well-drained, xeric-mesic. Sands, loams & clays.
Slender-stem bitterweed *Hymenoxys scaposa*	x x x x	Wildflower 3"-6" Perennial	Showy yellow daisy-like flowers. March-Oct.	Achenes. June-Nov.	Full sun, part shade	Grows on dry calcareous soils & on caliche banks throughout much of western Texas.	Well-drained, xeric. Sands, loams, clays, limestone-based & caliche-type soils.
Tahoka daisy *Machaeranthera tanacetifolia*	x x x	Wildflower 6"-12" Annual	Showy magenta daisy-like flowers with yellow centers. March-May	Achenes. May-July	Full sun, part shade	Occurs on gravelly soil flatlands, fields, prairies in the Rolling Plains, High Plains & the Trans-Pecos.	Well-drained, xeric. Sands, loams, clays & caliche-type soils.
Texas snakeweed *Gutierrezia sarothrae*	x x x x	Wildflower 1'-3' Perennial	Showy tiny yellow flowers. Sept.-Nov.	Achenes. Oct.-Dec.	Full sun, part shade	Grows in open areas, prairies, fields, meadows on poor, dry soils; also along roadsides.	Well-drained, xeric. Sands, loams & clays, limestone-based & caliche type soils.
Yellow plainsman *Hymenopappus flavescens*	x x	Wildflower 1'-3' Biennial	Showy yellow flower heads. May-Sept.	Achenes. July-Nov.	Full sun, part shade	Grows in open fields, meadows & plains in the High Plains & the Rolling Plains.	Well-drained, xeric. Sands & loams.

Species	Ornamental Value	Wildlife Value
Purple coneflower *Echinacea angustifolia*	This showy coneflower has several close relatives that freely hybridize with one another. Colors range from pink to white to a rose-purple. The flower stays attractive for a long time.	Purple coneflowers provide copious nectar to bees & butterflies in your garden. Ripe achenes are eaten by small seed-eating birds.
Red gaillardia *Gaillardia amblyodon*	This is a marvelously easy wildflower to grow & it comes in various coloration patterns from mainly yellow to mostly reddish. Blooms most of the season from spring to late fall & provides lots of color to a wildflower meadow.	Indian blanket attracts bees, butterflies & several other varieties of small insects who forage on the nectar. Ripe seed heads are favorites with many species of seed-eating passerines like the Painted Bunting.
Slender-stem bitterweed *Hymenoxys scaposa*	This bright yellow daisy-like flower atop a slender scape is graceful & elegant as it peppers a landscape. The species works well in a rock garden & appreciates good drainage. The plant is highly aromatic.	Bees, butterflies & other small insects forage for nectar from the flowers. Ripe achenes are eaten by small seed-eating birds. Foliage is bitter & not highly prized by herbivorous animals.
Tahoka daisy *Machaeranthera tanacetifolia*	This absolutely beautiful wildflower produces thick continuous blossoms for about two months before they fade. These plants work well in a shortgrass meadow or on a rocky hillside. The plant also does well in a rock garden. They love good drainage.	Tahoka daisy attracts many small bees, butterflies & other insects that are attracted to the nectar. Ripe achenes are sought after by several species of seed-eating birds.
Texas snakeweed *Gutierrezia sarothrae*	This golden bushy plant does very well in poor dry soils & requires very little water. Looks great in a rock garden. Fields are covered in the fall with solid balls of rich golden yellow which last until it freezes.	Many smalls insects, including syrphid flies, small bees & butterflies are attracted by the nectar. These clumps provide great cover for small animals. Seed-eating birds such as finches & sparrows eat the ripe achenes.
Yellow plainsman *Hymenopappus flavescens*	Very striking deep yellow wildflower with pale gray-green leaves which are furry on the underside. These plants look great in a wild-flower meadow. Yellow plainsman is quite drought tolerant & needs no extra watering.	Bees, butterflies & other nectar-loving insects spend a great deal of time foraging atop these flowerheads which serve as landing platforms. What seed does not serve as food for granivorous birds will self sow for the next year.

Table A.5
Native Plants of Texas

Please note that each two-page "spread" is divided into a top half (with plants' growing information) and a bottom half (with plants' ornamental and wildlife values). Numbered regions correspond to the Texas Ecoregion map on page 11.

Species	Ecological Region										Habit Height	Flower	Fruit	Sun Exposure	Habitat	Soils and Moisture Regime
	1	2	3	4	5	6	7	8	9	10						
Yellow zinnia *Zinnia grandiflora*									x	x	Wildflower 6"-8" Perennial	Showy yellow flowers. May-Oct.	Achenes. May-Oct.	Full sun, part shade	Grows on dry calcareous substrates in the Trans-Pecos & the Plains country.	Well-drained, xeric. Sands, loams, gravelly limestone-based soils.

Vervain Family – Verbenaceae

Species	1	2	3	4	5	6	7	8	9	10	Habit Height	Flower	Fruit	Sun Exposure	Habitat	Soils and Moisture Regime
Prairie verbena *Verbena bipinnatifida*	x	x	x	x	x	x	x				Wildflower 6"-12" Annual	Showy magenta to purple flowers grouped in 2"-flower heads. March-Dec.	Capsule-like fruit, dry (Schizocarp). May-Dec.	Full sun, some shade O.K.	Prefers prairies & fields throughout most of Texas, except for Trans-Pecos.	Well-drained, xeric to mesic. Sands, loams, clays & limestone-based soils.

Waterleaf Family – Hydrophyllaceae

Species	1	2	3	4	5	6	7	8	9	10	Habit Height	Flower	Fruit	Sun Exposure	Habitat	Soils and Moisture Regime
Baby blue-eyes *Nemophila phacelioides*	x	x	x								Wildflower 10"-28" Annual	Showy lavender & white flowers. March-May	Fruiting calyx with seeds. May-July	Full sun, part shade, dappled shade	Grows in sandy soils & open woodlands in East & Southeast Texas.	Well-drained, mesic. Sands & sandy loams.
Blue-curls *Phacelia congesta*	x	x	x	x	x	x	x	x		x	Wildflower 1'-3' Annual or biennial	Showy purple to blue-lavender flowers. March-June	Capsule, ovoid. May-Aug.	Full sun, part shade, dappled shade	Occurs in sandy, gravelly or rocky areas, distributed throughout Texas except for Pineywoods.	Well-drained, mesic. Sands, loams, clays & limestone soils.
Purple phacelia *Phacelia patuliflora*	x	x	x								Wildflower 10"-12" Annual	Showy purple & white flowers. Feb.-May	Capsule with seeds. May-July	Full sun, part shade	Prefers sandy soils in fields, prairies, openings & edges of woods, also along stream banks in Southeast, South Central and Coastal Texas.	Well-drained, mesic. Sands & sandy loams.

Species	Ornamental Value	Wildlife Value
Yellow zinnia *Zinnia grandiflora*	These flashy yellow flowers infuse brilliant golden color to the landscape. This is a great erosion control plant as the tightly-packed needle-like leaves form thick mats over the soil. Yellow zinnia works very well in a dry gravelly-soil rock garden.	Bees, butterflies, diurnal moths, syrphid flies are attracted to the flowers.
Vervain Family – Verbenaceae		
Prairie verbena *Verbena bipinnatifida*	Prairie verbena makes a great low-growing ground cover. Looks very good in rock gardens. Prefers full sun & limestone soils but will survive in others.	Prairie verbena is an excellent butterfly plant. When in bloom it is always attended by them as they daintily park on the conveniently shaped landing-platform-shaped flower heads.
Waterleaf Family – Hydrophyllaceae		
Baby blue-eyes *Nemophila phacelioides*	Baby blue-eyes forms a beautiful carpet of lavender blue. Can be upright to straggling with attractive blade lobed or divided leaves irregularly toothed.	Bees & butterflies are attracted to the flowers & forage on the nectar.
Blue-curls *Phacelia congesta*	Blue-curls is an elegant erect, branching plant with dissected leaves & pretty blue-lavender flowers. Does well on almost any soil, but does appreciate a little extra moisture. Best to keep them out of direct hot sun.	Insects, especially bees are highly attracted to Blue-curls. Butterflies will also sip nectar from this plant.
Purple phacelia *Phacelia patuliflora*	This attractive low growing wildflower grows in clumps. Flower color varies from lavender to purplish-violet. They are an attractive addition to any garden.	Bees & butterflies are highly attracted to these flowers.